STYLE & SEDUCTION

*The Tauber Institute Series
for the Study of European Jewry*

JEHUDA REINHARZ, General Editor
CHAERAN Y. FREEZE, Associate Editor
SYLVIA FUKS FRIED, Associate Editor
EUGENE R. SHEPPARD, Associate Editor

The Tauber Institute Series is dedicated to publishing compelling and innovative approaches to the study of modern European Jewish history, thought, culture, and society. The series features scholarly works related to the Enlightenment, modern Judaism and the struggle for emancipation, the rise of nationalism and the spread of antisemitism, the Holocaust and its aftermath, as well as the contemporary Jewish experience. The series is published under the auspices of the Tauber Institute for the Study of European Jewry—established by a gift to Brandeis University from Dr. Laszlo N. Tauber—and is supported, in part, by the Tauber Foundation and the Valya and Robert Shapiro Endowment.

For the complete list of books that are available in this series, please see www.upne.com

Elana Shapira
  Style and Seduction: Jewish Patrons, Architecture, and Design in Fin de Siècle Vienna
ChaeRan Y. Freeze, Sylvia Fuks Fried, and Eugene R. Sheppard, editors
  The Individual in History: Essays in Honor of Jehuda Reinharz
Immanuel Etkes
  Rabbi Shneur Zalman of Liady: The Origins of Chabad Hasidism
*Robert Nemes and Daniel Unowsky, editors
  Sites of European Antisemitism in the Age of Mass Politics, 1880–1918
Sven-Erik Rose
  Jewish Philosophical Politics in Germany, 1789–1848
ChaeRan Y. Freeze and Jay M. Harris, editors
  Everyday Jewish Life in Imperial Russia: Select Documents, 1772–1914
David N. Myers and Alexander Kaye, editors
  The Faith of Fallen Jews: Yosef Hayim Yerushalmi and the Writing of Jewish History
Federica K. Clementi
  Holocaust Mothers and Daughters: Family, History, and Trauma
*Ulrich Sieg
  Germany's Prophet: Paul de Lagarde and the Origins of Modern Antisemitism
David G. Roskies and Naomi Diamant
  Holocaust Literature: A History and Guide

*A Sarnat Library Book

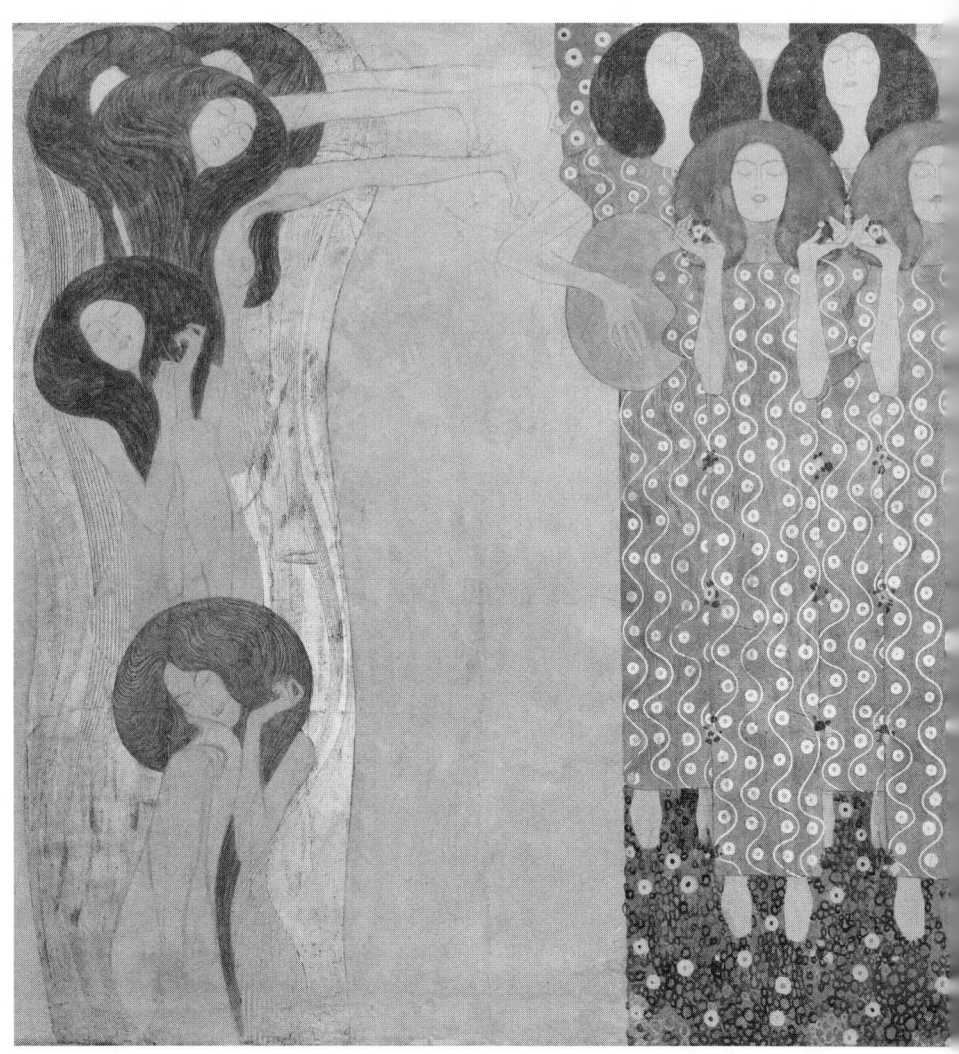

ELANA SHAPIRA

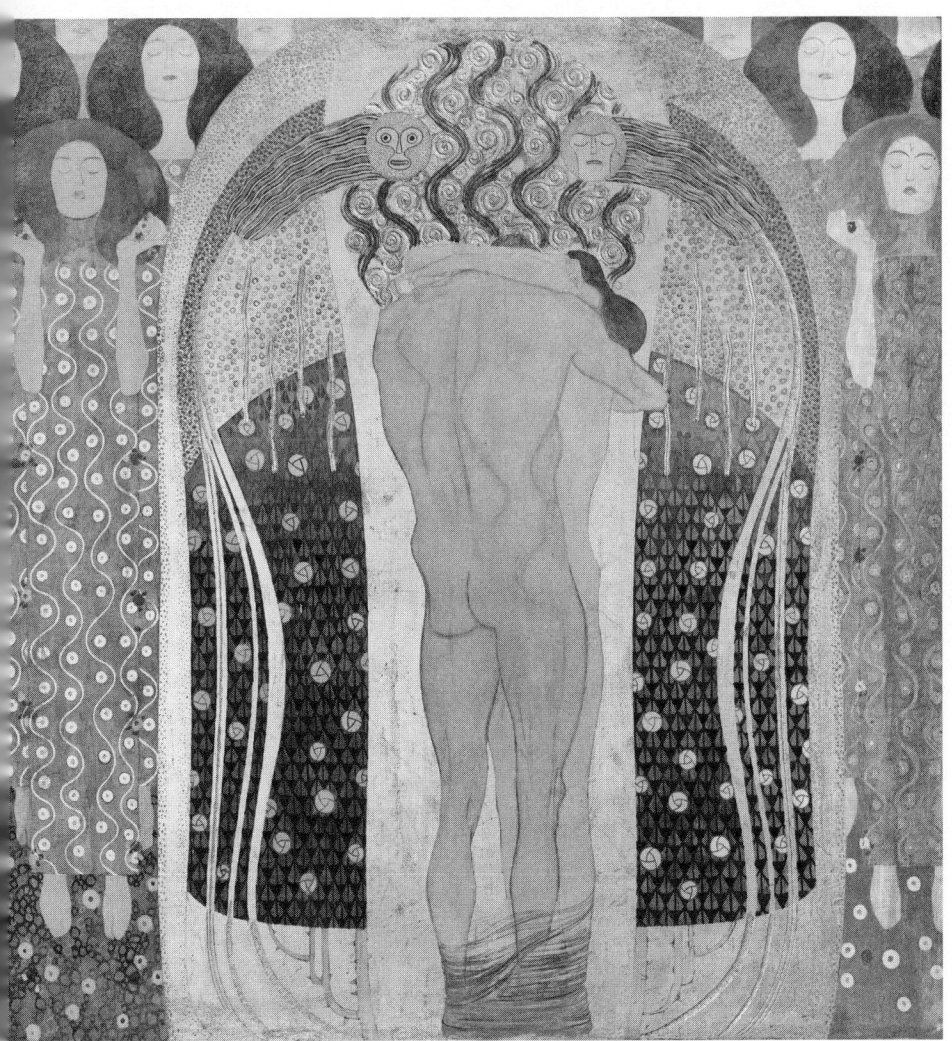

STYLE & SEDUCTION

Jewish Patrons, Architecture, and Design in Fin de Siècle Vienna

BRANDEIS UNIVERSITY PRESS } WALTHAM, MASSACHUSETTS

BRANDEIS UNIVERSITY PRESS
An imprint of University Press of New England
www.upne.com
© 2016 Brandeis University
All rights reserved
Manufactured in the United States of America
Designed by Eric M. Brooks
Typeset in Whitman by Passumpsic Publishing

For permission to reproduce any of the material in this book,
contact Permissions, University Press of New England, One Court Street,
Suite 250, Lebanon NH 03766; or visit www.upne.com

The illustrations used as a design element on the title page and
chapter openings are details of Figure 15: Gustav Klimt, *The Kiss*, from
his *Beethoven Frieze*, Secession House, 1902, © Belvedere, Vienna.

Library of Congress Cataloging-in-Publication Data
Names: Shapira, Elana, author.
Title: Style and seduction: Jewish patrons, architecture, and design
   in fin de siècle Vienna / Elana Shapira.
Description: Waltham: Brandeis University Press, 2016. | Series:
   The Tauber Institute series for the study of European Jewry | Includes
   bibliographical references and index. | Description based on print version
   record and CIP data provided by publisher; resource not viewed.
Identifiers: LCCN 2015047436 (print) | LCCN 2015041804 (ebook) |
   ISBN 9781611689693 (epub, mobi & pdf) | ISBN 9781611689204
   (cloth: alk. paper) | ISBN 9781611689211 (pbk.: alk. paper)
Subjects: LCSH: Architecture and society—Austria—Vienna—History—
   19th century. | Architecture and society—Austria—Vienna—History—
   20th century. | Architects and patrons—Austria—Vienna—History—
   19th century. | Architects and patrons—Austria—Vienna—History—
   20th century. | Design—Austria—Vienna—History—19th century. |
   Design—Austria—Vienna—History—20th century. | Jews—Art patronage. |
   Vienna (Austria)—Civilization—19th century. | Vienna (Austria)—
   Civilization—20th century.
Classification: LCC NA2543.S6 (print) | LCC NA2543.S6 S535 2016 (ebook) |
   DDC 720.1/03—dc23
LC record available at http://lccn.loc.gov/2015047436

5 4 3 2 1

CONTENTS

List of Illustrations } ix
Acknowledgments } xiii

Introduction } 1

1 THE HISTORICISTS, 1860S–70S
Eduard von Todesco, Gustav von Epstein, and
Their Neo-Renaissance Palaces on the Ringstrasse } 21

2 THE SECESSIONISTS, 1897–1902
Ludwig Hevesi, Karl Wittgenstein and the Secession House,
and Friedrich Victor Spitzer's Music Salon } 57

3 THE MODERNISTS, 1902–7
Isidor Singer and Heinrich Kanner and the Telegraph Office
of *Die Zeit*, Fritz Waerndorfer's House for the Art Lover, the
Wiener Werkstätte and the Cabaret Fledermaus, and the
Richard Beer-Hofmann Villa } 115

4 THE AVANT-GARDISTS, 1908–11
Peter Altenberg's Portrait in the American Bar and
Leopold Goldman and the Goldman & Salatsch House } 167

Conclusion } 219

Notes } 231
Bibliography } 279
Index } 305

Color plates follow page 110

ILLUSTRATIONS

Figures

6	1. Ludwig Förster, caryatid with a tiara and a Star of David, Palais Todesco façade, 1864
7	2. Gustav Klimt, *Judith I*, oil on canvas, 1901
26	3. Christian Griepenkerl, coronation of Esther, ballroom ceiling, Palais Ephrussi, 1873
33	4. Ludwig Förster, Hercules supporting the side alcove, Palais Todesco façade, 1864
36	5. Caricature "Die Ringstrasse des Lebens," *Die Bombe*, 1873
37	6. Carl Rahl, *The Judgment of Paris*, sketch for Palais Todesco dining room ceiling, 1863–64
44	7. Theophil Hansen, Palais Epstein façade, 1872
45	8. Gustav Gaul, portrait of Gustav von Epstein, oil on canvas, 1858
49	9. Theophil Hansen, Alexander frieze, winter garden, Palais Epstein, 1872
52	10. Christian Griepenkerl, *Birth of Venus*, ballroom ceiling, Palais Epstein, 1872
62	11. Joseph Maria Olbrich, Secession House, 1898
79	12. Caricature "Die Secession," *Der Floh*, 1898
85	13. Koloman Moser cover for Ludwig Hevesi, Österreichische Kunst im 19. Jahrhundert, 1903
87	14. Ferdinand Schmutzer, photo of Karl Wittgenstein, 1908
97	15. Gustav Klimt, *The Kiss*, in his *Beethoven Frieze*, Secession House, 1902
98	16. Palais Wittgenstein, music room with Max Klinger's Beethoven sculpture
101	17. Joseph Maria Olbrich, drawing for a wall decoration in the music room of David Berl, July 1899
106	18. Joseph Maria Olbrich, view of dining table and piano case, Victor Spitzer's dining room and music room, 1899
120	19. Otto Wagner, portal of the Telegraph Office, 1902

122	20. Karl Kraus, "Die Europäisierung der 'Zeit' oder 'Der kleine Kohn ist weg!,'" *Die Fackel*, 1903
123	21. Josef Hoffmann, studio in the Waerndorfer House, fireplace corner with George Minne's *Kneeling Boy*, c. 1904–6
131	22. Margaret Macdonald, *The Seven Princesses* (detail), music room in Waerndorfer's house, 1906
135	23. Koloman Moser, bookplate for Waerndorfer, 1903
145	24. Josef Hoffmann, barroom of the Fledermaus Cabaret, Wiener Werkstätte postcard no. 74, 1907
157	25. Josef Hoffmann, Beer-Hofmann villa, 1906
160	26a. Beer-Hofmann villa, grand hall, interior facing arched gallery, 1905
161	26b. Beer-Hofmann villa, interior gallery facing glass cabinet in grand hall, 1905
163	27. Beer-Hofmann Villa, view of the library from the studio
178	28. Unsigned photograph of Peter Altenberg's room in the Hotel London, c. 1904–10
181	29. Adolf Loos, Gibson Room, Café Museum, April 1899
184	30a. Adolf Loos, American Bar, early photo of the interior, with Gustav Jagerspacher's portrait of Peter Altenberg, 1909
185	30b. Gustav Jagerspacher, portrait of Peter Altenberg, 1909
192	31. Oskar Kokoschka, *Ich bin der Voyeur am Notbett der europäischen Isolde*, 1909
201	32. Adolf Loos, front page of *Das Andere* with a Goldman & Salatsch ad, 1903
202	33. Unsigned photograph of Leopold Goldman, 1909
208	34. Adolf Loos, entrance hall, Goldman & Salatsch House, 1911
212	35. Adolf Loos, Goldman & Salatsch House façade, 1911
228	36. Adolf Loos, Goldman & Salatsch House, 1911

Plates

1. Gustav Klimt, *Judith I*, oil on canvas, 1901
2. Christian Griepenkerl, coronation of Esther, ballroom ceiling, Palais Ephrussi, 1873
3. Carl Rahl, *The Judgment of Paris*, sketch for Palais Todesco dining room ceiling, 1863–64
4. Theophil Hansen, Alexander frieze, winter garden, Palais Epstein, 1872
5. Christian Griepenkerl, *Birth of Venus*, ballroom ceiling, Palais Epstein, 1872

6. Joseph Maria Olbrich, Secession House, 1898
7. Koloman Moser cover for Ludwig Hevesi, *Österreichische Kunst im 19. Jahrhundert*, 1903
8. Gustav Klimt, *The Kiss*, in his *Beethoven Frieze*, Secession House, 1902
9. Joseph Maria Olbrich, drawing for a wall decoration in the music room of David Berl, July 1899
10. Margaret Macdonald, *The Seven Princesses* (detail), music room in Waerndorfer's house, 1906
11. Josef Hoffmann, barroom of the Fledermaus Cabaret, Wiener Werkstätte postcard no. 74, 1907
12. Gustav Jagerspacher, portrait of Peter Altenberg, 1909
13. Adolf Loos, Goldman & Salatsch House, 1911

ACKNOWLEDGMENTS

At the end of the twentieth century I was asked to write an essay on the family of the Viennese tailor Leopold Goldman, the owner of a renowned men's fashion firm and a client of the architect Adolf Loos. With Goldman's input, Loos would design the Goldman & Salatsch House, a celebrated modern architectural landmark at the center of Vienna. My essay was to appear in a catalogue accompanying an Oskar Kokoschka exhibition at the Albertina in Vienna, which was to be held in honor of Leopold Goldman's daughter, the charismatic artist and graphic designer Kitty Goldmann (1918–2001), the only member of her family to survive the Holocaust and exile. Though the exhibition never took place, the historical material collected, including an interview with Kitty Goldmann in Santiago, Chile, spurred an exploratory journey that culminated in this book on Jewish patrons and modern architecture and design in Vienna.

Two colleagues strongly supported my exciting exploration of Viennese Jewish history and modern architecture and design. I am deeply indebted to my friend and colleague the historian Lisa Silverman for her enthusiastic encouragement of my project of tracing Jewish patronage in Viennese modernism, for thought-provoking discussions concerning Jewish identities, and for her critical insights, which significantly contributed to this book. I am indebted to the architectural historian Christopher Long for his unfailing encouragement, for his willingness to share his broadminded critical understanding of Viennese architecture and its reception, and for his enlightening remarks, which contributed to the overall coherence of *Style and Seduction*.

Special thanks are due to the art historian Patrick Werkner, director of Collection and Archive at the University of Applied Arts Vienna, and to the art historian and artist Martina Pippal, a professor in the art history department at the University of Vienna, for their supportive guidance and critical remarks on my doctoral thesis, in which I presented my initial findings. While doing research into the Goldman family and the Goldman & Salatsch firm, I consulted with Georg Gaugusch, the owner of the fashion store Jungmann & Neffe in Vienna and a scholar specializing in Jewish genealogy in Vienna. I further consulted with the architectural historian and former curator at the Albertina, Burkhardt Rukschcio. An expert on Adolf Loos, he first traced the importance of Loos's clients—specifically Leopold Goldman—to Loos's work. I am grateful to both for generously sharing their knowledge with me.

I am grateful to Kitty Goldmann, Peter Kniže, and Emile Zuckerkandl, of blessed memory, and to Pierre Stonborough, for inspiring discussions. Particular thanks go to the many colleagues who contributed to my research and book, among them Beatrix Bastl, who is a historian and the director of the library and university archives of the Academy of Fine Arts Vienna; Andreas Bergbauer, a fashion historian and designer; Louise Hecht, Jewish historian at Palacky University, Olomouc, Czechoslovakia; Nicole Immler, a cultural historian and lecturer at Utrecht University; Katja Kaluga, the literary historian responsible for the publication of the collected works of Hugo von Hofmannsthal with the Freies Deutsches Hochstift / Frankfurter Goethe-Haus; Markus Kristan, curator for architecture at the Albertina; Eva Ottillinger, an art historian and the chief curator of the Imperial Furniture Collection in Vienna; Inge Podbrecky, Austria Federal Heritage Authority; Ursula Prokop, an independent architectural historian; Paul Rachler, a historian and archivist formerly at the Secession House and now at the Vienna Künstlerhaus; Benjamin von Radom, a photographer and researcher preparing a book on caryatids in Vienna's city center; Günther Schefbeck, director of the archives of the Austrian Parliament; and Christian Witt-Dörring, a design historian and former curator at the MAK–Austrian Museum of Applied Arts / Contemporary Art (Österreichisches Museum für angewandte Kunst / Gegenwartskunst).

For their help in collecting visual material for this book, I extend special thanks to Régine Bonnefoit, curator of the Fondation Oskar Kokoschka, Villeneuve, Switzerland; Grigkar Immobilien, Vienna; Heinz Lunzer, a historian and independent curator; Thomas Matyk, head of the reproductions department at the MAK; Andreas Nierhaus, curator for architecture at the Vienna Museum; Peter Prokop of the Picture Archives at the Austrian National Library; Benjamin von Radom; Cornelia Reiter, director of the Graphic Collection of the Academy of Fine Arts Vienna; and Günther Schefbeck. My research was supported in part by grants from the Department for Cultural Affairs of the City of Vienna and the David Herzog Fund at the University of Graz.

I thank Richard I. Cohen, Hebrew University of Jerusalem, for his critical and supportive comments on this book. I am indebted to Gabrielle Greenlee for her skillful editing and insightful remarks, which contributed considerably to this book. I am grateful to Phyllis D. Deutsch, editor in chief, University Press of New England, for her commitment to and enthusiastic support of this publication.

My deepest gratitude goes to my husband, Anton Legerer, for his unwavering support, encouragement, and inspiring talks, which contributed to this book, and to our four boys, Benjamin, Tomer, Uri, and Yuval, for their support and wonderful curiosity.

Earlier versions of portions of chapter 1 appeared in "Todesco, Förster, Hansen, and the New Hellenistic Jews on Vienna's Ringstrasse," in Beatrix Bastl, Ulrike Hirhager, and Eva Schober, eds., *Theophil Hansen: Ein Resümee* (Weitra: Verlag Bibliothek der Provinz, 2014); portions of chapters 2 and 4 in "Jewish Patronage and the Avant-Garde in Vienna," in Annette Weber, ed., *Jüdische Sammler und ihr Beitrag zur Kultur der Moderne / Jewish Collectors and Their Contributions to Modern Culture* (Heidelberg: Universitätsverlag Winter, 2011); portions of chapter 3 as "Modernism and Jewish Identity in Early Twentieth-Century Vienna: The Patron Fritz Waerndorfer and His House for an Art Lover," *Studies in the Decorative Arts*, 13, no. 2 (Spring–Summer 2006): 52–92; and parts of chapter 4 in "Tailored Authorship: Adolf Loos and the Ethos of Men's Fashion," in Rainlad Franz und Inge Podbrecky, eds., *Leben-Mit-Loos* (Vienna: Böhlau Verlag, 2008), and in "Adolf Loos and the Fashioning of 'the Other': Memory, Fashion, and Interiors," in *Interiors: Design, Architecture and Culture* 2, no. 1 (March 2011): 213–38.

I dedicate this book to my father, Sheike Shapira, of blessed memory and to my mother, Sara Jane Shapira.

STYLE & SEDUCTION

INTRODUCTION

This book examines the contribution of Jewish patrons to the development of modern architecture and design in Vienna from the mid-nineteenth century to World War I. It reconsiders the cultural meaning and relevance of buildings, interiors, and design objects that were financed, produced, and co-designed by Jewish businessmen, journalists, and authors and that continue to play an important role in Viennese culture today. The narrative recasts the roles of the period's protagonists—patrons, architects, and their friends—and, in looking at a selection and arrangement of public and private events, recounts their actions to provoke reflection.[1] The four chapters examine the progression of Viennese styles in relation to intense dialogues between Jewish patrons and their architects and between Jewish patrons and their friends in the different club circles they initiated or belonged to, identifying the patrons as historicists, secessionists, modernists, and avant-gardists.

Until the 1980s, scholarly discussion avoided addressing the role of clients in the making of Viennese architectural landmarks and design masterpieces. This could be understood in light of the modern romantic dismissal of the influence of patrons on artists.[2] Yet the reason for neglecting the Jewish identification of important patrons also had to do with the continual undermining of their contribution to Viennese modernity as individuals, not least because they were part of a collective Jewish Other. A notable exception would be the historian Steven Beller, who did emphasize the influence of bourgeois Jews on Viennese modernity: "There were, of course, many figures in Viennese modern culture who were not Jewish, or of Jewish descent, but it is my contention that the Jewish presence was so large and so influential that, as far as Viennese modernity was concerned, those in the artistic and intellectual élite who were not Jewish were essentially following and reacting to the ideas and problematic of the children of the Jewish bourgeoisie."[3]

Yet in an invited lecture titled "The Visual Arts in Vienna circa 1900, Reflections on the Jewish Catastrophe" at the Austrian Cultural Forum in London on November 17, 1996, the renowned émigré art historian Ernst Gombrich challenged Beller. Questioning the notion of "Jewish patronage," Gombrich expressed the misleading belief that there was nothing "Jewish" about "cultured Jews": "Of course I know of many very cultured Jews, but, briefly, I am of the opinion that the *notion of Jewish Culture* was, and is, an invention of Hitler and his fore-runners and after-runners. My brief is, of course, to talk about the *so-called Jewish Culture* and the Visual Arts, a problematic topic at the best of times."[4]

Gombrich's problematic argument was embraced by other scholars, who dismissed the Jewish identification of Viennese modernism's patrons.[5] Indeed, the scholarly discussion that developed in the 1980s and 1990s still largely supported the view that it was only the crisis of integration that ultimately forced acculturated Jews to reclaim a Jewish identification.[6] Scholars such as Carl Schorske and Jacques Le Rider have chosen to focus on the crisis as a motive for cultural production and reclamation of Jewish identity.[7] In contrast, this text analyzes the role of Jewish identity within a longer historical view, throughout the second half of the nineteenth century and the early twentieth century.

In light of the ambiguity following the Gombrich and Beller debate, the chapters in this book explore the longer history of Jewish and gentile relationships to provide a new semantics of modern Viennese architecture and design. Why a new semantics? It seems necessary to treat Jewish identification within Viennese modernism as a question of Jews actively fashioning new language to convey their aims of emancipation as well as claims of cultural authority.

In much of the relevant scholarship, the issue of patrons' Jewishness in the period is simultaneously acknowledged and dismissed either through generalized comments such as those that refer to "this group" of patrons or as an exotic feature of Viennese modernism in major exhibitions.[8]

Furthermore, when scholars have looked beyond the immediate political climate to interpret shifts in the aesthetic arena, delving further into the relationships of Viennese modernist architects with their clientele, there have still been generalizations or missed opportunities to bring to light the Jewish imprint on the process. Examining the prominent modern masterpieces of Joseph Maria Olbrich's Secession House, Josef Hoffmann's Purkersdorf Sanatorium, Otto Wagner's Postal Savings Bank, and Adolf Loos's Michaelerplatz Building in *Architecture and Truth in Fin-de-Siècle Vienna*, Leslie Topp does analyze the architects' pursuit of different notions of truth in relation to the compromises they reached in cooperating with their clients. Yet Topp ignores the relevance of clients' Jewish context and their artistic input from within that context. Though Topp describes in detail how Loos designed the Goldman & Salatsch House (also identified as the Michaelerplatz Building) to challenge the antisemitic critique of Jewish businesses, she does not mention Karl Wittgenstein in her analysis of the clients with links to the Secession House, nor does she discuss the authorial intent of Leopold Goldman in the fashioning of the Goldman & Salatsch House, or how both of these factored into the rise of Viennese modern architecture.[9] And where scholarship does get closer to the client-architect relationship and focuses on the Jews' role in modern architecture, there is still room to examine how tightly woven the working and social relationships were between Jewish patrons and their architects. This is the case in Fredric Bedoire's *The Jewish Contribution to Modern Architecture, 1830–1930*, which brings the subject to the fore but offers only limited insights into the importance of the relationships studied in the book.[10]

The culture that shaped modernist Vienna was one of collaboration, but participants' roles and interrelationships have not been fully recognized. Previously I have examined modern portraits of Jewish art patrons as examples of the search for cultural platforms shared by Jews and gentiles and in relation to shared concerns with artists in fighting antisemitic prejudice and supporting new psychological understandings.[11] This book examines Jewish patronage in Vienna within a broader cultural context, concentrating on patrons' contributions to architecture and design. Not only were Jewish clients and their architects simultaneously contributing to the new aesthetic, but equally significant was the simultaneous influence that the patrons of opposing historicist and modernist trends had in the changing city. Not only were the degrees and quality of relations between Jewish patrons and their gentile architects and friends represented in modern architecture and design, but within the Jewish community of patrons there were also degrees of relations and consensus.[12] The social negotiations—or the "quality of relations"—between Jews and gentiles and between acculturated Jews and assimilated Jews largely contributed to the cosmopolitan reputation of fin de siècle Vienna.[13]

The Jewish Dandy Fashioning Modernity

The author Stefan Zweig noted that Kaiser Franz Joseph I granted the Jewish bourgeoisie a sense of security and the illusion that they were not in any immediate existential danger.[14] In return, Jewish patrons demonstrated time and again their loyal support of the kaiser from the midnineteenth century until World War I. There was no conflict between the patrons' dependency on the kaiser and the well-being of the empire, on the one hand, and a critical Jewish influence on Viennese modernism, on the other hand. Jewish patrons continued to support the kaiser even after the election of the antisemitic Karl Lueger as mayor of Vienna. Lueger's hate rhetoric included a call to boycott Jewish stores, and his railing against other sources of Jewish wealth, influence, and power served the broader populist mission of liberating the Christian population from the fantasized hegemony of Jewry. Kaiser Franz Joseph I's failure to prevent Lueger from assuming his post proved his political weakness. Although Jews were aware of the antisemitic threat, they relied on the illusion of stability to continue promoting their progressive cultural politics.[15]

The year of Lueger's election, 1897, was not a turning point for leading Jewish patrons. The Jewish patrons who continued to support the kaiser's multicultural ideology offered a critical alternative to the populist mayor's xenophobic modernization. They continued to support contemporary art and architecture, yet they reconsidered their integration strategy of respect and preservation of European and local historical traditions. Thus, for the different patrons—the historicists, secessionists, modernists, and avant-gardists—the agenda was progressive. The younger generation would redefine its position in Viennese society and specifically within the Jewish élite through the promotion of revolutionary architecture and design.

The narrative in the following chapters, therefore, reconstructs the contribution of leading Jewish patrons to Viennese cultural development by analyzing their patterns of socializing and socialization as Jews among gentiles. Style is regarded here as the dynamic, ongoing process of fashioning. In the Viennese context, style was supported or directed by Jewish patrons—in collaboration with others—to project their constructed identities and social integration and to allow them to claim authority as producers of culture.[16] The protagonists are the historicists (the textile industrialist and banker Eduard von Todesco and the banker Gustav von Epstein) secessionists (the cultural critic and journalist Ludwig Hevesi, the steel industrialist Karl Wittgenstein, and the sugar industrialist and photographer Friedrich Viktor Spitzer), modernists (the publishers and journalists Isidor Singer and Heinrich Kanner, the textile industrialist Fritz Waerndorfer, and the author Richard Beer-Hofmann), and the avant-gardists (the author Peter Altenberg and the tailor Leopold Goldman).[17] The analysis of each man does not focus on a single identity but rather reconsiders a range of aspects or revelations of their Jewish identification in their public performances and their choice of style or styles in the management of their desired presentation in relation to previous generations of Jewish patrons, contemporary Jewish patrons, and the larger Viennese public.[18]

The historian Michael Pollak has suggested that assimilated Jews used aesthetic projects to stabilize their identity by shifting the criteria of identity from the group to the individual.[19] In contrast, when I refer to the identities that Jewish patrons constructed for themselves, I argue that some of these Jewish businessmen and journalists grasped the symbols of modernity to fashion new progressive group identities. The standard narrative is that most Jews erased all outward traces of Jewish history and culture to integrate. However, I claim that the relationships between Jewish patrons and their artists and architects formed a new cultural program that embedded the Jewish micronarrative firmly in the macronarrative of European history, so that Jews and the aspects of Jewish culture they chose to retain would become part of the fundament of Viennese high culture. To this end, this book uses the term "Jewish identification" rather than "Jewish identity." The former implies a more dynamic process whereby patrons, through their investment in modernist art, design, and architectural objects, directly or indirectly redefined what Jewish culture meant.[20]

Georg Simmel, a German sociologist of Jewish origin, was an authority on the relation between the individual and society with regard to fashion and culture in Vienna in this period.[21] Toward the end of his essay on style, published in the applied arts journal *Dekorative Kunst* in 1908, Simmel stated: "What drives modern man so strongly to style is the unburdening and concealment of the personal, which is the essence of style."[22] Jewish patrons discussed in this book entertained the possibilities of "Jewishness" and reconstructed a Jewish self-identification through their fashioning of Viennese style. The terms "Jewish self-identification" and "Jewishness" are used here as aspects of identity that defined the relationship of acculturated Jews to Jewish culture in separate ways: "Jewish self-identification" is self-determined cultural identification based on Jewish heritage and critical public discourse, whereas "Jewishness" is a projection of the daily confrontation with the Christian majority and its irrational antisemitic attitudes.[23] Jewish self-identification is represented, for example, in the caryatid with a tiara decorated with a Star of David (Fig. 1) among the twenty-six caryatids decorating the upper floor of the Palais Todesco (1864). Appearing at the corner on the front façade, facing Vienna's Opera House, she can be identified as the beautiful Jewish Queen Esther. The biblical heroine was chosen as an identification symbol for Jewish salon women in nineteenth-century Vienna (discussed in chapter 1). Sim-

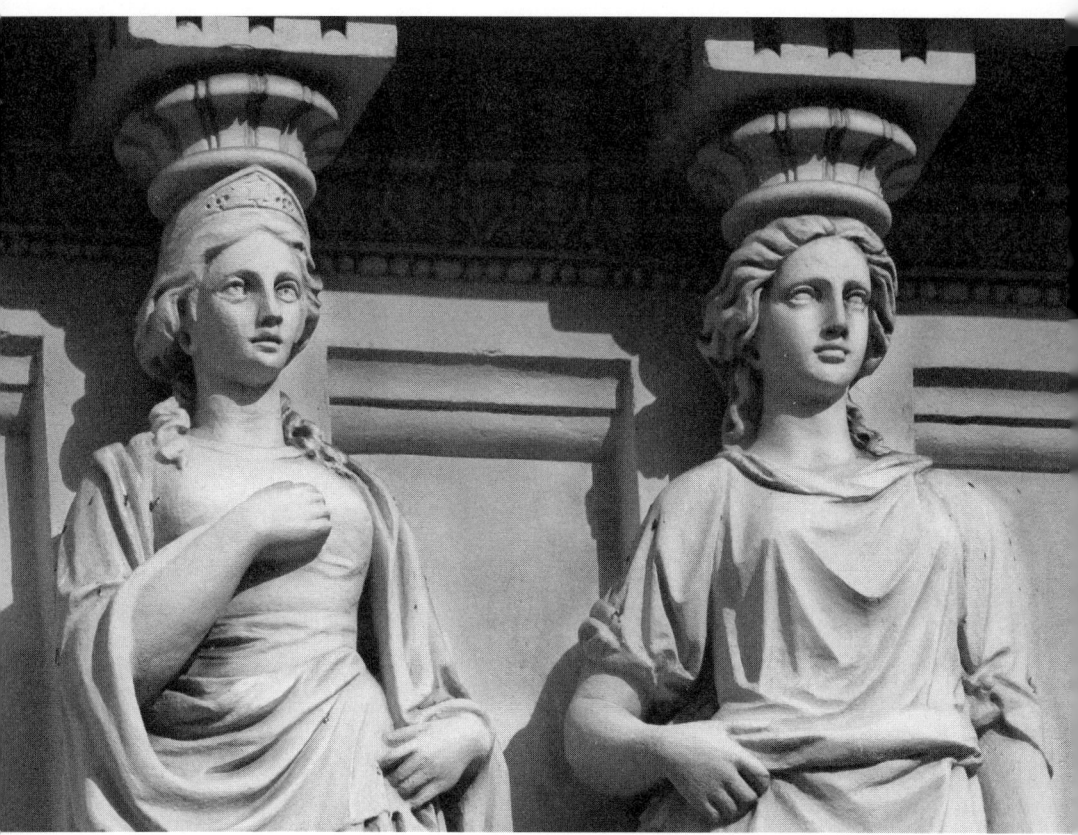

FIGURE 1. *Ludwig Förster, caryatid with a tiara and a Star of David, Palais Todesco façade, 1864.* Photo: © 2010, Benjamin von Radom.

ilarly, another caryatid in this series whose hair is covered and who carries a book close to her could be identified as a devout Jewish woman and therefore an allegory of devotion.[24] Positioned within a larger group of caryatids, those representing Jewish self-identification are successfully camouflaged.

This strategy reveals a subtle play of exposure and concealment in representing the Jewish self, in which the Jewish figure (or the Jewish viewer) has control over her reading as Jewish. In contrast, for example, in Gustav Klimt's *Judith I* (1901, Belvedere, Vienna) (Fig. 2, Plate 1), the female figure is adorned with Oriental symbols in overt reference to a "Jewishness" that is imposed on her reductively. Judith appears as a *femme fatale* with a provocative expression of sexual ecstasy on her face and with her breasts exposed. Her open mouth, showing her teeth, evokes the threatening image of the *vagina dentata*. Klimt transformed a biblical character identified as a Jewish

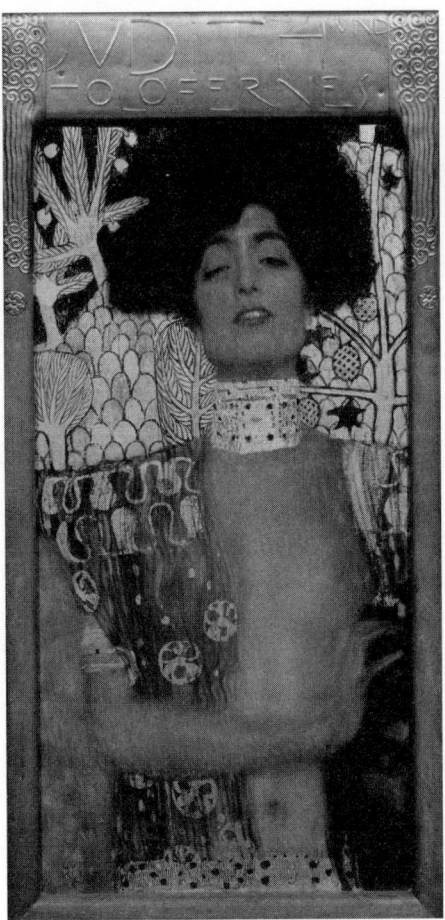

FIGURE 2. *Gustav Klimt,
Judith I, oil on canvas, 1901.
Ludwig Hevesi, Österreichische
Kunst im 19. Jahrhundert
(Leipzig: E. A. Seemann, 1903).*

devout woman, representing chastity and humility, into a shameless and striking temptress in accordance with the transformation of the iconography of this subject toward the end of the nineteenth century.[25] Klimt's exaggeration of the reference to "Jewishness" was a provocation against those who dismissed his art as representing "Jewish taste."[26] He inflated the reference to "Jewishness" to expose and challenge, or even capitalize on, the stereotype of Jewish Otherness as Oriental, exotic, and sexually promiscuous. His Jewish patrons continued to support him, perhaps because in his tactic of capitalizing on "Jewishness" they identified the possibility of transforming common prejudice against them into a demonstration of cultural accomplishment.

To expand the limitations of "Jewishness" and embody a Jewish self-identification, it was crucial for the Jewish patron to exhibit good taste. In this way he could claim authority. In Vienna around the end of the nineteenth century, the template for a figure of style, taste, and connoisseurship was the dandy. The historical persona of the dandy, who presented his aesthetic through dress and appearance, originated in the legendary gentile British social climber George Bryan "Beau" Brummel, whose sartorial ideal was one of gentlemanly discretion and lack of ostentation. The persona was later elaborated on by the gentile French author Charles Baudelaire, who promoted the idea of beauty in everything. The English literature scholar Rhonda Garelick examines the social phenomenon of dandyism, pointing out that the dandy's influence required a vast system of communication, which would convince others to grant him the title of dandy: "Dandyism, then, does not just merge the real and the fictional; it creates a contagion of style and seduction. Texts about dandies strive for dandyist appeal; critics' writings about dandies fall easily into dandyist style and succumb to its charms. This is, of course, how all celebrity works; and dandies are among the earliest celebrities. One cannot declare oneself a celebrity any more than one can simply state that one is charming and influential. Celebrity and influence require a vast system of communication, a network of opinion and desire."[27]

In her portrayal of the British author Benjamin Disraeli, a self-styled dandy and eventual prime minister of Britain, the philosopher and social critic Hannah Arendt called attention to a statement made in his novel *Tancred* (1847): "What is a crime among the multitude is only a vice among the few."[28] According to Arendt, this statement documents Disraeli's recognition that Jews could have no better chances of integration (or claims for authority) than in circles that pretended to be exclusive and to discriminate against them. The reason for this is that these circles could allow Jews to transform their supposed crime—namely, "Jewishness"—into a more attractive vice. Arendt's observation about Disraeli's integration strategy, for example, can be seen as an example of the formula of style and seduction and the dandy's ability to charm his way through the social mix. The dandy, the influential celebrity, can turn certain relationships or dynamics upside down, so that a Jewish man can have access to exclusive gentile clubs, or rather support and initiate new exclusive clubs and thereby reshape crime into an attractive vice. Furthermore, we can newly analyze the authority of Jewish patrons in the Viennese movement in light of Garelick's observation of how the dandy model allowed them to transmit ideas and emotions. The dandy's transformative role as someone adept at style and beauty allowed the Jewish man of certain means to redeem the negative associations the broader culture imposed on the Jew and become an arbiter of taste; a negative perception was bypassed and a positive, modern perception replaced it in this form of seduction.

The leading protagonists discussed in this book invested ideas and money and transformed their "Jewishness," considered by the gentile majority as a crime, into progressive patronage of architecture and design; in these cases, the Jewish dandy-cum-celebrity was appreciated as showing an attractive vice.[29] Jewish patrons' conscious process of self-styling was a clear example of a Jewish self-identification and a formula that allowed them new access and influence.

How Did Jewish Patrons and Their Artists and Architects Refer to the Seductive Power in Their Designs to Reshape the Modernist Imagination?

In his 1903 lecture "The Metropolis and Mental Life," Simmel raised the central question of "how the personality accommodates itself in the adjustments to external forces."[30] The film historian James Donald notes how Simmel critically acknowledged the danger that accompanied strategies of coping with the overwhelming impressions of the city: "As their senses are bombarded, as urban life becomes increasingly mediated and as fellow citizens become, of necessity, more self-interested, suggests Simmel, individuals resort to stratagems of inward retreat and social distance. A blasé, intellectualizing attitude is one such strategy for self-protection. This reflects less indifference than a reserve cultivated to contain the aggression inherent in urban relations: 'a slight aversion, a mutual strangeness and repulsion, which will break into hatred and conflict at the moment of a closer contact.'"[31]

A direct expression of how the subjective perspective bridged the gap between the self and outer reality was the choice of proper dress.[32] Dress represents identity but also a claim to distinction, and proper dress can be a defense strategy to deflect violence. Moreover, in the context looked at here, dress became a central criterion for measuring the success of integration of minority groups, specifically Jews.[33] The correct dress could also serve as a healing tool, bridging the gap between a person's experience in the external world and an ideal projection of that same experience in the interior world. As such, the topic of dress is treated in this book as more than just a reference to clothing and fashion; it is also brought up frequently in reference to other types of coverings (and uncoverings). Not only are we interested in the dandy's apparel, but we also want to consider how a building façade or a painting, for example, can be seen to dress an underlying structure and examine what that form of covering tells us.

The dynamic of covering and uncovering was crucial to the social games examined in this book. Moreover, it exhibited a strong erotic appeal. Each of the protagonists presented in this book consciously or unconsciously engaged in the social game that Simmel described as "flirtation," and for each of them, as Jewish patrons, flirtation was part of their coproduction of a new Viennese style.[34] Their flirtations mirrored their experience of not wanting to —or their bitter acknowledgment that they would never—be fully accepted in Viennese society; their authorial creative license is symbolized in this posture of appearing in public half turned away,[35] championing their Otherness. The dandy role allowed Jewish patrons to expose themselves by engaging in a newly sanctioned form of flirtatious performance in social encounters. The dandy Jewish patron, furthermore, used personal charisma, creative thinking skills, and finances to channel flirtation toward larger, more permanent performances grafted onto architecture and design.

Rethinking Viennese Modern Architecture and Design

The modern movement in Vienna began in the early 1890s with the art theories of Hermann Bahr and continued with the publication in 1896 of the architect Otto Wagner's *Moderne Architektur (Modern Architecture)*.[36] Wagner's antihistoricist manifesto for modern architecture was followed by the foundation of a new art association, the Vienna Secession (1898). This in turn inspired the foundation of the Wiener Werkstätte (Viennese Arts and Crafts Workshops) in 1903. In 1905, Klimt left the Secession after the split in the Secession between the group of the artist Josef Engelhart and that of Klimt. In 1908, the modern period was concluded.[37]

To understand the context of modern Vienna considered in this book, it is important to review the previous period. In the historicist period of the second half of the nineteenth century, the Ringstrasse was the central construction project. The project began after Kaiser Franz Joseph I ordered in December 1857 that the walls separating the city center from the suburbs be torn down, a decision that has been identified as the official push that began the expansion and modernization of Vienna. However, it was not the first act of expansion. Since the early nineteenth century there had been different expansion projects in which a progressive architect, Ludwig Förster, played an important role. Förster presented his ideas in lectures and in his journal, *Allgemeine Bauzeitung*, through which he promoted the systematic reception of the latest European trends.[38] He was known and respected for introducing international trends to Vienna, and his progressive liberal perspective on architecture was integrated into the Ringstrasse construction project. The

Ringstrasse architecture's historicist agenda (historicist style is an eclectic composition of different historical styles such as classic, Gothic, Renaissance, and baroque), aligned with contemporary European liberalism, was represented through the French neo-Gothic style of the Votiv Church, the Parliament's Greek revival style, the City Hall's Gothic style, the Court Theater's baroque style, the State Opera's French Renaissance style, the Museum of Arts and Industry's neo-Renaissance style, and the neo-Renaissance style of the Stock Exchange House. The architectural program further promoted the positivist *Weltanschauung* that with the help of science and education and a knowledge of history, the people's standard of living would improve and society would be structured and directed in a progressive manner.

An early Förster contribution to the Ringstrasse was a whole block of houses on the corner of Kärntnerstrasse and the Kärntner Ring for gentile and Jewish patrons. This decision to mingle different population groups can be interpreted to correspond to the classical, Gothic, Renaissance, and baroque architectural styles of the buildings' façades.[39] Förster shared his European liberal agenda with his young partner and son-in-law, Theophil Hansen. Significantly, Hansen had arrived in Vienna from Athens after working on central projects there patronized by Simon Sina, a Greek Orthodox art patron. In Vienna, Sina lived in a neighborhood at the center of the Jewish community and closely cooperated with Jewish patrons.[40] Hansen promoted a Hellenistic style as a pan-European one, and his rejection of the possibility of a national style reflected a progressive leaning that was in line with his liberal gentile and Jewish patrons alike.[41]

Working in Hansen's circle as the master builder for the Palais Epstein was Otto Wagner. Wagner began his architectural career on the Ringstrasse, and though he endorsed the European perspective he would turn against the eclectic historicist style. Redirecting the liberal positivist Weltanschauung, he rejected the educational program of the historicist period in favor of art nouveau aesthetic schemes and the critical consideration of hygienic conditions (the use of easy-to-clean materials, air circulation, and the installation of bathrooms) and technological advantages (new materials). In his book *Moderne Architektur* (*Modern Architecture*), Wagner argued for modern-looking houses and the supremacy of functional architectural forms. An early realization of this was his design of Vienna's underground stations, which effectively connected the city center with the suburbs. In turn, Wagner's assistant, Joseph Maria Olbrich, would design the first striking modern masterpiece, the Secession House, an exhibition building for the Vienna Secession (Association of Austrian Fine Artists), of 1898. Positioned between Hansen's historicist Academy of Fine Arts and Wagner's art nouveau underground station in Karlsplatz, the Secession House followed Wagner's construction model for the underground stations and was further adorned with exotic Oriental decoration, a detail worth noting because it is suggestive of a cultural past that Viennese Jews would have a historical association with. Olbrich created two more modernist landmarks, villas for Max Friedmann, a businessman and politician of Jewish origin, in Hinterbrühl (1898) and for the cultural critic Hermann Bahr in Vienna (1899).

Wagner's, Olbrich's, and Hoffmann's cooperation in designing the Austrian exhibit at the Paris World's Fair in 1900 confirmed official Austrian art's public change of direction. The success of their exhibit followed the appointments of two modernists to cultural posts in Vienna, Arthur von Scala became the director of the Austrian Museum of Art and Industry (1897) and Felician von Myrbach became a professor for illustration in the School of Applied Arts (1899).[42] However, the introduction of international schools in the eighth Secession exhibition substantially enriched the formation of a modernist movement: "the Four" from Glasgow (Charles Rennie Mackintosh, the Macdonald sisters, and Herbert McNair), Robert Charles Ashbee from London, Julius Meier-Graefe's firm La Maison Moderne from Paris, and Henry van de Velde from Brussels. While Hoffmann's design for the Paris exhibit had shown the influence of Belgian art nouveau's curved lines, by 1901 the geometric lines and spatial concepts of his four villas in the Hohe Warte artist colony showed the English influence of Mackintosh, Ashbee, Mackay Hugh Baillie-Scott, and Charles Voysey.[43] In further developing the Wagner and Olbrich modernist agenda, these villas did not present a stylistic unity but offered primary forms for spatial and furniture designs that would become sources for a future aesthetic program.[44] Hoffmann's breakthrough role was in founding the Wiener Werkstätte in 1903, in cooperation with the designer Koloman "Kolo" Moser and the businessman Fritz Waerndorfer, who actively encouraged the group's aesthetic.[45] The Wiener Werkstätte's first major groundbreaking project was its design for the Sanatorium Purkersdorf of Victor Zuckerkandl, brother-in-law of the Jewish journalist Berta Zuckerkandl, near Vienna in 1904–5. Hoffmann's architectural plans and the decorative interior design of his colleagues at the Wiener Werkstätte represented the sanatorium's therapeutic aims. The keywords were air, sun, nature, cleanliness, training, and modern technology.[46]

The next significant modern construction was Otto Wagner's Postal Savings Bank on the Ringstrasse in 1906. In his earlier 1902 design for the Telegraph Office and art gallery of the newly founded newspaper *Die Zeit*, Wagner had radically developed his ideas concerning functional construction, illustrating the functional aspects as decorative schemes, and this new bank building on the Ringstrasse would be a monumental adaptation of those lessons learned. The canonized masterpiece that followed was Adolf Loos's 1909 business and residential building across from the Hofburg (the imperial court), commissioned by his tailor, Leopold Goldman, who was the owner of the men's fashion firm Goldman & Salatsch. Loos used reinforced concrete as a frame system, following the earlier example of Jože Plečnik's Zacherl-House, a residential and business building for the gentile industrialist Johann Zacherl (1905). Like that building, the Goldman & Salatsch building elevated functional form into monumental architecture. But Loos added more innovation to the spatial plan by combining a grand store setting with adjacent tailoring workshops while also retaining residential space above it, so that commerce and industry were closely linked to living space.[47] Loos also critically considered hygienic conditions, choosing ceramic tiles to protect the small inner court's walls. And he reduced the exterior decoration, using only plaster for the upper floors, to convey modern social ideals: privacy through anonymity and lack of ostentation, or equality, in the social sphere.

All of these architects who encapsulated Viennese modernism worked with Jewish clients, and the Jewish contribution to the architecture of the period bears a direct relationship to the development of the period styles. Modern architecture in Vienna was the result of cultural currents that allowed Jews to fashion an ideal self-image in a societal context that would formerly have been closed to them.

In contrast to contemporary gentile patrons—for example, Nicolaus Dumba who seemed to tailor his patronage to suit his personal interests—Jewish patrons of historicism and opposing modernist trends preferred to serve a template for a collective group.[48] Consequently, Jewish patrons co-produced designs that encouraged a creative play between exposure and concealment of their interests, specifically their Jewish identification. Similarly, the gentile patrons Albert Klein and Heinrich Drasche (both referred to in chapter 1), whose interests were directly related to the promotion of their businesses, expressed specific professional and bourgeoisie class agendas; their counterpart Jewish patrons demonstrated their professional and class interests in the decoration of their houses, only these interests were presented in direct relationship to their Jewish identification.[49] If historicist patrons were considering how far they could stretch the limitations of Jewish identity without provoking anger and challenges to their authority, modernist patrons were refashioning their Jewish identification as a modern statement of Otherness and a progressive culture.

Within the construct of Otherness, another group—women—can be considered as testing social boundaries through aesthetic conversation. For example, Berta Zuckerkandl addressed the relationship between integration and modern aesthetics in her supporting reviews of Klimt, Hoffmann, and the Wiener Werkstätte. She also published an article concerning women's fashion (Zuckerkandl is discussed in chapter 2). In this article, Zuckerkandl consciously encouraged the development of a feminist consciousness by pointing out the possibilities offered by modern aesthetics.[50] The leading gentile feminists Marie Lang and Rosa Mayreder contributed to the public discourse concerning modern architecture, as discussed in chapter 2.[51] Mayreder and Lang supported different modernist styles, and while they did not perceive these styles as critical instruments for the promotion of the feminist movement in Vienna, their entry as women into a discussion dominated by males invariably introduced the question of feminism.

Through their demand to take an active part in public discourse and contribute as producers of culture, Jews and women alike threatened the status quo. According to the historian Alison Rose, "The perceived Judaization and feminization of Viennese culture gave rise to hostility toward women and Jews."[52] Rose further mentions the belief in the femininity of male Jews and the accusation that they were responsible for the "so-called feminization of Viennese culture."[53] Jews were identified as feminine, materialistic, sexually deviant, aggressive, and immoral. Jewish men, according to Rose, handled antisemitic rhetoric by displacing "anxieties of their own sexual difference onto women. The gender stereotype created by Jewish men in their representations of women assisted them in negotiating their way through the changes and challenges of modernity."[54] A historical witness to these developments was the author Otto Weininger, an assimilated Jew who was well known to both intellectuals and patrons among his contemporaries, and whose work was widely reviewed by scholars. Weininger compared the conflict between man and woman to the conflict between the Aryan and the Jew in his best-selling *Geschlecht und Charakter* (Sex and character), published in 1903.[55] Several scholars have related the motivation behind Weininger's vicious rhetoric against women and Jews in this book to his doubts about his own Jewish masculine identity.[56] My suggestion is that the discourse concerning Jewish masculinity in Viennese modernism was skillfully transformed in the context of Jewish patronage into a driver of new creative architecture and design toward the end of the nineteenth century. Jewish patrons discussed in this book deflected the negative associations of being Jewish or effeminate (immoral, uncultured, and so on) and instead inhabited the cultural space created by these categories, from these spaces claiming the creative freedom to modernize the city. By appearing in the Viennese society as Jewish dandies, they sidestepped prejudices and secured a new authority to command new artistic networks, initiating change at a safe distance from Austrian provincialism in the guise of seductive men or of men promoting seductive artistic design.

Recasting the Protagonists

When we speak of group achievement in this context it is necessary to allow nuance, because the members of the Jewish collective certainly had differing motivations on the individual level. In this book, each chapter's specific focus on two or three Jewish patrons highlights their particular Jewish self-identification and also points to differences in their approaches toward patronage and the design process. The question of whether a coherent, unified semantics appears in the successive styles or in parallel existing styles that Jewish patrons helped produce remains a conspicuous one throughout this book. In other words, the extent to which the Jewish patrons of Vienna's architecture and design fashioned an imagined Viennese community or encouraged the creation of imagined Viennese communities (à la Benedict Anderson) through modern styles remains unquantifiable even though we reach a more qualitative understanding of what the Jewish experience within the community entailed.[57] What can be said is that the individual patrons contributed to a new vocabulary without which emancipation and a new cultural authority could not be envisioned.

Chapter 1 introduces the patrons who supported the historicist style in the buildings of the Ringstrasse in the second half of the nineteenth century. It focuses specifically on the cooperation between Todesco and Epstein with Hansen, the star architect of the Ringstrasse, on their neo-Italian high Renaissance palaces. It demonstrates how Hansen adapted his original façade and decorative plans to fit his clients' cultural identification with the heritage of Jews in antiquity who embraced Hellenist culture. To set the pieces of these social relationships in place, we should note that Todesco and Epstein did not have similar reputations in Viennese society. Todesco was a brilliant businessman but was mocked for his wrong and embarrassing use of foreign words in his speech. Despite his eventual bankruptcy, Epstein was known and celebrated, even after his death, for his noble posture, elegant appearance, and superb taste in matters of art and design. Yet the two historicist patrons hired an architect identified with the classical style since the Hellenic was a cultural platform they shared with their Christian neighbors that encouraged mutual respect. By examining various contemporary publications, this chapter outlines the terms of Todesco's and Epstein's cultural convictions and shows their concern that not only the exterior of their palaces but also their interiors reflect identification with Jewish Hellenist heritage. Chapter 1's examination of the historicist period is critical to understanding how the formation of a new Jewish consciousness defined cultural networks that contributed to the modernization of Vienna. Vienna's young literary circle of the early 1890s, called Jung-Wien (Young Vienna), was also key in the transition between the historicist and secessionist periods, as it facilitated the absorption of modern trends by the Viennese fine arts.

To understand Jewish patrons' contributions to the public discourse on a new aestheticism, it is helpful to look at their coproduction of new architecture and design through an initial Jewish disadvantage, which they managed to turn into identity progress in both Jewish and Viennese cultures. Chapter 2 analyzes how the Jewish patrons of the Vienna Secession, the first avant-garde movement in Vienna, initiated new acculturation through modernist design. Promoted by journalists such as Hevesi and Zuckerkandl and by patrons such as Wittgenstein and Spitzer, the secession directly reacted to the antisemitic movement's exclusionary politics in Vienna and sought more tolerance of outsiders. The simultaneous propulsion of new ideas of cultural progress by artists, architects, patrons, and media alike at this period would bring Vienna and its ideas into the modern age. To that end, Hevesi's fashioning of a new critical awareness in support of Jewish emancipation is better understood in relation to Wittgenstein's financing of the Olbrich-designed Secession House and his support of secessionist artists: while Hevesi was reshaping the argument with prose, the patronage of a figure such as Wittgenstein was supporting the secessionist aesthetic that embraced cultural difference or Otherness through design. In Olbrich's design, architect and patron reached further back to the Near East (or the Orient, as the cultural mainstream would designate it). The Oriental motifs in secession design were reminders to acculturated Jews of their origins in the Near East, which could also be seen in the Moorish-style synagogues built in Vienna at the second half of the nineteenth century.

The secessionist *Gesamtkunstwerk* (total artwork, representing a synthesis of music, drama, and art) offered a decorative artistic setting for a new brotherhood between artists and patrons. Olbrich's interiors for the coal industrialist David Berl and Spitzer, his brother-in-law, in buildings positioned on or near the Ringstrasse (and later in Spitzer's villa in Hohe Warte), further supported the stylistic change from historicist to secessionist. In these later structures, the Jewish identification with a new romantic spirit (inspired by Richard Wagner's ideal of Gesamtkunstwerk) can be seen. In a further analysis of Spitzer, we see his patronage of the new secessionist designs as a means by which he "seduced" his way into society, offering a cultural stage for various flirtatious societal dramas in his music salon.

Chapter 3 begins with Singer and Kanner's hiring of Otto Wagner to design the Telegraph Office and art gallery for *Die Zeit* and reviews how modern aesthetics became a shared platform for an ambitious civilizing project. The chapter compares two Jewish patrons who influenced the evolving concept of Viennese modernism in completely different ways: Waerndorfer and Beer-Hofmann. Both men invested in modern architecture to reposition themselves in Viennese society, but they stylized themselves as two very different kinds of Jewish dandies. The chapter also includes analyses of Waerndorfer's new design of his private house in Vienna's eighteenth district (1902); his contribution to the Wiener Werkstätte (1903), which he helped finance and codirected; and his support of the creation of a new Gesamtkunstwerk in the Cabaret Fledermaus, which he founded in 1907. The chapter looks at how Waerndorfer, through his aesthetic choices and his investments in architecture and cultural venues, such as the Caberet Fledermaus, inhabited a critical Jewish identification that dangled perilously between prejudiced, stereotyped notions of Jewish acculturation and a forward-looking, modernist sensibility. The cabaret becomes a transformative venue, where critical theater skits addressed the subject of Jewish acculturation, and where modern dance performances commented on issues of body image and notions of masculinity, femininity, and—particularly of interest for the subjects of this book—the Jewish male body. Waerndorfer is seen through the study of the body image, for example, and his investment in the cabaret is presented as evidence of his desire for reclamation of the body. In contrast, Beer-Hofmann, a representative of the Jung-Wien modern literary movement, encouraged the architect Hoffmann to decorate his house in Vienna's eighteenth district (1906) with abstracted classicist architectural elements to challenge the Oriental allure of the secessionist movement, and to revert to the Jewish identification with the Hellenistic Jews to further develop the ideal. While Waerndorfer showed a revolutionary approach by exchanging religious dogma for aesthetic inclinations, Beer-Hofmann's charisma as a Jewish dandy and his involvement with modern aesthetics reconstructed his cultural and religious Jewish identification. Both men promoted and supported the Wiener Werkstätte and adapted the modernist style to multiple levels of experience and for different progressive social gatherings.

Altenberg's and Goldman's cooperation with the architect Loos resulted in two classical architectural masterpieces that challenged notions of intimacy and masculinity in Vienna. Chapter 4 examines in detail the relationships between Loos and Altenberg and Goldman. Loos was a member of the coffee house intellectual circle of Altenberg and Karl Kraus—the much feared publisher and editor of the journal *Die Fackel* (The torch)—and the chapter carefully examines Kraus's role in promoting Loos's modern designs. Loos and Kraus were both critical of the Jewish acculturation process in Vienna. Loos furnished his design of Vienna's American Bar (1908), an intimate elitist men's club, with a portrait of Altenberg that hung on the wall opposite the entrance. This decision showcased design and identity as closely tied in the culture; the portrait indicated the desire to grant the men's club a cultural exclusivity, confirming the presence of the leading Viennese poet (whose exclusivity, it must be noted, hinged on both his "Jewishness" and his dandyism). The chapter argues that Altenberg's portrait in Loos's club serves as a gateway to understanding the relationship between Loos and his Jewish clients, which depended on a desire for a brotherhood of modern men united by the appeal of modern aestheticism. The chapter reexamines the fruitful cooperation between Goldman and Loos in the construction of the revolutionary Goldman & Salatsch House opposite the Hofburg in the inner city and analyzes the iconography of its modernist design. Loos's avant-garde contribution was represented in the novel treatment of spaces and flat surfaces and his skillful matching of austere plaster with the natural textures of wood and marble. The public scandal caused by the "monster of a house" (as it was called by its critics because of its undecorated and smooth painted upper façade) lasted for almost two years and led to the recognition of Loos as the father of a new avant-garde school in Vienna.

Four central motives are identified as integral to the authorial intent of the patrons discussed in this book. First was their need to represent themselves in a heightened capacity in public and to demonstrate self-mastery to counter antisemitic prejudices; second was their ambivalence toward—and their loyalty to—their Jewish identification and heritage; third was their use of style to assert a Jewish element in the progressive collective; and fourth was the belief that modern architecture and design granted them historical redemption and an eternal aesthetic proof of their achievements, both for themselves and for their chosen social and artistic group, in the chronicles of Vienna.

The conclusion of the book reconsiders how Jewish patrons and their architects and designers contributed to change in Viennese styles and the facilitation of a shared aesthetic identity and platform of communication between Jews and gentiles. Though the underlying culture ensured a certain distance between Jews and gentiles, the Jewish patrons discussed throughout the book were modern actors who used modern languages of representation—such as the fashioning of the dandy—to rewrite the macronarrative of Viennese society. If in many instances Jews and gentiles clearly showed their separate identities—their respective Otherness and their preservation of micronarratives—there was also an undeniable impetus toward a fraternity of cultural progressives. The identification of Jewish patrons as Others encouraged them to embrace styles that confirmed their uniqueness within Viennese society yet managed to mitigate hostility toward their "Jewishness" (for a time). If the Jew was seen in terms of negative, mostly antisemitic, associations and his Otherness was viewed as a threat or temptation to Christians, the Jewish patron seemed to take refuge in the outsider label and use it as a point of departure. In this sense, the Jewish patron did not reclaim his Jewish identification because of a sharpening of antisemitism or a failure in liberal politics. Rather, he reclaimed it because it had always been there, it was always the subtext, and the historical moment had arrived when "Jewishness" could be used for all its imposed negative attributes and reworded in a modern language of representation. The conclusion outlines this process of reclamation in the domain of the arts, translating it in terms of these patrons' Jewish self-identification.

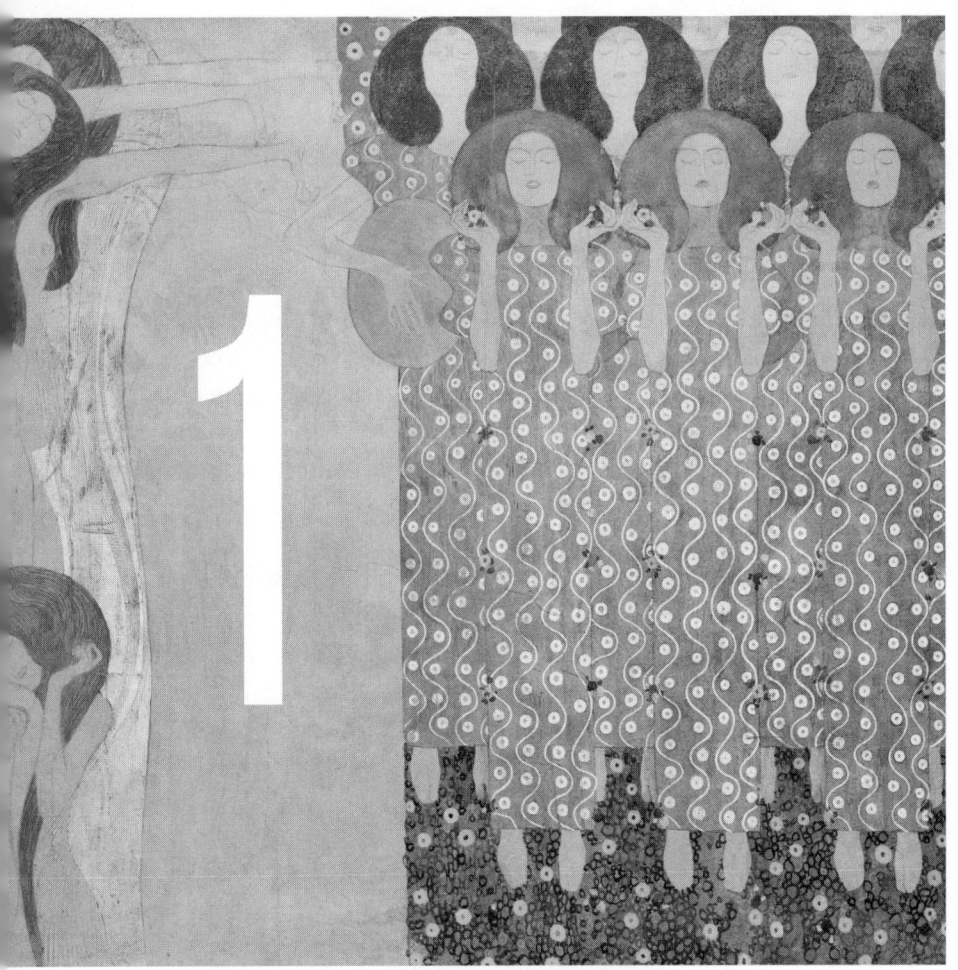

THE HISTORICISTS
1860S—70S

Eduard von Todesco, Gustav von Epstein, and Their Neo-Renaissance Palaces on the Ringstrasse

In Vienna in the second half of the nineteenth century, a highly publicized collaboration between leading Jewish patrons and architects shaped modern Vienna and strongly affected a shift in the perception of Jewish culture. The Jewish patrons Eduard von Todesco (1814–87) and Gustav von Epstein (1827–79) fashioned their identification as art patrons and cultural producers when they hired the prominent gentile architects Ludwig Förster (1797–1863) and his younger colleague and former partner Theophil Hansen (1813–91) and, together with them, became integral to the modernizing of Vienna. Todesco, a textile industrialist and banker, worked on the Palais Todesco at Kärntnerstrasse 51 with Förster and Hansen, in the design of the façade and on the interior décor, respectively. Similarly, Epstein, a banker, worked with Hansen in the design of the Palais Epstein and his apartment interiors.[1] Through these collaborations the two Jewish patrons were able to claim a certain celebrity as producers of Viennese high culture at a time when prejudice against Jews was widespread.

Through a conscious visualization of their cultural setting, and in a manner of self- identification that mined the heritage of Hellenistic Jews,[2] Todesco and Epstein refuted worn stereotypes of Jews as solely wielders of money and fashioned for themselves new roles as critical and influential patrons in Vienna. As an arbiter of taste, Todesco asserted himself through his humorous (and somewhat reckless) approach to cultural holy cows. He belonged to a literary club with strict codes of secrecy that may have allowed bawdy humor and social transgressions inside the club, but its members could not allow such behavior to be publicized. Yet in the late 1860s and early 1870s Todesco allowed humoristic and society journals to report his jokes and perhaps invent anecdotes at his expense. Because he was a prominent banker and society man, his misbehavior encouraged critical reflection on the Jewish acculturation project, specifically the expectation that Jews would fully conform to the constructed image of historicist culture. In contrast, Epstein successfully achieved cultural and artistic distinction and was much more cautious about his public image as a tastemaker. After the completion of his grand palais he mastered the role of celebrity patron, inviting art critics to admire his grand apartment's interiors and presenting his art collection in public.

Prologue: A Triumphant Historical Reunion of a Jewish Queen with a Greek Prince

Todesco's public persona was deeply rooted in Viennese tradition. At the end of the 1830s, he had become a member of a Viennese literary circle called Soupiritum (the "supper" was a reference to the members' regular Wednesday dinner parties), which disbanded in 1848.[3] In 1848, the year of the failed liberal revolution, Todesco was already a well-known personality in the city with enough courage to try to intervene in local politics.[4] He had just become the director of the bank called Hermann Todesco's Söhne; ten years later, in 1858, his older brother, Max, would transfer to him and to his younger brother, Moritz, the ownership of the textile factory in Marienthaler in Lower Austria. Between 1852 and 1874, Todesco belonged to a literary club called Baumannshöhle (Baumann's cave), later called Gnomenhöhle (Gnomes' cave), which also met in the Palais Todesco from 1864 to 1874. The club's aim was to encourage sociability (*Geselligkeit*) between Jews and gentiles.[5] The influential Austrian authors Franz Grillparzer and Eduard Bauernfeld were prominent members of this club. Todesco's social stature in the broader Viennese culture was improved when he was ennobled by Kaiser Franz Joseph I in 1861. And in 1864, after the completion of his palais, Todesco became a leading partner in the Marienthaler und Trumauer Actien-Spinn-Frabriks-Gesellschaft, a textile factory. He received the title *Freiherr* (baron) in 1869.

By many standards, then, Todesco was a central figure in Vienna's financial scene. Yet the point of departure for examining Todesco's self-fashioning as a celebrity Jewish patron is his wife, Sophie (1825–95). Sophie demonstrated her command of society through smartly orchestrated cultural gatherings. On April 1, 1868, she presented a carefully directed cultural event in Palais Todesco's salon: a series of *tableaux vivants*, including a reconstruction of the German artist Eduard Julius Friedrich Bendemann's painting *The Mourning Jews in Exile* (1831–32). Sophie's choice of Bendemann's painting revealed her aim of introducing a Jewish historical perspective to her guests, and the event was analyzed as a new construction of Jewish identity.[6] The wish to return to Zion was more romantic than realistic at the time, but the intention was to make a public statement. It was Sophie's role to preserve cultural ties with high aristocracy for her husband's literary club and certainly it is Sophie's intent as a producer of culture that is grafted onto the caryatid positioned on the upper part of the front façade of Palais Todesco: the caryatid can be identified as the Jewish Queen Esther, but it reflects Sophie von Todesco's claim of high social status and cultural aspirations (Fig. 1). On multiple levels, Esther would have been a significant symbol to Sophie and Eduard, and they would at times embrace representations of the Jewish queen or look beyond them in their negotiations with the broader Viennese culture. The book of Esther is read in the synagogue on Purim, the holiday that celebrates the deliverance of Jews from ancient enemies.[7] It tells the story of the beautiful Esther, the niece of the wise Mordechai, who was chosen by the king of Persia, Ahasuerus, to be his second wife. Encouraged by her uncle, Esther hinders the plans of Haman, an advisor to Ahasuerus, to destroy the Jewish people. In April 1866, in his review of the eager cooperation between the architect Hansen and the genre painter Carl Rahl on the design of the Todescos' grand apartment, Ludwig Speidel noted that Eduard von Todesco had rejected the idea of painting the story of Esther in his dining room and instead had chosen a Greek theme. Speidel mentioned that the Greek saga of Paris had not been Rahl's first choice but rather Todesco's. Speidel, who was also a close friend of Rahl, explained that the artist had recommended the memorable story of Esther, honoring Purim ("'Tage des Wohllebens und der Freude,' heißt es in der Schrift," or Purim "as a day of feasting and joy," it says in the scriptures), as more fitting to the pleasures of the dining table and to the national identification of the Todescos. But, according to Speidel, Todesco had argued against this national subject in favor of the Greek one, not because of a preference for a Hellenistic glorification of life but to avoid hurting the feelings of his guests with "other beliefs" ("Rücksicht auf andersgläubige Gäste," or considering of the faiths of other guests).[8] The fact that Esther appears on the Palais Todesco's façade and yet was passed over as a suitable representation for an interior space points to the various types of negotiations a Jewish patron made when deciding how to visualize his or her Jewish identification.

The dramatic judgment of the Trojan prince, Paris—who was asked to judge who was the most beautiful of Aphrodite, Pallas Athena, and Hera, and whose choice led to the Trojan wars—was instead chosen for the Todesco's dining room ceiling. Todesco preferred to show the tragic outcome of a Greek legend of temptation instead of the happy end of a Jewish biblical story of temptation, since presenting the story of Esther in his dining room would also mean reminding his guests of the threat of antisemitism. Todesco insisted on maintaining control over the design of his house and thus had the last word on the identity he was conveying through art. His choice of Paris further represented his wish as a liberal patron of the arts to match art with European *Bildung* (historical knowledge presented through a blend of art and science). In claiming a preference for the Greek story, Todesco evoked a Hellenistic Jewish heritage, the merits of which he saw as providing a shared cultural platform for himself and guests he would have at his palace. Sophie von Todesco supported her husband's choice to create this new European cultural platform to be shared by Jews and gentiles and contributed to the fashioning of a new liberal Jewish identification on the Ringstrasse.

Todesco's aim was supported by relatives who perceived the reclamation and study of their Hellenistic heritage as part of a Jewish emancipation project to fight prejudice against them and advance Jewish culture. Three days after Speidel published his review, Theodor Gomperz (1832–1912), a renowned Jewish philologist and Sophie von Todesco's brother, concluded a lecture in the German Schiller-Stiftung in Brünn (now Brno in the Czech Republic, where the family Gomperz originated) titled *Traumdeutung und Zauberei: Ein Blick auf das Wesen des Aberglaubens* (The interpretation of dreams and sorcery: A view of the essence of superstition), declaring that his mission was to clarify and eventually bury historical superstitions: "And we who were born later could only free ourselves from the overpowering influence of the past by recognizing it thoroughly."[9] Thirty years later, in 1896, in an essay titled "Der Zionismus" (Zionism) that appeared in the Viennese liberal newspaper *Die Zeit*, Gomperz would argue against the new Jewish national movement and for acculturation. Gomperz advocated fruitful dialogue between Jews and gentiles, a tradition dating back, according to him, to the post-Alexandrian Hellenistic period.[10] It was this ideology of acculturation that would shape Vienna as a modern city.

The story of Esther nonetheless echoed through the Todescos' involvements with culture. In 1871, Sophie and Josephine Wertheimstein, her sister, together with other society ladies, founded the Grillparzer Prize to celebrate the eightieth birthday of Franz Grillparzer, author of the 1863 play *Esther*.[11] In October 1888, the Burgtheater performed Grillparzer's *Esther* fragment on opening night along with the German Friedrich von Schiller's classic, *Wallensteins Lager*. Grillparzer's stage adaptation of the story focuses on a psychological examination of Esther. The decision to perform *Esther* on opening night may have been a tribute to the gentile author and salon woman Fanny von Arnstein, a role model for Viennese Jewish salon women who had achieved a high position in gentile society through marriage to Jewish businessmen and who wished to shape Vienna's cultural life and express their political claims for emancipation.[12] In Grillparzer's *Esther*, Esther informs her uncle that the

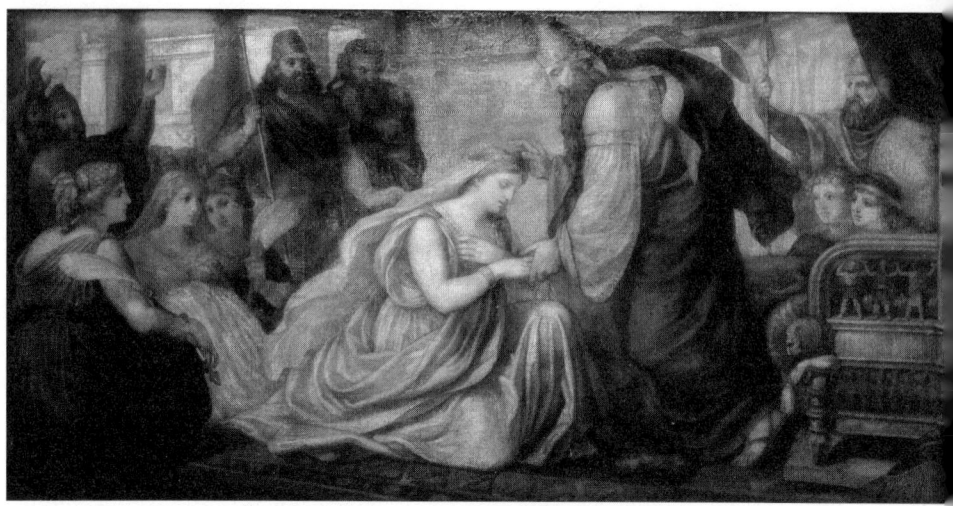

FIGURE 3. *Christian Griepenkerl, coronation of Esther, ballroom ceiling, Palais Ephrussi, 1873. Photo: © 2014, Benjamin von Radom.*

Jewish nation has been saved, and her uncle responds with a long monologue about Jewish history and the threats against the Jews. The play informed the crowd about the existential threat to the Jews and their perspective on it. Eduard von Todesco had died a year before this performance, but it may have been patrons such as Sophie von Todesco and Adolf von Sonnenthal, a Jewish actor who was artistic director of the theater at the time, who supported the choice of *Esther* for the opening night.[13] Clearly Jewish patrons in their rental apartment palaces on the Ringstrasse played a part in fashioning Viennese historicist style and were adherents of a progressive liberal Austrian ideology, but their commitment to the past was also strongly driven by a desire to fight superstitions against Jews[14] while preserving their collective identity. Sophie and Eduard von Todesco contributed to a new historical narrative of the Jews by embracing the historicist trend in Viennese culture at the time, and specifically by drawing on the positive acculturation connotations of the Hellenistic Jews.

A case that mirrored that of the Todescos in that it also touches on the figure of Queen Esther is that of the Jewish patron Ignaz von Ephrussi. After rejecting the idea of the Greek subject—the marriage between Venus and Adonis—to decorate his ballroom, Ephrussi chose the coronation of Esther (Fig. 3, Plate 2) and the trial of Haman.

Ephrussi was married to Eduard von Todesco's niece and lived in the neighborhood of the Palais Todesco before moving to his neo-Renaissance rental apartment palace at Universität-Ring 14 (designed by Hansen and built in 1872–73).[15] In contrast to the Todescos' preference of a Hellenic theme (at least most unequivocally in the interior spaces of their palace), his choice emphasized his Jewish identification. The two scenes Ephrussi chose depicted Esther's moment of glory at her coronation and the trial of Haman, which would have confronted his guests with the story of antisemitism in an earlier historical context. The architectural historian Mara Reissberger notes that the presentation of Esther as a subject is unique expression of Jewish identification. She sees Ephrussi's choice to celebrate the triumph of Judaism over antisemitism as a rejection of assimilation.[16] And while that choice can be seen as quite assertive of a Jewish separateness, especially when contrasted to Todesco's choice to neutralize the differences between himself and his gentile guests, I argue that the issue is not assimilation or nonassimilation but the attitude of self-fashioning: both Todesco and Ephrussi were shaping their Jewish identification and doing so in a historicist vein. Moreover, a renowned Viennese rabbi at the time, Rabbi Joseph Samuel Bloch, identified the book of Esther as a defense of the ancient Hellenistic Jews, pointing to a shared cult of sensuality and celebration of woman's beauty. The story of Esther, after all, championed her as an ideal, the "beautiful Esther" (in contrast to the rebellious Vashti).[17] Rabbi Bloch, highly respected for his fight against antisemitism, theorized that the book of Esther had been written in the time of the Maccabees (164–63 BC) as an apologetic text in defense of Hellenistic Jewish culture.[18] Ephrussi's choice to have a gracious blonde Esther in his ballroom therefore was consistent with the Hellenistic display of a grand sculpture of Apollo, the Greek god of music and poetry, in the inner court of Ephrussi's palace. Furthermore, the façade of the building is decorated with protruding heads of Hermes on the ground floor and caryatids on the top floor.

Ephrussi and Todesco (and other Jewish neighbors such as members of the families Auspitz and Lieben) shared a desire to assert their Jewish self-identification, and it was through the specific choices they made in their patronage that they were able to balance notions of Jewish identification and Europeanness. The fact that in 1888 the renowned Burgtheater included *Esther* in its opening performance suggests that the Todescos' and Ephrussis' Hellenistic Jewish evocations had made specifically Jewish references and representations acceptable in broader Viennese culture. The performance of *Esther* at the Burgtheater acknowledged that the Hellenistic Jews in Viennese society had triumphed in shaping a new representation of Jewish self-identification.

The New Europeans

> But [the stranger's] position in this group is determined, essentially, by the fact that he has not belonged to it from the beginning, that *he imports qualities* into it, which do not and cannot stem from the group itself.[19]

Jewish patrons of the Ringstrasse did not become Europeans in Vienna. Their families had adopted a progressive German culture in different cities in the Habsburg monarchy (which became the Austro-Hungarian Empire in 1867) at least one generation before they moved to the city. Yet after the patrons received the right to purchase land and settle in Vienna, they publicly displayed their becoming European to their gentile neighbors to express their belonging in the city, thereby claiming the right to take part in the city's cultural production. For leading Jewish families in the second half of the nineteenth century, demonstrating their Europeanization meant adapting the fashionable historicist style for their houses. Yet the patrons mentioned in this chapter distinguished themselves within the Viennese Jewish minority and from Viennese gentile society by celebrating their Hellenistic Jewish past with the use of Hellenistic visual elements. Through their esteemed ancestors, these Jewish patrons claimed an old European inheritance as a means of entering contemporary European society.

In 1888, the same year *Esther* was performed at the opening night of the Burgtheater, Friedrich Uhl, the editor of the *Wiener Zeitung*, offered this comment on the Ringstrasse's Jewish patrons, who had received equal rights only in 1867:

> Enthusiastic competition caught the citizens of Vienna and the rich Jewish bankers, those who received through the emancipation—at last!—the right to be people, to possess their own house, their own home. They showed their pride by building luxurious houses and, moreover, rental-apartment houses. They allowed their magnificent buildings on the Ringstrasse to be built by first-class artists to show: Here we are, here we're going to stay, here it's beautiful, here we want to build our palaces! Rothschild, Todesco and Springer, Wiener and Schey, Königswarter and Epstein, as they were all called, became house owners on Vienna's Ringstrasse—they, the men who were not allowed to own houses and land before 1848.[20]

It was no small matter to have a place on the Ringstrasse. In June 1858, the author of the *feuilleton* series "On the New Design of Vienna" in the liberal newspaper *Die Presse* noted there should be a plan for the new street around the old city to group the important political, economic, and cultural institutions more closely around the court buildings of the Habsburg monarchy. The aim was to present the visitor to Vienna from the provinces with an ideal architectural portrait that glorified Austrian power.[21] Jewish patrons who built on the Ringstrasse experienced in a short period a change from being excluded to becoming part of the newly fashioned and self-aware circle of power. Palais Todesco was among the first buildings built on the lucrative land that became available after Kaiser Franz Joseph I ordered in December 1857 that the walls separating the city center from the suburbs be torn down.

The stylistic choices represented in the public buildings reflected a European liberal education program. For example, the Gothic style of the City Hall evoked "its origins as a free medieval commune";[22] the early baroque style of the Burgtheater (Court Theater) commemorated "the era in which theater first joined together cleric, courtier, and commoner in a shared aesthetic enthusiasm";[23] and the university's Renaissance style served as a symbol of liberal culture.[24] Following Carl Schorske's observations about the public buildings on the Ringstrasse, the specific Renaissance-Greek façade and interiors of the Palais Todesco can be read as cultural constructions apart from merely physical constructions. One of the first palaces built on the Ringstrasse, the Palais Todesco was fashioned as I argued above with the political and cultural agenda of the Todesco and Gomperz (Sophie von Todesco's maiden name) families. These families established themselves on the Ringstrasse not just to partake of the glory of the new Vienna but also to promote a new Jewish cultural center that would be open to Jews and gentiles, parallel to the synagogue but not exclusively for Jews.

Looking further back, the choice of architectural style had long been central to the acculturation project of Jewish patrons. In 1848, Adolf Jellinek—later rabbi of the second Ashkenazi synagogue in Vienna, the Leopoldstadt Temple (1858)—had expressed in the Jewish journal *Der Orient* (The Orient) the opinion that a modern and aesthetic appearance could make Jewish religious practice look more attractive and consequently improve the humiliated position of Jews in the city.[25] Following Jellinek's recommendation, Jews saw the challenge as how to build synagogues that were attractive and still maintained a distinct and individual Jewish character. In fact, the first Ashkenazi synagogue in Vienna had already offered Jewish patrons a Jewish stylistic model to help fashion future Viennese styles. The first Ashkenazi "German synagogue," which became the City Temple, had been consecrated in 1826 in Vienna in Seitenstettengasse, financed by the bankers Nathan von Arnstein, Bernhard von Eskeles, and Michael Lazar Biedermann.[26] According to the building regulations at the time for non-Catholic sacred houses, the façade of the synagogue had to be inconspicuous, blending in with the environment like a residential building.[27] Searching for a fashionable look for their synagogue, the leaders of the Jewish community in the early nineteenth century (at that point still not recognized officially as a community) had chosen a famous Viennese architect, Josef Kornhäusel, to design it.[28] Kornhäusel placed a single decorative Greek meander motif under the cornice separating the ground and first floor.[29] Below the meander motif, the entrance to the synagogue was marked by a biblical citation. In the interior, Kornhäusel transformed the prayer hall into a splendid Biedermeier public hall. Besides the façade's meander motif, the interior's Ionic columns—six columns on each side leading to the bimah (a raised area in the synagogue used for the Torah reader)—evoked a Greek temple, but collectively the twelve columns referred to the twelve tribes of Israel, symbolizing Jewish national identity. In April 1826, a reviewer in the *Wiener Modezeitung* (Viennese fashion journal) described the interior as a "sacral theater" and praised the tasteful design of the new synagogue, noting that its style could compete with any other house of the time.[30]

This was the broader context out of which arose Eduard von Todesco's interest in further developing the Greek revival in the design of his house. Furthermore, Hermann Todesco, Eduard's father, had donated a Torah curtain to the City Temple made from the wedding dress of his daughter, who had been married there.[31] In his own building project, Eduard hired Förster as his architect.[32] Prominent patrons of Eduard's father's generation had cooperated with the Förster and Hansen team. In choosing Förster, Todesco was also following the examples of the brothers Ludwig (also known as Louis) and Adolph von Pereira-Arnstein, grandsons of the famous Jewish salon woman Fanny von Arnstein, and Salomon Mayer von Rothschild. Ludwig von Pereira-Arnstein had asked Förster to build his palace in the first district at Weihburggasse 4 in 1840. In 1844, a year after it was completed, Förster designed a palais at Renngasse 6 for Ludwig's brother Adolph (1844–47). Förster also redesigned the Palais Rothschild at Renngasse 3 in 1847 so that it could house the Rothschild Bank.[33] The style of these houses was classicist, using elements from Greek temples and early Renaissance architecture, such as channeled Corinthian pilasters to flank the windows in Weihburgasse and Renngasse, but adapted to the reserved tone of the Biedermeier era. The Todescos were aware of the rich tradition of the Pereira-Arnstein salons. Sophie von Todesco fashioned her salon on the model of Fanny von Arnstein and Fanny's daughter, Henriette von Pereira-Arnstein.

In choosing Förster, whom the Pereira-Arnstein brothers had used for their city palaces, the Todescos made their mark according to the grand classicist (Greek classicist) heritage of the Viennese Jewish patrons of the Biedermeier era. This post-Biedermeier, younger generation would more effectively secure their place as cultural producers in modern Vienna. It is worth noting an example, though, of the extent to which Todesco's father, Hermann, was associated with a classical heritage. In the memorial book for Hermann's funeral, the elder Todesco's cultured identity is documented in an illustration that shows a stylistic mix that his sons would later develop further: within a Gothic architectural frame two Greek gods, Athena and Hermes, are shown on the left side of the illustration as a couple observing a city landscape beyond a terrace. At the center of the illustration, in an oval-shaped garland, the name Jehova is written in Hebrew letters, rising like the sun above a dancing figure surrounded by angels.[34] This cultural blend of Greek heroes and Jewish religion would be championed in the younger Todescos' cultural club in their palais on Kärntnerstrasse.

Changing conditions of visibility dictated the fashioning of new styles. The literature scholar Aleida Assmann describes the replacement of old style with the new as a result of a competition between social groups.[35] In the battle over social visibility played out in the Viennese Ringstrasse landscape, while a minority of Jewish patrons—Todesco, Epstein, and Ephrussi—chose the German Förster and the Danish Hansen to design elaborate neo-Renaissance façades with specific Hellenistic references, the majority of Jewish patrons chose to work with the Italian-Austrian Johann Julius Romano and the Austrian August Schwendenwein to design low-key and reserved buildings with Greek revival elements grafted onto a neo-Renaissance style.[36]

Romano's and Schwendenwein's neo-Renaissance designs were praised for their solidity and elegance (the Biedermann family's house on Burgring was described as "soliden Eleganz," (solid elegance) and the Königswarter family's houses on Burgring as "Solidität und Eleganz") (sobriety and elegance). In contrast, Förster's façade for Palais Todesco was described quite differently, as "especially striking because of its rich decoration in which the beauty appears to be almost too much for the house."[37]

So why did the Todescos and a handful of other Jewish patrons choose the more ostentatious architecture? While, as noted above, the Todescos were not the only Jewish family establishing an architectural presence with historicist elements, they saw the Palais Todesco as the first clear articulation of the new Ringstrasse patrons' unique cultural characteristics. The fact that relatives settled around them further allowed Eduard and Sophie von Todesco to make a mature statement about their cultural identity, with their more ornate façade an articulation of a Jewish self-identification that adamantly evoked a Hellenistic Jewish legacy.

In the striking Renaissance Hellenism of the Todescos' cultural club, they emerged as cultural leaders of a new small Jewish settlement around the intersection of Kärntnerstrasse and Kärntnerring.[38] The patrons who bought lots in the area where the original Kärntner gate to the inner city had stood were Jewish industrialists and bankers—the Todescos and Eduard Wiener—and two gentile industrialists, Heinrich Drasche (1811–80) and Albert Klein (1807–77). Soon after that, Max Springer, Eduard Todesco's brother-in-law,[39] bought a lot from Albert Klein, situated between the future Palais Todesco at Kärntnerstrasse 51 and the future Palais Wiener at Kärntnerstrasse 55 and Kärntnerring 1. Eduard Wiener and Springer asked Förster to design their houses to look like a unified whole.[40] Essentially, Förster would design the whole corner block, with façades adorned in different rich and subtle decorative schemes.

On the top floor of the Palais Todesco were twenty-six caryatids, eighteen on the front façade facing the Opera House and four on each side façade (at Mahlergasse 1 and Walfischgasse 2). Holding the cornice up with their heads, these sentinels were intended to give the palace a visible social and cultural prestige. The Austrian archaeologist Anton Bammer argues that, in the context of modernizing Vienna in the historicist period, the aristocracy represented history but the bourgeoisie were "writing history."[41] According to Bammer, Todesco, Epstein, and Ephrussi would have used caryatids, among other symbols, as a way to "write history," displaying a cultural authority that was exclusive and formidable and that granted them the cultural authority that came with the classical Greek (in their case, specifically the Hellenistic Jewish) tradition. In this way they meant to secure a rapprochement between Jews and gentiles in Viennese society. In choosing caryatids as one of the outer expressions of their Bildung, the Todescos and others like them were creating a provocative, protective barrier against the working classes to emphasize their own inclusion as the newcomers in bourgeois society and guarantee their presence in an exclusive circle of power. The many Palais Todesco caryatids were bold presences, rich in their poses and allegory: three of them hold books, two have doves with open wings on their right shoulders, two are crowned by wreaths of flowers, two are crowned with tiaras, and so on.[42] The caryatids as a group can be interpreted as an ideal self-identification for Sophie von Todesco, reflective of the poem "Woman of Valor" (Proverbs 31:10–31) supposedly written by King Solomon and cited before the Friday evening dinner. Indeed, Jewish salon women and the wives of prominent pa-

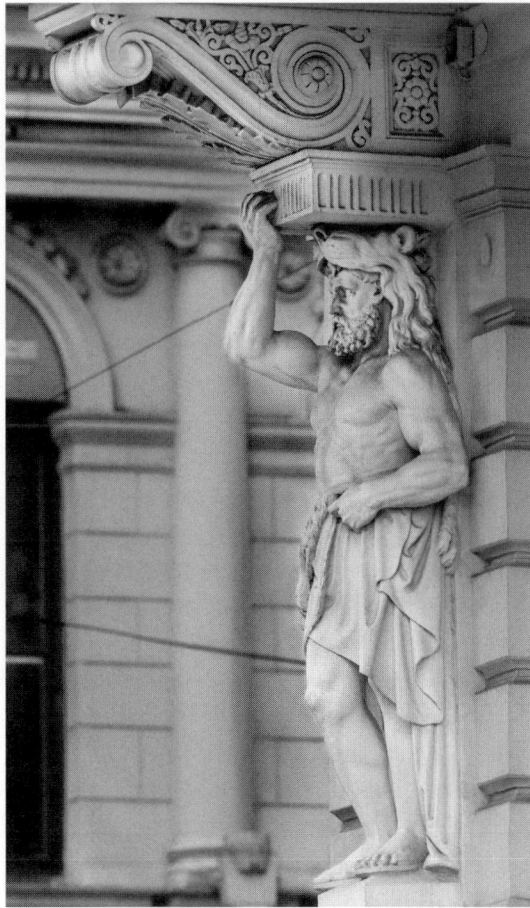

FIGURE 4. *Ludwig Förster, Hercules supporting the side alcove, Palais Todesco façade, 1864. Photo: © 2013, Benjamin von Radom.*

trons could have identified with the caryatids as role models for "carrying the weight of their house": "Another woman figure from classical antiquity comes to mind. Who does not know the female caryatids on the façades of palaces, which carry heavy loads on their shoulders? The Greeks invented these female figures, but Jewish women realized them in life. . . . The biblical poet sang of these women: 'Who can find a woman of valor? She is worth more than pearls.'"[43]

The caryatids and the Hercules figures supporting the alcoves in the Todesco structure also related its façade to a specifically Viennese tradition (Fig. 4).[44] Förster used similar decorative elements on the façades of his buildings, such as the meander motif and running dog patterns and protruding lions' heads, but he made sure to include individual elements as well in each palace. But Förster's plan for the façade of the Palais Todesco was a livelier adaptation of Greek architectural heritage, displaying the caryatids in different poses and arrangements of dress.[45] These caryatids wear Greek chitons that cling to their bodies and emphasize the curves of their legs or fall loosely in erotic tension between the suggestively revealed or concealed female body. Förster's use of channeled Corinthian pilasters between the windows of the first and second floors were a further development of his designs for the classicist Palais Ludwig Pereira and Palais Salomon Rothschild. In the Palais Todesco the pilasters did not frame the windows but were used as an ordering measure in a more elaborate decorative scheme, which included Renaissance, winged female couples placed at the arched windows who, playing a game of exposure with their dress, flirt at times with the viewer.

To complement the cultured or erotic caryatids holding up the cornice, Förster and the Todescos chose the bearded, strong, and masculine warriors Atlas and Hercules to serve not as erotic decoration but as culturally authoritative and intimidating bodyguards. While the caryatids appear singly or in pairs, holding different poses—with crossed hands, grasping their dress, holding books, or with a tilted head leaning on a raised hand, evoking the self-conscious and cultivated woman—the male figures supporting the alcoves were meant to represent the status of the owner of the house.[46] The choice of Hercules to support the alcoves could be seen as a reflection of Eduard von Todesco's important and powerful role in the economic scene as well as an identifier of the Todescos' Hellenistic Jewish heritage.[47] Eduard would have been familiar with the figure of Hercules as a recurrent heroic motif in the Finance Ministry at Himmelpfortgasse 8. Eduard's relationship with the ministry house reflected both his importance in the economic scene in Vienna and his social position in the city.[48]

While critics welcomed the role model of cultivated Jewish women patrons, they were quick to point out the outsider position of Jewish men patrons. For example, in his *feuilletons* in the *Neue Freie Presse*, the Jewish columnist Daniel Spitzer remarked how the noses of the members of Parliament hardly looked Greek enough to match the building's Hellenistic style, while the red boots of another member seemed ironically to complement the polychrome Greek architecture.[49] The Swiss cultural historian Jacob Burckhardt would have criticized the Greek caryatids on the façades of the Todesco, Epstein, and Ephrussi palaces, since in his private letters he questions the right of "ugly Jews" in Germany to adorn their houses with the beautiful (Greek) caryatids.[50] Though Jews were supposedly protected as part of the new Austrian multiethnic landscape, pointing out the supposed disparity between their Jewish looks and their claim to cultural authority became a popular antisemitic strategy, especially after Vienna's stock market crashed in 1873 (Fig. 5). Even if their intention was to "opt in," the media's undermining of their authority as producers of culture forced Jewish patrons to confront the possibility that they would be forced to "opt out"—unable to choose as they might have done in an earlier stage of the dialectical process of fashioning style.[51]

The Gesamtkunstwerk in Palais Todesco and the Beauty of Belonging

Despite prejudice, and perhaps because of it, Jewish patrons like Todesco carefully constructed their belonging to a Viennese Europeanness and encouraged, in turn, a desire on the part of their guests to belong to their club (as reflected in Garelick's analysis of the dandy's network of seduction, mentioned in the introduction).[52] Jewish patrons created a cultural program by relating their houses to public buildings they wanted to be identified with, as well as maintaining close associations with houses of relatives and other Jewish patrons. The Todesco and Gomperz palaces shared a subtle "family resemblance," for example, through the four allegorical figures of the arts.[53] Possibly following Hansen's suggestion, Carl Rahl, who painted the artistic themes on the ceilings of the interiors and also on the ceiling and walls of the dining room in the *bel étage* of the Todescos' grand apartment, visually echoed the female allegories of the arts that Förster had used on the Palais Gomperz's façade at Kärntnerring 3.[54] Through this iconographic link, the Todesco and Gomperz families presented themselves as art patrons in a collective framework and further secured their family network.

As has been noted, Eduard von Todesco's wish to use a Hellenistic Jewish identification for his apartment interiors—specifically choosing figures easily identified with a deep appreciation of Greek culture—was related to his aim of establishing a shared cultural platform for gentiles and Jews. However, the subject of temptation, or the idea of seduction, also played a special role. Todesco wanted *The Judgment of Paris* to decorate the ceiling,[55] and Reissberger suggests that Eduard may have identified with the idea of the tempted man who is offered the most beautiful woman.[56] Yet the idea of offering or possessing beautiful women was a symbol of a more complex seduction in the Palais Todesco. No doubt the choice of *The Judgment of Paris* for the center of the ceiling, framed at the corners by four goddesses (Hope with an anchor, Fortuna with a horn of plenty, the avenging winged Nemesis riding a chariot drawn by a griffin, and Fate or Destiny writing on a scroll),[57] was to play a

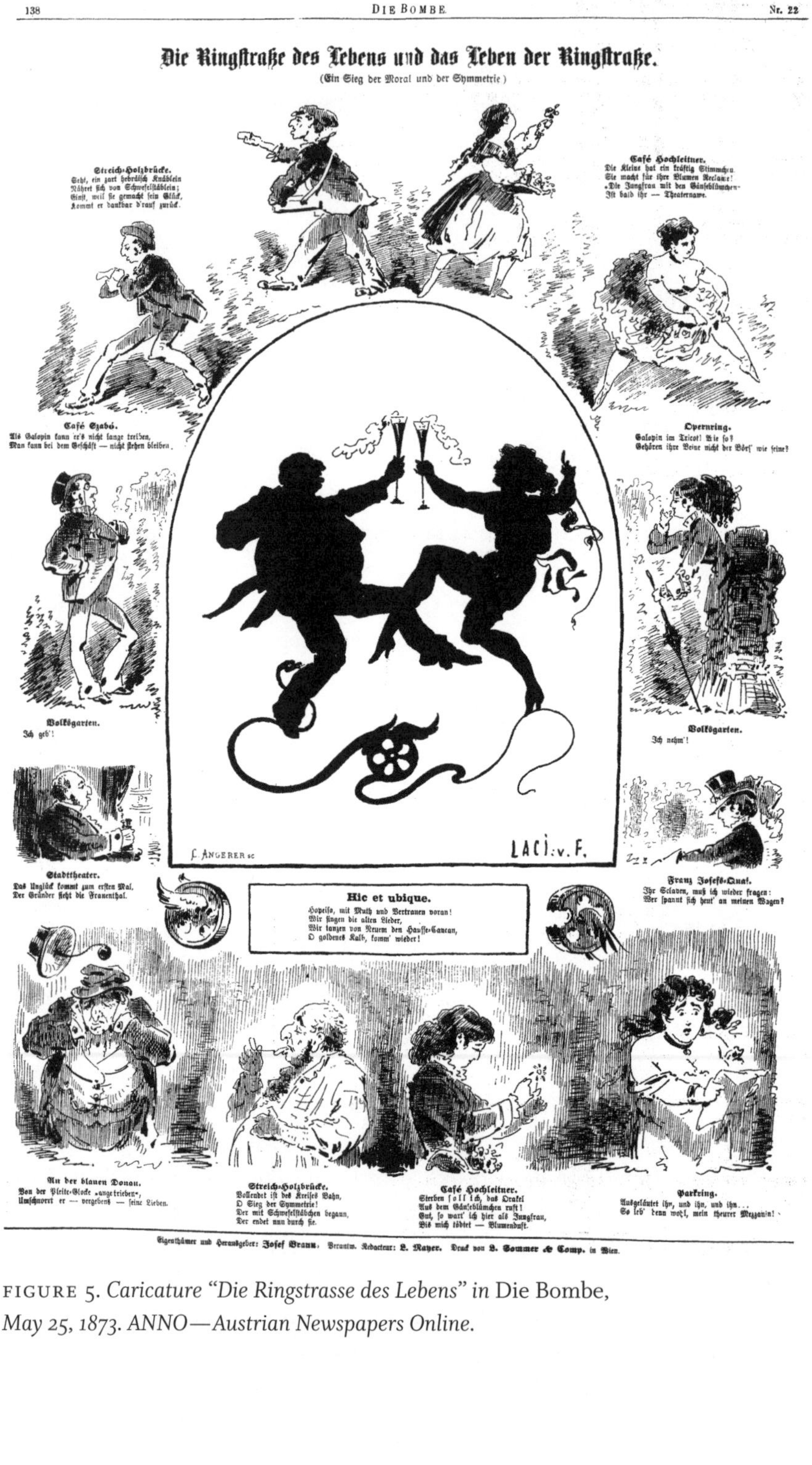

FIGURE 5. Caricature *"Die Ringstrasse des Lebens"* in Die Bombe, May 25, 1873. ANNO—Austrian Newspapers Online.

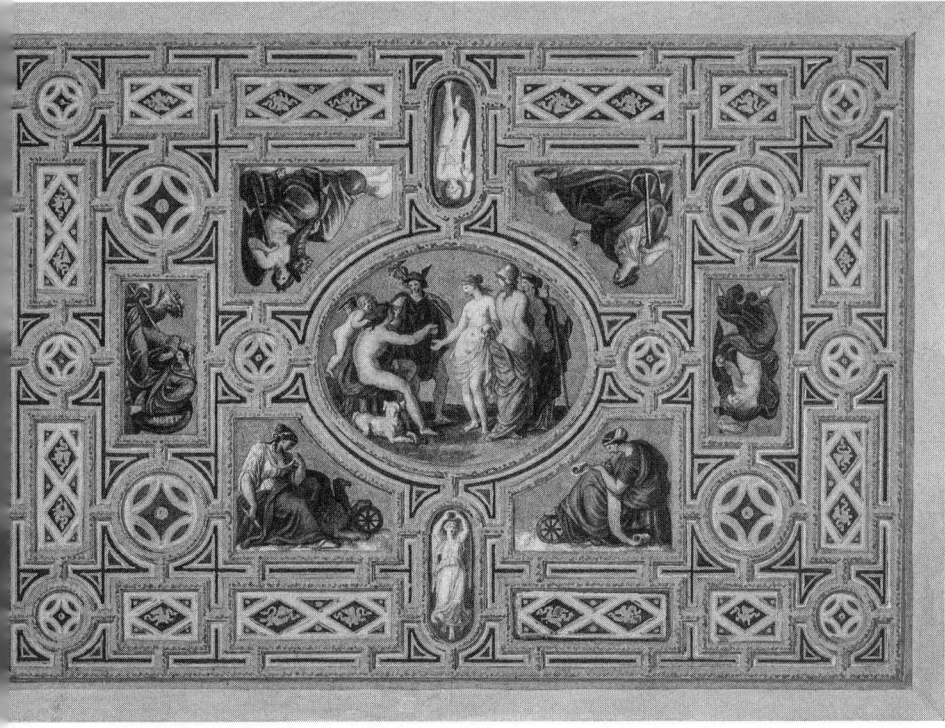

FIGURE 6. *Carl Rahl,* The Judgment of Paris, *sketch for Palais Todesco dining room ceiling, 1863–64. Library of the Academy of Fine Arts, Vienna. Inv. no. 20.165.*

special part in constructing Eduard's role as the host of his guests, but also in the construction of the Todescos' society. The Greek myth of Paris's life and the Trojan wars that decorated the ceiling and the walls in the dining room demonstrated the Todescos' distinguished cultural identity.[58]

The central part of the ceiling shows Paris, bribed with the promise of receiving the most beautiful woman on earth, choosing Aphrodite as the most beautiful of the three goddesses and handing her the apple (Fig. 6, Plate 3). Of course, on the surface level of association, the ceiling's mythological beauty contest can be seen to symbolize the host's desire to claim that he had the most beautiful dining room. The goddesses at the corners, calling on hope, fortune, and destiny, could be seen as sincere expressions of the host's wishes for himself and his guests. However, the question "who is the most beautiful?" may also be seen in the context of the typical caricatures of the time that aimed to portray the ugliness of Jews, and thus *The Judgment of Paris* can be read as a cultured and culturally fluent act of countering provocation with authority. Todesco's dining room was indeed seen to exemplify good taste, as Karl Grün noted—not that of Todesco, but of his architect Hansen: "The dining-room at [the Palais] Todesco with the wall and ceiling decoration, windows with fitted curtains, stylishly designed furniture, doors that are based on drawings, and finally his chandeliers, everything is devised by Theophil Hansen . . . the master of good taste for high bourgeois families."[59]

The Todescos did receive some acclaim, however. A writer in the journal *Kunst-Chronik* praised the beautiful example set by the Todescos in fashioning a new awareness among the Viennese bourgeoisie.[60] Furthermore, the journalist Uhl noted that no other public room surpassed the beauty of the Todesco dining room.[61]

Todesco's Authorship: The Art of Acculturation and Challenging the Cultured Fetish

The concept of the Todescos' dining room, which had relatively little natural light, was ambitious. The architect Hansen conceived of the interplay of the gold-framed ceiling paintings with the oval centerpiece of *The Judgment of Paris*, together with the series of educational wall paintings of central scenes in the Paris saga, as an adaptation of the richly framed ceiling paintings and monumental wall paintings in the Council Hall of the sixteenth-century doge's palace in Venice.[62] The dining room featured decorated pilasters with Corinthian capitals, denoting the room's importance as a public space and legitimizing the use of outer architectural elements in accordance with the late Empire style.[63] Hansen's pairing of the artistic Greek identification (of the Paris myth) and the grand European Renaissance design scheme would be a model for the Jewish Viennese taste for grandeur and the high bourgeois lifestyle. But the question at the center in the survey of the Palais Todesco architecture revolves around the authorship of design and where the attribution for the fashioning of this Viennese bourgeoisie style lies: was it indeed Hansen's Gesamtkunstwerk, within a comprehensive aesthetic motive, or was it Todesco's self-styling in the name of a new cultural club?

Todesco arranged his public rooms carefully. The fact that beauty and aesthetics were at least prominent considerations or concerns for Todesco can further be determined by his interest in painting. The first paintings known to have been purchased by Todesco were acquired a year after he married Sophie. In 1846, he bought two paintings by the contemporary Austrian artist Friedrich Gauermann and exhibited them at the Wiener Kunstverein.[64] Several paintings showed different aspects of Eduard's developing cultural perspective. A painting by J. O'Connell depicted Psyche and Amor; another painting by an unknown artist showed the mythological Ganymede as a beautiful young man in a golden frame.[65] A further indication of an aesthetic quest, as well as another reference to Eduard von Todesco's identification with Italian Renaissance nobility, were the portraits of a Venetian nobleman and of Doge Marcantonio Trevisani, both attributed to Tintoretto.[66] But he was also interested in political subjects, as in the depiction of the general and statesman Lamoral, Count Egmont, by the Belgian painter Louis Gallait. Egmont, who opposed the Inquisition in the Habsburg Netherlands, was executed after a false accusation of heresy. Other paintings Todesco owned had Christian iconography, such as Pieter Brueghel the Younger's copy of his father's monumental *John the Baptist*, which Todesco had bought by the end of the 1860s and which was inherited by his daughter Yella von Oppenheimer (1854–1943).[67] And another ambitious Christian theme in the Todesco collection was the painting after Titian's *Pope Julius II* (also identified as, or perhaps referring to, a painting after Titian's *Pope Paul III*).[68] In 1883, Todesco was the first client to purchase a painting by the impressionist Olga Wisinger-Florian, buying her "Field Flower Bouquet," which was exhibited in the Künstlerhaus that year.[69] Todesco's wish to keep his collection up-to-date and to show works by both old masters and contemporary artists is evident. A few questions arise from a consideration of the paintings mentioned above. Did Todesco purchase Christian paintings to give his guests of other beliefs a feeling of familiarity in his home (a view referred to above regarding his choice of subject for the dining room)? Was the Hellenistic identification chosen as a barrier against Christian iconography, or was it a transitional phase in the process of assimilation, leading toward conversion to Christianity? The Hellenistic identification legitimized the Jewish creation of a shared cultural platform for rapprochement between Jews and Christians, and the art exhibited in the public rooms or donated to art museums was meant to secure the social position of the Jewish patrons.

In 1888, one year after Todesco's death, Ferdinand von Saar, a close friend of Josephine Wertheimstein (née Gomperz; 1820–94) and her daughter Franziska, wrote *Seligmann Hirsch*, a tragic story of Jewish acculturation in which the unruly Jew Hirsch is rejected by his daughter and son. Saar's hero, the secular self-made Galician Jew, Seligmann Hirsch, who moves to Vienna with his children after the death of his religious wife, declares: "But I tell them, I have style—I must have style, since I socialize in Vienna in the best society. Of course out in the country, where nobody knows me, I let myself go."[70]

Saar disclosed the aspiration of Jews to obtain manners and "style" as an entry ticket to the finest Viennese society. Hirsch, his hero, further recognizes the disparity between the pretentious salon orchestration of his newly ennobled son and cultivated daughter-in-law and their respected guests' prejudice against them as Jews.[71] Hirsch's son eventually changes his family name from von Hirsch to von Hirtburg. The Ringstrasse patrons were enthusiastic about the book. Sophie Todesco's sister-in-law, Louise Auspitz-Gomperz, recommended that Saar send his book to different critics for review.[72] Most of the reviews complimented Saar on his psychological portrayals, and some pointed out that there was no trace of antisemitism.[73] However, Saar's wish to confront the cultivated children, the Viennese patrons, with their Polish father, echoed a romantic yet dangerous tendency, since it did not fit their migration history. Most of the Ringstrasse's Jewish patrons had come from German-speaking cities in Moravia, Bohemia, and Hungary or from Germany. The fathers of the Jewish patrons Todesco, Gomperz, Lieben, and Auspitz were well educated and respected for their progressive Western Weltanschaaung and achievements. By referring to the Polish father, Saar may have adapted an antisemitic strategy of undermining the Western European identification of these patrons and confirmed the prejudice against the Jewish patrons of the Ringstrasse as supposedly new (Western) Europeans who did not really belong. Another possible interpretation is that through the relationship of the cultivated children and their Polish father, Saar was actually portraying the relationship between the patrons and a stereotypical personification of the Jewish population, exposing the patrons' ambivalence, shame, and yet strong sense of commitment to the Jewish collective. Given the creative freedom to challenge social taboos, which was permitted in his literary club, Todesco may have consciously chosen to act out time and again the role of the invented Polish father.[74] Though this story was written after Todesco's time as a cultural producer in Vienna, it can be said that he would have appreciated the character who questioned a certain art of acculturation and might have reveled in the iconoclastic unruliness of the self-made Galician Jew.

In contrast to his demonstrably shrewd economic, political, and art patronage skills, in Viennese society Todesco chose to identify himself as a foreigner or fool. This is documented in many reported anecdotes, such as those about his flouting of his secretive literary club's rules, and the caricature of him that appeared on the front page of the journal *Der Floh* on June 12, 1870. In this caricature he is identified as a staff member of *Der Floh* and is shown looking suspiciously at a dictionary of foreign words held in his left hand, while he makes a desperate gesture with the right hand, possibly asking "what does this mean?" The caricature mocks the claims of acculturated Jews to be versed in other European languages such as French and English.[75] Certainly

Todesco enjoyed provoking people time and again. During a dinner party in which many famous people from Vienna's theater scene were present, he is reported to have whispered to his neighbor, "Who is this Shakespeare who is being discussed here? I have never heard of this man before."[76] Yet Todesco's provocative challenge to Jewish acculturation—the public display of Europeanization—was also used to challenge his authority as a Viennese art patron.

In 1888, the year when Saar's novel appeared, Cornelius Gurlitt published an account in his book *Im Bürgerhause* of an event he had witnessed in the Todesco dining room.[77] Gurlitt's anecdote supposedly shows Hansen's pride in his Gesamtkunstwerk and recalls Hansen's angry outburst when he noticed that Todesco was using a tablecloth that did not fit in with his aesthetic program, shouting at the owner for "ruining" his design:

> We were sitting at the table of the richly decorated house of a Viennese banker, not far from me sat his friend, the famous master-builder, who had "furnished" him. The lively discussion at the table was suddenly interrupted when the artist in an excited tone shouted at his host: "What's the idea of having such an ugly cloth in my room! You are ruining the whole place for me!" Everyone looked around. There on the side table was a tasteless, overly colorful tablecloth. The servant hurried to remove it. Yet the master-builder found it difficult to calm down. "What will people think of me, when you are ruining the whole atmosphere with your aniline colors. You must consider that I am an artist and I can't allow my work to be ruined!" "I meant" . . . the banker started to explain. "Oh, who cares what you mean! I have already received your promise that you should ask for my permission before each planned change in the room. This is the minimum I can demand, that not everyone who wants—could ruin my work. What would you say," he asked his neighbor, an excellent portrait artist, "if someone placed in your portrait a red nose, like the tablecloth there." Everyone was smiling and kept silent, and the banker did not feel so good in his stylish dining room.[78]

Reissberger assumes that the event took place in Todesco's dining room. Historians have used this anecdote as evidence of Todesco's reputation as a philistine.[79] This anecdote contains certain presumptions about the relationship between a Jewish patron and his designer, at least as far as that relationship was generally seen in Vienna. One is the myth of the patron's total reliance on the architect, which would later also be paraphrased in Adolf Loos's criticism of the parvenu who purchased a secessionist Gesamtkunstwerk design.[80] Another is that the designer could rudely question the patron's personal additions to his design—his questioning, as recalled by Gurlitt, would confirm the prejudice against Jews as not having art, culture, or taste. To this, one could add the prejudiced stereotype of Jewish newcomers (parvenus) as crude, which would be a personal insult directed toward the owner. In Vienna at that time, this could have been allowed and possibly even expected due to his Jewish identity. Was the designer afraid that his design would be regarded as the product of Jewish taste (meaning bad taste), an accusation Karl Kraus would use against the secessionists in the early twentieth century)? Gurlitt hints indirectly at the patron's Jewish identity by quoting the architect comparing the patron's personal contribution to the interior, the striking tablecloth on a side table, to a nose painted red and standing out in a beautiful portrait. The red nose does not necessarily echo the stereotypical identification of the striking Jewish nose and could suggest a drunken man, but the vast subtext of antisemitic caricatures would certainly have permitted such a connection.[81]

The insult in this case was meant to reverse the roles of master and servant: the craftsman who served the patron reemerges as his master. Was it the case that Todesco was challenged in claiming authority over the grand design of his palace? But then what are we to make of the initials S(ophie) E(duard) T(odesco) that appear above the side entrances of his ballroom, leading to the studio on one side and to the reception room on the other side? And the repetition of their initials to decorate the golden rail of the grand staircase leading to their private apartment? Todesco made sure to leave his authorizing signature.

There is another aspect to Gurlitt's story of the colorful cloth. It may have been a calculated provocation by Todesco himself: an expression of his wish to act out the role of the "Polish father" and challenge the fetish of Western culture. Here we move away from the architect's role as manufacturer of a Gesamtkunstwerk and return to the role that Todesco had in self-styling his cultural identity. Georg Simmel argues that "the social game has a deeper double meaning—that it is played not only *in* a society as its outward bearer but that *with* the society actually 'society' is played. Further, in the sociology of the sexes, eroticism has elaborated a form of play: coquetry, which finds in sociability its lightest, most playful, and yet its widest realization."[82] Todesco's choices of artwork, in the case of the wall paintings in the dining room, are proud representations of societal games: the judgment of beauty and status, the enticement through bribery and compromised reward, and the mediation of love and triumph. Todesco reveled in the power of connotation of the imagery in his interiors, which could mirror his guests' considerations of leaving or staying. The imagery on the walls as much as the social engagement of his guests was a flirtatious game of consent or denial played out to avoid reaching a decision.[83] Todesco tantalized his guests with the cultured setting just to ruin the impression with a provocative statement.

As a host, Todesco surely felt committed to making sure his guests felt comfortable in his house, but his provocative humor and statements supposedly exposing his ignorance guaranteed a certain distance between him and them. Todesco chose to expose the artificiality of his beautiful and cultured Hellenistic Renaissance setting as a conscious act of acculturation. He placed himself in the embarrassing position of an ignoramus or a man without taste—also possibly through the "colorful tablecloth"—and each time forced himself, his wife, and their guests to reaffirm their bond through the shared cultural achievements of Viennese society. Through his reckless approach to cultural icons, Todesco challenged the aims of Jewish acculturation —namely, the necessity of proving an identification with and participation in Western European culture.

"Be Who You Appear to Be"

An admirer of the Todescos' cultural productions and grand display of beauty in their house was the patron Gustav von Epstein.[84] Epstein, who built one of the most impressive historicist neo-Renaissance palaces on the Ringstrasse, at Burgring 9 (today Dr. Karl Renner Ring 1), chose the motto "SIS QUI VIDERIS" (Be who you appear to be) for his coat of arms in 1866.[85] Painted on the ceiling of the small cupola over the entrance hall of his rental apartment palace built (1868–71), this coat of arms and motto greeted his guests.[86] The Palais Epstein was conceived as a physical symbol of the banker's cosmopolitan outlook, enlightened patronage, and wealth.[87] It was also the product of an intense dialogue between Epstein and his architect, Theophil Hansen.[88] Following the fashionable dictates for rental apartment palaces on the Ringstrasse, Hansen modeled it after Italian Renaissance palaces but made a monumental addition in ordering the Czech-Austrian sculptor Vincenz Pilz to create the caryatids on high pedestals guarding the palace entrance and supporting the balcony of the *bel étage* (Fig. 7). The four caryatids, two on each side of the arched portal, protrude into the public sidewalk.[89] In contrast to the caryatids in the side entrance porticos of Hansen's later Austrian Parliament, built next to the palace, which were a direct reference to the caryatids in the Erectheion on the Acropolis in Athens, Epstein's caryatids do not have the same pose and therefore do not appear to be frozen in

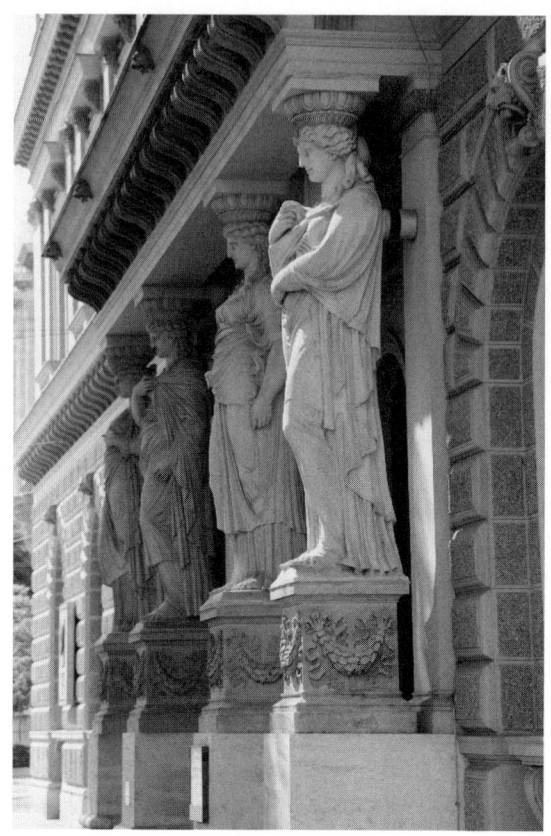

FIGURE 7. Theophil Hansen, Palais Epstein façade, 1872. Photo: © 2015, Benjamin von Radom.

time. Epstein's robust, somewhat masculine-looking, monumental caryatids look as though they are adjusting their Roman garments in front of guests and passersby.

The façade plan submitted for approval to city authorities in the winter of 1868 shows a bearded and elegantly dressed man with a fashionable hat and a cane standing close to a caryatid, yet his head does not even reach the decorated upper part of her pedestal. His elegant appearance set against the caryatids' monumental stature is meant to underscore their grandeur.[90] Epstein had rejected the more feminine and delicate-looking caryatids in Hansen's early sketches, and the final caryatids reveal the extroverted character of the owner. Epstein's preference for more imposing caryatids reflected his consciousness of the modern woman and his wish to modernize Vienna's landscape through allowing the sculptures of women to evoke the impression of live performance. A nude putto on top of the arched entrance, representing a

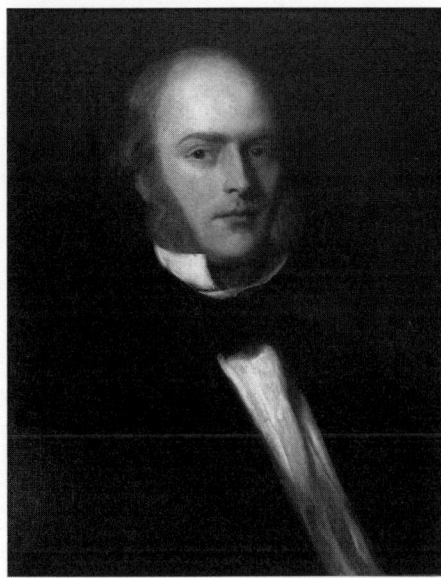

FIGURE 8. *Gustav Gaul, portrait of Gustav von Epstein, oil on canvas, 1858.* © *The Austrian Parliamentary Administration. Photo: Christian Hikade.*

promise of prosperity and leisure, is a complementary contrast to the stylish display of the four dressed women. Yet as figures securing the entrance with their body structures, two to a side, they also appear as Greco-Roman female guards for the seductive treasures within Epstein's house.

In contrast to the robust appearance of his entrance caryatids, Epstein's portrait from a decade earlier shows a mature and self-assured yet delicate-looking and reserved man at the age of thirty with a pale face emerging from a somber background (Fig. 8). It was made on the occasion of his marriage to Emilie Wehle in August 1858 by the Austrian painter Gustav Gaul, and it hangs in his old office in his palace, which is owned by the Austrian Parliament today. Epstein has red hair, a high forehead (due to a receding hairline) and a slight moustache. His warm brown eyes are determined, and his smart smile elevates the contours of his face. He looks at his viewer with confidence, inner serenity, and the authority of a gentleman. The modesty of his white shirt, the black tie around a high collar, and his black jacket confirm his identification as a man of style. In comparing his portrait, with its presentation of a reserved and serene gentleman, to the far more imposing figures of the caryatids at his palace's entrance, the viewer can trace the intricacies of Epstein's self-styling, expressed by the motto "Be who you appear to be." Appearance and presentation are carefully gauged and offered to the public in multiple layers.

A Humanist and an Art Lover: The Patron Epstein

"Sis qui videris," and indeed, he is what he appears to be! "He wants, he has, he does" says a German poet from the Middle Ages, who presents all the cleverness of ambition, possession and handling of a gentleman (Herrn): one can say the same about Gustav Ritter von Epstein, who uses the rich resources available to him, realizing [them] in a way that now grants him unconditional recognition of his surroundings, and secures in no less a manner the general admiration of future generations in the highest degree."[91]

The monumental caryatids on the front of his new palace positioned Epstein next to Todesco as an advocate of the new Jewish self-identification in relation to a Hellenistic Jewish heritage, and Epstein's fame in Vienna as one of the best representatives of Jewish society was further secured. His identification with the Greek tradition was further expressed in the modest smiling Hygeia in an arched niche of his palace's inner court. Vicenz Pilz, sculptor of the entrance caryatids, was also responsible for this sculpture in white marble. Under the inner court's glass roof, Hygeia, half-naked with a raised leg, poses on top of a garlanded base above the water fountain.[92] However, this Hygeia, holding a chalice in her right hand as a snake curls over her left, failed to fulfill her promise to protect the good health of the owner and his family.[93]

The art historian Friedrich Dahm describes how Epstein asserted his authority over Hansen in his selection of Hansen's drawings. The caryatids Hansen had designed to decorate the balcony of the *bel étage* were moved to the ground floor to guard the entrance, and Epstein replaced the architect's original vision of erotic caryatids with monumental and masculine ones. Furthermore, it was Epstein's choice to paint the coat of arms in the entrance hall cupola. He also rejected the placement of decorative vases on the bel étage balcony, which would have emphasized the floor's importance—marking its hierarchical distinction as the one occupied by the owner of the house. Dahm's suggestion is that this stylistic change, stressing the bel étage and second floor equally, shifted the design from Romantic historicism to a strict historicist style.[94] The intense dialogue between patron and architect gave Hansen the necessary stimulus to innovate stylistically.

Compared to the powerful place of Todesco in the cultural network of Vienna, Epstein, who was a few years younger, appeared more of a newcomer. However, in a very short period he achieved the reputation of a powerful rival. When the brilliant Jewish chess player Wilhelm Steinitz provoked him during one of their games, Epstein shouted at him: "Do you know who I am?!" Steinitz told him he knew he was the "Epstein" of the stock exchange, but here playing chess he, Steinitz, was "the Epstein."[95] The "Epstein of the Stock Exchange" became the "Epstein on the Ringstrasse" through the carefully designed palace, the interiors of his apartments on the first floor, and the reputation of his art collection. Epstein's house near the Parliament building belongs to the Parliament today, and his memory is highly regarded and publicized in the chronicles of the institution. The link between the two buildings was secured visually through their "family resemblance": the caryatids guarding the Palais Epstein's entrance correspond to Hansen's later designs for the classical caryatids guarding the Parliament building's side porches.[96]

Like Todesco, Epstein inherited a fortune from a charismatic father.[97] Lazar Epstein (1798–1864) was described as "not such a fine man" but very smart, and through his looks and character he became one of the prominent figures in Vienna.[98] He began his career as a supplier to the Austrian army during the Napoleonic wars and founded a cotton-printing factory in Prague after the wars.[99] In 1840 Lazar opened a textile merchandising business in today's Judengasse near the headquarters of the Jewish community in Vienna, and progressed, through his sharpness and social skills, from selling printed textiles to banking. After his father's death, Gustav von Epstein sold the textile factories and concentrated on the bank business. He was known for his generosity. Following Austria's humiliating defeat by Prussia in 1866, he gave a huge grant through the state to the poor and orphans, for which he received his noble title and the order of the Eisernen Krone 3, becoming Gustav Ritter von Epstein in November 1866.[100] Clerks in a small room at the entrance to his bank (on the ground floor of the future Palais Epstein) granted financial help to the needy in a discreet manner, dispensing yearly sums equivalent to $1 million today.[101] After Epstein erected his grand palace, his poor health led him to retire from business and transfer the management of the bank to a procurator. He dedicated himself to the design of the palace and his fast-growing art collection, and in January 1872 he moved to the finished *bel étage*. He continued to hold representative roles in different firms in Vienna, Prague and Budapest, and he held the honorary position of consul in Vienna of Grand Duke Nikolaus Friedrich Peter von Oldenburg.[102] From the time Jews received equal rights in 1867 until his death in 1879, Epstein was a member of the committee headed by the president of the Jewish community.

In the biographical essay on Epstein in the *Biographisches Lexikon der Wiener Weltausstellung 1873* (Biographical lexicon of Vienna's world exhibition 1873), the author noted that Epstein gained his rich knowledge and experiences and built his distinguished appreciation of art during his travels in

Europe, especially in Italy, and through the Orient.[103] The meeting of Italian and Oriental aesthetics was on display in the architectural setting of Palais Epstein. Epstein was an art patron before he built his palace, but it was through his city palace that he promoted his reputation as a humanist and a Renaissance man rather than as a businessman.[104] To demonstrate his high aspirations, Epstein helped found, and contributed to, the Austrian Museum of Art and Industry; was a founding member of the Association for the Promotion of the Applied Arts School (Gründungsmitglied des Vereins zur Förderung der Kunstgewerbeschule); and helped found the Society of the Friends of Music (Stifter der Gesellschaft der Musikfreunde).

Carl von Vincenti, a contemporary art critic, praised Palais Epstein as one of two brilliant examples of Hansen's talent and understanding of Renaissance art. Vincenti was a careful observer, noting the play of red, black, and white in the stairway: "Two Veronese red marble columns on high black marble bases and with white Corinthian capitals. The walls shine in gray and red stucco lustro."[105] Vincenti further praised the palais's organic style, achieved through repeated motifs.[106]

The contemporary art critic Emerich Ranzoni played a special role promoting the Renaissance style as the new Viennese style on the Ringstrasse through his architectural reviews in the liberal newspaper *Neue Freie Presse*. In 1873, the year of the World Exhibition in Vienna, Ranzoni praised Hansen's Gesamtkunstwerk in the Palais Epstein, describing its interiors in detail in his book *Wiener Bauten* (Viennese buildings).[107] The author described entering though red marble columns, climbing up the grand staircase, and entering the winter garden. One would have used the winter garden, with its floor of black-and-white mosaic—a repetition of the star paneling parquet in the ballroom—to enter Epstein's apartments.[108] The most celebrated space identifying Epstein with the heritage of Hellenistic Jewish culture was the winter garden, with its frieze of Alexander the Great's army parade (Fig. 9, Plate 4). Walking through or sitting in the winter garden, a guest's thoughts would have been elevated by the sight of the frieze, which would have put him in appropriate frame of mind to enter Epstein's more private rooms. The frieze was a copy of a relief by the Danish sculptor Bertel Thorvaldsen, which shows the victory parade of Alexander the Great in Babylon.[109] The original, commissioned by Napoleon in 1811, is in the Appartamento Napoleonico in the Palazzo Quirinale in Rome.[110]

This area was designed as an open space. It served as the music room during evening events, when the mirrored doors would be pushed open and disappear into the walls of the ballroom, and the audience would sit facing

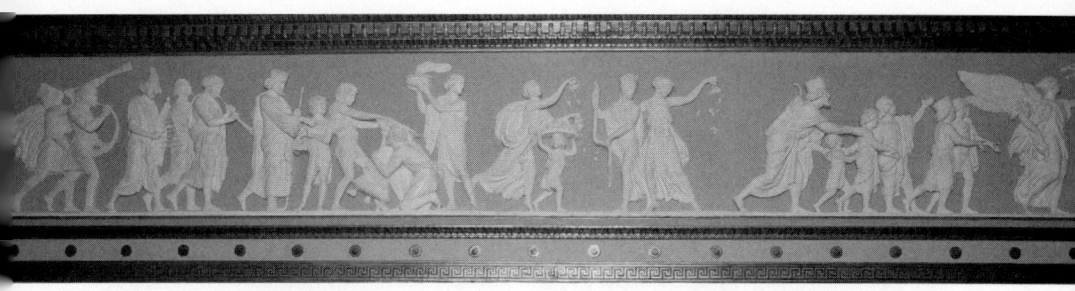

FIGURE 9. Theophil Hansen, Alexander frieze, winter garden, Palais Epstein, 1872. © The Austrian Parliamentary Administration. Photo: Christian Hikade.

the inner court.[111] In Epstein's time this space was decorated with Italianate vegetation, and in the middle of the window niche a guest would encounter a red marble fountain in the shape of a shell with the statue of a faun by the Parisian sculptor André le Brun (1783).[112] The faun of Greco-Roman mythology is half-human, half-goat (the human head has goat's horns), a forest god who could be a source of fear in the forest or of benevolence, such as when guiding travelers.[113] The cooperation between Hansen and Epstein was praised for reviving antiquity and bringing it back to life in a lively manner.[114]

In his description, Ranzoni continued from the winter garden to Epstein's studio, commending its tasteful "wooden architecture" (later revealed to be a plaster imitation), and its decorated ceiling, which included a copy of Rubens's *Venus and Amor*, whose original he suggested might be in Florence.[115] The author of the biographical essay on Epstein in the *Biographisches Lexikon der Wiener Weltausstellung 1873* took the display of prestigious books stored in built-in bookcases and on the desk in the library next to the studio as evidence of Epstein's high culture: "In the tall bookcases, superbly finished in cherry wood, exquisite works of all literatures welcome book lovers, on the desk a rare old book in Latin lies open, as well as a historical lexicon by a famous author. Apart from books, the room is decorated with archaeological and ethnographic peculiarities, marble busts, and folkloric items, costumes, etc."[116] Epstein owned prints and graphical works mainly by Dutch masters, which he also kept in his library. The library seduced the educated visitor with its offer to engage in a European cultural treasure hunt.

Displaying his authority as a learned humanist patron was crucial for Epstein. Reissberger note that Epstein's intense dialogue with Hansen was further evident in the office or studio Epstein designed just before resigning from his business positions. With their shared interest in reviving the aesthetic of antiquity, Epstein worked with Hansen to refashion himself: he did not want an office but a gentleman's studio in his palace, with windows directed toward Parliament. He refused a décor allegorizing the sources of his fortune—industry, trade by rail and sea, and other commerce—in favor of a more cultured humanist scheme.[117] Hansen had offered him a coffered ceiling with similar to the planned coffered ceiling for the future large hall of the stock exchange building, yet Epstein rejected it. In contrast to Todesco's office in his palais—with its painted allegories of wealth and the branches of his business: trade, industry, the railway, and shipping[118]—Epstein preferred to identify himself as a humanist, seducing his audience with a copy of Rubens's *Venus and Amor* on his studio's ceiling. This seduction then revealed the patron Epstein's intellectual world, but—much as Todesco did with his Greek theme—it anchored his Jewish patronage as a historicist in a cultural heritage that could be shared with the broader Viennese or European culture.

Ranzoni continued his tour from the studio, turning right and entering the corner room—the smoking or billiard room—that looked out over the Ringstrasse. The ceiling decoration in this room followed the decorative scheme of the ceiling of Santa Maria dei Miracoli in Venice, but in accordance with the room's profane atmosphere, the decorative frame was borrowed without the religious Old Testament imagery.[119] Vincenti described the colorful coffered ceiling in this room (noting that it was a copy of the ceiling of the Venetian Renaissance church) as having an "oriental colorful style."[120] In addition to establishing orientation and uniformity through the rhythmic application of pilasters,[121] the smoking room was decorated with eight beautiful wall paintings by the landscapist Josef Hoffmann, which Ranzoni described as "one of the most ORIGINAL achievements" in landscape painting.[122]

In September 1870, Hansen had written to Hoffmann that Epstein liked his sketches very much and wanted to buy the landscape paintings.[123] The landscapes allowed Epstein to bring the world into his smoking room and invite his guests to virtually travel with him. The smoking room with the borrowed—once sacred, now profane—ceiling presented a cultlike setting for a virtual journey. The large paintings were set in wooden frames against the dark blue wallpaper, with black wood paneling on the lower parts of the walls. The paintings depicted ancient pilgrimage sites, among them Ellora (a mountain temple in India), Philae (a temple to Isis on an island in the middle of the Nile River in Egypt), and Athens and Rome. For Epstein these landscapes could have further meant connecting Vienna—represented by a painting of it and a view of the street—with other pilgrim or tourist destinations around the world. This arrangement also championed the stranger's need, according to Simmel, for a dialectical experience of "placement" and "displacement"[124]—and this virtual journey may have been Epstein's way of remembering his journeys to Italy and the Orient.

Continuing through the smoking room, the guest entered the dining room with its distinguished display of old masters. While the Palais Todesco dining room ceiling, as noted above, followed the decorative scheme of the council hall ceiling in the doge's palace in Vienna, the Palais Epstein dining room ceiling followed the decorative scheme of the San Lorenzo fuori le Mura basilica in Rome.[125] The coffered plaster (imitating the coffered wood in the original sacred space) granted a sense of elevation and formality to the old masters hanging on the room's red lustro walls. As Todesco had chosen the prestige of Rahl's Troy decorations for his dining room, so Epstein chose the prestige of old masters for his dining room.[126] When he offered to show his old masters at the Austrian Museum of Art and Industry in Stubenring, Epstein made a clear public statement that he wanted a role in shaping the public discourse on art. In 1865, he donated seven books to the museum, mainly albums of sketches by the German neoclassicist Karl Friedrich Schinkel and an impressive two-volume folio by Jules Goury and Owen Jones titled *Plans, Elevation, Section, and Details of the Alhambra*, published in London in 1842–45.[127]

The next room at the front of the palais was the grand ballroom, which had a lighter appearance than the other public rooms because of the sand color of the imitation marble walls. The pilaster decorations in this room also cited the Santa Maria dei Miracoli. The pilasters were decorated with fantastic vegetation and animals, birds, and dolphins and crowned with a variation of a Corinthian capital bearing a naked winged putto sitting in the middle with crossed legs. There was a smart play of "placement" and "displacement" through the arrangement of pilaster, window (opening to the balcony at the front), pilaster, mirror, pilaster, window, pilaster. As if the owner or his guest were invited to look out to Vienna and back in to the room, the mirror united the owner or his guest with the setting of the room at the same time. This arrangement allowed the visitor to choose if he wanted to "opt in" to the Palais Epstein or to "opt out" to the Ringstrasse, thus exposing the owner's methods of fashioning his style. Epstein's offer to his guest to "opt in" or "opt out"—or to remain hanging between the two possibilities—contradicts Reissberger's suggestion that the mirrored doors to the winter garden, which disappeared into the walls when opened, may have evoked, when closed, the impression that this room was a hermetic environment.[128]

It was, instead, an environment very conducive to expansive thought and associations—namely, within the classical tradition. The spandrels above the three doors leading into the dining room, the winter garden, and the recep-

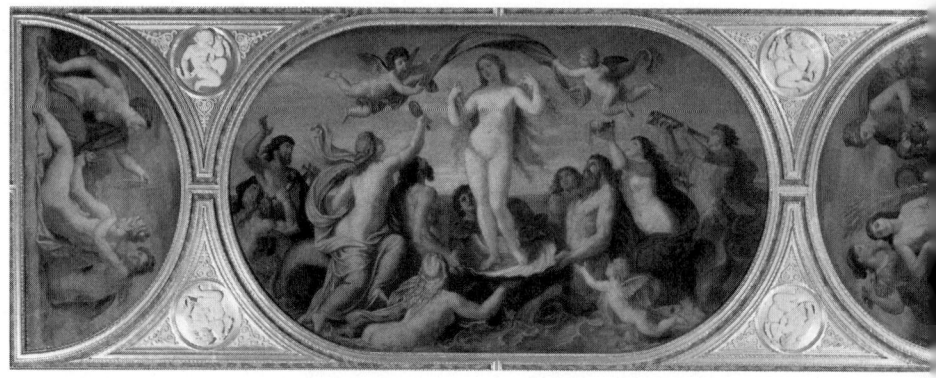

FIGURE 10. *Christian Griepenkerl*, Birth of Venus, *ballroom ceiling, Palais Epstein, 1872. © The Austrian Parliamentary Administration. Photo: Christian Hikade.*

tion room were decorated with reclining naked bacchantes, who turned to face each other and held chalices in their outstretched hands as if raising glasses to the joys of life. Ranzoni noted that despite what he considered a waste of gold and marble, this room achieved the most beautiful decoration through the spiritual paintings of Rahl's students, Eduard Bitterlich and Christian Griepenkerl, who executed Rahl's drawings with the central ceiling painting of the *Birth of Venus* (Fig. 10, Plate 5).[129] Hansen and Rahl had conceived the original thematic program for the palace of Grand Duke Nikolaus Friedrich Peter von Oldenburg.[130] Oldenburg rejected the artistic program because of its expense, and it is possible that Epstein, wanting to have something to fulfill his aristocratic ambitions, asked Hansen to realize the scheme on a smaller scale in his ballroom. Epstein knew the grand duke through a journey they had made together to Italy, and he was also his consul in Vienna. A portrait of the grand duke and his wife also hung in Epstein's studio.[131] Perhaps Hansen, not wanting to waste an existing art program, offered it to Epstein. Whatever the case, the central *Birth of Venus* panel fit well with Epstein's self-fashioning. The frieze on the ceiling depicted the power and triumph of Amor (love).[132] In Hansen and Rahl's explanation of the program, Venus is identified as the ideal of beauty. The paintings in the flanking lunettes show the graces, who grant morals and charm, and the nature goddesses, who grant gifts of nature. To the right, below the graces, is the depiction of the wedding of Amor and Psyche; to the left, below the nature goddesses, is a lively dance of the muses. On the elongated frieze leading toward the winter garden, Apollo appears, playing his lyre among shepherds. On the other side, toward the street, another elongated frieze shows Bacchus transforming water into wine.¹³³ The parade of classical figures was intended to serve as a stimulus, encouraging the visitor to engage in dancing. The red star motif on the parquet floor—similar to the black star motif on the winter garden floor—was framed with the meander motif.¹³⁴

Epstein's European and Jewish Cultural Networking

Epstein's modernist identity was expressed through a combination of daring wall colors, his choice of art, and the borrowed historicist sacred setting. His art of flirtation provoked abundant speculation. Where was the original Rubens painting that was copied on the ceiling of his studio (Florence or Paris)? Who was the ceiling of the ballroom actually planned for? (If for the grand duke's castle, what was the relationship between Epstein and Oldenburg, who often traveled to Italy together)?¹³⁵ Who else bought paintings by the Dutch artist Frans Hals (and did the Rothschilds have more old masters than Epstein did?)? Such discussions among Epstein's guests, journalists of his day, and later historians helped fashion Epstein's reputation as a brilliant aesthete—and as "the Epstein on the Ringstrasse."

The Palais Epstein smoking room's citation of the Renaissance Santa Maria dei Miracoli made it, according to Reissberger, into an exhibition object alongside the existing landscape paintings, transforming this hall into part of an imaginary museum.¹³⁶ Reissberger explains that this arrangement of an "art depot" suggests a culturally imperialistic "trophy collection." Her argument is that to own art—in the form of citations, copies, and originals—served the members of the "second society" as demonstrations of richness, not in the form of obtained capital, but in the form of obtained cultural goods.¹³⁷ Reissberger suggests that Epstein's interiors represented a wish to mask and compensate for his lack of a distinguished past—to shift attention from his history (his origins) to the history of the acquired design and art objects.¹³⁸ In contrast, I argue that as in the case of Todesco's Greek subjects in his dining room, Epstein's carefully orchestrated public rooms made a claim on history, precisely from his own Jewish history—a Hellenistic Jewish history: he fashioned his self-image not by looking past his origins but by identifying an origin that was shared with other Europeans. Using sacred models such as references to a Roman basilica as decorative schemes and employing the prestige of old masters and representations of Hellenistic culture, the two Jewish patrons shaped a modernist identity.

Compared to the Palais Todesco, the Palais Epstein's façade was more reserved, apart from the caryatids, and represented a rather rigid historicism.

However, there was a respectable competition between the grand interior of the Palais Todesco and the Palais Epstein's entrance and *bel étage* apartments. If Todesco used the figure of Hercules, supporting the alcoves on the *bel étage*, to relate his palace on Kärntnerstrasse to the Ministry of Finance building in Himmelpfortgasse, Epstein used the caryatids guarding his entrance to refer to the Parliament building.[139] He may also have accepted Hansen's suggestion to establish a visual relation between his palace and the Oriental striped walls of the staircase in the Stock Exchange (whose design Epstein influenced as a member of the construction committee).[140]

When we consider the Oriental style in the stripes of the palace staircase, we may infer that Epstein perceived Orientalism as integral to Jewish style, but the pervading theme remains the historicist, the Hellenistic, and (in his self-fashioning) the Hellenistic Jewish style. The caryatids would also appear in Epstein's future second building, next to the stock exchange building, though only decorating the side balconies.[141] Epstein was praised in various publications accompanying Vienna's World Exhibition in the spring of 1873 as a model art patron, thereby securing fame for himself in Vienna's chronicles.[142]

The historian Brigitte Hamann claims that the design of the Palais Epstein was not meant for Jewish society since, she argues, Epstein's artist friends were mainly gentiles.[143] Yet Epstein not only identified himself as a Jew; as a gentleman he engaged with Jewish causes and was a member of the board governing the Jewish community. When Rabbi Moritz Güdemann met Epstein at a charity event in the Palais Todesco, Epstein told him, according to Güdemann's memoirs: "I will not consider my house officially opened until I welcome you in it."[144] When his palace was being constructed, Epstein mediated between the master builder, the young architect Otto Wagner, and the orthodox Jewish community in Pest (now Budapest). In an action indicating his links to the Jewish community and the broader Viennese one, he may have recommended Wagner as the architect for the future synagogue of the orthodox community in 1867–68.[145] The grand two-volume work on the Alhambra that Epstein gave to the Austrian Museum of Art and Industry's library, recognized as a standard source on the Moorish style, would serve as Wagner's main inspiration for the decoration of his synagogue in Pest.[146] Did Epstein recommend Wagner to turn to the Alhambra book in his search for inspiration?[147]

Epstein was on a trip in Italy when the stock market crashed in Vienna during the World Exhibition, in May 1873. He was called back to Vienna, where he learned that one of his bank clerks had speculated away all his fortune. In the process of paying back his debts and upholding his reputation as a gentleman, Epstein lost all his possessions.[148]

Toward a Modern Viennese Style

While the patrons of historicism were themselves fully invested in the Viennese cultural milieu, it is certain that they would have acknowledged a prevailing prejudice against them. The predisposition of many people to dismiss Jewish patrons as lacking in style, however, was not enough to discourage the patrons, and they would achieve their cultural aims despite it. Furthermore, rather than negating their Jewishness—and any hindrances this might lead to in Viennese society's perception of who could claim to have style or not—they consciously retained their Jewish identification.

In his 1893 text accompanying a series of eleven tableaux vivants, addressed to the acculturated Jewish public in the salon of Sophie von Todesco and her daughter Yella von Oppenheimer, salon in the Palais Todesco, the young Hugo von Hofmannsthal (1874–1929) contrasted the new Jewish aristocracy with the established gentile elite: "Ihr habt nur Leben, sie—sie haben Stil" (You have only life, they—they have style).[149] The sentence concluded a passage that presented style as the ultimate factor separating Jews and gentiles: "And even if several possessions could be identified as related [similar] / one thing, I see clearly, must separate you and them / how could I formulate in short what is actually a lot? . . . / You have only life, they—they have style."[150] The original (but subsequently erased) last lines of Hofmannsthal's epilogue explained that gentiles have style since they do not have the fear and confusion that Jews have "running in their blood," while the Jews will never understand the eternal sense of serenity and great harmony that gentiles enjoy.[151] The performance of *Esther* in the Burgtheater, embraced by Jewish patrons and the Viennese cultural establishment alike, could be seen as a public reminder of Jewish existential fears. Hofmannsthal's prejudice against his patrons' lack of style is important to the discussion of Jewish patrons' contribution to modern style in Vienna.

When Oppenheimer staged these tableaux vivants in the presence of her mother in 1893, many of the performances were expressions of the patrons' wish to position themselves in a constructed European narrative: the figures were more broadly European, such as Empress Theodora, the lovers Romeo and Juliet, and characters from the Medici court. However, and significantly, the first tableau vivant was an imitation of the contemporary Hungarian Jewish artist Adolf Hirschl's *Jacob and Rachel*. Members of the Jewish elite participated: Anna Auspitz, Elsa von Gutmann, Adrienne Hakim (future sister-in-law of the patron Fritz Waerndorfer, subject of chapter 3, on the modernists), and Ilse von Lieben. By opening her tableaux vivants with a biblical scene, Oppenheimer was integrating her family's Jewish identity into a European cultural context in a positive manner.[152]

Oppenheimer's deliberate exposure of the family's Otherness through the Jacob and Rachel tableau vivant and her father Eduard von Todesco's sometimes apparently foolish behavior in the midst of his calculated cultural investments give the lie to Hofmannsthal's "You have only life, they—they have style." Rather, Todesco's and his daughter's negotiations of the Viennese cultural scene, dallying with their Jewishness and simultaneously reworking themselves within European history can be seen as a brilliant art of sociability and socialization. Father and daughter critically foregrounded prejudices against them and understood the advantages of concealing or alternately exposing their "Jewishness" to authorize new styles. Todesco fashioned his Jewish self-identification through the aesthetic choices he made for his palace. Its historicist and Hellenistic Jewish attributes seemed to anticipate—or perhaps obviate—the contemporary cultural clashes taking place outside its walls in Vienna. Furthermore, the cultural effect of his palace, rich with art, allowed Todesco some leeway to behave in a way that may have seemed contrary to but that perhaps was a direct outcome of his aestheticism: the many anecdotes of Todesco's alleged ignorance suggest that he had the social power and social acuity to undermine what was acceptable social behavior.

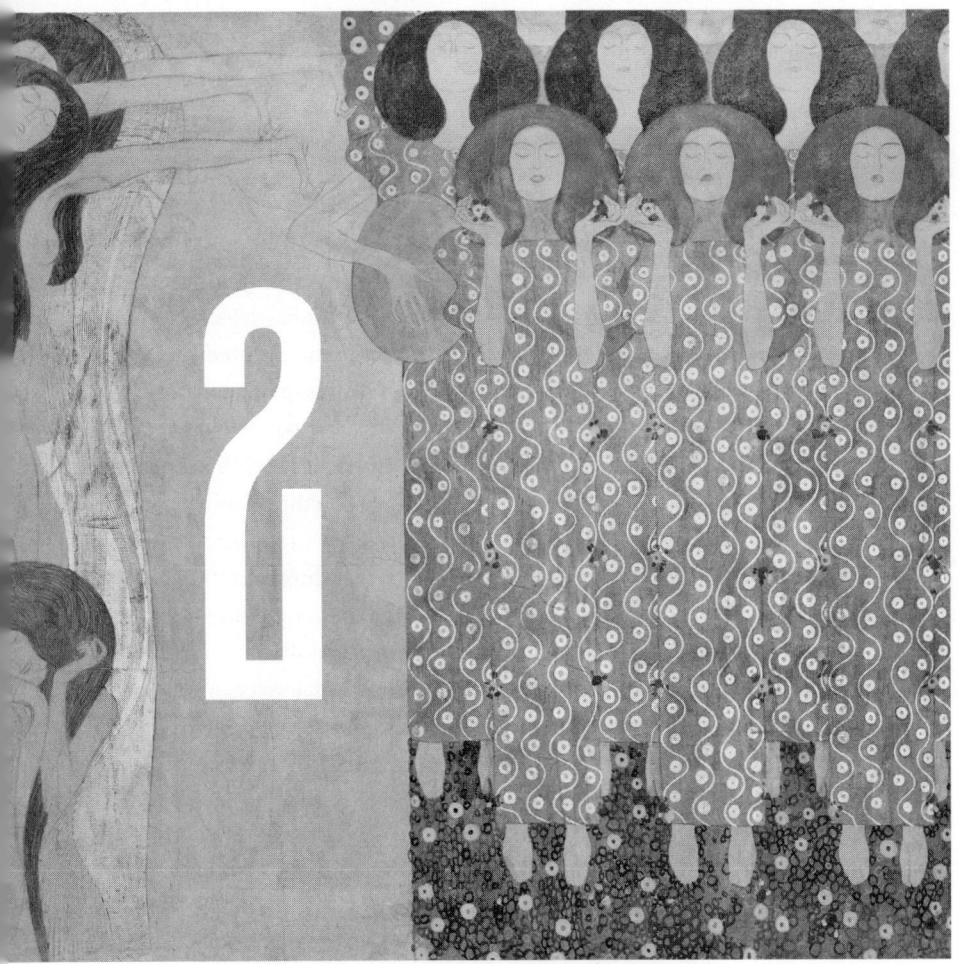

THE SECESSIONISTS
1897–1902

*Ludwig Hevesi, Karl Wittgenstein
and the Secession House, and Friedrich
Victor Spitzer's Music Salon*

Modern architecture and design were how Jewish intellectuals and art patrons exchanged their ideals of lifestyle and defined their social visibility in Vienna. The public media, newspapers, and journals shaped these exchanges further. The Jewish journalist and editor of the journal *Die Wage* Rudolf Lothar, praised the new Secession House as a stage for *Streitkultur* (the culture of debate).[1] Lothar and *Die Wage* would serve as models for the Jewish cultural critic and publisher Karl Kraus (1874–1936) to further fashion a critical Viennese culture of debate in his journal *Die Fackel*. The public debate between Kraus and the Jewish art critic Berta Zuckerkandl, who published in the *Wiener Allgemeine Zeitung* as well as in other liberal and arts journals, revealed not only their positions for or against the secessionist movement but also their perceptions of the relationship between Jewish acculturation and the visualization of modernity. Kraus considered Gustav Klimt's paintings and the secessionist style as championing a kind of "Jewishness," or representing "Jewish taste."[2] In contrast, Zuckerkandl perceived Klimt's secessionist art and Wiener Werkstätte designs as a shared cultural platform for rapprochement between the city's Jews and gentiles. She saw the secession movement as a modernist cultural platform that Jewish and gentile aesthetes could stake a claim on, similar to the way the historicists had established a Hellenistic—or European—cultural platform through which prominent Jewish patrons had established historical relations to Hellenistic Jewish culture and thus refashioned their place in the social network.

The ideal of the Gesamtkunstwerk was integral to the new secessionist style and represented a new Jewish acculturation project that further transformed Jewish and Viennese traditions. The irony is that the new agenda originated in the theoretical work of a German composer who rejected Jewish acculturation and had also coined the term "Judaization."[3] In his 1849 "The Art-Work of the Future," Richard Wagner defined the ideal Gesamtkunstwerk: "The Great Gesamtkunstwerk must contain all the branches of art in order, as it were, to use up, to destroy them for the benefit of attaining their common purpose—namely, the absolute, unconditional portrayal of perfected human nature; he [the artist] conceives of this great Gesamtkunstwerk not as the act of an individual will [*willkürlich mögliche That des Einzelnen*] but rather as the necessary collective work of the humans of the future."[4]

The art historian Juliet Koss argues that Gesamtkunstwerk "describes both the work created by the interrelation of the arts and—just as significantly—its effect on an audience. It presents a model of artistic production and aesthetic reception that is active, communal, political, and fundamentally utopian."[5] The secessionist Gesamtkunstwerk, promoted in Vienna by Jewish patrons and journalists alike, was an attempt to create a new cultural platform through a shared aesthetic experience. Jewish patrons wanted to be included in the grand cultural project and define new understandings of patronage as well as new ideas of artistic reception. (Many patrons were also admirers of Wagner's music.)[6] In the early years of the twentieth century, ideas about the role of art in society were shifting in Vienna. By October 1907—on the occasion of the opening of Cabaret Fledermaus, designed by Josef Hoffmann and the Wiener Werkstätte—Berta Zuckerkandl could look back with pride on a decade of development in Viennese art and design. Paraphrasing Wagner's ideal of Gesamtkunstwerk, she stated: "For a decade now our city has united elements that, through a strong shared feeling, through a special active creative force, indeed, through a mutual aesthetic and ethical creed have been closely connected to each other. The art culture, on the crystallization of which they have been working, produced powerful seeds of progress [disseminated] far beyond our country."[7]

Zuckerkandl's claim to be a coproducer of the secessionist Gesamtkunstwerk is supported by her promotion of the secessionist artists in her newspaper articles and her talented networking and through events in the artistic world. In 1902 her husband Emil Zuckerkandl (1864–1945), a respected professor of anatomy at Vienna University, invited the French sculptor Auguste Rodin to a light meal at the Prater, a large park in Vienna's second district that had been open to the public at no charge since the end of the eighteenth century. It was a beautiful July day, and everyone in the secession movement, according to Berta's report, had gathered. Berta laid a blanket in the greenery. Klimt, the president of the Vienna Secession, was in a splendid mood. Next to him sat Rodin, who could not stop admiring the handsome Viennese carriage drivers. Next to Klimt sat two beautiful thin models who also attracted Rodin. Nearby the renowned Jewish pianist Alfred Grünfeld sat at the piano in a large hall with open doors (perhaps the Lusthaus, a renowned public hall in the Prater). Klimt asked him to play something by Franz Schubert. Grünfeld, as

Berta reported more then thirty years later in her memoirs, with a cigarette in his mouth "dreamed" Schubert. Then Rodin turned to Klimt, saying: "I have never felt before the way I feel here at your place! Your Beethoven frescoes [in the secessionists' Beethoven exhibition of 1902], which are so tragic and spiritual; your unforgettable temple-like exhibition [house], and now this garden, these women, this music! Around you and in you [is] this childish happiness! What is it?" Berta, who knew French, translated Rodin's words, and Klimt replied with only one word: "Austria!"[8] This social event, recalled so vividly by Berta Zuckerkandl, may have been inspired by Klimt's painting *Schubert at the Piano* and therefore could be interpreted as Zuckerkandl's successful attempt to create in writing a tableau vivant. This idea of an elevating and all-encompassing live work, reveals how the Zuckerkandls took part—initiating, mediating, and reporting—in producing Austrian Gesamtkunstwerk.[9]

Yet Berta's Austrian national agenda was not directly relevant to three other prominent supporters of the secession movement, Ludwig Hevesi (1843–1910), Karl Wittgenstein (1847–1913), and Friedrich Victor Spitzer (1854–1922), who aimed to promote the secessionist Gesamtkunstwerk as a cultural platform that Jews and gentiles in Vienna could share. For Hevesi, a cultural critic and journalist, the secession style was a modern style identified with Vienna's special character as the center of the Austro-Hungarian Empire. Wittgenstein, a steel industrialist, perceived the secession style in relation to his position in the Viennese social elite; consciously or unconsciously he projected onto the relationship between Vienna and the Secession House the power relationship between European colonial powers and the Near East, perhaps indirectly redefining the relationship between Viennese society and its Jewish minority. Spitzer, a sugar industrialist and photographer, exhibited his art photographs in other European countries, but he perceived the new style mainly in relation to local cultural production and the possibility of his securing a leading role in Viennese art scene.

The Secessionist Dandies Hevesi, Wittgenstein, and Spitzer

Through their support of the scandalous modern Secession House and the secession artists, the patrons Hevesi, Wittgenstein, and Spitzer fashioned the Jewish dandy role as an integration strategy, joining exclusive clubs where they could transform the supposed crime of their "Jewishness" into an attractive vice. In their public appearances in the media, exhibition halls, and private salons, each man played a different social game of exposure and concealment of his "Jewishness." Their patronage juxtaposed secessionist style and public opinion: in a positive manner, they encouraged critical reflection on discriminatory social patterns, and in a negative manner, they transmitted ideas and emotions of style and seduction, challenging the norms of social respectability.

The founding of the secessionist movement played a crucial role in forming a new secessionist social club of members and friends of the secession movement. Hevesi and Wittgenstein supported the building of the Secession House and, through media reports and financial assistance, radically redefined the terms of integrating or representing the process of Jewish acculturation within Viennese culture. Much like the patron Eduard von Todesco did before them, these new Jewish patrons would invest in cultural platforms, or styles, that could be shared by Jews and gentiles yet that would allow some way for them to reflect their cultural difference. Both Hevesi and Wittgenstein were aware of the growing cultural and social tensions between Jews and gentiles in Vienna. The rise of German nationalism and the new antisemitic discourse in Vienna in the 1880s and 1890s forced acculturated Jews to rethink their integration path. Reports of the Dreyfus affair in France (1894–1906) and the election of the antisemite Karl Lueger as mayor of Vienna in 1897 had proved the failure of liberal politics in Europe, and new options had to be created for future generations of Jews to thrive. The inhospitability of the Viennese political climate to the Jewish minority, however, cannot explain the renewed interest in Jewish identification. The art patrons discussed in this chapter saw in the secessionist style a way to access Jewish identification through the guise of the modern. If Jewish identification in the past had been a liability, with the modernist style it would be avant-garde and progressive. In the domain of art and design, the secessionist style would permit a positive exposé of Jewish cultural difference while positioning itself as modern art. The secessionist Jewish patrons would choose symbols for their designs and media that highlighted their historical relationship with the Orient, and perhaps it should not be forgotten that Zionist leaders were doing the same thing at the same time.

Given the prestige Joseph Maria Olbrich achieved through the celebrities associated with the Secession House (Fig. 11, Plate 6), access to him as an architect became an entrée to an exclusive club of friends of modern art. Spitzer used Olbrich's *Jugendstil* interiors for his apartment in Schleifmühlgasse, near the Secession House, as an original setting for this creative brotherhood of artists, critics, and patrons. Spitzer secured the romantic sense of togetherness with the help of the modern setting. At the same time in this distinguished collective and exclusive setting, he felt comfortable enough to

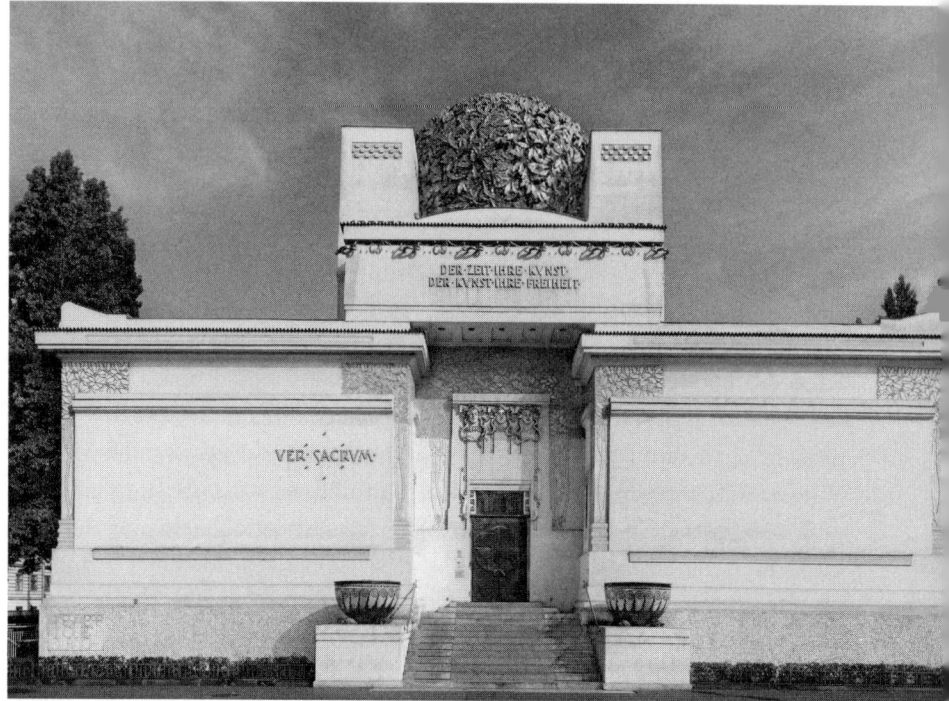

FIGURE 11. *Joseph Maria Olbrich, Secession House, 1898.*
Photo: © 2015, Benjamin von Radom.

expose the cultural difference between Jews and gentiles in the form of flirtatious dramas in his salon.

For Wittgenstein, Hevesi, and Spitzer, the artistic brotherhood of Vienna's secessionists offered new possibilities of refashioning Jewish identification as a positive, modern Viennese and European identification. The imagined secessionist community of friends of the arts was bound together more forcefully by the challenge of turning "Jewishness" in its negative connotations into a more alluring identification, an attractive vice. This translated into different scenarios for each of the three men. For Hevesi, it was fighting the antisemitic view of Jews as ugly with an all-inclusive aesthetic ideology; for Wittgenstein, it was provoking the Jewish patrons on the Ringstrasse and maintaining a powerful economic and cultural position in relation to them by flaunting his Jewish identification as an exotic trait; and for Spitzer, like Hevesi, it was fighting the exclusion of ugly and disrespectful Jews from the German romantic impression of Wagner's Gesamtkunstwerk and encouraging flirtatious dramas in his salon.

An Artistic Rebellion

In November 1896, Eugen Felix, a conservative artist, was elected president of Vienna's Künstlerhaus.[10] Misusing his political power, Felix censored the Künstlerhaus exhibition of the younger generation's modernist impressionist and symbolist works and withheld invitations to foreign exhibitions from the members of the new modernist group.[11] Ambitious artists among them began to consider an alternative exhibition space and requested a small but prominent site on the Ringstrasse across from the Austrian Museum of Art and Industry for their new exhibition house.[12] They may have asked for this prominent place because the Österreichischer Kunstverein (Austrian Art Association) had built a temporary exhibition building there.[13] The secessionists may also have wanted to benefit from the support of their neighbors, the Ringstrasse patrons. Their proposal was presented in a meeting of the city council at the end of March 1897.[14] When Hevesi published his first report that same month on the founding of the group, he described the gathering of young artists with modern blood as a "fighting society,"[15] an expression of their determination to succeed. In early April 1897, they received the approval of the city council, and the next day they published a public declaration that they had founded a new artists' association, the Vienna Secession. While the group still did not plan to break away from the Künstlerhaus,[16] the public exposure prompted further restrictions by its president and precipitated a final separation.[17] On April 24, 1897, a month before the modernists resigned from the Künstlerhaus, the Jewish genre painter Isidor Kaufmann received the Königswarter Prize (named after a prominent Jewish patron of the Ringstrasse, Baron Moritz von Königswarter) for his painting *Sabbath* (current location unknown), which depicted a Shabbat service at the temple and which he exhibited in the annual exhibition of the Künstlerhaus.[18] The Viennese conservative art scene appreciated Kaufmann's realistic art, with its subtle handling of Jewish cultural difference.[19] On May 25, however, a group of nineteen modernist artists resigned in official protest against the Künstlerhaus's exhibition politics and perhaps the choice to give an award to this particular painting. If the choice of Kaufmann's *Sabbath*, showing the interior of a temple with Jewish congregants, was meant to provoke the modernists with its conventional religious subject and expression of gratitude to Jewish historicist patrons (Königswarter had died five years earlier, but his desire to show the relevance of Jewish culture to Viennese modernism was still honored), then the Secession House, which resembled an Oriental temple and would be completed a year and a half later near the Karlsplatz, may have been meant as a protest against the acculturation attempts of the Ringstrasse patrons. Ironically, the Secession House's provocations against the acculturation aims of the European historicist architectural ideal restated Königswarter's aim and more ambitiously showed the relevance of Jewish culture to the formation of Viennese modernism.

When the artists and architects Gustav Klimt, Josef Engelhart, Joseph Maria Olbrich (1867–1908), Josef Hoffmann (1870–1956), and Koloman Moser officially founded the Vienna Secession in May 1897, it was a rebellion against Felix's conservatism and a condemnation of the Künstlerhaus's commercial character. Hevesi and another cultural critic, Hermann Bahr, closely followed developments in this emancipation and secured a positive reception for it in the Viennese media. Hevesi observed that the Viennese secessionists had adopted the Munich secessionists' aims: to serve the needs of modern society, reestablish a connection with the international art scene, and reject commercial interests to promote pure art.[20] Klimt, one of the first Viennese artists to absorb the Munich secessionist Franz von Stuck's pessimistic romanticism, as witnessed in his 1895 painting, *Love*,[21] was elected as the first president. The appointment was also due to his connections with prominent patrons of the Ringstrasse.[22] In March 1897, before the Vienna Secession's founding, Hevesi reported that payment to secure the Secession House's future construction had been given by private donors, later identified as Karl Wittgenstein. The funding would also secure the existence of the Vienna Secession for the next ten years.[23] This was months before the permanent place for their house was approved, in mid-November 1897; its final location would be behind the Academy of Fine Arts, next to Naschmarkt and near Karlsplatz —a few blocks from the Ringstrasse.[24] Their new place allowed the secessionists to make a radical stylistic statement against the historicist style of the Ringstrasse.

Wagner, Olbrich, and the Orient: A Temple, a Church, and a Modern Art Museum

It was the father of modern architecture in Vienna, Otto Wagner (1841–1918), who was first criticized for importing Oriental architecture to the city. The "invasion" of Oriental symbols in Vienna was perceived as an attack on the Hellenistic heritage of Western tradition and strongly opposed. The art historian Margaret Olin also points to a pervasive antisemitism that aligned itself with the defense of Hellenistic heritage, noting the Viennese art critic Josef Strzygowski's antisemitism in a 1902 essay: "Evoking Delacroix's *Mas-*

sacre at Chios, he compared the spotless maiden of Greek independence, abducted by a ruthless Turk in the painting, to the beautiful maiden of Hellenic art who sells herself to an 'old Semite.' The Semite keeps her as the jewel of his harem, surrounded by the 'Semitic pack' teeming with silk, gold, and jewels. This hedonistic art culminated in proliferations of flat patterns that 'celebrated their orgies in the Arabesque.' To capture the tenacity of the race that created it, Strzygowski cites the phrase 'der ewige Jude' (Eternal Jew), thus uniting Jew and 'ruthless Turk' in a narrative that had little to do with either."[25]

In a later publication independent of his critique of the Orient—though perhaps related to it, in that his sinister attitude seemed to apply broadly—Strzygowski criticized Otto Wagner as a master of disguise.[26] In contrast to Strzygowski's negative evaluation of the Orient as set against the Hellenistic culture (and Germanic culture), I suggest that Wagner's use of Oriental allure was crucial to the development of modern Viennese architecture. What Strzygowski dismissed as "architectural disguise" and an impairment was to Wagner a new principle of design—namely, his "new principle of clothing," as I describe below. The principle of clothing, defining the architectural surface, was what Gottfried Semper formulated as "cultured dress" in his book *The Style* (1863).[27] The new principle of clothing was, according to Wagner in his booklet *Modern Architecture* (1896), an "attractive mask."[28] Wagner may have first formed his "principle of clothing" when he designed the Orthodox Rumbach Synagogue (in Rumbach street) in Pest (the eastern and largest part, with two-thirds of the territory, of Budapest, separated from Buda, the other part of the city, by the Danube River) early in his career.

As noted in the previous chapter, the Viennese patron Gustav von Epstein may have been the one to recommend that the Orthodox Jewish community choose Wagner as the architect of its synagogue. Wagner had designed the Villa Epstein in Baden (1867), had planned a brick factory for Epstein in Laaerberg that was never constructed, and was the master builder of Epstein's Ringstrasse palais at this time (1868–72).[29] Wagner's drawings for the official competition won first prize in March 1868. Wagner designed the synagogue to have a Byzantine-Moorish façade. Following Ludwig Förster's monumental example of the Leopoldstadt Temple in Vienna (1858), Wagner (who had been apprenticed to Förster) chose a tripartite façade and angle turrets. Yet in competition with Förster's monumental Dohány Synagogue in Pest, designed for the Reform Jewish community, Wagner searched for a more authentic Eastern inspiration. The art historian Ines Müller points out that Wagner used Owen Jones's book on the architecture of the Alhambra for his colorful interior design of the synagogue—a book Epstein that had given to the library of the Austrian Museum of Art and Industry in 1865 and that Förster had also used—differently and fashioned the smaller Orthodox synagogue in a more beautiful manner, offering an appropriate source of identification to the Orthodox community.[30] Wagner's octagonal plan for the new temple shared a symbolic relationship with monumental architecture in Jerusalem —namely, the Muslim Dome of the Rock (AD 688–92)—as well as with recent Jewish sacral architecture in other parts of Europe, such as the Györ Synagogue in Hungary (1866).[31]

Concluding her analysis of Wagner's Rumbach Synagogue in Pest, Müller repeats the argument that the historicist architect Gottfried Semper's Dresden Synagogue (1838–40) greatly influenced Wagner's works.[32] Semper had combined two different styles in his Dresden Synagogue, a Moorish interior and a neo-Romanesque façade, expressive attributes of Jewish heritage (the Moorish designs identified the Orient, the birthplace of Judaism) as well as the religion's integrative aims (the neo-Romanesque represented Western Jews' desire to be part of European society). Most architects and scholars, however, have focused on the splendor of the Moorish interior. Through his design of the Rumbach Synagogue, Wagner succeeded in readapting the essence of Semper's "principle of clothing." The architectural historian Anthony Alofsin best describes Wagner's revolutionary modern approach in the synagogue, referring to his use of cast iron and thin masonry walls instead of thick load-bearing ones: "Ornament in combination with light structure creates an openness of space associated with modern innovation. The walls become tapestry held up by delicate columns, making the room a sort of tent."[33] Alofsin further argues that the synagogue provided the members of the Orthodox community with "luxury, novelty, scale and visibility."[34] And Müller notes Hevesi's commentary on the Rumbach Synagogue's influence over Wagner's Jugendstil design at the end of the 1890s:[35] he praised Wagner for his ability to stimulate the soul through the senses, through what was unknown in the West and yet still "appears Viennese."[36]

In the same article in the October–November 1900 issue of the *Zeitschrift für bildende Kunst*, Hevesi mentions that he had reminded Wagner of his quasi-Moorish brick Rumbach Synagogue, with its colorful elements, but the architect's reaction was that this achievement had almost vanished from his memory.[37] Hevesi saw Wagner as the only architect who could adequately design a modern synagogue. Eighteen months earlier, in April 1899, Hevesi had published a critical article regarding the latest debate on the style of the future grand Pest synagogue (possibly Kazinczy synagogue).[38] Hevesi's preference was no longer a historicist-Moorish style, but a modern one. If he had seen the Moorish style as necessary for the Jewish temple to avoid figural details, the modern aesthetic could now take its place. Hevesi clearly imagined Wagner conceiving a synagogue in a modern Jugendstil style and concluded his April 1899 article with a recommendation to have Wagner design the synagogue, which would meet the expectations of modern Jews.[39]

In her examination of the influence of the Pest synagogue (Rumbach synagogue) on Wagner's later works, Müller suggests that Wagner repeated the synagogue's practical design—in particular, its toilets, wardrobes, heating system—in the Steinhof Church (1903). Müller also suggests that for that church, Wagner adapted the formal structure of other famous synagogues, such as the one in Florence, as well as his own previous designs, such as the thin entrance and pulpit pillars in the Rumbach synagogue. Furthermore, Wagner borrowed the Oriental visual allure identified with nineteenth-century synagogues for the church, such as its golden cupola and Byzantine-like interior coloring.[40] The golden cupola could be read as a further curious reference to an authentic Oriental source, the golden cupola crowning the Dome of the Rock. Ákos Moravánszky notes that one can describe the Steinhof Church as an expression of abstract architecture, which could also be identified with Byzantine architecture.[41] Wagner's Pest synagogue and Steinhof Church both met practical demands (for example, for a heating system) and shared visual associations (for example, integrating the Star of David into the synagogue's interior décor and integrating the cross as a decorative pattern into the church's ceiling), and in their linkage they became interesting examples of how function and design would unexpectedly become foundational to Wagner's modern semantics.

Similar to Förster—who had projected the Moorish-Byzantine style onto the designs of the Villa Pereira in Greifenstein in lower Austria (1843–47), the Protestant Gumpendorfer Church (1846), the Arsenal (1850–56), and finally the Leopoldstadt Temple (1858)—Wagner would, consciously or unconsciously, use the same style as a platform for a new aesthetic while addressing the cultural variables in the Vienna and the Austro-Hungarian Empire of his time.[42] The exotic Moorish-Byzantine style of Wagner's Rumbach Synagogue can be viewed as the foundation for his Jugendstil abstraction. (In fact, in 1911, Wagner was still proud to include the Pest synagogue and Steinhof Church in his list of achievements on his visiting card.[43])

Wagner's "principle of clothing," exemplified through the exotic Moorish dress patterns projected onto the façade and interior of his Rumbach Synagogue, gave the Orthodox community an attractive house that identified the origins of the Jewish nation in the Orient. The following question then arises: if we can interpret Wagner's Rumbach Synagogue as homage to a Jewish historical narrative (a nation that originated in the East) and as an aesthetic structure that visualizes integration, can Olbrich's later Secession House be understood in a similar fashion? And would this exotic Orientalist style be seen as a direct threat—and how so—to the Italian Renaissance-Hellenistic heritage that Viennese historicism had promoted?

Around 1869, the journalist Joseph Weyl wrote a humorous version of the lyrics to Johann Strauss's famous *Blue Danube* waltz:

> Whoever has not seen
> Our beautiful Vienna city for a long time
> Will almost be unable to find a house
> Wherever you look is a palace!
> The Ring is a jewel—there lives the whole of Israel,
> In ten years they will comfortably
> Build there a New Jerusalem.[44]

Weyl may have wanted to mock the Jewish patrons on the Ringstrasse as a collective with a Jewish agenda. He provocatively points out the threat of "their" plan to transform "our . . . city," to "build there a New Jerusalem.["][45] Weyl was probably also aware that the historicist patrons were not interested in being reminded of their national identification, represented in the Jewish prayer that expresses a wish to return to Jerusalem. Yet it would be almost three decades before the presumed fears of Weyl's lyrics were realized—and then not by the Ringstrasse patrons but by Karl Wittgenstein, their rival, with the Secession House. The Orientalist character of the house was not an expression of Jewish national identification but a gesture of rebellion against the Ringstrasse's historicist European culture, replacing the ideal of acculturation with a clear representation of cultural difference. While the narrative of Jewish patronage during the second half of the nineteenth century had been directed toward Hellenization or Europeanization, the patrons of the early twentieth century did an about-face. With the intent to lure an avant-garde audience of both Jews and gentiles, the Secession House's Orientalist character—with its ostentatious display—embodied nonetheless a narrative of cultural difference between Viennese Jews and gentiles, in a manner similar to Förster's Moorish Temple (1858) and Stiassny's Polish Synagogue (1862) in the second district.

In 1894, Olbrich had been called back to Vienna from a study trip in Italy to help Wagner meet the challenge of designing the city's new underground stations.⁴⁶ Olbrich returned, but only after a short visit to Tunis.⁴⁷ Subsequently he became Wagner's chief draftsman, and it has even been suggested that he designed the exterior of the Hofpavillon (the court pavilion) next to Schönbrunn castle (1897–98).⁴⁸ At the end of March 1897 an early drawing by Olbrich for a small temporary exhibition building for the secessionists was presented to the city council.⁴⁹ The building had an elongated rectangular form with a grand façade. The façade and the cupola crowning the entrance hall might remind one of the Hofpavillon station. After the rebellious group's official resignation from the Künstlerhaus, Olbrich offered a more monumental design for their structure, once again following an (Otto) Wagnerian model. According to Clark it was a combination of Wagner's villa in Hütteldorf and Vienna's favorite church, the Karlskirche (St. Charles Church): "At either side of the entrance were to be two immense, free standing columns of an unorthodox order, each supporting a ceremonial tripod."⁵⁰ The structure would have a more traditional, projected decoration: "the walls were decorated with a simulation of rustication and a generous supply of swags and urns."⁵¹ In late September 1897, a further sketch for the Ringstrasse lot presented, for the first time, the idea of white walls for the façade. The cubic form and the white walls were in accordance with Olbrich's architectural impressions from the south of Italy and Tunis as well as with the new tendencies in the architecture of Charles F. A. Voysey.⁵² The abstract projection of white walls would be disturbed by the huge decorated pylons with "bronze busted females ('Nature' and 'Poetry'), whose long robes read like pilaster flutes, or visa [sic] versa,"⁵³ flanking the entrance. A pattern of laurel branches and leaves crowned the entrance with a great triumphal arch. Olbrich adapted classical antiquity's architectural elements such as the triumphal arch and caryatids, like those that also guarded several Ringstrasse palace entrances and the Parliament building, into a modern art nouveau relief-like decoration.

In mid-November 1897, the secessionists received approval to build at the new location, behind the Academy of Fine Arts and next to Karlsplatz.⁵⁴ Olbrich further refined his Secession House sketch, adjusting the size of the cupola and the columns flanking the entrance, before he began working on the final stages.⁵⁵ In another early drawing, the cupola rises above four pylons, suggesting the form of an altar. In a subsequent sketch, the cubic shape with white walls was crowned with an unusual dome, which was to be foliated.⁵⁶ In this series of sketches, the triumphal arch turned into a triumphal cupola or crown. The combination of a tripartite façade and the cupola suggested the architect's conception was of a place of worship. Furthermore, a space allowing for an inscription was added above the entrance. The design submitted to the building commission in mid-March 1898 showed a further abstract geometric variation on the cubic building with a foliated cupola rising from four pylons. This sketch was approved in early April 1898. Clark classified the composite of symmetrical composition, dome, and moldings as "Secessioniststil."[57] The idea of breaking the façade in the middle with a shallow recess and narrow doorway may have been inspired by an early archaic temple in a sketch by Klimt.[58] The sketch of a blank façade without openings could have been adapted into the developing scheme and secured the ultimate nudity of the temple's outer walls. Yet whereas Klimt's sketched temple might be interpreted as a continuation of the historicist heritage of the Ringstrasse, the finished house projected a radical modern revelation with its striking golden cupola in contrast to the white walls and the formal combination of three geometric elements—the cubic base structure, round cupola, and triangular glass constructions on the roof. The cupola immediately gave the house an Oriental identity in the eyes of contemporary viewers, and this identity is directly related to the authorial intention of both Hevesi and Wittgenstein as supporters of the Secession House.

Hevesi's attempt to define the terms and subtly prepare the recipe for the future secessionist style is documented in his first essay on the Secession House, where he positions its modernity in relationship to contemporary trends in other leading European cities.[59] Two days later he published his review of the Secession House itself. After describing in detail the construction of the golden cupola, he identifies it as a magical impression—a piece of the Orient in Vienna.[60] He notes that there is nothing similar in the world. He also mentions a plan (which was never realized) to build stairs to the cupola to allow for its close inspection.[61] Hevesi identified the cupola, representing a golden laurel tree, as the true symbol of the secession movement. Hevesi's reviews embraced the Secession House as modern and Oriental, which contrasted to an earlier critical reception of it in the *Neue Freie Presse*. There, the Austrian feminist activist Rosa Mayreder, using the pseudonym of Arnold Franz, criticized the architects of the "new direction" as threatening the good old Viennese style and emphasized that when one looked at the Secession House coming from Kärntnerstrasse (we can imagine her passing by the Palais Todesco) one immediately saw the golden cupola as an "Asiatic silhouette!" Moreover, in contrast to the good old Christian culture, it demonstrated the invasion of barbarity (a hybrid between a store and a temple)—Mayreder underlined her rejection of the house by associating it with "money making" (a store).[62] Wittgenstein, though, had no problem if the Secession House he had helped finance was associated with money making. He may have appreciated the fact that the house with the golden cupola connected with his name could be regarded as a lucrative investment.

Style and Prejudice

In the late 1890s, the wish of secessionist patrons to overcome religious, ethnic, and even racist frictions in Viennese society is evident in the fact that a few prominent critics and patrons joined Freemasons' lodges. There was a growing sense of the need to create a Viennese collective consciousness to project new stylistic claims. Heinrich Gomperz, son of Theodor Gomperz and nephew of Sophie von Todesco, remembered having the following discussion with the Hungarian Jewish lawyer Géza Winter:

> One day [Rudolf] Lothar met me on the platform of a tram. He wanted to convince me quickly to join a Freemasons lodge he belonged to. Since I asked why and for what aim, he referred me to the "Master of the Chair" [*Meister von Stuhl*]. I searched for this man and found an informal, fat, tedious, Hungarian Jewish lawyer [Winter]. He made the following disclosure to me on the essence and aim of Freemasons in general: "See for yourself, humanity is divided into nations and confessions. For several centuries smart men have said: 'humanity is divided into nations and confessions, therefore we want to establish an association and say to people: . . . and so on with no end. The membership is also very practical, since every man is responsible for the others, and the brothers really hold to each other in a brotherly manner." I asked: "How does this look in reality? Here is Rudolf Lothar, the publisher of *Die Wage*, and here is also, as you said, Hermann Bahr, the publisher of *Die Zeit*. These are two competitive enterprises; how does this brotherhood express itself?" He answered, "This is precisely a great example! Recently Bahr wrote a negative critique of a play by Lothar. Lothar came to me to complain: 'Meister, how can brother Bahr write like this about me?' I called brother Bahr to me and said to him: 'How can you write this way about our brother Lothar?' And now look at Bahr's critique of Lothar's last play: brilliant![63]

The gentile Bahr and the Jew Lothar—both publishers and journalists and both members of the Freemasons' lodge Freundschaft (Friendship), discussed below in relation to the patronage of David Berl—were united in promoting the new secessionist movement as a shared cultural platform and encouraged a Viennese culture of debate. The Jewish patrons of the previous generation, with their Hellenistic Jewish vision, had embraced historicism with a liberal ideology that held that they could secure their integration and become Europeans through science, education, and aesthetics. The exotic Orientalist design of the Secession House near Karlsplatz was a reaction to that. In accordance with a new and urgent political agenda against antisemitism that had digested the failures of the integrationist historicists, the Secession House offered new and old religious symbols as a shared cultural platform.

The house was a symbol of the world of the artist. Koloman Moser's angel in the large circular window by the inner entrance hall personified the arts' protective role over society, its lotus flower dress decoration recalling Egyptian art.[64] The angel watched over the people in the grand exhibition hall as their new protector. Around the window's perimeter was a quote from Bahr that expressed the secessionist ideal of art as transcending history: "The artist displays his world, the beauty that is born with him, that has never been and will never be again."[65] Expressing his belief in beauty as a form of salvation, Bahr first presented this romantic statement in an article on the secessionist movement in the journal *Die Zeit*.[66] Two Jewish journalists, Isidor Singer and Heinrich Kanner, had invited Bahr to be editor of *Die Zeit*'s arts, theater, and literature sections and, together with Bahr, formally founded the journal in 1894.[67] Importantly, a few months before he joined Singer and Kanner in founding the journal, Bahr had completed a book titled *Der Antisemitismus*. He had dedicated it to his "dear friend Dr. Emil Auspitzer,"[68] the secretary of the Lower Austria Trade Union, whose relationship with Bahr had inspired and enabled the author to publish. In 1891, Bahr had introduced himself to Auspitzer, who was also chosen as chairman of the board of the planned theater and music exhibition in the Prater.[69] Following their meeting, Auspitzer offered Bahr his first journalistic job as a theater critic for the *Deutsche Zeitung*, published in Vienna.[70] Edited by Emil Auspitzer and Wilhelm Auspitzer, the newspaper expressed German national ideas and competed with the liberal paper *Neue Freie Presse*. The respectable monthly salary Bahr received from the newspaper allowed him to travel in Europe to interview prominent personalities on their feelings and responses to antisemitism. The interviews were first published in the *Deutsche Zeitung* between March and September 1893. In the introduction to his book, Bahr interpreted the psychology of antisemitism as the ordinary gentile's preference for attributing his problems to the Jewish population. Bahr's assessment was that if there were no Jews, the antisemite would need to invent another scapegoat or object of hatred.[71] He further referred to the use of antisemitism by demagogues, supporting his argument with the example of the composer Richard Wagner, whom he admired, but who used antisemitism to master—meaning to manipulate—

the emotions of the masses.[72] Bahr noted that there was no way to challenge antisemitism with reason, since anyone who hates Jews hates them with a passion. Moreover, the masses would not give up their passion for any reason except perhaps for another ideal (and a mass movement), and Bahr says that socialism might be the only medicine against antisemitism.[73] Just before the book was published, and months before helping found *Die Zeit*, Bahr resigned from *Deutsche Zeitung*. In 1894, the *Deutsche Zeitung* was sold to new antisemitic owners, who fired the Jewish editors and turned the paper into the propaganda organ of the future mayor Karl Lueger.

Bahr's resignation and the antisemitic takeover of the newspaper may have encouraged Bahr to transfer the political battle onto Vienna's art scene. In his articles in *Die Zeit*, Bahr reported passionately and in detail on the conflicts in the Künstlerhaus between two groups, the youngsters he identified as the modern ones against the members of the old school. These conflicts would lead to the breaking away from the Künstlerhaus of the modern artists, headed by Klimt, and the founding of the secessionist movement. Bahr, like Hevesi, enthusiastically supported the new movement.[74] He saw it as the triumph of youth. The journalist Karl Kraus claimed that Olbrich's artistic "Empfindungen" (perceptions, emotions) expressed Bahr's "Vorempfindungen" (pre-perceptions, presentiments).[75] It is possible that before presenting the Secession House as his dream of ideal beauty,[76] Olbrich had heard from Bahr the idea that an artist should help his public to seek self-improvement and beauty.[77] To what extent did Olbrich intend the Secession House to represent the world of the artist alone, instead of wanting it to represent the shared experience and expectations of the secessionist community?

The new aesthetic did not solely represent artistic beauty or Olbrich's view of artistic beauty; it also manifested the social negotiations the artist was a part of. These included the irrational tensions and optimistic aspirations of other artists and the patrons who hired him. One can look at Bahr, as one of the secession movement's leading gentile supporters, as an example of the complexity of the cultural experience in Vienna at the time. Bahr seems to have strongly identified with acculturated Jews, and he was certainly part of an elite circle that included Jewish intellectuals, but he also comes across as ambivalent toward, or even harboring a sense of disgust at, acculturated Jews.

Bahr's history reveals the insidiousness of antisemitism and how Jews and gentiles, intellectuals and artists alike, negotiated it as a reality. In March 1883, Bahr had been the provocative spokesman at a memorial event for Richard Wagner at Vienna University. He had made an enthusiastic speech about Wagner and had even mentioned Wagner's antisemitism in his praise of the composer's German ideology. Another prominent journalist and a colleague of Bahr's, Theodor Herzl, an ambitious author and playwright, who would cover the Dreyfus trials in France for the liberal newspaper the *Neue Freie Presse* more than a decade later, resigned his membership in the German Albia fraternity in response to Bahr's speech. While Herzl did not have a problem with the nationalistic fraternity's objection to the Jewish spirit or its promotion of total assimilation, which would have led to the disappearance of Jewry into the Germanic nation, he did object to the new promotion of racial antisemitism.[78] In this cultural battleground, Bahr and Herzl understood Jewishness as it was expressed and seen in the Viennese culture from different perspectives. Notably, Herzl would channel his different perception of the state of Jewry into the political fight for Zionism.

In 1897, Herzl and Bahr would face off once again on the same subject when Herzl published his play *Das neue Ghetto* (The new ghetto).[79] The play describes the failed attempts of a young Jewish lawyer, Jakob Samuel, to integrate into Viennese society. In the Vienna of 1893, Samuel is portrayed as being forced to choose between defending corrupt Jewish speculators and denying his Jewish identity. He is rejected by his close friend, who then joins an antisemitic party. In an attempt to save his pride, Samuel ends up losing his life in a duel. In his early January 1898 review of the performance of *Das neue Ghetto* for *Die Zeit*, Bahr expressed his enthusiastic support for the new Zionist movement.[80] Yet because of Bahr's history of support for the antisemitic Wagner and the prevailing distaste for assimilation among certain members of the gentile elite, Herzl may have perceived this praise for a separate Jewish state as an insult. Bahr's review of Herzl's play and his support of Herzl's Zionist project were actually reminders of the failure of Jewish integration in Vienna. In his review, Bahr argued that assimilation forced Jews to question their own self-assurance and actions, making them appear "uncanny" (strange, not familiar, threatening) to others: "In understanding they are German: they have German ideas and German concepts. But they don't have German instincts. They also no longer have Jewish instincts, so how should they live? They go about as half-humans here and there, deprived of their power, reduced creatures with empty understanding, uncanny to others, and a torture to themselves."[81]

According to the critic, assimilated Jews were suspended between two different cultures and belonged to neither. However, this suspension—which Bahr regards as a source of torment—may actually have served as a creative stimulus for Jewish patrons of the arts. It was their uncertain, in-between status that allowed Jewish patrons to engage in cultural productions that on the one hand sought to create shared cultural platforms to accommodate the difference between Jewish and gentile cultures and on the other hand aimed to define Jewish cultural difference in an attractive way. It was this acknowledged suspension (and the painful acknowledgment of their exclusion as Orientals and foreigners) that resulted in the activity of new, nonconformist, Jewish patrons. The secessionist style that Jewish patrons helped produce would offer three solutions to this suspension between cultures: it advocated a new decorative Gesamtkunstwerk that would override the differences between the cultures; it embraced difference as an aesthetic virtue, as the Secession House's Oriental character would reflect; and it championed a new shared cultural platform of youth adoration—an embracing of the new, the modern—that encouraged the open-minded reception of the latest European trends and emancipation (freedom from dead histories) for the new art.

In his opening article in the new secessionist journal, *Ver Sacrum*, in January 1898, the same month he published his review of Herzl's *Das neue Ghetto*, Bahr stated three maxims for the (or his) secessionist program, supporting the rapprochement between artists, critics, and patrons:

> The first is that whoever wants to achieve something innovative should not be afraid to make a fool of himself. Everyone who has eventually triumphed, and every subject that has gained momentum here, was first laughed at for years. It seems that it does not happen any other way in Vienna. The second rule is that one has to understand about making oneself hated. *The Viennese have respect only for those whom they actually find disgusting. Only through hate does one achieve power.* The third is one should not allow oneself to be weakened. The Viennese has the habit, when someone demands something from him, to offer him half of it. When it appears that one is satisfied with that half, then it is taken away again after a while. But if one insists and does not give up, then it becomes uncomfortable for him [the Viennese], and he offers more than the initial demand. Everything or nothing must be the slogan.[82]

Bahr familiarized his readers (artists and patrons) with the avant-garde rhetoric (agitation, nonconformism, and an unyielding stance) by calling on their shared innermost and painful memories of the experience of rejection. The compensation for this rejection was the creation and appreciation of pure art, supposedly beyond capitalist interest. Bahr's emphatic remarks may be read as a call to arms for the dispossessed or the disempowered with an idealistic artistic slogan. The new art would unite creators, consumers, and art lovers in a new fraternity, the *Künstlerschaft* (artistic community).[83] The

Gesamtkunstwerk of secessionist architecture and design would promote an aesthetic experience that was multilayered and all-encompassing. Prominent Jewish patrons and sympathetic journalists understood this integral experience to symbolize the potential of a new integrated culture that would spurn rejection (on other cultural fronts) in favor of inclusion.

Nonetheless, an incident with Bahr's most renowned protégé in the Jung-Wien literary circle, Hugo von Hofmannsthal, would reflect how difficult surmounting religious or cultural stereotypes and prejudices could be. Hofmannsthal, who came from a renowned Jewish family whose members had converted to Christianity, had his own Jewish acculturation ideal, subsumed in German idealization, that looked to antiquity to fashion a better self-image: "We even more than other nations, approach antiquity as a magic mirror in which we expect to see our own faces in a foreign, purified guise."[84]

Hofmannsthal's text is a poetic echo of Olbrich's "dream of beauty" for his Secession House.[85] Bahr wrote similarly about the artist-hero who projects his own eternal ideal beauty, as captured in the large round window inside the Secession House that praises Olbrich's achievement. But when Bahr's romantic claim that the Secession House represented the beauty of the world of the artist[86] was attacked and undermined in a humorous journal, a caricature was made not of Olbrich but of the protégé Hofmannsthal. It was an easy target to attack modern aesthetics by relating it to Jewish looks. To ridicule the secessionist art movement, Berthold Löffler, a student at the Kunstgewerbeschule (School of Applied Arts, where Klimt had studied and Josef Hoffmann and Koloman Moser taught), had drawn a caricature of Hofmannsthal with the title "Narcissos" (Narcissus) in *Quer Sacrum, Organ der Vereinigung bildender Künstler Irrlands* (Skewed spring, journal of the Association of Fine Artists of Crazy-Land), published by him and four fellow students. The title *Quer Sacrum* was a play on *Ver Sacrum*. The students' journal was distributed at the Prater, in Vienna's second district, during the parody exhibition called "Secession Village," arranged by Pauline Sandor von Metternich in early June 1899. In the caricature, in which the figure does not actually resemble him, young Hofmannsthal is seen in his slippers, half-naked, looking at a Greek water basin on a tripod.[87] He has a small hooked nose, and a forelock covers his high forehead. There is something forced and feminine in his pose. He is very thin and smiles in a rather evil way at his "reflection." Yet the basin cannot reflect his image since it is empty. His shirt hangs down, and his suspenders fall between his legs, creating a disordered impression and contributing to his unattractive appearance. The text next to the caricature reads: "Narcissus: Deep in the reflecting surface [he] looks with joy at his image. Caught in his dream he stares down, the soap suds slide drop by drop; like a whimsical flowerbed, sparkling blossoms creep around the wash basin;—Narcissus."[88] Hofmannsthal's claim about his nation's need to be reflected in the foreign, purified guise of antiquity is ridiculed in this caricature. While Hofmannsthal's and Olbrich's artistic wish to be reflected in antiquity is attacked, it is Hofmannsthal's appearance as a supposedly Jewish dandy that is specifically targeted in this caricature (as was the case in Burckhardt's jealous and bitter attack on the Jewish patrons who adorned the façades of their houses with beautiful caryatids).

Hevesi's Magic Mirror: The Jewish Pallas Athena

In his reviews of the Secession House, Hevesi may have molded his readers' hopes in a manner similar to Hofmannsthal's—looking to antiquity as a mirror that would reflect modern man in a foreign, purified guise. Figures from other corners of Viennese culture commented as well on the building's classical Greek model and the metaphors within it. The activist Marie Lang, cofounder of the Austrian feminist movement, praised the Secession House in her essay in the *Wiener Rundschau* in 1898, comparing it in merit to a Greek temple. Lang argued that while the Greek temple offered an ideological message about clear beauty, the Secession House, also a temple, offered a parable of modern man's battles and triumphs. She proclaimed that modern man, and the building that represented his modern struggle, "can not tolerate anymore the comedies and masquerades, and naked as he is, and even if it is at the expense of beauty, appears before us."[89] It is surprising, however, that Lang saw the house as representing a naked man. The house was only partly naked. It was seductively adorned with what can be seen as feminine fashion accessories such as belts with golden coins and a bas relief depicting "embroidery" work, and with imagery relating to seductive biblical and Greek mythology scenes. Striking symbols such as the owl, gorgons, and the golden helmet of the central orb hint at a phantom of Pallas Athena enclosed in the monumental house (a parallel suggestion is that the representation is of Daphne's transformation into a tree).[90] By identifying the golden cupola—that is, what I suggest can be compared to Athena's golden helmet—as representing the Orient in Vienna, Hevesi consciously or unconsciously highlighted the foreignness of this guise of Athena, identifying her as a Jewish (Oriental) Athena.

During his successful journalistic career, Hevesi, who was born into a Hungarian Jewish family, had also contributed to the Viennese humorous journal *Der Floh*.⁹¹ The journal included attacks on patrons of the Ringstrasse and had specifically and repeatedly targeted Eduard von Todesco in the early 1870s. Hevesi was therefore aware of the risks he took as a Jewish critic in describing art as a mirror and a reflection of his and his readers' shared self-image. Ridiculing Jewish looks and body language had become a popular tradition in *Der Floh*, and the founding of the Vienna Secession inspired new caricatures. Shortly after the opening of the Secession House, Jewish patrons' enthusiasm for it was ridiculed in another *Der Floh* caricature. This one shows two religious Jews with ugly noses standing in front of the building. One, looking surprised, asks his friend: "What, did you also become a friend of art?" His smiling friend answers: "Nu, when the whole world shouts 'See it [a misunderstanding of the word "Secession"], see it,' I also want to see it" (Fig. 12).⁹² In a caricature titled "At Fregoli," which appeared in *Der Floh* in January 1899, a husband with strikingly Jewish facial characteristics asks a famous transformation artist if he could "beautify" (transform) his ugly Jewish wife: "Are you the famous master of metamorphosis?" "Si Signor, how can I help?" "Can you do me a favor and transform my wife somehow? How much will it cost?"⁹³ This explicit desire to transform Jewish looks was an interpretation of the excitement of Jewish patrons about the new secessionist movement. In another *Der Floh* caricature titled "The Secession at Home," a Jewish husband addresses his wife, who sits at the mirror coloring her eyelids with a long paintbrush: "What are you dabbing on your face, Malvine? Are you transforming yourself into a pointillist work?"⁹⁴ Hevesi challenged this popular antisemitic tradition in his ideological promotion of the secessionist aesthetic revolution and forced his readers to reflect on it. Defending modern secessionist aesthetics, he explained: "It is when one wants, a piece of wallpaper in completely faded colors that have no impact [had expired] because of their fineness. At least they [the new paintings] offer some color—and this is not a little thing. The philistine will say: 'Wallpaper? In God's name, must the wallpaper have such a long nose [associated with some color]?' This is because he is used to wallpapers with short noses [associated with faded colors]."⁹⁵

By comparing the secessionists' striking colors to long noses, Hevesi raised the question of how to react to new experiences and challenged his readers' reliance on familiar aesthetic experiences. The rejection of the implied Jewish factor (the prominent long nose) was analogous to the rejection of or hesitance about the new aesthetic revolution, and Hevesi was suggesting that ugly looks as much as newness in art and aesthetics was something the philistine would have to get over to assume cultural prestige. Bahr and Hevesi

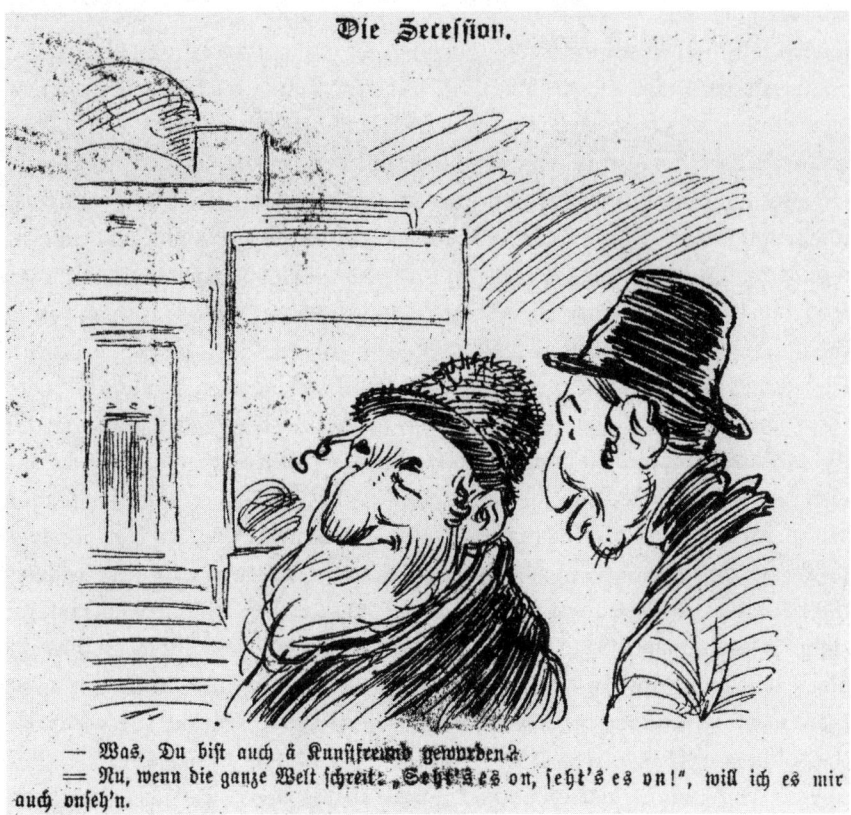

FIGURE 12. *Caricature "Die Secession," Der Floh (November 27, 1898): 5.
ANNO—Austrian Newspapers Online.*

recognized the need to transform rejection into a source of authorial claims as cultural producers. As a cultural critic, Hevesi was able to use his reviews to fashion readers' expectations of the new secessionist movement and, ideally, create a new place for Jews on the cultural stage. He presented to his readers art as a mirror of their ideal self-identification. The Greek goddess Athena embodied in the Secession House was a personification of his high expectations.

Establishing a space such as the Secession House to facilitate a culture's shared self-reflection was crucial. If architectural structures in the changing Vienna could be seen as mirrors of the culture, what was the process of cleaning or purifying this mirror to seduce its viewers? How much would the understanding of these structures need to be guided to remove negative stereotypes of "Jewishness" associated with their patronage and presentation?

Furthermore, can we say that this type of purification process was a form of Jewish self-identification?

Jewish patronage and the idea of purification in relation to the presence of "Jewishness" in Viennese culture was far from buried in the culture's subconscious; rather, it was topical and meted out in the media and the visual arts. One does not have to dig far to find examples of the dangers associated with Jewish presence or patronage in Viennese culture. For example, the Jewish female icon, Judith, was reworked in different guises as a personification of Jewish patrons in Vienna. The notorious Judith was presented at this time as the dangerous and flirtatious biblical Jewish woman who killed her admirer, Holofernes. Though alluring, she was not without menace, and she became the embodiment of dangerous seduction in Viennese popular culture at the time. She was captured memorably in Klimt's *Judith I* (Fig. 2, Plate 1). Judith had been invoked similarly in an earlier decade. In a review of an event at the Palais Todesco in April 1868, the journalist Ludwig Speidel referred to the beautiful women in the salon, with their biblical attributes: "Indeed the ballroom, at the end of which a small stage was set, was a breathtaking sight. When a man looked over there, when his gaze was caught by flowing black hair or met with shining dark eyes, he could be moved in a strange manner. One understood at once the deep biblical exegesis, the words of the soldiers of Holofernes, as they looked at Judith, and spoke among themselves: 'The Hebrew nation should not be disrespected, because they have beautiful women.'"[96]

Speidel expresses an admiration for the Jewish women in the room by reflecting on the unforgettable Judith, but in so doing he brings danger or at least complication into the context of this presumably sedate cultural event at the home of a Jewish patron. Hevesi also referred to the Judith dynamic, though in a contrasting fashion. In a short satirical story from 1906 titled "Der Aristopath," Hevesi documents the self-fashioning process of the modernist dandy who exorcises his "Jewishness" (if he is Jewish) or his fear of the destructive power of "Jewishness" (if he is gentile) by projecting the negative onto the figure of the Jewish femme fatale, Judith. Hevesi introduces his modern art collector not as an aristocrat but as an "Aristopath" (perhaps a combination of "aristocrat" and "psychopath") who enjoys only an extreme "nervous art."[97] The Aristopath's enemy is none other than Judith, whose portrait hangs in his bedroom.[98] The aristopath refuses to commit himself to any woman and prefers to flirt with different women in cafés. However, he must contend with the phantom of Judith of the black hair, big eyes, and cold lips when she abandons her portrait and threatens to decapitate him.

Hevesi's dandy's fear of Judith ensures that he will never commit himself to a woman, so he is condemned to eternally flirting with them. It is not clear if the short story was an autobiographical text explaining Hevesi's own decision to remain a bachelor or if Hevesi was expressing in a humorous way what he observed in other Jewish and gentile men who were haunted by the ghost of the Jewish Judith and therefore could not commit themselves to any woman.

The idea of promoting a positive Jewish cultural difference was just as important for Hevesi as the idea of establishing a new creative brotherhood. The first Secession exhibition took place in the Gartenbaugesellschaft (Horticulture Society) on the Park-Ring in spring 1898. As the movement's didactic message was expressed through the introduction of foreign contemporary trends, only a few of the artists were Austrian.[99] The aim was to inspire local artists to proceed in similar directions. In his review in *Ver Sacrum*, which introduced and noted the jury members' different tastes in the first exhibition, Hevesi quoted them as still unified in their intent: "We are a party and we want to remain a party until stagnant relationships are brought back to life and Austrian artists and the Austrian public get a picture of the modern art movement."[100] This political and cultural movement did not promote style, however, but regeneration. Hevesi further claimed in another review that in the same manner that "secession" meant the emancipation of the collective, to be a "secessionist" meant to claim one's freedom within this collective.[101] He saw in modern art the possibility for the realization of an ideal form of emancipation, whether personal, religious, political, or something else. This art legitimized no style, no formula—nothing other than the promotion of artistic emancipation. Moreover, Hevesi noted that it was not the theme but the personal color, meaning the personal truth, that had been emancipated in modern art, and he declared that "all these different truths are equally true."[102] For Hevesi, the emancipatory tenet of secessionist art allowed him to reshape and advance his role in Viennese society, to be a leading figure in the production of culture.

Hevesi worked hard to fashion himself as a leading commentator on the Viennese cultural scene. In December 1890—when he was forty-seven, and fifteen years after moving to Vienna[103]—the writer (son of a medical doctor, Samuel Löwy, and his wife, Marie née Rottenstein) officially changed his surname from "Löwy" to "Hevesi." He adopted his birthplace Heves in Hungary as his surname. A few days after changing his name, Hevesi converted to Christianity in the Evangelist Reform Church in Budapest.[104] However, he continued to be acclaimed as a Jewish author, and he continued to identify himself as Jewish in his official registration.[105] Furthermore, he used his insider knowledge of modern Jewish culture to promote modernist architects.[106]

When, in the first issue of *Ver Sacrum*, the secessionists invited the public to join them to "be educated," they identified themselves as "knowledgeable, appreciating, understanding, adepts, and masters over the spirits!"[107] They saw themselves as the chosen minority with a mission to educate the ignorant majority. What was Hevesi's role among the new chosen minority, these new masters over the spirits? If the patron Wittgenstein marketed himself, as discussed below, as a new American entrepreneur in Vienna, suggesting a new manner of doing things, Hevesi promoted the Secession House as promising of a new world, inviting the many onlookers who admired the small house with a monumental impression from the outside to come inside and make themselves comfortable.[108] The new world promised equality for all and invited onlookers to witness a new religious narrative.

The Secessionist House's foundation stone was put in place at the end of April 1898. The building was completed six months later and officially opened for the second Secession exhibition on November 12, 1898. During construction the original ideas presented on paper were modified. Additions included stucco walls decorated with flora, owls, and spiny stalks emerging from stucco urns, the foliage crowning the entrance and the office windows. The original golden cupola that had appeared on Olbrich's drawing titled "First Sketch for the House of the Viennese Secession" (1897) was transformed into a cupola crowning the entrance hall, seen only from the outside, and made of three thousand gilded laurel leaves and seven hundred berries.[109] Alfred Roller's symbolic drawing of "a small tree, whose roots were breaking through the bands of its constricting container, reaching out for more freedom and new nourishment,"[110] explained the idea of the foliated cupola. In July 1898, however, Olbrich trumped this description when he published a vignette in *Ver Sacrum* depicting a tree with fruits, calling to mind the tree of knowledge or the tree of life in the Garden of Eden. (In Central and Eastern Europe, the tree of life is a striking symbol frequently sculpted on Jewish gravestones. The gravestones of various Jewish personalities—the editor of the *Fremden-Blatt*, Isidor von Klarwill, whose gravestone was designed by Olbrich in 1898, and Josef Marmorek, whose gravestone was designed by his brother, Oskar, in 1902—were crowned with foliated cupolas.[111] In the context of the Jewish gravestone, this motif refers to the future life in heaven.)[112] In addition, the presence of the snakes made it clear that it also represented a return to the traumatic scene of the temptation and original sin. Othmar Schimkowitz's sculpted lizards (biblical snakes) flanking the top of the copper entrance doors would confirm Olbrich's suggestion that the tree foliage was not merely a triumphal crown but a promise of the return to the Garden of Eden. Above the entrance, Schimkowitz's sculpted gorgon heads were allegories of the arts of painting, architecture, and sculpture, as noted in golden inscription below, and integrated Greek mythology and the biblical temptation narrative. In Greek mythology gorgons were female figures with snakes for hair who had been punished for committing sexual sins in the temple of Athena. Yet the idea of returning to the place of sin, whether a biblical or a classical reference, was a reason for celebration and not meant to provoke fear, as confirmed by Koloman Moser's rhythmic frieze of dancing maidens bearing golden wreaths at the rear of the museum.[113] These serial presentations of painted dancing maidens with exposed breasts, evoking through their profiles and flatness ancient Egyptian and Greek art, can be seen as types that replaced the performance of the caryatids displaying their dresses in the Palais Epstein façade and the cultivated caryatids with different attributes decorating the Palais Todesco. This regression in time was countered by Hevesi's quote in golden letters, set above the entrance: "To every time its art and to art its freedom," declaring the secessionists' demand for the freedom of expression.[114] The Secession House did not attempt to reconstruct a historical style, but in combining visual references to ancient Egyptian art, Near Eastern architecture, imagery from Greek mythology, and art nouveau design, it showed how modernization was rooted in Western and Eastern traditions.

Hevesi not only wrote the motto above the entrance doors to the Secession House, but he further—as he claimed—defined the progressive program of Viennese modernism.[115] At the same time, Hevesi saw the Secession House as a modern physical metaphor for a love object. The new beautifully stylized architecture had a masculine cubic body with white skin, but was highlighted —as noted above—with feminine clothing accessories, like belts with golden coins and white embroidery work, and it exhibited attributes of the Greek goddess Pallas Athena—the three owls of wisdom on the structure's sides, the gorgons above the entrance that refer to the gorgon head on her shield, and the golden helmet rising in the midst of four pylons. Viewers were physically attracted to the new house. Hevesi noted that viewers who saw the house drew the curved outline of the top of the building with their fingers and touched the chased copper door with their hands in the late evenings.[116] This flirtation can be said to have become more concrete when one noticed— and it is difficult to notice immediately—the image of the vulva-leaf placed in the golden cupola. It transformed the house into an uncanny female presence

—displacing the vagina from the lower part of "her" body to "her" head was a trap that insiders knew about.[117]

I suggest that the visual dialectic between the structure's naked white body and its dressing decoration was developed, however, not only to connote erotic attraction but also to continue a program familiar in Vienna's architecture, that of the caryatids that also populated various Jewish patrons' historicist palaces on the Ringstrasse. The Secession House took the gesture of the caryatids playing with their robes in front of the Palais Epstein one step further. As those figures handled their dresses, parted their pleats, and physically supported the Viennese architectural structures of the historicist period, the Secession House was itself a figure holding "her" dress and sustaining "her" structure by bringing the lightness of fashion to bear on the severity of the modern architecture.[118]

This new stylization of a beautiful architectural body represented the transition from the patrons of historicism to the patrons of modernism, from the old historicist rental apartment palaces to the future modern buildings. This difference in attitude toward the entire architectural structure—the change to seeing it as a figure in itself—marked the transition. If the building as a form had not been treated differently, the break with the historicist aesthetic might not have been significant, since the Secession House in some of its imagery still made visual reference to the past, which the historicists would have approved. My suggestion as noted above is that the white-skinned house, with the golden laurel cupola or cap, is a paraphrase of Athena and her golden helmet. The owls on the sides of the house and the gorgons on top of the entrance door are her symbols, starkly set against the stucco walls. It is not clear who decided—the critic, the architect, or the patrons—that an abstraction of the Greek goddess was more impressive than a representational image.

Hevesi may have supported this leap of conceptualization. According to him, Athena should have served as a symbol of continuity between the old and the new styles. However, his vision rested on having representations of the goddess made on the structure's wall space. In his early review of the planned Secession House on the Ringstrasse,[119] Hevesi noted a plan to add a mosaic of Pallas Athena inlaid with precious stones by the historicist sculptor Artur Strasser to the final Secession House near Karlsplatz. When the house opened, at the end of November 1898, Hevesi reported twice on the plan to add the figure of Pallas Athena to the front façade—a plan that was not realized.[120] So how was the leap made from visualizing Athena through imagery to having a structure that seemed to actually embody the goddess?

Hevesi was a generation older than the secessionist artists, and they ac-

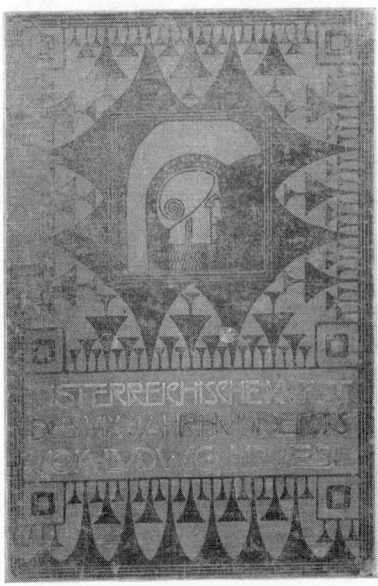

FIGURE 13. *Koloman Moser cover for Ludwig Hevesi,* Österreichische Kunst im 19. Jahrhundert *(Leipzig: E. A. Seemann, 1903). Library of the Academy of Fine Arts, Vienna.*

cepted him as a father figure.[121] Olbrich clearly expressed his respect for Hevesi and his comments on Olbrich's design. In fact, Olbrich asked the critic to write the text for the first monograph on his work. The first edition of *Ideen von Olbrich, Text von Ludwig Hevesi* was published in Vienna in 1900.[122] It is interesting to note why Hevesi praised Olbrich as a modern talent: "The comfort of the surface is felt again, and the cleanliness of the line, the finesse of the curve. How much new there is to do again! The whole curving art of modernity is something new. And [it is] something endless, since its delicate or powerful melody cannot be exhausted. New lines, new articulations, [and] new color tones in new contrasts or complimentary combinations: in all this foments the modern talent."[123]

Hevesi complimented the abstract characteristics—clean lines, curves, arrangements, and colors. Yet as the case of the representation of Athena shows, Hevesi also tried to interfere in the iconographical program for the Secession House decoration. Could it be that he supported both an iconographical program and an abstract conceptualization to achieve both a representation of a Jewish Athena and a purified architectural abstraction?

Hevesi further reclaimed the heroic image of Athena as a symbol of continuity between past and present to promote his book on Austrian art, *Österreichische Kunst im 19. Jahrhundert*, published in 1903. At the end of 1902, Hevesi asked the designer Koloman Moser to design the book cover (Fig. 13, Plate 7). Moser drew the head of Athena in profile in a square frame within a larger frame, which in the future would resurface with the Wiener Werkstätte geometric carpets and their decorative patterns of sharpened triangles, as well as in the sharpened triangles of Klimt's portrait of Adele Bloch-Bauer (1907). While the cubic body of the Secession House may have manifested Athena's masculine character as the goddess of war, the sharpened triangles framing Athena's head in Moser's cover for Hevesi's book may have symbolized her aggression. For Hevesi the transition from the figurative image of Athena to her decorative geometric abstraction on the Secession House was a reference to the continuity between historicism and modernity.

Wittgenstein's Rebellion

Just as Hevesi may have sympathized with the authority of the historicist patrons, the industrialist and patron Karl Wittgenstein identified with cultured European society to an extent. However, he provoked his social circle by challenging their architectural achievements on the Ringstrasse with the modern Orientalist Secession House. Though Hevesi and Wittgenstein may have had the same modernist expectations of the Secession House and seen its ideal representation as a purified architectural abstraction, compared to Hevesi, Wittgenstein was less of a theoretician, observer, or commentator and more of an actor.[124] He may have wanted to challenge what he perceived as the Jewish elite's tendency to conform to European tradition, yet his impulse to embrace modernist architecture can also be understood as enacting an imagined Jewish identification in relation to the heritage of the new Hellenist Jews on the Ringstrasse. He shared little with the Jewish community in his immediate surroundings but in many ways was invested in a Jewish identification.[125] In this sense, as a Viennese cultural producer Wittgenstein made a significant contribution to the conflation of Jewish identity and modernity in Vienna.

In 1897 Wittgenstein was invited by Max von Gomperz to join the lucrative Ringstrasse patrons' club—the board of the Rothschild Credit-Anstalt Bank.[126] Nonetheless, he claimed an outsider position in relation to both the Ringstrasse club and wider Viennese society, which was enhanced when he supported the Secession House's construction during the period of cooperation between him and Gomperz. That cooperation, however, would not last long. At the beginning of 1898, following other industrialists' growing opposition to his business methods (including his managing a powerful cartel and manipulating share prices), Wittgenstein resigned from his post as the central director of the Prague Iron Industry Company. He also resigned from all his

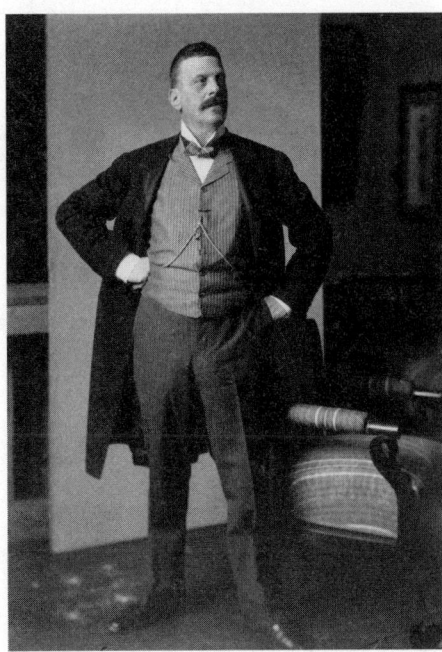

FIGURE 14. *Ferdinand Schmutzer, photo of Karl Wittgenstein, 1908. Österreichische Nationalbibliothek, Vienna.* LSCH0147.

steel companies' boards. In May 1898, an anonymous satirical item in Rudolf Lothar's journal *Die Wage* titled "Wittgenstein's Abschied" (Wittengenstein's farewell) presented an imaginary dialogue between Gomperz and Wittgenstein, prophesying their ultimate break.[127] The item expressed Gomperz's disappointment with Wittgenstein after his resignation from his official posts in the steel industry and his fear that Wittgenstein's retirement would have a bad impact on the industry and shares. Gomperz's fears would be realized only after the Secession House was finished, at the end of 1898 and in early 1899.

Like Todesco, Wittgenstein made sure to challenge the Jewish acculturation ideal, but Wittgenstein chose to provoke people by exposing his Jewish outsider identity in a different manner. Photos of the steel tycoon, who entered Vienna's art scene as a major player at the end of the nineteenth century, emphasize his attractive appearance. As a young man, Wittgenstein appeared in profile in these photos, proudly showing his straight nose. In 1908, the photographer Ferdinand Schmutzer showed him posing with his hands on his hips—standing in front of a white screen in Schmutzer's studio (Fig. 14). Wittgenstein demonstrates his physical fitness and strength to the viewer. According to his daughter Hermine (1874–1950), his motto was: "There is no shame in wealth."[128] Wittgenstein turned the condemnation of the wealthy Jew on its head by showing off that he could enjoy wealth.

He had made his fortune by profiting from stock-market transactions—for which Jewish businessmen were frequently condemned—and he flirted with the fact that people simply knew about his Jewish origins and most certainly criticized his Jewish business network.[129]

The Wittgensteins acknowledged their Jewish heritage by displaying portraits of Karl's Jewish paternal grandparents in their salons: "The portraits of Moses Meier Wittgenstein and his wife Brendel Simon, stiff and patriarchal and remote, still hang in the Viennese villa of their great-great-great-granddaughter but little is recalled about their originals."[130]

Karl Wittgenstein was born in Gohlis, near Leipzig, in 1847; four years later the family moved to Vienna. Karl did not do well in his studies, and in 1865, at the age of eighteen, he ran away to America with his violin. He worked there for two years as a waiter, bartender, and tutor of mathematics and German.[131] Yet after he returned to Vienna, he achieved what he perhaps had witnessed in America—the capitalist dream. He started studying at a technical college and simultaneously worked in a machine factory of the State Railroad Society. A year later he left his studies and held a series of temporary jobs. In 1872, he proved himself when Paul Kupelwieser hired him as a draftsman for the construction of the Teplitz Rolling Mill.[132] Wittgenstein made a good impression on Kupelwieser by finding buyers when the market was slow. At the same time he bought shares of the mill's stock. His sources of funds were his mother, Fanny, and his wife, Leopoldine Kallmus, whom he married in 1874.[133] It was his early fascination with the stock market that would bring him in contact with prominent Jewish patrons, eventually granting him exclusive control over the steel industry and consequently his great fortune.

Wittgenstein would have known Todesco's reputation. He may have heard about the magnificent interiors of the Palais Todesco from his children's tutor, the gentile Eduard Wessel, who also worked for the Todescos and other prominent families (in January 1879, Wessel's death notice in the *Neue Freie Presse* was signed by the Wittgenstein, Gomperz, Wertheimstein, Todesco, and Ephrussi families).[134] Karl Wittgenstein may even have been invited to see the Palais Todesco's interior by Max von Gomperz, who (as Todesco's brother-in-law) lived there. In any case, in 1879, Wittgenstein rented an apartment in the historicist neo-Renaissance palace belonging to the banker Eduard Wiener (a former neighbor of Todesco), at Schwarzenbergplatz 2.

If we remember that nineteenth-century historicist Europe was the background for Jewish acculturation, we should see Wittgenstein's self-stylization through a modernist attitude as an attempt to reframe that context. As noted in the first on the historicist patrons, Aleida Assmann claims that the dialectic of new and cliché patterns or decorations, as well as the dialectic of collectivity and individuality, always led to new battles over social visibility.[135] This notion helps explain Todesco's and Epstein's support of the historicist aesthetic with a nod to Hellenistic Jewish heritage, in contrast to the more common type of Jewish patronage among their contemporaries—the less striking, more solid neo-Renaissance houses on the Ringstrasse. In a similar fashion, Wittgenstein's support of the new secessionist movement, specifically the financing of the Secession House, was an attempt to claim the stylistic lead in the battle of social visibility over the historicist patrons. Wittgenstein knew how to tap into Vienna's Jewish network. Though he had the security of no longer belonging to the Jewish community, since his parents— Hermann Wittgenstein (1802–78) and Fanny Figdor (1814–90)—were baptized as Protestants before their marriage in Germany, Jewish network was still accessible to Wittgenstein. Despite having already planned their baptisms, his parents had first married in Vienna's synagogue, possibly to become members of Vienna's Jewish elite or to receive the blessing of Fanny's father, Wilhelm Figdor.[136] Karl Wittgenstein was aware of the Jewish and the gentile elites' high regard for the Figdor family and quickly learned how to impress and specifically use Jewish networks in Vienna to advance his career. As the following anecdote proves, he relied on his relations with Jewish businessmen to achieve social visibility from the start.

An important figure in Wittgenstein's business network was the Galician Jewish businessman Jacob Rappaport (1840–86), a newcomer to the Ringstrasse who bought the celebrated Palais Schey there in 1881. He was an important financial expert, chairman of the supervisory board of leading banks (including the Depositenank and Bodencreditanstalt), and a major player in the stock market.[137] As well as having novel business and media enterprises, Rappaport was the representative in the Austro-Hungarian Empire for the Bohemian Mining Company's owner, the gentile French banker Paul Eugène Bontoux.[138] In 1884, Rappaport arrived fifteen minutes late for a meeting with Wittgenstein to negotiate the sale of the bankrupt Bohemian Mining Company. Wittgenstein demanded that Rappaport compensate him by inviting him for dinner at the luxurious Sacher restaurant, rejecting the other restaurants Rappaport suggested.[139] Wittgenstein cleverly calculated this way of advancing his social position in Viennese society, as the Sacher restaurant was known as the meeting place for the city's aristocrats. He did not have problems associating with Rappaport, the Polish newcomer to the Ringstrasse's social elite, in public and perhaps made a point of doing so. Wittgenstein's purchase of the Bohemian Mining Company made him a powerful figure in the steel industry because he became a competitor of the largest company, the Prague Iron Industry Company. In the summer of 1885, impressed by Wittgenstein's performance, Max von Gomperz, a generation older than Wittgenstein and head of the Prague company's governing board as well as a member of board of the Credit-Anstalt bank, approached Wittgenstein to take over management of the Prague Iron Industry Company.[140] Gomperz's request paved the way for Wittgenstein to form a very powerful cartel, of which Wittgenstein wanted full control. Once again he approached Rappaport to purchase shares of stock in the Prague Iron Industry Company.[141] Wittgenstein's purchase of the major part of the shares in the Prague company improved the stocks' share price immediately, leaving all participants in this deal satisfied. The move, prompted by Gomperz's request and accomplished with Rappaport's help, enabled Wittgenstein to reach a financial status almost equal to his previous business competitors, the Gutmann and the Rothschild families. It is difficult to establish how indebted Wittgenstein was to Rappaport for the advancement of his career or the exact nature of their relationship. After Rappaport's untimely death, Wittgenstein also bought the Alpine Mining Society (now called the Alpine Industry), which Rappaport had founded.[142]

Wittgenstein was not afraid to play a provocative leading role among Vienna's rich, acting as an unheralded newcomer in his patronage of the Secessionists as well Georg Simmel argued in his 1908 essay "The Stranger" that "the stranger" secures the experience of intimacy as long as he succeeds in convincing his guests of his uniqueness, as in the case of having had a great love affair.[143] Wittgenstein marketed himself as both a newcomer and outsider to the Viennese and was identified by friends also as an American who conformed neither in his business conduct nor in his manner of socializing; he created his own style.[144]

Wittgenstein may have claimed an imagined Jewish identification to improve his position as an industrialist and a patron in Vienna. He made his career by associating himself with leading Jewish patron families on the Ringstrasse and both relying on and successfully competing against leading Jewish industrialists. He was definitely aware of the importance of accessibility and made his association with them a public matter in Vienna. Therefore, he made a marked effort to be seen with Rappaport in the Sacher restaurant at a crucial time in his career (as discussed above) and further collaborated with the Gutmann, Rothschild, and Gomperz families at the same time he patronized the secessionists, for which he was criticized. Wittgenstein positioned himself exactly at the center of Vienna's business and cultural scene. For more than a decade, he rented an apartment at Schwarzenbergplatz 2, in the Palais Wiener von Welten, where he witnessed how Wiener followed the grand Todesco tradition of arranging cultural evenings in his salon.[145] He could also have witnessed David Gutmann, his competitor in the Bohemian steel industry, make his aristocratic claims with his grand palace at Schwarzenbergplatz 10. In 1890, Wittgenstein purchased a historicist neo-Renaissance palace on Alleegasse (today Argentinierstrasse 16)—not far from Schwarzenbergplatz or the palaces of the Rothschild brothers in Prinz Eugenstrasse. The architect Friedrich Schachner had designed this palace for Duke Nakó in 1872.[146] Wittgenstein also had as a role model a most celebrated art patron in his own relative of the same generation, the banker Albert Figdor (1843–1927).[147] A highly respected collector of art, applied arts, and Judaica, Figdor had offered in 1891 to donate his whole collection to the Kunsthistorisches Museum (Museum of Fine Arts), but he was refused because of his Jewish origins.[148] It was in early 1890 that Wittgenstein entered the cultural scene as a patron.[149] His patronage was connected to the reputation of his mother, Fanny Figdor.

Fanny, the daughter of a rich Jewish family (she may have been named after the renowned Jewish salon woman Fanny von Arnstein), established her own exclusive Viennese salon and was also a role model for Karl in his desire to take an active part in the Viennese cultural scene. Leading authors such as Ignaz Castelli, Eduard Bauernfeld, and Ludwig August Frankl were guests at the salon of Fanny's parents, Wilhelm and Amalia Figdor; these authors were also invited by Eduard von Todesco to his literary club.[150] Fanny's parents were buried in the renowned Währinger Jewish cemetery in Vienna.[151] Among the prominent Jewish patrons buried in this cemetery are two prominent Ringstrasse patrons, Gustav von Epstein and Jonas von Königswarter. Following her family's tradition of patronage, Fanny is memoralized on a plaque as one of the founders of the Künstlerhaus. She also sponsored young musicians until her death in 1890.[152] Fanny was not a warm person, and a strong hierarchy in the family kept a distance between her and her grandchildren, Karl's children. According to her granddaughter, Fanny Figdor was a dominant figure in the Wittgenstein house, and she modeled the role of patron with which Karl had to come to terms.[153]

Wittgenstein always kept one foot in the Ringstrasse, moving his business office to an apartment in the Palais Schey there around the end of the nineteenth century.[154] The palace offered Wittgenstein a nostalgic connection with the poet and novelist Ludwig August Frankl (1810–94), the charismatic secretary of Vienna's Jewish community. Frankl had lived from 1882 until his death in 1894 in the apartment that Schey, and later Rappaport, had designated specifically for authors. The Wittgenstein family respected Frankl's memory. He was the tutor of Gustav, brother of Fanny Figdor. The family preserved his poems describing young Fanny, Karl's mother.[155] Though Frankl was the secretary of Vienna's Jewish community, he was a secular Jew. His book *Nach Jerusalem!* (*To Jerusalem!*, 1858) reports on his 1856 trip to Jerusalem and his efforts there in the name of the Viennese Jewish patron Elise Herz to establish a modern Jewish school that would teach both religious and secular studies. Frankl describes in detail his distaste for the Eastern European Orthodox Jews in Jerusalem who opposed his project, and at the same time he romanticizes Sephardic Jews as the positive exemplar of the Oriental.[156] Frankl's romantic image of the Orient was represented in the trophies collected during his journey. Like other Jewish intellectuals since the late eighteenth century, Frankl used his constructed, romantic image of an ideal Orient to distance himself from religious Ashkenazi Jews and to support his secular Jewish identification.[157] With his connection to figures like Frankl, Wittgenstein maintained a direct relationship to the long histories of Jewish patrons and the Jewish heritage of the Ringstrasse.

A few years after his mother's death, Wittgenstein began to continue her tradition of patronage, but he later fashioned a novel patronage style partly in rebellion against her. His regard of art as a form of compensation was shared with his older brother Paul. It may have been Paul and Karl's daughter, Hermine—two amateur artists—who introduced him to the secessionist movement. Karl became very attached to his art collection. When he remained in his city palace in Alleegasse during the winters, he kept his paintings close to him, only lending them to other museums when he was not staying in the palace.[158] His carefully designed setting was integral to his well-being. Given his need to establish an intimate relationship with his possessions, the question arises, why did he invest in the Secession House? Was it a rebellious act of emancipation from his mother and the historicist patrons (for example, Gomperz, who may have played a fatherly role in his life) to secure his position as a leading producer of culture in Viennese society?

Wittgenstein's art patronage distinguished him as an aesthete and allowed him to be part of both Christian and Jewish progressive patronage in Vienna. In the Viennese battle for social visibility, Wittgenstein claimed a position superior to that of the Jewish historicist patrons by confronting them with the failure of their acculturation project—namely, a failure to acknowledge their Jewishness outside of the European (Hellenistic) Jewish tradition. Wittgenstein saw his Jewish neighbors' disavowal of a cultural heritage with roots in the Orient (specifically, the semitic Middle East) as a weakness on a par with their being targeted by the media for their Jewish "looks" and their riches. For them to distance themselves from cultural identification with the Orient was an attack on their "Jewishness" along the same lines. Wittgenstein may have therefore supported Olbrich's new Oriental cultural pilgrimage site of the Secession House as an affront against the more acceptably European roots that the Jewish Ringstrasse patrons were trying to recall. His secessionist provocation partly succeeded in challenging the old elite's rule of cultural affairs.

Through his nonconformist patronage and willingness to embrace aesthetics beyond the traditional European historicist model, Wittgenstein was fashioning an adopted and imagined Jewish identity.

Wittgenstein and Vienna's Temple of Modern Art

For Wittgenstein art, specifically his investment in the new Secession House, served as an exciting replacement and perhaps an alternative to the Christian religious experience.[159] If the church's emphasis on original sin (especially the fall) was its central narrative, the Secession House provided references to the same primary scene—the tree of knowledge, the lizard crawling down the sides of the entrance door, and the temptation of the Egyptian or Greek dancers on the house's back—countering the fall of Adam with the rise of modern man (or modern art). In contrast to Todesco and Epstein, who rewrote their historical narrative as Europeans by demonstrating their relation to the Hellenistic Jews, Wittgenstein was not afraid to refer to a Jewish Oriental heritage. However, he also had the luxury of fashioning his reputation by testing the European Christian narrative since he could draw, to some extent, on both traditions. Wittgenstein's patronage included his purchase of paintings, among which were traditional naturalist paintings (for example, by Rudolf von Alt) as well as impressionist and symbolist ones (by Giovanni Segantini and Gustav Klimt). The church was ambivalent about the interpretation of religious themes in works shown at the Secession House (for example, in the case of Max Klinger's *Christ on the Olympus*), but Wittgenstein continued to support the Vienna Secession.[160] Moreover, Wittgenstein also bought paintings that may have evoked discomfort and even critical reflection in their viewers. The first painting he bought, displayed in the first Secession exhibition (which opened at the end of March 1898), was *The Source of Evil* (1897) by the Italian-Swiss painter Giovanni Segantini.[161] It was reproduced in *Ver Sacrum*'s May–June 1898 issue next to the second Segantini painting in the exhibition, *Angel of Life*, which depicted a harmonious mother-and-child composition. Wittgenstein's choice, *The Source of Evil*, is described by the Italian historian Luigi Villari as "a nude figure of the most exquisite grace and charm, bending forward over a little pool of water, leaning with one hand over an overhanging ledge of rock, and with the other spreading out her masses of wavy hair, so as to see them better reflected."[162] In his introduction to the painting, Villari identifies its subject matter with a popular legend, "according to which vain women who constantly look at themselves in the glass end by seeing the devil."[163] Villari views the picture as a moral work representing the artist's attempts to subdue his own vanity. Did Wittgenstein see his first secessionist purchase similarly—as a representation of his own vanity or devilishness? Is this what he searched for as a secessionist patron?

Financing two-thirds of the cost of the Secession House with 50,000 gulden, Wittgenstein was the building's main patron. An article by Georg Günther, his friend and former business associate, described Wittgenstein's generosity toward every kind of art—this might be an allusion to his commitment to the Gesamtkunstwerk—and stated that the Secession House "owed its origin to him."[164] James Shedel refers to the report of two leading artists, Josef Engelhart and Moll, who said they received 70,000 gulden for the building from "patrons and friends of art," some of which may have come from Nikolaus Dumba and Fritz Waerndorfer, but Shedel concludes that Wittgenstein was the chief supporter of the Secession House in the early days.[165] The architectural critic Otto Kapfinger and the architect Adolf Krischanitz refer to three sources on the financing of the house. The first is the catalogue of the second Secession exhibition, which recorded the artists' gratitude to the "friends of art." The second is Hermine Wittgenstein's "Familienerinnerungen," in which Hermine noted that her father was granted the title of cofounder in return for his generosity, listing him together with artists. The third source is Christian. Nebehay's book *Ver Sacrum 1898–1903*, which mentions the state of lower Austria as an additional source of support.[166] The claim that without Wittgenstein's financial guarantee the Vienna Secession would not have received permission to build the house[167] is supported in Wittgenstein's obituary in 1913: "When permission was sought for the new artistic movement to build its own house, and the officials of the city expansion fund and the police made their permission conditional, requesting a large financial guarantee, it was Karl Wittgenstein's generous gesture that almost alone accounted for the largest part of the sum."[168] While there is firm evidence that Wittgenstein's role in the funding of the Secession House was crucial, it is less clear whether his patronage influenced its design. But perhaps the question of whether or not he interfered in the design is less important than the impact he made by investing in the modernist house designated for the friends of modern art.[169] According to his daughter Hermine's memoirs, the secessionist artists approached Wittgenstein,[170] presumably before their break with the Künstlerhaus. Hoping to keep his interest in their future project alive, they may have even shown him the different versions of Olbrich's plans.

Just as the historicist patron Gustav von Epstein had resigned from his bank positions before dedicating himself to art patronage, in the spring of 1898 Wittgenstein took a three-month trip to several British colonies after resigning from his business positions in the steel industry. His itinerary included Egypt, southern India, Ceylon, Singapore, and Hong Kong. In April 1898, the month the secessionists laid the foundation stone for their house, Wittgenstein published an article in the *Neue Freie Presse* about the English government in these countries.[171] After his return to Vienna, he might have observed Olbrich's sketches with a fresh eye—at least he would have seen them with the eye of a man who had just visited those British colonies. He might have supported the evolving Oriental look of the house to give the Austrians the illusion of being colonizers in relation to the new building. Wittgenstein seemed to champion the process of starting from the weak position of the stranger and Other and turning it into a position of triumph and conquest.[172]

Similarly, the striking visual statement of the golden cupola atop the white temple-like cuboid might have expressed a colonial desire—meaning the desire of a country to possess colonies.[173] Using a colonial perspective to emphasize the attractiveness of a representation of "Jewishness" in Vienna's landscape was part of a tradition that had begun with Förster's Moorish synagogue in the Leopoldstadt (1858) and had reached a climax in Klimt's portrait of Adele Bloch-Bauer, set against a golden background with Oriental symbols (1907). The colonialist association would have been confirmed through a reference to Near Eastern architecture, such as the Dome of the Rock in Jerusalem, at this time under Turkish rule. The cupola further related the building to the uniqueness of new Oriental synagogues in the city, such as the Polish Synagogue by Wilhelm Stiassny in the second district (1892), which also had a golden cupola.[174] The owners of the historicist houses in the neighborhood of Karlsplatz would have seen the modern temple as an affront. With its Oriental character, it appeared to contemporaries and later to art historians as displaced in its surroundings. It remains to be asked whether the Secession House represented an "Oriental invasion"—a term used by Hevesi in an early review of the building,[175] as a reference to an imagined colony in the Near East—or whether it was interpreted as an ideal, as in Weyl's projection of a future "New Jerusalem." Furthermore, if the new house challenged the Catholic authority represented in the nearby baroque Karlskirche, as suggested above in Mayreder's contemporary review, was Wittgenstein challenging both the Jewish acculturation project and the Catholic authority in Vienna?[176]

For Wittgenstein, I suggest, the Secession House represented a temple to the arts, a place where he could also negotiate the terms of his imagined Jewish identification. But it was a new kind of a temple, one for a close and exclusive art club. Scholars have noted that the naked cubic body of the house, with its flat golden tree decoration, did not communicate with its immediate environment. Moreover, it is defensively closed off from its surroundings.[177] The highlight in the development of the secessionist movement was the first Gesamtkunstwerk exhibition in 1902, when the conductor of the neighboring Royal Opera House, Gustav Mahler, performed Beethoven's ninth symphony. This performance officially celebrated the relationship between the Opera House on the Ringstrasse and the Secession House just a few blocks away. Mahler had supposedly been depicted as "the artist-savior" in Klimt's *Beethoven Frieze*, which was on display in a room off the hall where Max Klinger's provocative sculpture of Beethoven was on display. Klinger's and Klimt's works, particularly, conveyed a messianic ideology that could also be read back into the building's golden cupola and the golden tree it suggests. Klimt's *Beethoven Frieze* included the final scene of *The Kiss* (Fig. 15, Plate 8) —a reunification of lovers that is part of the restoration of the bliss of the Garden of Eden—and invoked the story of the redeemer coming to Zion (Isaiah 59:20). Within the messianic message was another one of danger or threat. Klimt portrayed destructive forces in the central part of the frieze with interesting choices: the allegory of gluttony was a scowling fat woman, half-naked, with bare sagging breasts. This negative figure is decorated with golden jewelry and a lavish golden belt inlaid with precious stones, offering a caricature matching Aubrey Beardsley's drawing "Ali Baba" on the cover of *The Forty Thieves* (1897) and Klimt's own Oriental femme fatale in *Judith I* (1901; Fig. 2, Plate 1). The simultaneous inclusion in the frieze of the Jewish hero Mahler and a caricature of a Jewish seductress in the allegory of gluttony both ennobled and rejected the Jewish involvement in the secessionist project.

For Wittgenstein as an investor, the opening of the exhibition was a moment he had waited for and a climax in his patronage. At the end of the exhibition he purchased a smaller version of Klinger's sensational Beethoven

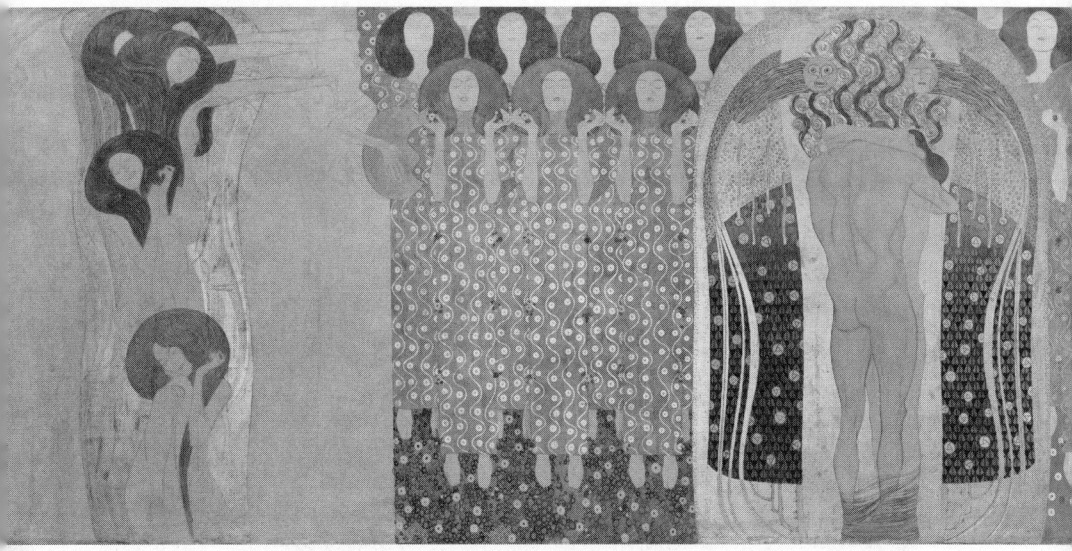

FIGURE 15. *Gustav Klimt,* The Kiss, *in his* Beethoven Frieze, *Secession House, 1902. © Belvedere, Vienna.*

sculpture (Museum of Fine Arts, Boston) and proudly allowed it to be photographed in almost every public room in his historicist palace in Alleegasse.[178] Aware of the importance of promoting art and music, he strove not only to support their creation but also to promote public discourse about them.[179] His purchase of Klinger's sculpture would also advance his strategic positioning of himself as a shaper of culture in the city. The press originally reported that Wittgenstein bought the version of Klinger's sculpture that the city had refused to buy, since the council had criticized its indecent partial nudity. One council member even identified Klinger's art as a product of "Jüdische Effecthascherei" (Jewish sensationalism).[180] But Wittgenstein had actually bought another version, depicting the naked upper body of the composer by the same sculptor. He wanted Beethoven's genius to be part of his household — he wanted to claim that he had his own Beethoven, possibly since his competitor and partner in the steel cartel, Wilhelm Gutmann (David Gutmann's brother), had built a house in Beethoven-Platz, where a monumental Beethoven memorial by Caspar Ritter von Zumbusch had been placed in 1880.[181] The seductive allure for visitors of Wittgenstein's home would have been the sculpture's association with the original Beethoven exhibition; he had also bought six plaques in the exhibition by an artist whom he ordered to come to his house to complete the work appropriately, with his signature.[182] While

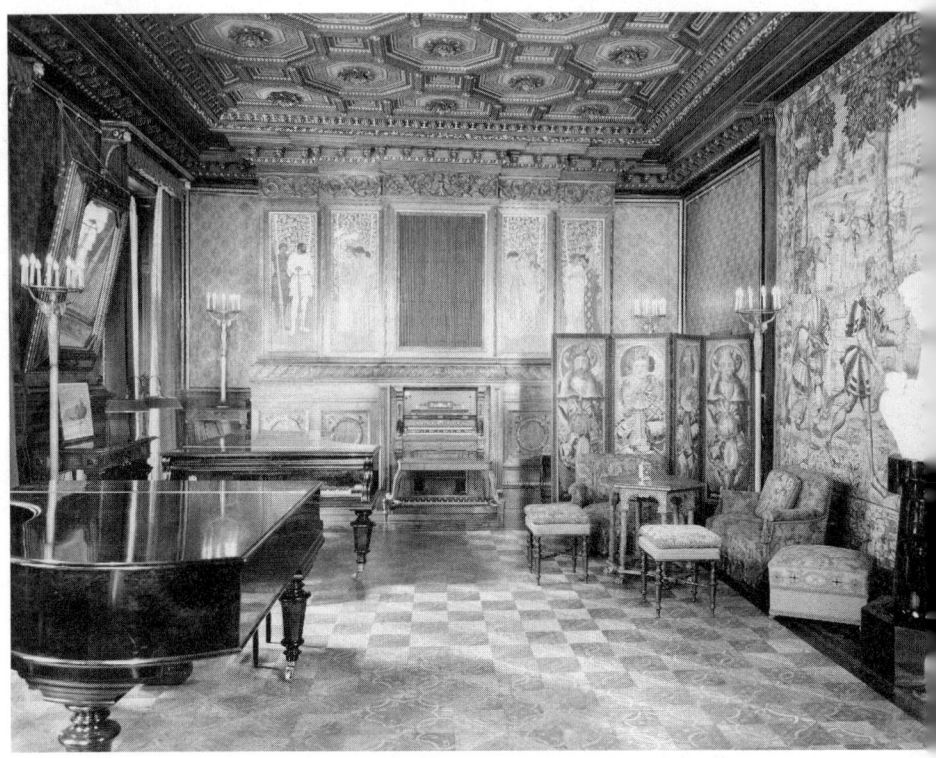

FIGURE 16. *Palais Wittgenstein, music room with Max Klinger's Beethoven sculpture, photo before 1909. Österreichische Nationalbibliothek, Vienna. 294.384-D.*

the Gutmanns had their monumental Beethoven outside their house on the square, Wittgenstein made sure that his grand marbled (modernist) Beethoven would be integrated into the interior of his cultured household (Fig. 16.)

Wittgenstein's patronage was carefully constructed, and he wanted a full return on his investments. The conductor Bruno Walter, who Mahler invited to be his assistant in 1901, specifically noted his appreciation of the Wittgenstein salon for its gratifying "all-pervading atmosphere of humanity and culture."[183] Wittgenstein's Beethoven sculpture linked his household to the famed fourteenth Secession exhibition and to his purchase of Klimt's painting *Das Leben ein Kampf* (Life [is] a battle, Aichi Prefectural Museum of Art, Nagoya, Japan), which had been exhibited with the title *The Golden Knight* at the Viennese Secession exhibition in 1903. This was a variation on the golden knight savior in Klimt's *Beethoven Frieze*. The idea of being identified as a golden knight appealed to Wittgenstein, and the painting, which showed a puppet knight standing erect on a black horse, was hung for a while at the top of the grand staircase at Wittgenstein's palace.[184] His association with the golden cupola of Olbrich's Secession House and the golden knight from the *Beethoven Frieze* were Wittgenstein's golden visiting cards, proving his success at cultural speculation and serving as seductive invitations to his cultured club.

Even after he began to support the secessionist movement, though, and in his own intimate surroundings, Wittgenstein was careful not to cut his ties to the historicist tradition. He may have used the novelty of modern design to assert a leading role in fashioning a new Viennese style, but in his economic relationship with artists he was locked into an older paradigm. The framework of his patronage, in contrast to the aesthetics he promoted, seemed to draw on quite traditional European models of labor relationships. His aristocratic pretense even while dismissing the offer of an aristocratic title is documented in a photo (in a private collection) taken during a garden party at Neuwaldegg Villa, the Wittgenstein residence in Vienna's outskirts, which presents family and guests in Biedermeier costume, circa 1905. Wittgenstein further demonstrated his aristocratic flair through heavy investment in architecture when he asked Hoffmann to redesign his hunting lodge in lower Austria 1906–8.[185] In a letter to Josef Hoffmann in July 1908, Fritz Waerndorfer, patron and financier of the Wiener Werkstätte, reacted to Wittgenstein's newly designed hunting lodge by imagining a similar design for the legendary Fugger family in the Middle Ages. Picking up on Waerndorfer's association, the art historian Franz Windisch-Graetz linked the interior with a *studiolo* (man's studio) belonging to Duke Federigo da Montefeltro in his Urbino palace.[186] Thus, when it came to the ultraluxurious modernist interior of two public rooms in his hunting lodge—the entrance room and living-dining room—Wittgenstein, in the scale of his patronage, evoked the aristocratic prestige of a grand Italian heritage just as the historicist patrons of the Ringstrasse had done. Furthermore, like Todesco, Wittgenstein wanted to assert in his relationship with artists that he was the master. He had no problems complaining in front of young artist Ivan Meštrović, whom he discovered in a Secession exhibition, about the ugliness of his women's faces. In April 1908, Wittgenstein asked Meštrović to send him photos of the sculptures Meštrović was creating for him since he did not like a particular *Crouching Woman* he had seen in the exhibition or *Eve*, and "he could not show a collection of ugly women in his house."[187] Wittgenstein seemed to walk the line between being a cultural catalyst, helping shape and promote modernist art in Vienna, and residing comfortably in the world of old Vienna—the stratified and perhaps already decadent historicist Vienna.

A Viennese Gesamtkunstwerk: Alma Flirting with Alexander in Spitzer's Music Salon

> Evening at Spitzer. He [Alexander von Zemlinsky] played and sang—I played and sang. It was *marvellous* being two. Only in the music can I be happy.[188]

The experience of listening to classical music together in an elevated cultured setting was integral to establishing shared cultural platforms and claiming cultural prestige in the salons of Wittgenstein and other industrialists and patrons such as David Berl and Friedrich Victor Spitzer. A drawing from July 1899 for a wall decoration in the music room of the coal merchant and Künstlerhaus patron David Berl (1838–1903) that depicts the architect Olbrich's blend of two national styles, French art nouveau and German nineteenth-century romanticism (Fig. 17, Plate 9).[189] The drawing shows two sirens guarding a tribute to the German composers Beethoven and Richard Wagner, whose names are encircled with laurel wreaths. Karl Kraus admitted sarcastically that the relationship of Berl to the secessionist brotherhood, mediated by the artist and gallery director Carl Moll, cannot be dismissed as a mere idle fantasy: "Just as every aristocrat used to keep his Jew-in-residence, so today every stockbroker has a Secessionist about the House. Herr [Carl] Moll is known to be the art-agent to the share pusher Zierer and the coal-usurer Berl. . . . This rapport between modern art and idle-rich Jewry, this rise in the art of design, capable of transforming ghettos into mansions, occasions the fondest of hopes. . . . Those who had the opportunity to admire the burgeonings of the celebrated *goût juif* at the recent Secessionist Exhibition will not dismiss such dreams as merely idle."[190]

Berl lived in a grand apartment in the neo-Gothic building on the Ringstrasse called Sühnhaus, on Schottenring 7, built in 1882–86 by Friedrich von Schmidt. In January 1888, Berl had been accepted into the Freemasons' lodge Friendship, and in 1889 he cofounded a philanthropic organization initiated by the lodge, Health Recovery House for Poor Women. Other prominent members of this lodge were its founder, Emrich Engländer (1832–1905), the uncle of Peter Altenberg; and the Zionist Jugendstil architect Oskar Marmorek. Marmorek had been accepted in April 1891. In that same year Berl became a *Redner* (speaker) at this lodge, meaning that he made sure regulations were observed and took part in the lodge's judicial proceedings. In October 1899, Berl cancelled his membership in the Künstlerhaus after having approached Olbrich to design the interiors of the public rooms in his apartment. For Berl, his association with Olbrich and the Vienna Secession was an extension of his membership in a Freemasons' lodge. Bahr, who had

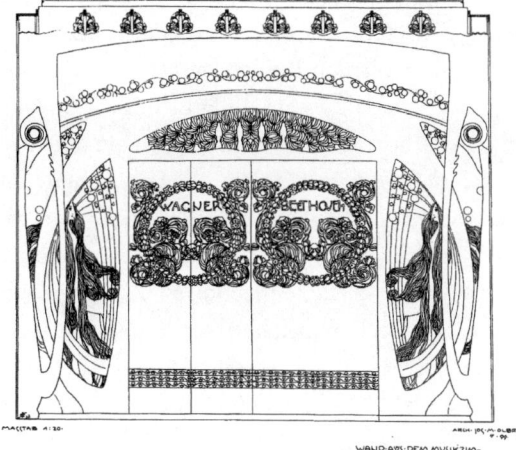

FIGURE 17. *Joseph Maria Olbrich, drawing for a wall decoration in the music room of David Berl, July 1899. Joseph Maria Olbrich, Ideen von Olbrich, Text von Ludwig Hevesi (1904; repr., Stuttgart: Arnold'sche, 1992), 19.*

belonged to the lodge since April 1897, may also have mediated Berl's hiring of Olbrich.[191] Also in October 1899, in the festively decorated temple of the lodge, Bahr, Marmorek, and Berl may have heard a lecture by the Jewish writer, editor, and secretary of the Austrian Industrialists' Association, Johann Auspitzer, on "What is modern and what is fashionable?"[192]

The question might have provoked much thought in Berl regarding patronage. If Berl and Marmorek had both belonged to the same lodge, why did Berl ask Olbrich and not Marmorek to modernize the historicist rooms in his apartment? From the 1890s, Marmorek had been in high demand as an exhibition designer. His most successful design was "Venice in Vienna," a popular entertainment park created in Vienna's Prater for the Jewish entrepreneur Gabor Steiner.[193] The patron Berl and the architect Marmorek were also representatives of the highest-ranking figure in their Freemasons' lodge, Geza Winter: Berl was his first representative and Marmorek his second.[194] Perhaps Berl wanted to distance himself from Marmorek, who had "violated the codes of honor" of the lodge and who was officially identified with the Zionist cause and the popular entertainment site in the Prater. After being forced to leave the lodge for "violating the codes of honor" in January 1899, however, Marmorek was still asked to design the interiors of the lodge's new assembly room in the first district, at Grünangergasse 2, in December 1900.[195] Perhaps, then, it was the romantic admiration for Richard Wagner and the elitist aspirations of the friends of the Vienna Secession that Berl shared with Olbrich that made their relationship stronger than any relationship with Marmorek.[196] Olbrich offered Berl what Wittgenstein had claimed

THE SECESSIONISTS, 1897–1902 { 101

in his association with the Secession House—a recognized stylistic advantage in the battle for social visibility in Vienna.

Similar to the declared aim of the German-French entrepreneur of art nouveau, Siegfried Bing, Olbrich wanted to liberate design from the burden of historicism with the help of natural imagery. In an article on art nouveau published in the American journal *The Craftsman* (1903), Bing explained that the representation of nature was meant to chase off "old memories" and "rejuvenate our spirits."[197] In Olbrich's drawing for Berl's music room, nature serves to glorify a romantic cult of music. In the realization of his design, approaching the idea of the Gesamtkunstwerk, Olbrich intensified spiritual aspiration through his use of color. According to the art critic Ludwig Abels, the furniture in this room was stained dark blue, with walls covered in matching silk, evoking an elevated mystic atmosphere.[198]

David Berl's brother-in-law, Friedrich Victor Spitzer, did not belong to a Freemasons' lodge but was a prominent member of the community of artists and friends of the Vienna Secession. He had just moved to Schleifmühlgasse 4 from the university area, where he had lived for a few years next to his workplace at a chemical laboratory. Schleifmühlgasse was only a ten-minute walk from the new Secession House. Spitzer would hire Olbrich to design the public rooms and the bedroom in his apartment in Schleifmühlgasse in 1899. Spitzer remained at this address for little more than two years and then moved, together with his Olbrich interiors, to his new villa in the artists' colony in Hohe Warte.[199] Photographs of interiors of Spitzer's apartment were published in at least three major German or Austrian design and architecture journals in 1900–1901.)[200]

Spitzer's father, David, was a friend of the renowned Gomperz family (the family Sophie Todesco came from), whose members had helped fashion the culture of the Ringstrasse. The Spitzers and Gomperzes came from the German-speaking city of Brno in Moravia. When David Spitzer died in November 1895, his son inherited his father's sugar factory, Spitzer und Söhne.[201] In a portrait taken by his photographer colleague Heinrich Kuhn, Friedrich Spitzer appears as a stout, elegantly dressed man. In contrast to Schmutzer's 1908 photo of Karl Wittgenstein (Fig. 14), who appears as a master, standing up straight with his right fist at his waist, Spitzer appears almost like a servant waiting to be given an order, with his left hand hidden behind his back while his right hand grasps the back of a chair. Wittgenstein wears a somewhat badly tied bow tie in his photo, yet he looks with satisfaction up to the right. Spitzer's photo shows him with a dotted tie, also not straight, yet he is lost in thought, with perhaps just a hint of a sly smile underneath his mustache.

A talented amateur photographer and an art patron, Spitzer would become a prominent member of the new secessionist friendship club. His entry ticket was his cofounding of and membership in the Wiener Camera Club and his collaboration with the Trifolium photographer's group (1898–1903), which included Hugo Henneberg, Heinrich Kuhn, and Hans Watzek. They specialized in variants of the complex gum bichromate process and signed their art photos with a three-leaved clover.

Spitzer's sensitive photographic portraits of his friend Klimt and his close acquaintance, the young Alma Schindler, stepdaughter of Carl Moll (who was, according to Kraus, also Berl's artistic advisor) captured the two Viennese celebrities and frequent guests at his salon in a reflective melodic moment, lost in their thoughts. The photos are documents of the intimate relationship between Spitzer and his two subjects, but it is the silent meditation of the moment that fascinated Spitzer. He was also interested in the relationship between figure and architecture. Two of his scenic photos, reproduced in the journal *Photographische Rundschau* (1904), reveal this: *Before the Church* shows a small crowd outside a church, praying in front of its entrance, and *Chapel Court* shows a woman farmer from the back, in Sunday dress, standing frozen in the chapel court. Did Spitzer represent his relationship as an outsider to the Christian church—which he did not join after he renounced his Jewish religion—through these photos of piety? In both compositions the individuals remain anonymous (most are seen from the back; only one is seen bowing in profile), and the architecture is simple, unornamented, with uncanny dark openings. Beginning in 1897, Spitzer participated in exhibitions in different cities, including Berlin, Hamburg, Krefled, Leipzig, Munich, London, Den Haag, and Paris.[202] He photographed famous society figures and artists such as Klimt, Ferdinand Hodler, and Jan Toorop. Besides photography he also chose to dedicate his free time to music.

In Spitzer's bachelor salon there were plenty of exciting musical evenings —spontaneous or organized with a planned program. On November 29, 1899, Alma Schindler (later Alma Mahler) reported in her diary on Spitzer's festive house warming at his newly designed apartment at Schleifmühlgasse, in Vienna's fourth district. Among the prominent secessionist personalities present were Josef Engelhart and his wife, Josef Hoffmann, and Spitzer's designer Olbrich. Alma first describes the white and light gray bedroom, which appeared to her "too virginal" for Spitzer's character but was in its own way "magnificent! with its overwhelming simplicity and geniality."[203] According to Alma, Spitzer's studio, however, was like a slap in the face with its old furniture. She associated the romantic art of Richard Wagner with the public rooms: "The dining room and salon blue. A peculiarly haunting blue (*eigenthümlich einen verfolgendes Blau*), like a Wagner motif. Also fine detailing. The piano is encased in wood, making a bit of a theatrical impression, with high lamps right and left. The stalks of laurels—it sounds also somewhat hollow."[204] That evening Alma was asked to play the piano, and so began her flirtation dramas in Spitzer's music salon. The architect Olbrich, with his great pride and endless vanity, reminded Alma of Richard Wagner. Spitzer remained in the background, watching a flirtatious scene between Alma and Olbrich.[205] The flirtation highlighted the sexual tensions and seductions that existed in tandem with the secessionist style and may have been enhanced by it. (Another example is noted above, of Zuckerkandl's afternoon at the Prater and her pride in Rodin's observation of Klimt's flirtation with his young models.) In this cultural context of seduction that seemed to be sweeping Vienna, it is perhaps only natural that Spitzer, the consummate bachelor, would have wanted to be host to it.

Spitzer remained a single man throughout his life. He appeared alone at public events and in his house, but he enjoyed and became engaged in what can be described as secessionist social dramas. He was not always the master of a situation, as witnessed in an anecdote recorded in Alma's diary, but he always knew how to turn disadvantage into advantage. The anecdote, referred to as "Mohrenhetz" (an African hunt), hints at Spitzer's insecure position in the secessionist friendship club, both as a single man and as a Jewish patron. More than ten days after the opening of the Secession House, at the end of November 1898, a festive evening was organized at the Molls' apartment with many prominent artists: Engelhart, Hoffmann, Olbrich, Theobald Pollack, Moser, and Klimt. Since the dining table was filled with couples and family, Spitzer had to eat with a group of other unmarried people in a side room. But he was bored and asked to join the main table. Alma suggested that they all cooperate to chase him away, and when the entire party ran to get hold of old halberds, Spitzer "ran like a tailor."[206] (Alma's phrase is a possible reversal of the idiom "Tapfer wie ein Schneider" [courageous like a tailor], based on a Grimm fairy tale called "The Brave Little Tailor." The tailor uses imaginative tricks to defeat two giants, catch a unicorn, and trap a wild boar and is allowed to marry the king's daughter. The moral of the story is that someone from the lower classes can achieve greatness if he is self-aware and creative. Spitzer supposedly "failed" to fulfil Alma's romantic expectation and "ran like a tailor.") One guest barked at him, and Klimt crowed "cock-a-doodle-doo." Then Spitzer was asked to return, but the game continued, and again they grabbed their weapons and threw him out of the dining room. Spitzer's role as an outsider in this group was exposed by the rather sadistic fancy of young Alma. His orchestration of flirtatious dramas in his own salon may have been meant to compensate for his exclusion and to secure the return of his guests. The dramatic romance between the gentile beauty Alma and the Jewish composer Alexander von Zemlinsky in Spitzer's salon demonstrate how he reshaped the drama by turning the seduction game into something that applied to others, making him a host instead of a participant.

In Spitzer's dandy apartment in Schleifmühlgasse, Olbrich created a continuous space between the dining room and the music room by removing a wall and replacing it with a folding screen, to be set aside when the owner or a guest played the piano. A contemporary art historian claimed that the color (blue, according to Alma) in this room "evokes Spirits, which imitate directly the emotions evoked by modern paintings, transferring coloristic qualities onto the spatial art: a whole new principle!"[207] In the drawing for the dining room Olbrich stained the wood paneling and furniture green, and the ceiling beams bore flowery green and red imagery. Olbrich transformed the ceiling beams into a kind of decorative element with rustic flair. In contrast, the pattern on the window curtains in the dining room was of intersecting circles, referring back to the pattern of the table cloth on the dining table, while the abstract imagery of fruits on the curtains in the music room referred back to the pattern on the screen dividing the music salon and the dining room; all these related elements a Gesamtkunstwerk. Both the music and dining rooms had elaborate decorative schemes highlighted by the flower imagery, suggesting that art and music and dining would come together to produce unique sensual and artistic sensations. The wood paneling on the lower part of the curving walls became part of a gridlike frame with the dado, giving Spitzer the ability to hang his paintings and photographs in every second frame. While the dining room table was simple and the backs of the chairs were decorated with horizontal lines, similar to the chairs in the dining room in Olbrich's Villa Friedmann (Hauptstrasse 27, Hinterbrühl; 1899), the grand piano was a special case. Its omega-shape curve and electric lights in the shape of metal clusters and glass flowers attached to the upper curve gave it a romantic flair (Fig. 18).[208] Flowery electric lights also appeared on the large buffet. The flower decoration and the lower curve form promoted a sense of festivity in contrast to the sharp rectangles of the upper wood paneling and dining table, which gave the rooms a sense of solemnity or pure simplicity. But the secessionists' claim of pursuing a tasteful environment provoked people. The architect Adolf Loos, an opponent of the secessionist movement,

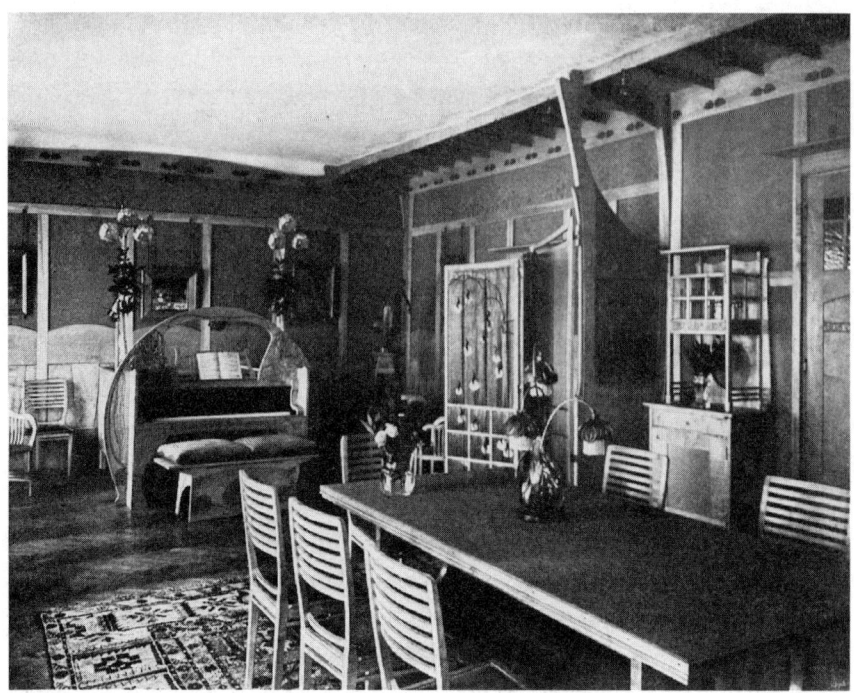

FIGURE 18. *Joseph Maria Olbrich, view of dining table and piano case, Victor Spitzer's dining room and music room, 1899. Joseph Maria Olbrich,* Ideen von Olbrich, Text von Ludwig Hevesi *(1904; repr., Stuttgart: Arnold'sche, 1992), 64.*

criticized Olbrich's interiors as pointless in a world of tragedy and drama: "Out with your pens, you describers of people and souls! Just describe how birth and death, how the cries of pain of an injured son, the death-rattle of a dying mother, the last thoughts of a daughter who wants to take her own life, describe how these will be played out, how they will look, in a bedroom by Olbrich.... Is the room where all this happens tasteful? Who's going to ask? Who's going to care? It's a room. Period."[209]

But Spitzer was among those who cared whether his rooms were tasteful. He consciously chose a secessionist designer to overcome his outsider position in the secessionist friendship club. Olbrich's tasteful setting for Spitzer's music room consciously supported Spitzer's wish to encourage seduction in his house—not the drama of birth and death, but the seduction of flirtation encouraged by the gaze of the dandy Spitzer. Spitzer's dandy charisma was a way for him to market his aesthetic lifestyle and maintain his single status as a director of seduction games for others. In the spring of 1900, Spitzer helped arrange an artistic collaboration between the young Hugo von Hofmannsthal and the composer Alexander von Zemlinsky for Hofmannsthal's ballet *The Triumph of Time*.[210] This was not the only match Spitzer encouraged. His music room, illuminated by flower lamps and decorated with the sculptural case of his piano, became the background for a famous short-lived love affair between Alma Schindler and Zemlinsky. If, as Simmel noted, modern man is driven to style to conceal and expose the personal,[211] then Olbrich's secessionist Gesamtkunstwerk can be regarded as a wish to conceal Spitzer's "Jewishness." In contrast, the presence of the Other—Zemlinsky—in Spitzer's music room represented a wish to expose his "Jewishness." Spitzer used this private theatrical orchestration to display his cultural difference.[212]

After her first meeting with Zemlinsky in Spitzer's apartment at the end of February 1900, Alma noted in her diary her fascination with the "ugly" Jewish composer.[213] They were sitting in the modernist dining room recently designed by Olbrich, and when the man sitting next to her on one side, Hans Fuchs, praised the Turkish smoking room and the modernist interior of the apartment, she lost respect for him and turned to converse with Zemlinsky, who was sitting on her other side.[214] The short but intense love affair that developed between Alma and Zemlinsky gave Spitzer's modernist music salon a certain authenticity, firmly establishing the Jewish dandy's network of desire. Alma's diary entries note that Spitzer played the observant, eager witness and even the director of this love affair. Alma learned to appreciate Zemlinsky during another afternoon event at the Spitzer apartment, when he sat down at the grand piano and played for her the prelude from Wagner's *Tristan and Isolde*.[215] Spitzer's instigating role in the affair is evident in the fact that he informed Alma at yet another social event, this one at the Hennebergs', that Zemlinsky had not appeared that evening as he had gone out to get drunk.[216] Toward the end of the affair, when Alma attended a Zemlinsky concert with Spitzer, she reported that Spitzer informed her that Zemlinsky had seen her and left. This hurt her feelings, which also led to an ugly antisemitic diatribe in her diary against Zemlinsky's new woman.[217] Spitzer was also present at the much-reported social gathering of 1902 when Alma met her future husband, Gustav Mahler, at the salon of the art critic Zuckerkandl.[218] The ensuing flirtation between Mahler and Alma soon resulted in marriage. Spitzer's interiors had given him a fine setting in which the dandy could confirm his position in the social drama of Viennese modernism.

Possibly following the recommendation of Olbrich, or following the example of three of his gentile friends—the artist and designer Koloman Moser; the artist Moll; and the photographer Henneberg, who hired Josef Hoffmann in 1900—Spitzer asked Hoffmann to design his villa in the Hohe Warte. In early May 1901, city officials approved Hoffmann's plans for Spitzer's future house, and in mid-May 1902, Spitzer and his friend and colleague Henneberg received permission to enter their villas. Hoffmann had designed artists' studios for Moser's and Moll's homes, and he designed photography studios for Henneberg and Spitzer.[219] Spitzer's villa, according to the architectural historian Eduard Sekler, was a more progressive achievement because of its sparing use of and unity of decorative elements. Sekler suggests that Hoffmann's achievement was due to Spitzer's insistence on including Olbrich's interiors in his house. This "cooperation" between Hoffmann and the earlier Jugendstil Olbrich design forced Hoffmann to create a more mature modernist ensemble.[220] Hevesi described the contrast in the interiors as expressing the fine taste of Olbrich's far-reaching fantasy in form and color and representing Hoffmann's strict rationalism, which left a distinct impression and achieved more with less.[221]

Spitzer consciously embraced the modernity of his interiors: both the Olbrich- and Hoffmann-designed rooms were filled with natural light. The striking flower lamps in Olbrich's music and dining rooms—either fixed to the ceiling or on the buffet or the side panels of the piano (Fig. 18)—are a direct reference to French art nouveau and, with the expressive flowers framing the entrance, specifically to Siegfried Bing's art nouveau gallery. In contrast, Hoffmann's lamps for the great hall—glass cubes hanging from the ceiling and mushroom-shaped lamps fixed to panels flanking the stairs going down to the large hall—may reflect the influence of the Scottish designer Charles Rennie Mackintosh (whose work was seen in Vienna during the eighth Secession exhibition in 1900). In accepting Hoffmann's masculine formal geometric design for his villa's public hall, with a reduced harmony of black, white, and gray, while insisting on the inclusion of Olbrich's feminine, flowery, and curved designs with the romantic blue color, Spitzer championed the meeting of the old secessionist figurative romantic style and the emerging secessionist geometric style.

In a 1903 essay about the artists' colony villas in Hohe Warte, the art critic Joseph August Lux noted the interdependency between the owner's "looks" and the designed environment: "And as the household belongings inside appear elevated, so the man achieves inside this space a greater importance and a stronger self-awareness, because everything here stands in visible relation to and dependence upon his appearance."[222] Lux's article was accompanied by detailed photographic documentation: Spitzer had allowed the photographer to record almost every corner of his villa. Spitzer programmed the design of his villa in a manner that would reflect his stature in Viennese culture. As his home's design expressed his sense of an aesthetic that would anchor the future, so Spitzer saw himself as an anchor or authority for a new generation of culture makers.

The Legacy of the Secession: Mastering "Jewishness" in the New Wittgenstein House

For the children of Karl Wittgenstein, part of coming to terms with their father's celebrity meant also engaging with the question of Jewish identification. Ludwig Wittgenstein's biographer argued that it was difficult: "Jews of assimilation, particularly in what became the German Empire, not only took pains to lose all traces of the old culture in themselves but viewed its manifestations in others and even viewed the race itself as a *sort of taint* from which only good fortune *and self-mastery* had managed to free them, *in so far as they were free.*"[223]

The secessionist style acknowledged Jewish cultural difference in the seductive gesture of Oriental inflections: the Secession House's golden cupola, which seduced with its gold allure and the suggestiveness of the golden orb's vulva; the similar enticement of the gold background in Klimt's *Judith I* (Fig. 2, Plate 1); and of course the seductiveness of Judith in all her complexity. The references seem to be to various attractions and detractions of the Otherness of "Jewishness" in Vienna at the time, not least to the way the exotic, excessive richness of gold was enmeshed with a more negative association of Jewish wealth, and to the equally challenging and provocative sexuality of "the Jewess" that was invariably tinged with danger. "Jewishness" was a category that in Vienna at the beginning of the modern age needed to be mediated by Jews and non-Jews alike, particularly by those Jews keen on acculturation. The older generation of Jews and—as this book examines—the Jewish patrons among them, as well as the younger generation of Jews and baptized Jews, had to come to terms with this cultural category, and patronage was key to their forming a new identification.

Hofmannsthal's pantomime story *Der Schüler* (The student), published in the *Neue Deutsche Rundschau* in November 1901, describes an abusive master who maintains control over the younger generation—in the characters of his daughter and his student—through a powerful ring.[224] The Jewish figures in the earlier version of this pantomime were the rabbi, Bochur (the student), and Taube (the rabbi's daughter).[225] The ring that the rabbi in the earlier version (the learned alchemist in the published version) possesses enables him to hypnotize and control the younger generation.[226] An early climax of the pantomime is when the rabbi (learned alchemist) hypnotizes his beautiful daughter with the magic ring and forces her to dance wildly, flirting with her viewers through playing with her loose hair as if it was a veil.[227] Her father, who in his command has repeated Herod's request to Salome, and the student, view the dance, but the daughter rejects the student because his body is too ugly.[228] To the men, her dance perhaps symbolizes their wish to liberate themselves from their old and ugly bodies, but the dancer prefers to free herself and her beautiful body from her abusive father and her ugly suitor, the student. The pantomime ends with her tragic death. After her father locks her up to prevent her from sending a love letter, she dresses up as him to escape her blind guard and leaves the house to send the letter. Coming back to her father's study to return his clothes, she is mistaken for him and killed by his rebellious student and a collaborator.[229] The symbol of the ring in the story of the rabbi and his daughter is interesting because it is inflected with many of the same associations that probably explained the secessionists' fascination with gold. The ring, which has been identified with the German Enlightenment author Gottlieb Ephraim Lessing's advocacy of religious tolerance in his play *Nathan the Wise*, is subverted in Hofmannsthal's pantomime to show the destructive powers of money (and "Jewishness")—and may also be a projection of the powerful influence the historicist Ringstrasse patrons had on his art. Identified as a Jewish author because of his prominent family and the network of Jung-Wien, Hofmannsthal may have tried coming to terms with the enigma of "Jewishness" by challenging the Jewish ideal of the teacher-student and father-daughter relationship in his work. Hofmannsthal expressed the stereotypical view that the Jews' intelligence, wealth (the ring), and ugliness were corrupting and could lead to criminal acts. In the published version of the same pantomime, he tried to generalize the identification of the threat by stripping the figures of their Jewish identification, perhaps because he felt it was too damning, too incendiary, and fed into stereotypes. More likely he felt that the audience could still make the same identification even without the specific labeling, particularly given the reference to Salome's dance of the seven veils, the ugly suitor and the hypnotic power of the ring.[230]

We might be reminded of Hofmannsthal's portrayal of the possessive relationship between the father and his beautiful daughter when we consider Karl Wittgenstein's hiring of Klimt to portray his daughter Margaret (1882–1958) on the occasion of her marriage to the American Jerome Stonborough in early 1905 ("Margaret Stonborough-Wittgenstein," Bayerische Staatsgemäldesammlungen, Neue Pinakothek, Munich).[231] Klimt placed the beautiful proud woman—wearing a sensual, white silk moiré dress—in a formal

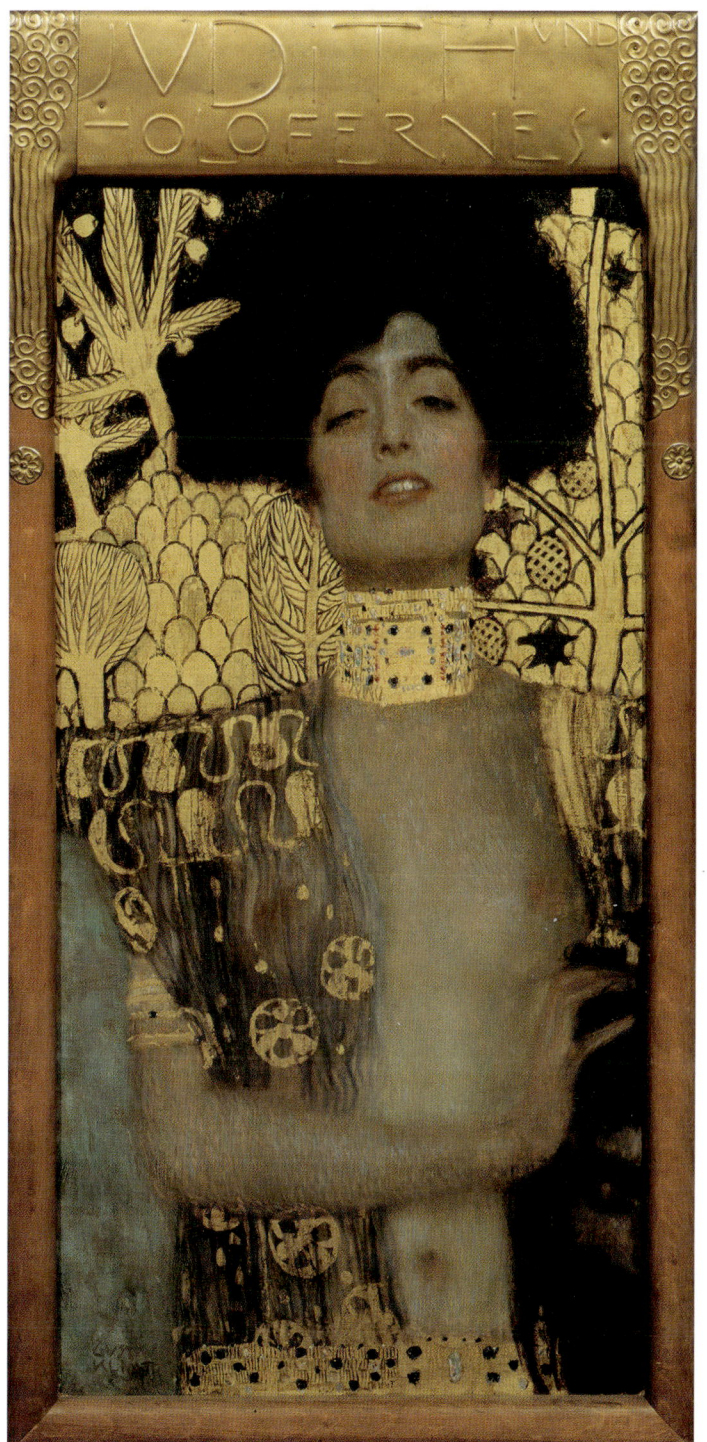

PLATE 1. *Gustav Klimt,* Judith I, *oil on canvas, 1901.* © *Belvedere, Vienna.*

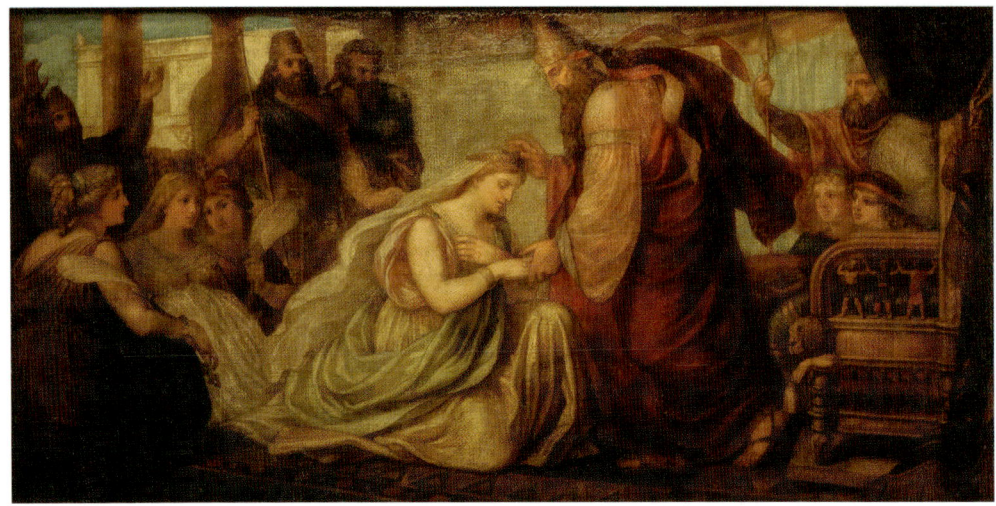

PLATE 2. *Christian Griepenkerl, coronation of Esther, ballroom ceiling, Palais Ephrussi, 1873. Photo: © 2014, Benjamin von Radom.*

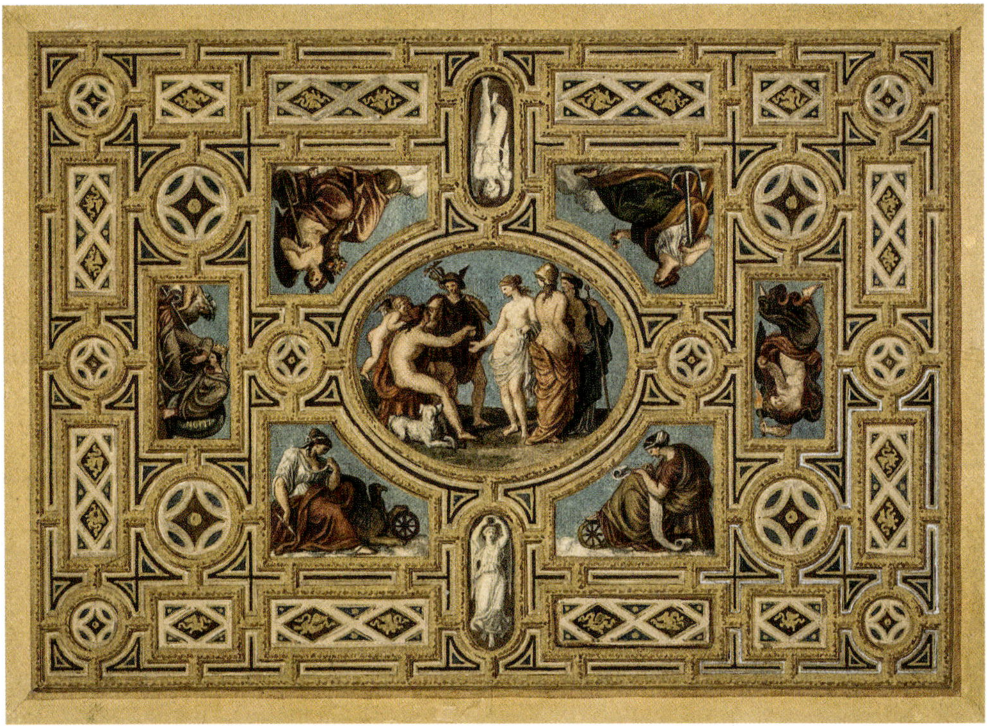

PLATE 3. *Carl Rahl,* The Judgment of Paris, *sketch for Palais Todesco dining room ceiling, 1863–64. Academy of Fine Arts Vienna, Kupferstichkabinett (Graphic Collection). Inv. no. 20.165.*

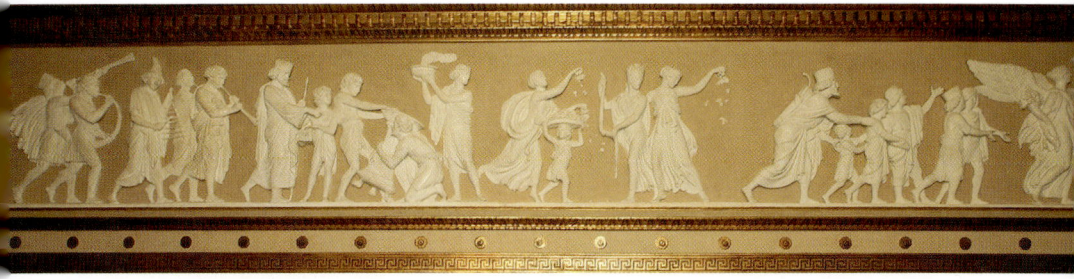

PLATE 4. Theophil Hansen, Alexander frieze, winter garden, Palais Epstein, 1872.
© The Austrian Parliamentary Administration. Photo: Christian Hikade.

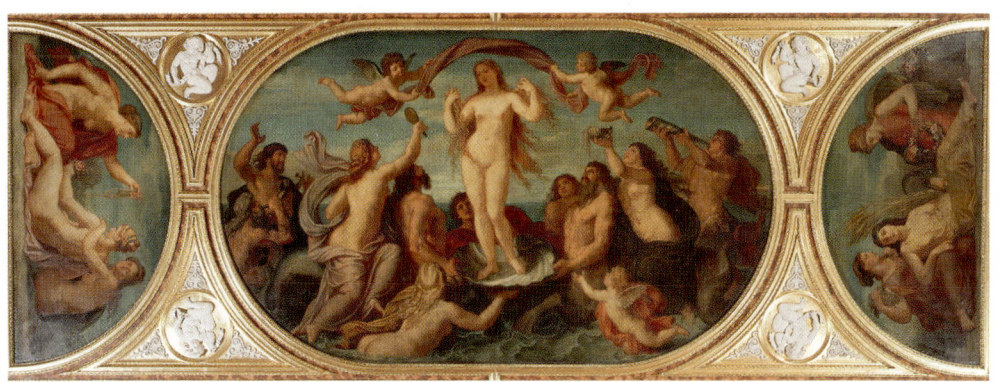

PLATE 5. Christian Griepenkerl, Birth of Venus, ballroom ceiling, Palais Epstein, 1872.
© The Austrian Parliamentary Administration. Photo: Christian Hikade.

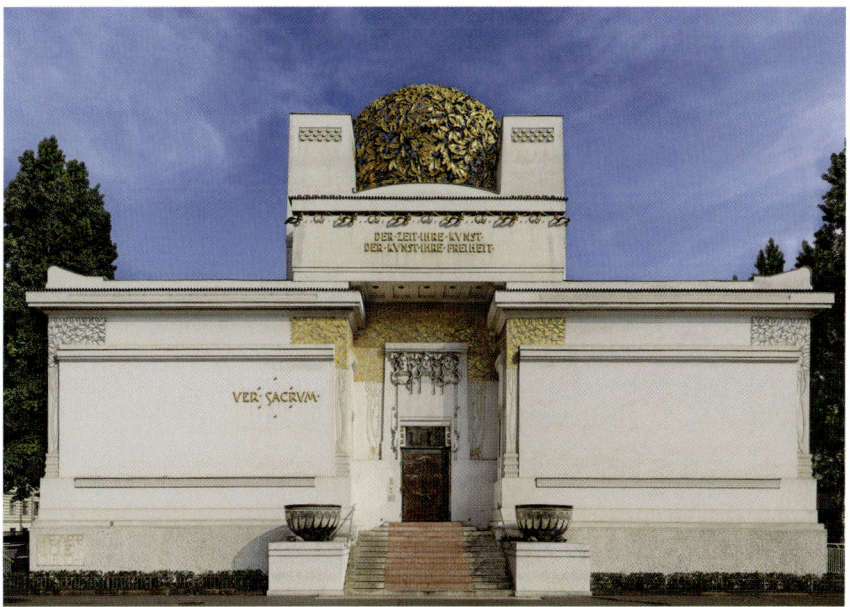

PLATE 6. Joseph Maria Olbrich, Secession House, 1898.
Photo: © 2015, Benjamin von Radom.

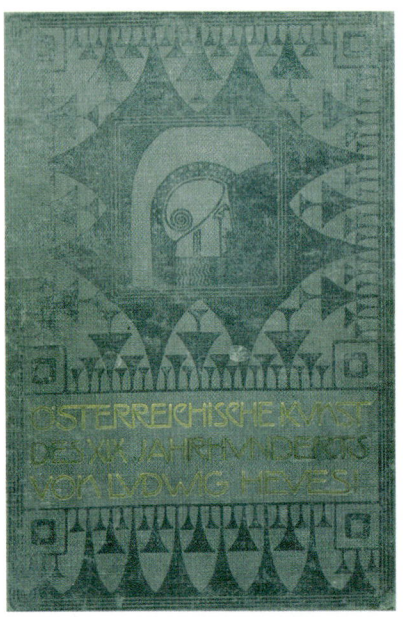

PLATE 7. *Koloman Moser cover for Ludwig Hevesi,* Österreichische Kunst im 19. Jahrhundert *(Leipzig: E. A. Seemann, 1903). Academy of Fine Arts Vienna, University Library.*

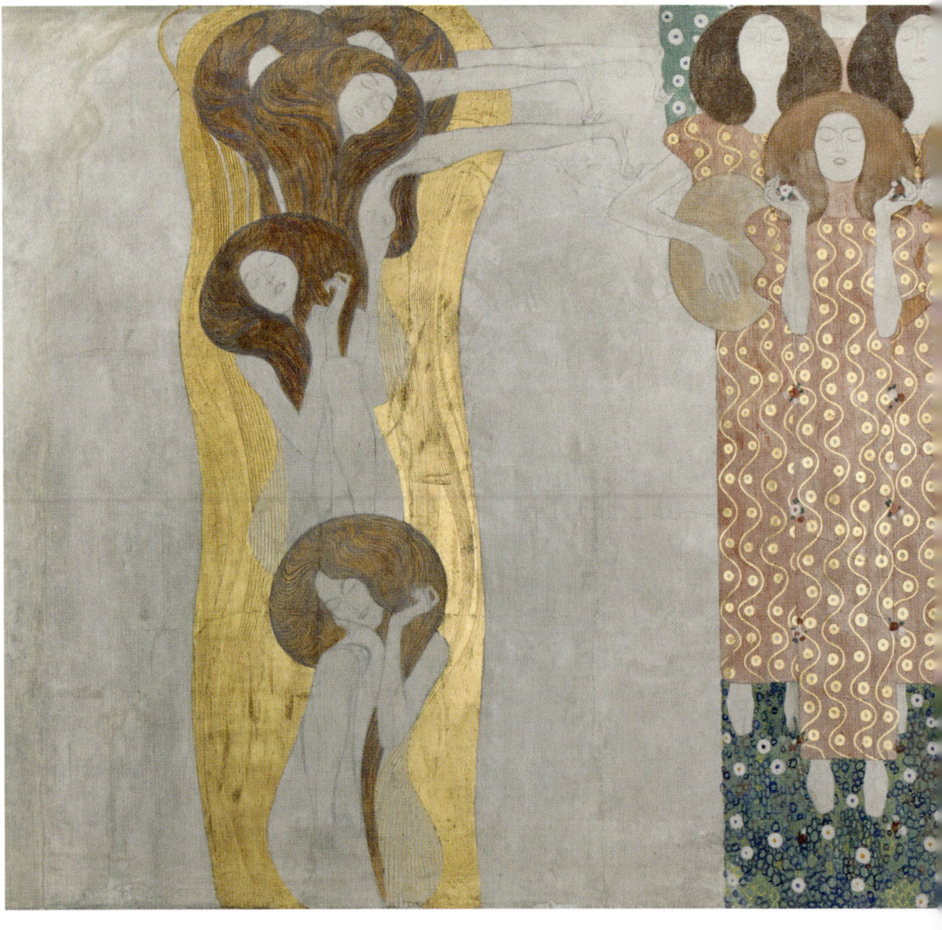

PLATE 8. *Gustav Klimt, The Kiss, in his* Beethoven Frieze, *Secession House, 1902.* © Belvedere, Vienna.

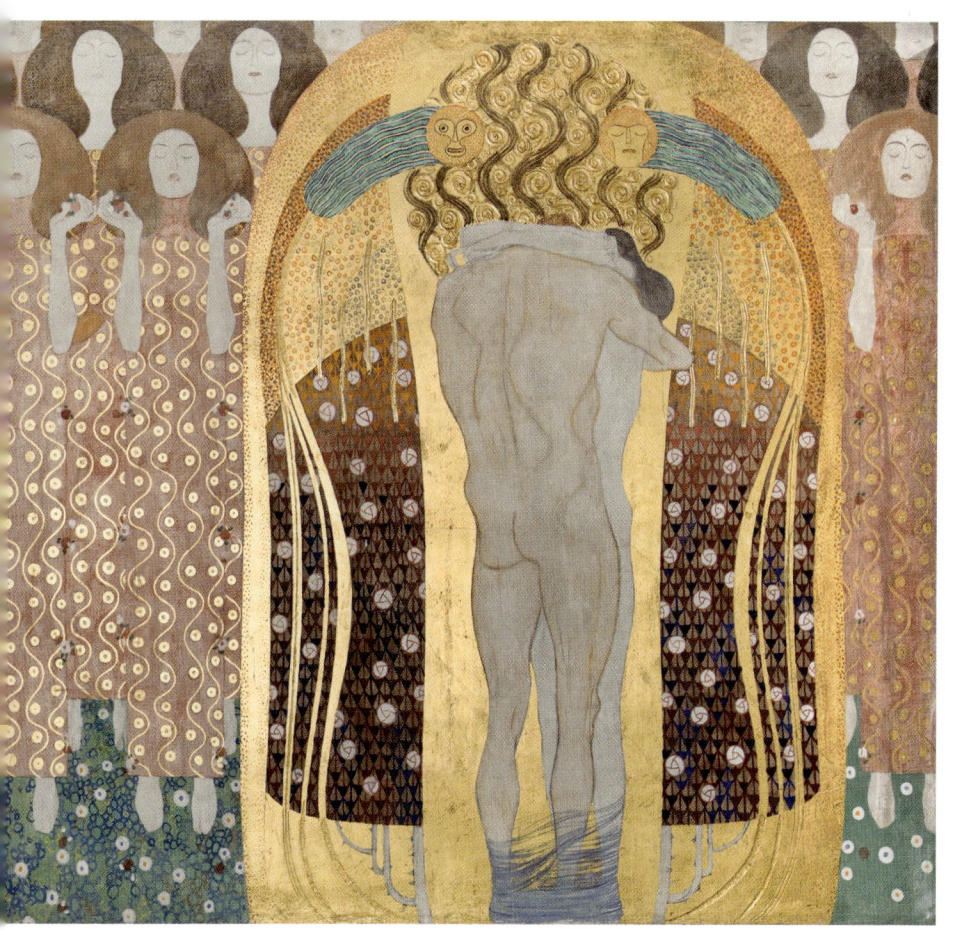

PLATE 9. *Joseph Maria Olbrich, drawing for a wall decoration in the music room of David Berl, July 1899.* Joseph Maria Olbrich, Ideen von Olbrich, Text von Ludwig Hevesi *(1904; repr., Stuttgart: Arnold'sche, 1992), 19.*

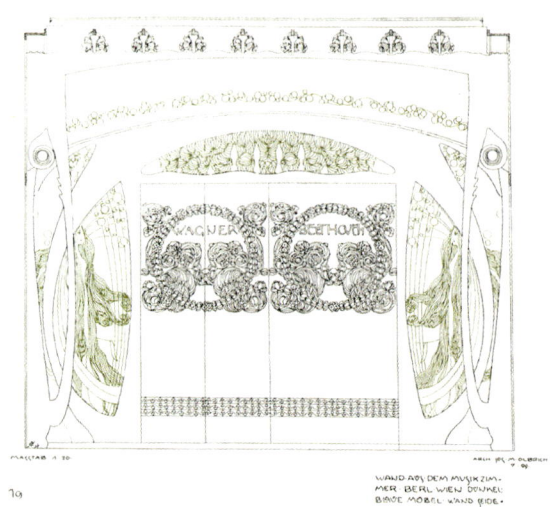

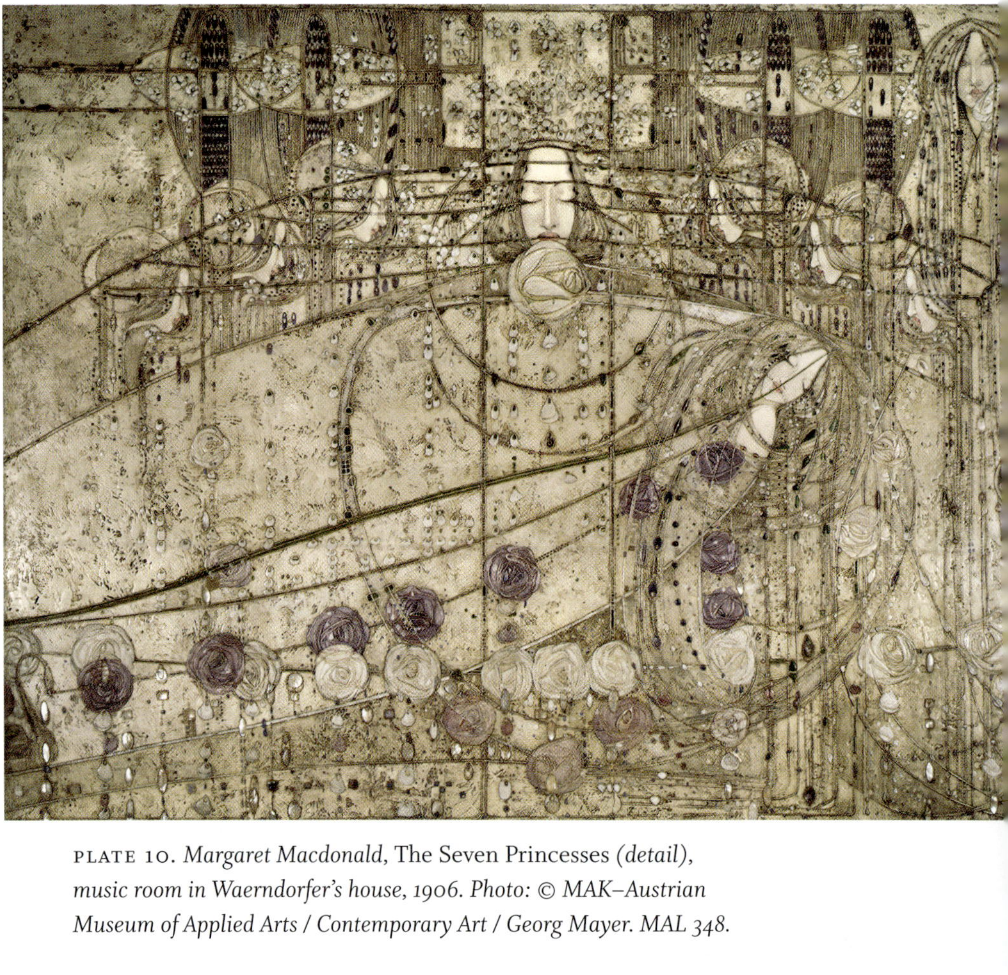

PLATE 10. *Margaret Macdonald,* The Seven Princesses *(detail), music room in Waerndorfer's house, 1906. Photo: © MAK–Austrian Museum of Applied Arts / Contemporary Art / Georg Mayer. MAL 348.*

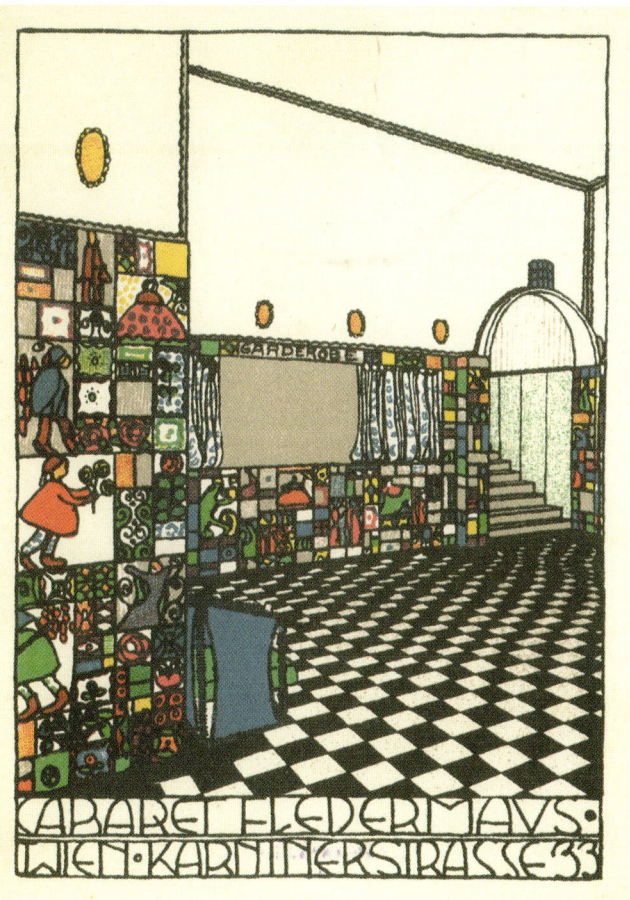

PLATE 11. Josef Hoffmann, barroom of the Fledermaus Cabaret, Wiener Werkstätte postcard no. 74, 1907. Photo: © MAK–Austrian Museum of Applied Arts / Contemporary Art. KI 13748-4.

PLATE 12. *Gustav Jagerspacher, portrait of Peter Altenberg, 1909. Wien Museum, Vienna. Inv. no. 094-715-001.*

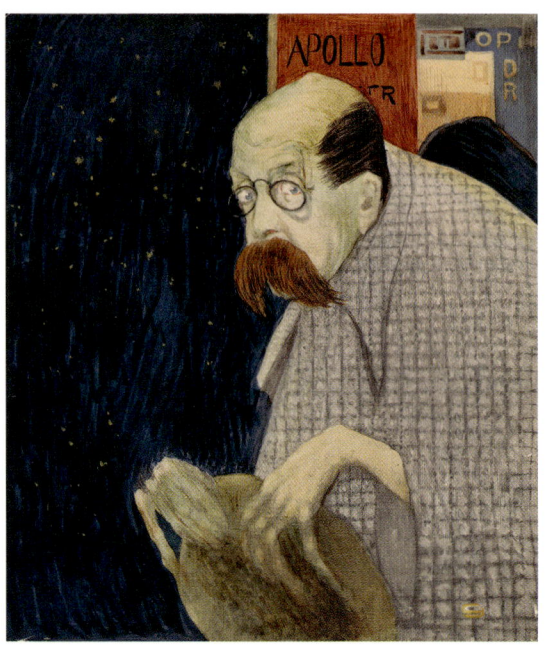

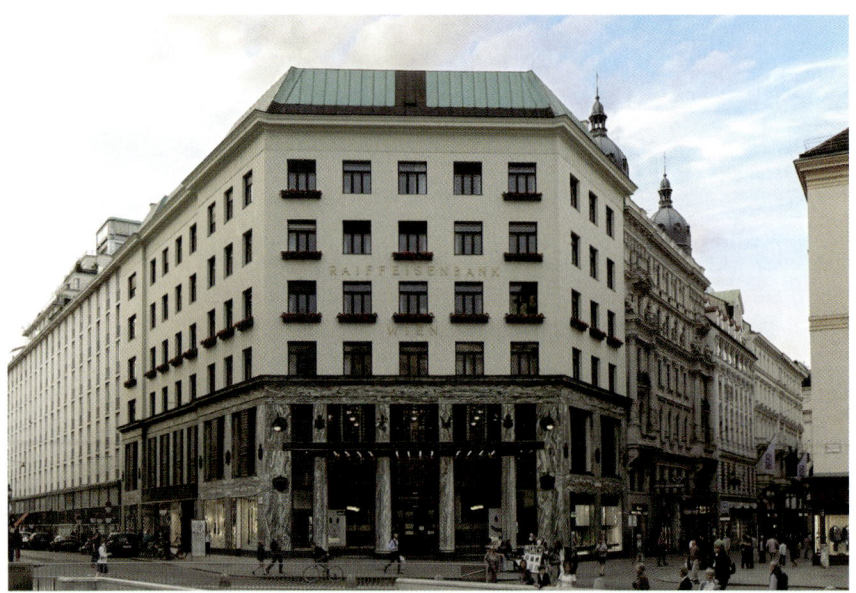

PLATE 13. *Adolf Loos, Goldman & Salatsch House, 1911. Photo: © 2015, Benjamin von Radom*

enclosure against a flat background setting, in a variation of a Wiener Werkstätte interior, and granted her a detached decorative halo at the same time. Though the portrait was of the young woman, it served as a tribute to Wittgenstein himself, as the grand patron of the secessionist movement and the Wiener Werkstätte, and it remained in his possession until his death in 1913. Perhaps displaying a likeness of his beautiful daughter was a way to secure his public reputation. The portrait, presented in exhibitions in Berlin (1905) and Rome (1911), did support the patron's reputation while placing his daughter Margaret's beauty on display. More than twenty years later, at the age of forty-four, no longer under her father's authority and disillusioned with her marriage, Margaret made her own grand contribution to the Viennese landscape with a new architectural landmark. Her city villa, designed by the family friend and architect Paul Engelmann and her brother Ludwig Wittgenstein, was completed in 1928. While the outer cubic appearance of the house was a development of earlier and contemporary works by Loos in opposition to the secessionist movement, the interior design's purist symmetrical arrangement realized a radical positivist philosophical perspective. Margaret's city villa, known today as the Wittgenstein House, entered the canon of Viennese modernist architecture with altered language. It negated the secessionists' stereotypical identification of wealth, sexuality, and "Jewishness" and replaced that with an emancipated imagined Jewish self-identification, demonstrating the positivist lesson that, with the help of science and education, it is possible to improve oneself and society. Karl Wittgenstein's children imagined their Jewish identification. In 1918, Margaret Stonborough-Wittgenstein wrote in her diary that she was still occupied with Jewish stories even though they were not very good, but the thought that she could have come from this milieu appeared to her unlikely and strange. She noted that the ideas in the Jewish religion fascinated her, but she could not decide if that was because they were so striking or because of her blood relations.[232]

The Wittgensteins and other Jewish patrons mentioned in this book championed the possibilities in their "Jewishness" through their fashioning of new Viennese styles. Their gestures of negation against Christian culture—for example, supporting the Oriental modern character of the Secession House instead of the baroque Karlskirche—meant keeping their identification as Others. In his financing of the Secession House as well as his ordering of Wiener Werkstätte interiors and purchase of various objects—and through his business relationships with Jewish patrons of the Ringstrasse—Karl Wittgenstein flirted charismatically with the question "Is he Jewish or not?"—or "Is he part of the Jewish elite of the Ringstrasse or not?"—and seemed only to improve his position in Viennese society by doing so.[233] He seemed to acknowledge and play with speculation concerning his identity.

In contrast, his son Ludwig (1889–1951) chose to enter a Jewish intellectual circle in Olomouc, where he was stationed toward the end of World War I, and where he also met the architect Paul Engelmann, possibly to solve the Jewish riddle of his family. In November 1920, Hermine Wittgenstein wrote Ludwig, her younger brother, a letter in which she notes that she understands his anger at being identified by others as "Ludwig Wittgenstein":

> That this discovery was unavoidable, I could have foreseen, but this does not make it easier for you to bear! I can only think for myself, that [the] new and unheard of will transform itself—change into [the] familiar—and you will be less of a phenomenon when they all know. [Better that] they all only guess that you *belong to another race*, [but] they must have already with God's will found out and *with this you were already a riddle for them*. This would not have exactly insulted me since *I was often a riddle for people* and could speak completely freely about it, since there was no secret involved. As I am finishing writing this, I see already the untruth [in it], since I also naturally search to make *my richness* a secret. . . . That people do not understand you naturally cannot be changed, but *they must respect you at least*, does this mean nothing to you?[234]

Hermine may have transformed the identity of Ludwig Wittgenstein, so that he belonged not to the Jewish race but to the Wittgenstein race, which is identified as another race.[235] The riddle is perhaps the riddle of their riches, but I suggest that they kept imagining their Jewish identity in relation to their riches in different forms. Ludwig handled the seduction of money and sexuality in his own way: he chose to negate the seduction of riches by donating his money to artists and to represent his (sexual) self-mastery.

The redesign of the Wittgenstein parents' summer villa in Neuwaldegg had been Engelmann's first project. His second assignment was to redesign Hermine's room in the Wittgenstein city palace in Alleegasse.[236] The Wittgenstein children's choice of the Jewish architect might have been a means of freeing themselves from the Jewish riddle, coming to terms with—and chasing away—the phantom of their overpowering father with the help of a real Jewish man with whom they could discuss ethics, whom they respected, and yet who they could easily direct.[237] The third assignment Engelmann received was to design Margaret's villa, for which he collaborated with Ludwig. Yet Ludwig's critical alterations of Engelmann's cubic arrangement of the house refashioned the Wittgenstein House according to Ludwig's ideal self-identification, defining modern style as purist within a totally controlled mathematical design.[238] This is in opposition to the uncontrolled desires projected onto the façade of the Oriental Secession House and its seductive gold crown.

The striking modern design may also have perpetuated the riddle of their wealth or of their race. Like the Secession House, Margaret's villa did not communicate with its immediate environment. The white cubic Wittgenstein House in the midst of historicist buildings presented an unapproachable (naked white cubic) body and monumentalized the outsider's claim. If the Orientalist inflections of the Secession House were a counterargument to the Hellenist heritage of the Palais Todesco more than thirty years after its construction, then the Wittgenstein House—thirty years after the Secession House and sixty years after the Palais Todesco—was a counterargument to the Secession House, refashioning modern Jewish self-identification in terms of the concretely modern. The rejection of an established European tradition and the offer of a more critical and self-conscious visual reference to the Oriental (Near Eastern or semitic) heritage were left behind. Engelmann's and Wittgenstein's new style demonstrated Simmel's thesis: "What drives modern man so strongly to style is the unburdening and concealment of the personal, which is the essence of style."[239] Their structure championed the Jewish dandy's social game of exposure and concealment of his "Jewishness." The new historical stylistic development actually continued the Jewish historicist and secessionist patrons' aims to create shared cultural platforms for Jews and gentiles based on a new self-consciousness and constructed Jewish perspective.

Jewish patrons in Vienna around the end of the nineteenth century used the secessionist style to transform Viennese and Jewish traditions to find a cultural platform they could share with gentiles for a rapprochement, while still allowing for cultural difference. The secessionist style would subsequently be reformed to redefine the Jewish dandy's social game of exposure and concealment by the next generation of prominent patrons, including the industrialist Fritz Waerndorfer and the author Richard Beer-Hofmann. Waerndorfer would purchase Klimt's scandalous *Pallas Athene* (1898), an act of rebellion against historicism's liberal and educational agenda. The painting, which was exhibited in the second Secession exhibition—the first exhibition in the new Secession House—transformed the goddess of wisdom, who represented the Bildung agenda of the historicist liberal patrons and was seen as a city protector, into a frighteningly seductive, redheaded femme fatale with a golden helmet. Her striking, hypnotic eyes, together with the disappearance of her body reflected the uncanny experience of confronting the threat of an uncontrolled persona. Klimt and the patron seemed to directly provoke the liberal bourgeoisie with the Medusa on Athena's breastplate, who sticks out her tongue to tease her viewer, a gesture multiplied in the round golden disks (gold coins) covering Athena's armor. Klimt consciously or unconsciously exposed the common belief that having money does not guarantee respectable conduct. In contrast to Waerndorfer, Beer-Hofmann would continue the heritage of the historicist patrons and, as a critically self-aware Jewish patron, reject the stigma placed on the Oriental style that was associated with secessionism. Both Waerndorfer and Beer-Hofmann constructed their Jewish identifications through a new style of architecture and design within the framework of new social dramas in their private houses and occasionally, as with Waerndorfer's cabaret, also in public.

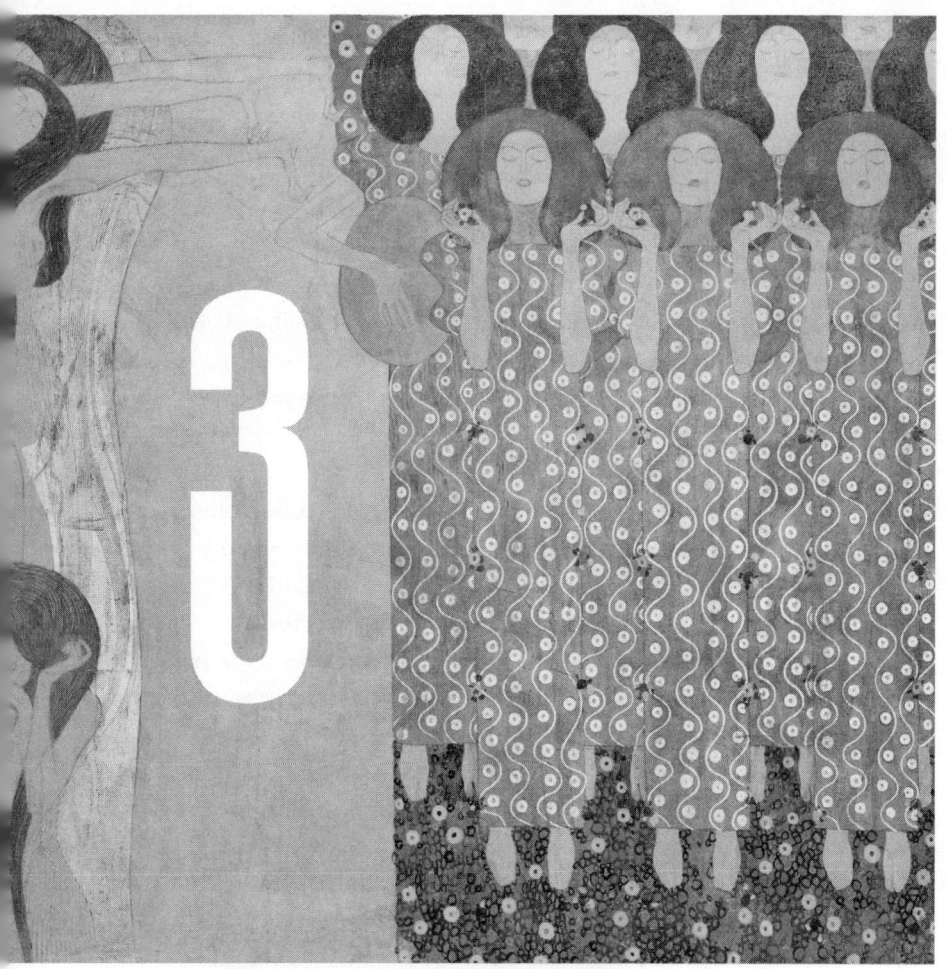

THE MODERNISTS
1902–7

Isidor Singer and Heinrich Kanner and the Telegraph Office of Die Zeit, *Fritz Waerndorfer's House for the Art Lover, the Wiener Werkstätte and the Cabaret Fledermaus, and the Richard Beer-Hofmann Villa*

This chapter examines how the publishers and journalists Isidor Singer (1857–1927) and Heinrich Kanner (1864–1930), in hiring the modernist architect Otto Wagner to design the Telegraph Office and art gallery for their newly founded daily newspaper *Die Zeit* in 1902, promoted liberal politics by continuing the modernization project of the historicists on the Ringstrasse and the secessionists in Vienna's center. Their design and culture renewal project was furthered by Singer's relative by marriage, the textile industrialist Fritz Waerndorfer (1868–1939), who promoted the latest European design trends—specifically British—in partnering with British and Austrian designers to renovate his house as a house for an art lover and encouraging the founding of the design workshop, the Wiener Werkstätte. Waerndorfer and his two partners, Koloman Moser and Josef Hoffmann, rebelled against the historicist tradition. This chapter reexamines Waerndorfer's aim to promote modern aesthetics in terms of his Jewish identification. Similarly, the author Richard Beer-Hofmann (1866–1945), offered his new house on the outskirts of Vienna as a modernist Jewish club for his colleagues in the literary circle of Jung-Wien (Young Vienna). Most of the members of Jung-Wien were Jewish authors who met in Café Griensteidel next to the Hofburg from 1890 to 1897; their modern literary achievement was in displacing meaning from outer relations between a person and his place and time to the mystery of inner relations, as manifested, for example, in Leopold von Andrian's *Der Garten der Erkenntnis* (The garden of knowledge; 1895) and Beer-Hofmann's *Der Tod Georgs* (The death of Georg; 1900). Waerndorfer and Beer-Hofmann thus secured their positions as cultural producers via new platforms for performance designed by Hoffman: the central hall of Beer-Hofman's house and the Cabaret Fledermaus. Waerndorfer suffered from, yet successfully managed the possibilities of, his "Jewishness," while Beer-Hofmann reconstructed his Judaism in a novel manner for his Jewish and gentile guests, using creative strategies in a modern style to both manifest and bridge cultural differences. The two patrons furthered the cultural regeneration of both Viennese and Jewish traditions.

Kohn's New Looks

Design was perceived as an outward witness to character. The photographer Friedrich Victor Spitzer was not the only Jewish patron who used his designed environment to advance as a producer in the Viennese art scene; his followers also had concrete cultural programs to cultivate political or social clubs, modernizing Viennese society in the process.

Eight years before Singer and Kanner founded their newspaper, *Die Zeit*, they had founded a journal of the same name together with Hermann Bahr.[1] This liberal journal supported modern aesthetics. Bahr provided the journal's progressive perspective on art and literature and established its creative network.[2] Singer, an economist, financed and published the journal, perceiving it as an instrument to promote his social politics. Kanner, his younger partner, saw it as a version of the *Nation*, which was recognized by him as America's leading liberal weekly.[3]

Born in Budapest, Isidor Singer moved with his family to Vienna in 1861. They belonged to the Jewish *haute bourgeoisie*; his father, David, was a wholesale textile merchant, and his mother, Regina, was a daughter of Samuel Goldberger de Buda, owner of the oldest textile factories in Hungary.[4] Singer received his doctorate in statistics and became a professor of national economy at Vienna University. In 1881, he married his rich cousin Hermine, daughter of Emanuel Ritter Goldberger de Buda and Franziska Hellmann.[5] Bernhard Hellmann, Franziska's brother, would become the father-in-law of the patron Fritz Waerndorfer. Singer's marriage gave him the good fortune of owning several houses in Vienna. Heinrich Kanner, Singer's partner at *Die Zeit*, was born in Galati, in Romania. He had been Singer's student and was a journalist, but in contrast to Singer, Kanner came from a poor German-speaking family. He started his career as a correspondent for the *Frankfurter Zeitung* in Vienna. As publisher and editor of *Die Zeit*, Kanner behaved in an authoritarian way in relation to his employees.[6]

Singer and Kanner's two *Die Zeits*—the journal (1894–1904) and the newspaper (1902–18)—provided their readers with a critical consciousness concerning national and social matters. Singer's role model throughout his career was the charismatic liberal Jewish politician Adolf Fischhof (1816–93), who played a significant role in Austria's 1848 liberal revolution.[7] He and Kanner embraced Fischhof's ideas on federalizing the Austro-Hungarian Empire into a Central and Eastern European customs union with a high degree of autonomy for national minorities.[8] Their political progressiveness is further demonstrated in their pacifism during World

War I, which eventually led to the newspaper's censorship and its closure in 1918.

The two men had also consistently promoted socialism, with Singer vaunting the cultural transfer of socialist ideas from England to Austria. In 1891, he and Kanner were among the founders of the Viennese Fabian Society (Wiener Fabier Gesellschaft), the London Fabian Society having been founded eight years earlier.[9] The society believed in the gradual promotion of socialism rather than outright socialist revolution. When the journal *Die Zeit* published the British playright George Bernard Shaw's first article in German, "Illusionen des Socialismus" (The illusions of socialism) in October 1896,[10] there was swift critical reaction: a bourgeois publication like *Die Zeit* was not the proper place for socialists to discuss their opinions.[11] It was Kanner who, having come from a poor background, defended the journal and argued that having a bourgeois background did not prevent someone from sharing socialist attitudes. Kanner saw in England a model for promoting socialism among the middle classes.[12]

Singer and Kanner founded their new liberal newspaper for financial reasons and to compete with the liberal newspaper *Neue Freie Presse* by offering a socialist agenda. Among *Die Zeit*'s investors were prominent aristocrats whom Singer knew closely and with whom he shared his socialist ideals, such as Eugen Philippovich. Members of the newspaper's board included leading Jewish patrons such as Adolf Gallia, the brother of Moritz Gallia, who had supported the secessionists and the later Wiener Werkstätte; and Max Friedmann, a prominent Olbrich patron.[13] Singer was a respected member of the Austrian aristocratic elite—he would entertain other members in his inherited villa in Grundlsee—and had a secure enough position in Viennese society to embark on his progressive agenda with Kanner.

From the beginning, when Singer created a competition for the design of his newspaper's header in May 1902, his ambition was that the newspaper as a new cultural project would contribute to a modern Viennese aesthetic. The competition called for a design that would fit the modern feeling without any bizarreness (meaning extravagant forms or weird imagery).[14]

The free gallery at the modern Telegraph Office would champion the founders' socialist idea of transfers between nations, cultures, and social classes—in other words, it was intended to allow readers and visitors access to the latest headlines of international newspapers on the ground floor and also provide them access to contemporary photography and graphic art with, for example, such diverse subjects as Austrian art, images from the past of Serbia, and images of Japan and its people.[15] For Otto Wagner and the editors the new office's architecture reflected the newspaper's liberal progressive program. Singer supported rational modern architecture to demonstrate the newspaper's ethics of honesty, clarity, and intelligibility and to move Austria in the direction of a modern state.[16] In his design of Die Zeit's Telegraph Office, Wagner reformed his own attachment to secessionist decoration to seduce the viewer and offered a more coherent aesthetic representation of modernity.[17]

The now destroyed modernist Telegraph Office for Die Zeit on Kärntnerstrasse 39 would be a prelude to Wagner's grand Postal Savings Bank (1904–6). Referring to Wagner's wish to offer new architectural designs that would correspond to contemporary clothes, not only by using new building materials and techniques but also by applying new forms,[18] the design historian Rebecca Houze concludes that "together [new materials, techniques and forms] constituted a modern, contemporary 'style.'"[19] For Die Zeit's Telegraph Office, Wagner used the modern materials of aluminum and glass and applied modern technology in arranging electric light in the rooms. In the façade and interior Wagner avoided any flirtatious decoration associated with female clothing and accessories (such as those one might associate with the Secession House's façade, discussed in the previous chapter) and instead offered, through the pared-down geometric decoration and the rivets motif, a well-tailored gentleman's suit.[20] The office portal would be the first space in his architectural body of work to use the rivets motif.

The publishers celebrated the opening of their Telegraph Office and art gallery on September 26, 1902, the day before it was opened to the public (Fig. 19). A drawing of Wagner's Jugendstil aluminum and glass portal advertised the Telegraph Office and the gallery in the newspaper. The publishers declared that with the new office and their plan to show modernist photographs and artworks in their gallery, they would "cultivate our civilization," demonstrating cultural progress and offering practical ideas to anyone who wished to design his or her life.[21] They were also eager to promote Wagner's status as celebrity modernist aesthete to attract visitors to their art gallery in the mezzanine of same building. The journalists proudly announced that the first genuine exhibition object was Wagner's modernist design of the gallery itself—the initial step toward fruitful cultural progress.[22] The exposure of the rivets in the structure's aluminum-framed glass façade was a new development that made it radically different from more traditional façades. The newness of Wagner's design was also a clear symbol that the Telegraph Office gave the newest news reports.[23] Moreover, the functional metal fittings and mountings displayed a very progressive factory aesthetic. The compact,

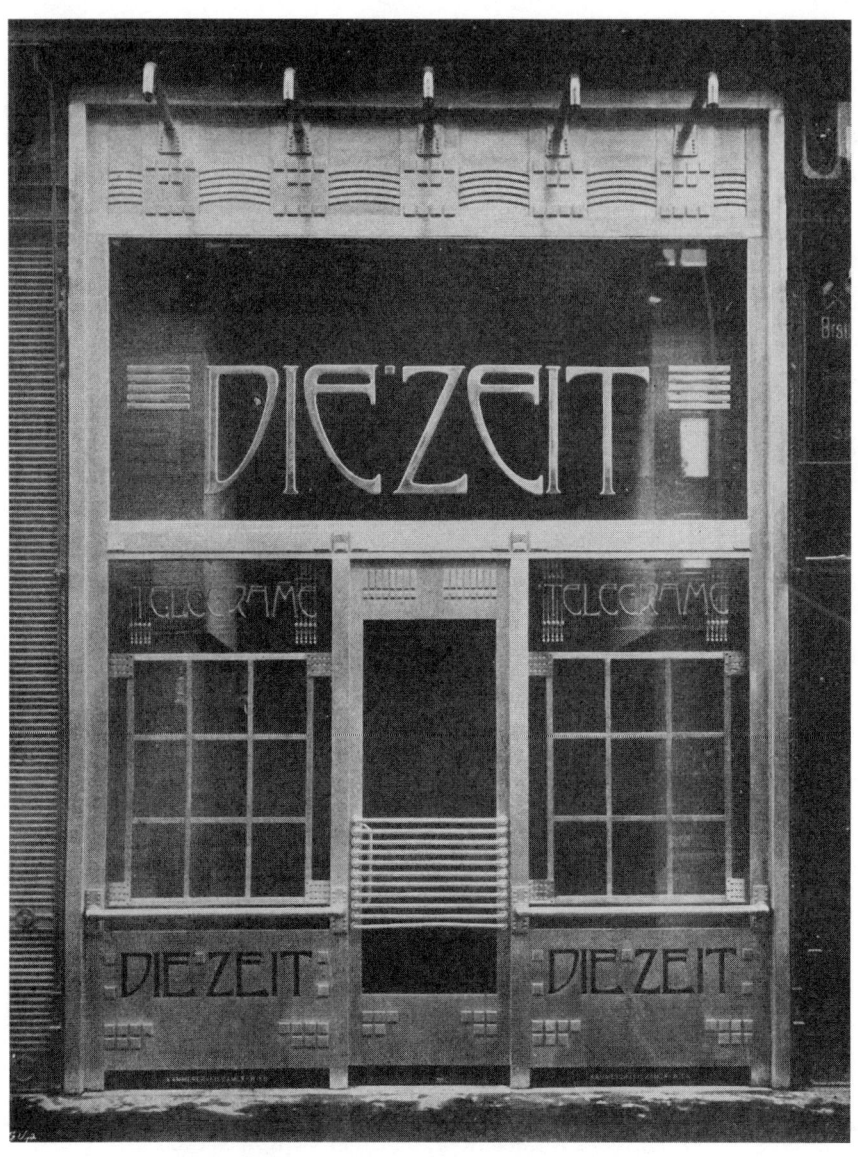

FIGURE 19. *Otto Wagner, portal of the Telegraph Office.*
Reproduced in Joseph August Lux, "Stilarchitketur und Baukunst,"
Der Architekt, no. 8 (1902): 47. Photo: © MAK–Austrian Museum
of Applied Arts / Contemporary Art. Bl. 12385-1902-47.

single office desk arrangement in the large gallery hall in the mezzanine was striking as well and was a forerunner for Wagner's counter-desks in the later Postal Savings Bank.[24] The vertical lines in the stained wood of the compact desk were matched by horizontal lines on the upper walls, as minimalist decoration. The gallery's ceiling lamp fixtures and the two tables in the center for displaying artworks were light and rational furnishings.

Singer and Kanner made their striking modernist architectural statement hoping to triumph in the battle for visibility. Their intention was to promote their newspaper in the city through the development of a new style. Moreover, the modernist Telegraph Office and art gallery were supposed to display an ideal shared front for the two men, whose differences in character and social position were striking. Singer's charismatic, flirtatious persona was admired, with his self-presentation as "somewhat bohemian. He had an attractive appearance and with intellect and humor succeeded in fascinating his discussion partners. He made a great impact on women."[25] Though he was a member of the Austrian and Jewish elites, his association with Kanner, from a poor German Jewish family in Eastern Europe, exposed him to attacks and made it easy for critics to disparage him as an uncultivated "Easterner." Singer would face harsh criticism of his and Kanner's newspaper from leading Jews. In the many critical commentaries that Karl Kraus published in his journal *Die Fackel*, he repeatedly labeled Singer and Kanner as "Easterners" who lacked culture, calling them "Eastern Jews" (Ostjuden), "the Galicians," and "the two energetic men who came from the East."[26] Even the jurist and politician Josef Redlich, who had invested a large sum in the founding of the newspaper *Die Zeit*, wrote a friend that he wanted to see it "more European."[27] By referring to the "loud" communication style and "search for sensation" in their reports, critics suggested that Singer and Kanner were undermining the Jewish acculturation ideals of "proper" communication style, which would prefer a "calm" tone and "moderate" arguments.

Kraus, a critic of the secessionist movement (as mentioned in the previous chapter), was convinced of his duty to denounce all the steps of assimilation that had gone wrong for Viennese Jews. In April 1903, he noticed that the newspaper *Die Zeit* had changed the looks of the newsboy on its advertising for subscribers from a "Jewish" looking boy to a "gentile" looking boy. He reported the change in *Die Fackel* and in the following issue juxtaposed the old and new advertisements under the title "The Europeanization of the 'Zeit' or 'Little Kohn has disappeared!'" (Fig. 20).[28] Kraus claimed that Singer had immediately ordered the change in the newsboy's looks after Kraus had pointed out his Jewish appearance in *Die Fackel*. Kraus exposed others' embarrassment

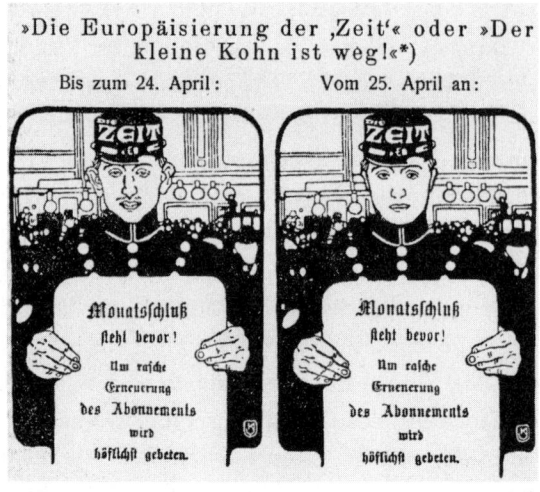

FIGURE 20. Karl Kraus, "Die Europäisierung der 'Zeit' oder 'Der kleine Kohn ist weg!,'" Die Fackel 5, no. 137 (1903): 17.

and ambivalence about their "Jewishness" and showed how they tried to cover up their "Jewishness" to secure European Jewish self-identification. When Singer and Kanner hired Wagner to design a modernist office and gallery and when, a few months later, they changed the "Jewish look" of the newsboy—in effect, putting him through plastic surgery to appear as a gentile boy—they reflected the belief of Jewish cultural producers seeking cultural authority that for public acceptance, the new Jewish self-identification in Austria required an aesthetic metamorphosis of their Eastern European Jewish identity. Singer invested his whole fortune in his newspaper to pursue his goal of fashioning a modern Austrian society. Yet his and Kanner's historical project of promoting a progressive European union as well as legitimizing socialist ideals and politics in a public architectural space has not been acknowledged as integral to Viennese modernism until today.

The Self-Styling of the Dandy Waerndorfer

In November 1898, the textile industrialist Fritz Waerndorfer resigned from his membership in Vienna's Künstlerhaus to prove his loyalty to and support for the new secessionist movement.[29] Waerndorfer became a leading modern art patron and producer of culture in Vienna through his correspondence with Hermann Bahr, through his help in organizing the secessionists' exhibitions, and through his purchase of art and design.[30] One of Waerndorfer's early purchases at the exhibitions was George Minne's *Kneeling Boy*, a sculpture of an Aryan-looking kneeling boy (Fig. 21). This kneeling boy can

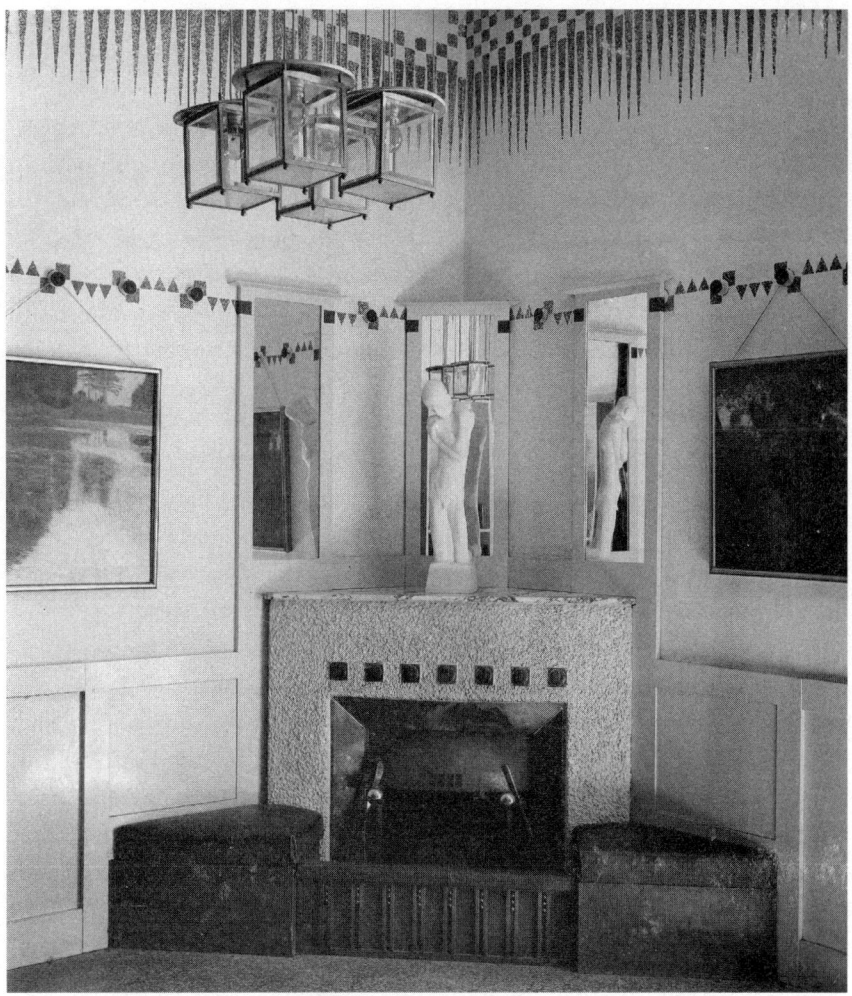

FIGURE 21. *Josef Hoffmann, studio in the Waerndorfer House, fireplace corner with George Minne's* Kneeling Boy, *c. 1904–6. Photo: © MAK–Austrian Museum of Applied Arts / Contemporary Art.* WWF 101-13-1.

be seen as symbolic of the transformation of Jewish identity (here in the frame of the secessionist club) that was apparent in the plastic surgery of *Die Zeit*'s newsboy, derisively named "Kohn" by Kraus (Fig. 20). The secessionist community fashioned itself as a religious group with the conscious choice of religious icons such as Minne's kneeling boy, who could be seen as a communal symbol. There were several copies of this sculpture and two photos and a self-portrait document its inclusion in the homes of Waerndorfer, Josef Hoffmann, and Carl Moll (see below). The boy was originally part of Minne's circular arrangement of five identical figures around a fountain, titled *The Fountain of Kneeling Youths*, exhibited in the Mackintosh room at the eighth Secession exhibition, in 1900. According to a review in *Ver Sacrum*, the journal of the Vienna Secession, he represented "a pious boy of the ancient church, who believes in the pious community, which unites in the sanctuary of art, innocent and elevated."[31] Before introducing Minne, the review's author wrote about people's longing for something impersonal yet personal on a higher level, a drive for something shared, for conventions that would restrain wild self-conceit, for quietness (serenity).[32] Waerndorfer, in his purchase of the kneeling boy, affirmed his longing to share this serenity. While his purchase of Klimt's *Pallas Athene* represented the secessionist revolt against historicist tradition, this purchase represented the ideal self-image of the secessionists, matching the love of art with the love of virginal youth.

Waerndorfer was a loyal reader of Singer and Kanner's liberal journal. He read Bahr's articles and corresponded with the critic; his first surviving letter to Bahr is dated a few months after Bahr's January 1898 review of Herzl's *Das neue Ghetto*, mentioned in the previous chapter. Bahr's prejudice against assimilated Jews (he regarded them as "misfits" and "reduced creatures" and pointed out their insecurities) was not viewed by his colleagues Singer and Kanner as a threat or as antisemitic.[33] This is surprising, considering that during 1898 *Die Zeit* regularly published articles covering the Dreyfus affair in France. Yet Bahr's vicious representation of the crisis of assimilated Jews, of their not belonging (to either the Jewish or the German identity), may indeed have influenced his readers. Helga Malmberg—with whom Peter Altenberg had a love affair and who was Waerndorfer's employee at the Wiener Werkstätte, which he helped found—described Waerndorfer as "a small, agile and dark type, quick to be excited about something and always a warm supporter of the ideas of his people."[34] Certainly, Waerndorfer was aware of his appearance, but in contrast to Bahr's accusative comments about a Jewish type, Waerndorfer seemed to view stereotypes with self-mockery. During the period of his house's redesign in 1902, Waerndorfer used a letterhead with a caricature by Marcus Behmer, a popular Jugendstil graphic artist who published in *Ver Sacrum*, that appeared above his name ("F. Wärndorfer") and his home address.[35] Behmer's caricature depicted a small, dark, peculiar animal with two short legs, a short tail, and a large head resembling a combination of a pig and a frog.[36] This caricature would seem to reflect Waerndorfer's negative perception of his looks and inferior position—reflecting Bahr's view of assimilated Jews as "reduced creatures"—in relation to the position of his secessionist friends.[37] Viewed in relation to Friedrich König's caricatures of secessionist artists as human birds—for example, Klimt's "der popopopo" (*popo* means bottom) depiction as a bearded head with a body shaped as a big ass—Waerndorfer's caricature is still striking as a representation of his "Jewishness."[38] Waerndorfer's disconcerting representation of his Jewish body was aligned with a rebellious antibourgeois trend among his friends to free themselves from the expectation that they would present a respectable appearance in society. Yet in the case of Waerndorfer, the disclosure of his natural state in the awkward animal on his letterhead should be compared to how Franz Kafka imagined Gregor Samsa's metamorphosis.[39] Through the grotesque caricature Waerndorfer's wish to reclaim his body is directly related to the liberation of his identity (even though the identity is a reduced animal). The Jewish industrialist, assuming that his new friends might perceive him as a "small, agile and dark type" as Malmberg did, made a joke at his own expense as an act of self-defense.[40]

In a letter to Bahr written in May 1900, Waerndorfer wrote that he always thought of Bahr as the publisher of the journal *Die Zeit*.[41] He also praised Kanner as the best political journalist in town.[42] In his first letter to Bahr in early May 1898, Waerndorfer had presented himself proudly as a cosmopolitan observer who could compare the cultural developments of different empires, yet in the end he undermined his standing by dismissing it as the position of a provincial Viennese. He complimented Bahr on his lecture titled "Kunstgewerbe und Wiener Stil" (Applied arts and the Viennese style)[43] and challenged the superiority of the old Viennese symbols such as the Kahlenberg (which offered the most famous view of Vienna in the nineteenth district) and the Palais Liechtenstein (an important example of baroque architecture in Vienna). Furthermore, he picked up on Dutch and British adaptations of colonial ornaments in their renewal of national design and recommended that leading secessionist artists such as Josef Engelhart and Koloman Mosser search for inspiration in Bosnian art and other Austrian "colonies" to renew Austrian art.[44] Waerndorfer was enthusiastic about the idea of renewal through cultural discourse, and it would be in his own house that he would succeed in offering a space for Western European cultural discourse.

In June 1896, Waerndorfer had bought a cottage-style house at Karl Ludwig Strasse 45, in Vienna's eighteenth district, close to his parents, who lived at Karl Ludwig Strasse 35.[45] In November 1896, at the age of twenty-eight, he had married Lili Hellmann.[46] Lili was the second daughter of Bernhard Hellmann and Lina née Singer, who had five children in all.[47] Well educated (besides German, she spoke English, Italian, and French[48]), Lili was the ideal cultured European partner for Waerndorfer. In 1902, he hired four prominent Austrian and Scottish architects and artists identified with the latest modernist European design to redesign his house: Hoffmann, Moser, Charles Rennie Mackintosh, and Margaret Macdonald. These artists from both the Austro-Hungarian and the British Empires created for Waerndorfer an impressive European house for an art lover. Although Hoffmann closely advised Waerndorfer, the industrialist deliberately chose a patchwork Gesamtkunstwerk arrangement of interiors designed by the four architects and artists, rather than a Gesamtkunstwerk conceived by one.

Waerndorfer wanted to establish his importance in the Viennese avant-garde scene by shaping a new artistic agenda, but he would also use modernist redesign to form a new identity as an assimilated Jew.[49] Indeed, the revolutionary modernist design of his house for an art lover evolved from his desire to form a new Jewish identification. With this in mind, and in tandem with his approach toward modern design, he identified with the character of the dandy to turn his life into a theatrical artistic spectacle.[50] He was not satisfied with merely dressing elegantly; he also recognized the existential condition of dressing up for a chief theatrical role, and he claimed to possess a passionate quest for quality.[51] Waerndorfer's dandyism was expressed through his selection of milieu (both friends and spaces), careful direction of his theatrical appearances in his house, and his iconoclastic leanings as a producer of modern culture. His new home reflected an aspiration to cultural self-improvement and his struggle to leave behind what he considered an embarrassing Jewish inheritance. Three mirrors in Waerndorfer's studio located strategically above the corner fireplace testified to the owner's identification with the fashionable persona of the dandy at this time (Fig. 21). Waerndorfer expected to improve his appearance by surrounding himself with beautifully designed pieces and avant-garde art, and Hoffmann's design of his house interior was meant to express this appearance.[52] Waerndorfer believed that, as Hoffmann and Moser put it, "intercourse with beautiful things" could make one beautiful.[53] Hoffmann was aware that Waerndorfer expected to make a complete break from historicist tradition and that the decorative scheme should highlight the patron's chosen artworks. When the architect Theophil Hansen had articulated the historicist model in Eduard von Todesco's studio on the Ringstrasse, he had projected Todesco's self-representation on the monumental Renaissance-style carved ceiling with allegories that related to that patron's professional ambitions.[54] In contrast, when Hoffmann projected Waerndorfer's temperament onto his house's decorative scheme, he identified his patron as a hedonist and perhaps an effeminate dandy, given the wall decoration's lighthearted geometric play of triangles and squares. And unlike the historicist patron Gustav von Epstein's choice to present a copy of *Venus and Amor* as the main attraction in his studio, Waerndorfer's star attraction in his room was the narcissistic *Kneeling Boy*. Epstein had decorated his ceiling to show his relation to Greek culture and his historicist credentials; likewise, Waerndorfer chose Minne's *Kneeling Boy* to show his membership in the secessionist club.[55] Two other prominent secessionists also showed Minne's *Kneeling Boy* in their home interiors as part of their crafted self-image. In his sitting room in his apartment at Neulinggasse 24, in Vienna's third district, Hoffmann placed his sculpture of the *Kneeling Boy* on a low vitrine next to the sofa. In a photo of his house, the *Kneeling Boy* is set next to a painting of Hoffmann's ancestor arranging the new idol and old relative together to complete the designed self-portrait. Moll's *Self-Portrait in the Studio* (circa 1906) shows how he positioned Minne's *Kneeling Boy* on a sideboard in the public room in his house in Hohe Warte. The young kneeling boy is part of the older Moll's metaphorical calling card.[56] The arrangement in Waerndorfer's studio could also be compared to the placement of Klimt's portrait of Marie Henneberg above the fireplace in the Henneberg House in Hohe Warte (designed by Hoffmann). However, in Waerndorfer's studio the altarlike design was not a tribute to the owner's wife but to the fashionable idol of youth, a prioritizing gesture that surely suggests at the patron's hedonism. The sculpture's feminine S-curve and its narcissistic gesture, with the boy hugging his shoulders, were stressed by its reflections in three mirrors, revealing the boy's back and two profiles. The reflections recalled the reflection from the water fountain in Minne's original circular composition, *The Fountain of Kneeling Youths*, in the Secession exhibition. Here, however, the play of reflections transformed the corner and the three-dimensional statue of a virginal boy, magnifying the object of adoration in an ambiguous space and allowing the owner in front of it to unite his own reflection with the sculpture's reflections.[57] Two late impressionist landscapes by Klimt flanked the Minne sculpture and served as a sensual contrast to the boy's virginal appearance.[58]

The young painter Oskar Kokoschka was hired to teach Waerndorfer's children drawing and visited Waerndorfer's house while writing his first expressionist poem, the text for his children's book *Die träumenden Knaben* (The dreaming boys.[59] The title may have been his response to Minne's *Kneeling Boy*. In contrast to the shy posture of the sculpture, however, Kokoschka's boy confesses having seven erotic dreams (yet in the last lithograph in his book, Kokoschka himself appears shyly, standing naked). The young artist was going through an identity crisis concerning his masculinity at the time.[60] Is it possible that Kokoschka, in his search for a masculine role model, found something to explicitly react against in the Waerndorfer home? Would he have been rejecting the effeminate sculpture and, by association, Waerndorfer the dandy? Kokoschka may have chosen to expose his disappointment with his patron in his poem. He refers to distancing himself from people living in a stagnant environment like inanimate objects; men who are like caged birds in locked rooms; and members of a sinful, large, and fearful congregation.[61] Nevertheless, Kokoschka's expressionist iconography is directly influenced by the works of Minne and the British graphic artist Aubrey Beardsley, which he saw and perhaps studied in Waerndorfer's house. The relationship between art and design in Waerndorfer's house may have evoked the impression of a gathering space for a sinful community (possibly secessionist or Jewish), yet in reality Waerndorfer was staging a private drama of body reclamation. Waerndorfer's identification as a dandy was an act of defiance not only against the patriarchal bourgeois order of his family but also against notions of masculinity, since stereotypes of Jewish men as feminine and lacking self-respect was another form of antisemitism at the time.[62]

Waerndorfer's Body Reclamation I: The Dead Virgin in His Music Room and the Pregnant Temptress in His Art Gallery

Following Georg Simmel's argument, and like Karl Wittgenstein, Waerndorfer claimed his uniqueness. He was "the Stranger" who sought to secure intimacy by convincing his guests of that uniqueness, as in the case of someone who had had a great love affair. Simmel treats the phenomenon of the wanderer as liberated from any given point in space, yet he confirms the importance of spatial relations as a condition of this phenomenon by describing how spatial relations are a symbol of human relations. Space, Simmel argues, can regulate nearness and distance both physically and culturally and also define the intensity of experience—which constantly alternates between "trust" and "estrangement."[63] Waerndorfer's new modern interiors illustrated Simmel's argument, redefining old notions of spatial relations.

At the end of 1902, Waerndorfer wrote to Hoffmann that he and his wife had not used their tickets to Richard Wagner's *Götterdämmerung* (Twilight of the gods) because Lili preferred to stay at home and arrange the newly delivered sideboard that Hoffmann had designed for the dining room.[64] The couple's investment in modernist design replaced the favored entertainment of acculturated Jews, such as going to a Wagner opera, and allowed Fritz and Lili to avoid gathering places frequented by friends for one evening.[65] Hevesi noted that the Waerndorfer's new dining room windows were not casements, but sash windows that were lowered and raised by leather pulls, like those in a luxurious train compartment: "These windows in the outer wall are an allusion, a pretension. Belts attached below the panes to lower them or raise them, like in a railway salon wagon of the Nice express. We are sitting in this salon as in a white marbled Pullman that is silently rolling forward. We are not in Karl Ludwig Strasse no. 45 anymore, but passing Genoa. Drifting along the Riviera. This white salon glides unnoticed and with no noise (Josef Hoffmann has built it in the Wärndorfer House) . . . gliding forward through imaginary zones."[66] Hoffmann had further added a visual reference to the Orient in the dining room—an illusionistic door opening in a built-in cabinet—the first evidence of ancient Egyptian influence on his work.[67] Simmel notes the stranger's dependence on uniqueness, since once his uniqueness and the uniqueness of the constructed relationship are challenged and compared to others, he loses his exclusive position as well as the security of being accepted.[68] Waerndnorfer was fashioning his uniqueness as a Viennese cultural producer not only as a Jewish *homme fatal* but also as a Jewish traveler.[69]

As a second-generation acculturated Jew, Waerndorfer was coming to terms with his Jewish identity. He used the interplay of modernist design and the artworks he exhibited in his house to further this self-exploration. The feminist idea of reclaiming the body, introduced by Hélène Cixous and Catherine Clément in *The Newly Born Woman*,[70] is useful in an examination of Waerndorfer's wish to elude the negative appraisal of others and find new terms for his identity. The art historian Bram Dijkstra links the artistic representation of "feminine evil" with the degeneracy of "the Jew."[71] In this ideological context, we can understand Waerndorfer's actions as a challenge both to the evaluation of his body by his patriarchal Jewish family, who expected him to conform to the bourgeois codes of respectable behavior, and to the distorted gaze of antisemites and members of the Christian majority—a gaze whose distortions materialized in antisemitic caricatures presenting a repulsive Jewish male physiognomy.[72] In traditional Western philosophy the body is what others see, and what its owner is expected to mirror. In the early twentieth century the female and the male body became the focus of a cultural power struggle with far-reaching ramifications. To free his body from its supposed inferiority, Waerndorfer tried to reclaim it, using the modernist redesign of his house to help him reject past associations, ease his physical discomfort, and display his body in an independent aesthetic unity (thereby achieving wholeness).

The prejudice against Jews provoked Waerndorfer. In his letter to Hoffmann of late 1902, he referred to the false accusations that Jewish patrons were egoists (as in Otto Weininger's *Geschlecht und Charakter*, a polemic against women and Jews) and cultural parasites (as in Richard Wagner's antisemitic *Das Judenthum in der Musik*): "When I look at my things sometimes it appears to me as if the whole secession was founded only for me. My two friends, respectively, Viennese species, I have through the secession. You have sent me to Glasgow—I would have no idea of Minne without you—in short I appear to myself as a pig fattened by your riches. Still, it does not matter."[73]

Waerndorfer was expressing here his awareness of the antisemitic cliché that the Jewish patron did not deserve respect for his merits but rather scorn because of his egotistical approach and his parasitical enjoyment—a "pig." He was afraid his new friends in the secessionist milieu would regard his reshaping of his identity as deceitful, so he kept confronting their prejudices, playing with their expectations in a most luxurious manner in his interiors —specifically his music room, designed by Mackintosh, and his art gallery, designed by Moser. Despite asking designers to create interiors to house his modern art collection, in his music room and art gallery his awareness of his Jewish origins seems to have surfaced in a calculated manner.

Waerndorfer's music room was designed to house a frieze titled *The Seven Princesses* by Macdonald, which depicted the central scene of the play *The Seven Princesses* (1893) by Belgian symbolist playwright Maurice Maeterlinck (Fig. 22, Plate 10). Mackintosh and Macdonald offered the patron an interior design invested with romantic and symbolic associations, presenting a remarkably appropriate setting for his identification as a dandy style setter. Waerndorfer ordered for this room a set of six of Mackintosh's high-backed chairs, four armchairs, and rugs and utensils like those exhibited in the International Exhibition of Modern Decorative Art in Turin, Italy, in 1902.[74] The high-backed chairs supported the impression of a medieval setting appropriate for Maeterlinck's archaizing plays. Thus, like the dining room, the music room evoked the experience of illusionary journeys. It also offered a radical example of Waerndorfer's need to encase any object to establish his possession of it. Even the piano placed opposite the fireplace was boxed like a rare art object in an extraordinary painted wooden case.[75] Like Spitzer, Waerndorfer allowed his designer to transform his piano into a modernist artwork.

Regardless of these other touches, the main attraction was Macdonald's *Seven Princesses*, and its multiple associations suggest Waerndorfer's consideration of his Jewish background. Seven has a special meaning in Jewish tradition and can represent the holiness of the sabbath. The protagonist of Maeterlinck's play is the seventh princess, offering further associations since the traditional opening ceremony of the sabbath on Friday evening includes

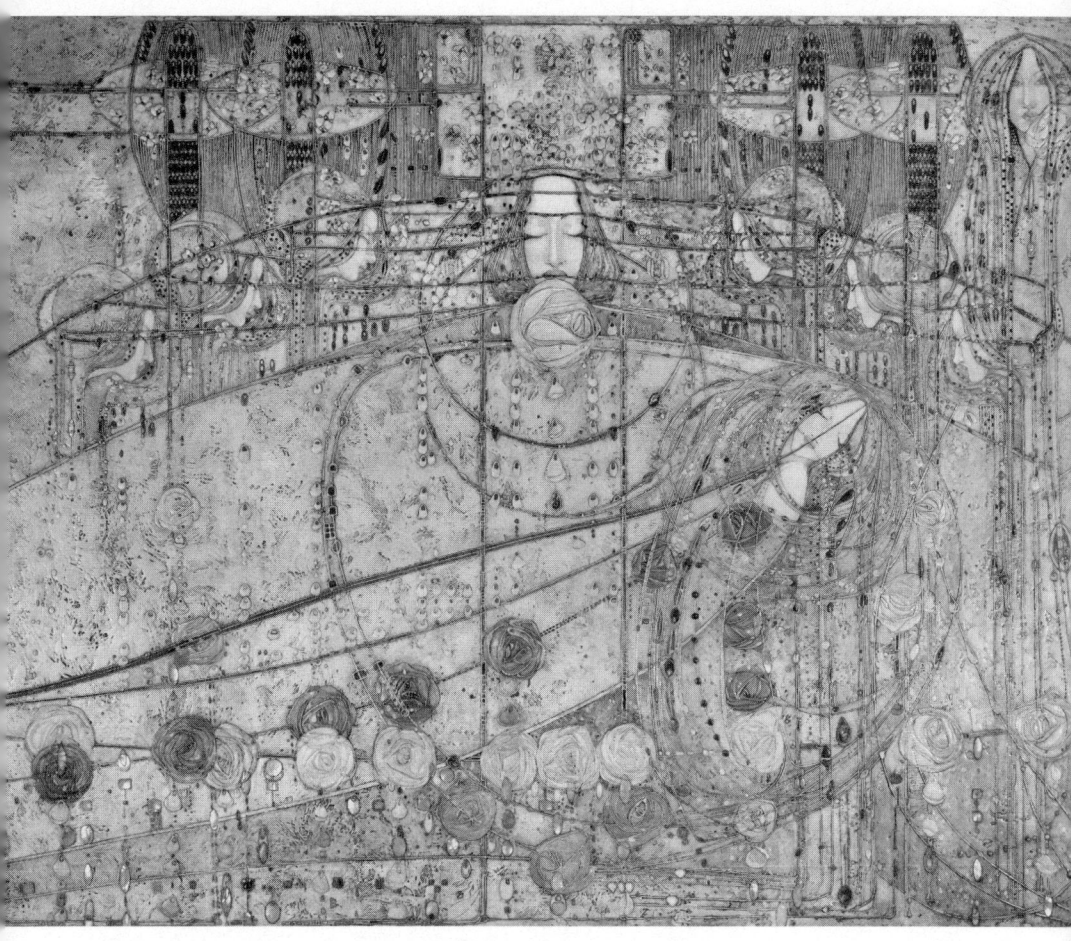

FIGURE 22. *Margaret Macdonald*, The Seven Princesses *(detail), music room in Waerndorfer's house, 1906. Photo: © MAK–Austrian Museum of Applied Arts / Contemporary Art / Georg Mayer.* MAL *348.*

a metaphorical reception of the bride, known as the Princess Sabbath.[76] Waerndorfer knew this tradition and mentioned it in a letter to Eduard Wimmer-Wisgrill, more than a decade after he had sold his house. In reference to the erotic aspect of Christian sacred architecture, Waerndorfer noted: "By the way, it is also demanded that Jews receive the Sabbath 'like a bride.'"[77] The message of Maeterlinck's play has to do with ideal love: Prince Marcellus will never unite with the seventh princess, Ursula. Thus, the seventh princess remains untouched, which also means pure and sacred. By asking Macdonald, or approving Macdonald's suggestion to visualize Maeterlinck's play, Waerndorfer may have hoped to associate the tragic fairy tale with the Jewish religious ceremony, expressing a Jewish nostalgia. The art historian Pamela Robertson has shown that Macdonald's frieze was meant to unify the interior and at the same time divide the room in a lower area of human activity and an upper spiritual sphere.[78] If the seventh princess is related to the ceremony of receiving the sabbath, the lower wall decoration, in which every second vertical wood strip is topped with a symbolic dark flame, might be further related to the Jewish ceremony of candle lighting on Friday evening. Through the representation of the romantic tale Waerndorfer created an atmosphere that could also have been a tribute to the holiness of the sabbath. Hevesi noted the sacral aspect of Macdonald's frieze and identified its role with that of a Muslim prayer carpet: "Seven princesses are awaiting the prince. He comes and finds the bride dead. Bending over the dead one, all of them—the prince and the six princesses—are crying. They cry in a fairy-tale manner, in an uncertain grayish harmony, in a swimming pale mouse gray and white melody. Calm like an old prayer carpet from the Orient, on which for a thousand years people prayed on their knees, hands, and forehead."[79]

It is interesting that Hevesi, himself an assimilated Jew, chose to use a Muslim carpet to make a religious allusion to the Orient. Given the second commandment's ban on making images, and the various interpretations of it by Jews in different countries over the centuries, as well as the wish of acculturated Jews to participate in European cultural production at the beginning of the twentieth century, modern poetry and art allowed Jewish collectors, musicians, and artists to distance themselves from a concrete physical image and from the particularity of Judaism's proscription on representation. Maeterlinck's rejection of historical truth in favor of a poetical representation was a point of departure for visual abstraction, allowing Waerndorfer to integrate his Jewish micronarrative into the celebrated macronarrative of European history, and to further promote it as part of Viennese high culture. As was the case with Spitzer, Waerndorfer's music salon would strengthen his new identity by becoming a place of artistic pilgrimage: "In its day, it was frequently described, even famous: one critic called it a 'place of pilgrimage for lovers of art, and for strangers coming to the city'—an interior in which 'each thought resolves itself as do the chords in music, till the orchestration is perfect, the effect one of complete repose filling the soul.'"[80]

In his review of the house, Hevesi noted that the artistic refinement of the music room expressed a pretentious claim, since it was "naturally not for philistines from Philistine or others from Central Europe."[81] Like Epstein's historicist public rooms, Waerndorfer's modernist rooms could be identified as art galleries.[82] If Epstein was proud to lend his excellent collection to public exhibitions, however, Waerndorfer removed from public exhibition works he preferred to keep in his residence and show only to a select audience. He promoted his home as a place of pilgrimage and a house for an art lover—a jealous one, at that.

With his purchase of Klimt's *Hope I* (1903), banned from display in a Klimt exhibition in the year it was painted, Waerndorfer cited his identification with the femme fatale. The painting of a naked pregnant woman shares several characteristics with the popular representation of the femme fatale around 1900. She is a redheaded seductress who looks boldly at her viewer with no shame but some curiosity. Hope (in German, the word refers to her pregnancy) challenged the bourgeois expectation that her sexual appeal and interest would be reduced by her advanced state of pregnancy. The art historian Robert Pincus-Witten identifies her as a femme fatale—that is, a wife of Satan or Satan's plaything.[83] In such provocative erotic artwork, the Jewish patron further supported Viennese modernism's match of style and seduction.

As noted above, Waerndorfer believed engagement with beautiful things would make him beautiful.[84] But he also chose beautiful things that evoked shock and disgust in their viewers. Two black-and-white photographs showing his picture gallery, documented in an undated Wiener Werkstätte furniture album, along with a Moser drawing of the window wall cabinet and published accounts by Hevesi and Malmberg, the Werkstätte employee, allow a glimpse of this area. Moser designed the small and narrow picture gallery on the ground floor, at the back of the house. He also designed the built-in cabinets and recessed display areas above them along the walls, and the waist-high cabinet in the center that was also a display counter. The wooden cabinets were finished in contrasting dark and light areas, possibly black and white. Large windows, though partially covered with white curtains, opened onto the rear garden, admitting plenty of daylight. Facing the windows hung three paintings, with Klimt's *Procession of the Dead* (1903) in the center. Each recessed area on this wall was framed by two tall climbing plants and by two white tapered columns with metal terminals, a further variation on the archaic motif of the columns in Waerndorfer's dining room. At the end of the room was a free-standing cabinet with a decorative grid and two glass doors, which housed Klimt's *Hope I*. Moser's design of the transparent glass cabinet "dress" was meant to enhance the redheaded female's fatal attraction. To connect the top of the cabinet with the continuous line of windows and display areas, Moser added seven small squares to each side of the end wall. The result integrated each display into an overall exhibition frame. On the windowsill to the left of the free-standing cabinet, Waerndorfer placed an expressive Minne sculpture called *The Bricklayer* (also known as *The Mason*), possibly symbolic of his membership in a Freemasons' lodge in Vienna.[85] The three allegories by Klimt in the picture gallery were *Hope I* and *The Procession of the Dead* (1903), as mentioned above, and *Pallas Athene* (1898). While the seventh princess in Macdonald's painting personifies purity, Klimt's naked pregnant woman in *Hope I* signifies something very different. Her red hair encircles her head, separating it from her body, and her feet are encircled by the tail of a mysterious, shadowy sea monster. Three female faces and a skull appearing to bite the woman's head are threatening elements, perhaps symbolic of the biological determinism of a woman's sexuality, doomed to procreation and death. With whom did Waerndorfer identify—the frightening phallic sea monster, the temptress, or both?

Waerndorfer's Jewish identification with the *homme fatal* can also be associated with the popular fictional Jewish femme fatale, as presented to Viennese audiences through Oscar Wilde's play *Salomé*. The story of Salomé, originating in the New Testament (Matthew 14:1–12 and Mark 6:14–29), is a classic antisemitic narrative of a Jewish woman whose actions lead to the martyrdom of the Christian John the Baptist. The German studies scholar Jacques Le Rider notes that in *Die Fackel* in 1903, Kraus passionately defended Wilde's *Salomé* against the liberal Christian critic F. Schütz, who detected antisemitic elements in the performance.[86] Kraus quoted Schütz's complaint that the play featured a staggering Jew with an ugly physique who gibbered in Hebrew, arguing that according to Schütz (and some liberal Jews), each work of art should present only one lesson—in this case, that there were no Jewish "bad habits."[87] Kraus protested Wilde's victimization in his trial and defended his own position as an outsider who was striving to create shared cultural platforms for rapprochement between Jews and gentiles in the Viennese cultural scene. Waerndorfer may have also expressed a special interest in the fatal attraction of *Salomé*. In 1903 Moser designed a bookplate (ex libris) for Waerndorfer (Fig. 23) that was a variation on two Beardsley illustrations for Wilde's *Salomé*, "The Woman in the Moon" and "The Eyes of Herod." To emphasize Salomé's fatal attraction, Moser added five phallic shafts with double spiral heads to his illustration. This might be a reference to a third illustration by Beardsley for *Salomé*, "The Climax," in which the body of Jokanaan (John the Baptist) is transformed into a stem and his severed head is held high by Salomé. Moser's bookplate makes no reference to the victim, Jokanaan, but in the five shafts detached from the human body instead alludes to male sexual arousal and to the castration fantasies associated with Salomé's fatal cha-

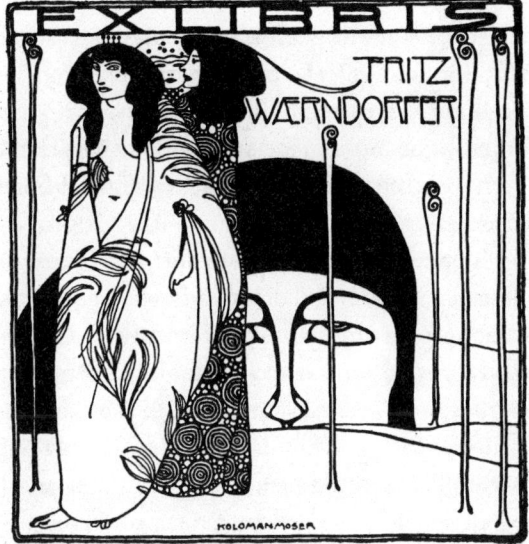

FIGURE 23. *Koloman Moser, bookplate for Waerndorfer, 1903.* Photo: © MAK–Austrian Museum of Applied Arts / Contemporary Art. WWGG 706-1.

risma. Yet the temptress dressed in an open robe can also be interpreted as an identification object for Waerndorfer. In her analysis on the relationship between secessionist style and women's fashion, Rebecca Houze identifies the open robe (and specifically Moser's drawings) as a cocoon out of which a larval woman emerges.[88] Perhaps the robe is only the shell from which Salomé needs to free herself (or, in other words, perhaps this echoes Waerndorfer's rediscovery of his true identity). Salomé's open robe is a symbolic repetition of the *Hope I* glass cabinet. The cabinet and the robe both seduce and trap with their flirtatious acts. The fact that the Jewish patron is personified through a half-naked or completely naked seductive woman is an end in itself, meant to simulate the experience of flirtation between the patron and his guests to avoid actual intimate relations between them.[89] This flirtation underlying the game of seduction was central to the project of Viennese modernism. In the process of helping to shape a sense of belonging for the secessionist group, the modernist Jewish patron Waerndorfer was trapped or trapped himself —willfully or not—in a Jewish stereotype of a seducer (the glass cabinet, the open robe). Waerndorfer was forced to sacrifice, or deliberately gave up, the personal, the experience of individual intimacy, to fit into the system of modern style—the Gesamtkunstwerk—that he helped produce.

When we consider the question of whether Waerndorfer identified with the frightening phallic sea monster or the temptress in *Hope I*, it should be noted that he kept pet snakes on the veranda of his house, next to the picture gallery. With his giant snakes he seems to have expressed his desire for omnipotence and taken delight in provoking disgust in his guests, which we can interpret as another instance of flaunting the prejudices against him as a Jewish art patron. On one occasion, he invited Malmberg to visit with her mother. He treated them in a most gallant manner and then showed them around his house. Drinking coffee on the veranda, Malmberg noticed huge and threatening poisonous snakes eating small white mice: "We took coffee in the terrace room, the large double doorway of which allowed a view to the garden. This room was almost completely filled with a large cage, which lodged to my horror giant poisonous snakes from foreign countries. The beautifully marked animals lay rolled together on tree trunks and were digesting their food, small white mice, whose pathetic remains could still be seen in a corner. Wärndorfer wanted to tell me about his 'darlings'; but I could not control myself, I turned away completely in disgust. It seemed to me most telling that he was keeping such house pets in particular. Yet I could not figure out if this was the fruit of a hobby or snobbism. I assumed that it was the latter."[90]

Noticing her reaction, Waerndorfer said he expected this from her, addressing her as a young and innocent lady. While this indeed may have been his hobby or an expression of his snobbery, it was also part of a calculated theatrical spectacle—a curious drive to express his corruptive power. Waerndorfer's wife, Lili, participated in his show of omnipotence as well. When Malmberg and her mother returned to the picture gallery to drink coffee from a beautiful fragile service, Lili opened the cabinet hiding the sensational *Hope I* and left her guests too shocked by the painting to enjoy their drink.[91] Not only did Waerndorfers' art evoke associations with femininity and seduction, but they clearly intended to shock their guests by questioning sexual taboos. This was expressed much earlier when Waerndorfer gave his copy of Arthur Schnitzler's *Reigen*, a play that portrays charged relationships between men and women, as a present to the secretary of the Vienna Secession in 1900.[92] Waerndorfer's house facilitated his provocations, the modernist interior a charming lure to draw his visitors onward. In his diary of June 1903, Bahr described the attractive tour that Waerndorfer had given him through the residence: "Rain. At Fritz Wärndorfer in the cottage: the wonderful room by Mackintosh (white, violet, blue, the high chairs). Beautiful dining room by Hoffmann (the lamps arranged so that there is only reflected light), and two Mienes [Minnes]. Showed me his original Beardsley (Lysistrata) and curious Betzmars. The uncanny letter by the dying Beardsley."[93]

This route would have ended with *Hope I*. In 1905, Hevesi noted that

Waerndorfer used the painting's forbidden attraction to flirt with guests.[94] His provocations, however, were a result of his failure to reclaim his body. He could not free his Jewish body from the distorted gaze of antisemites. Instead he disclaimed his body and reaffirmed through spectacle his identification as the Other, the stranger, the Jew. Prominent authors such as Kraus and Peter Altenberg referred to Waerndorfer simply as "the snob." Despite his sense of himself as an outsider in Vienna, less than three months after the completion of the redesign of his house, Waerndorfer backed the architect Hoffmann and the designer-artist Moser in their dream of creating the Viennese arts and crafts workshops called the Wiener Werkstätte.

Excursus: How Did the Secessionist Style Become a Modern Style? The Wiener Werkstätte's Narration of a Jewish Generational Conflict and the Kneeling Boy *on the Dining Table*

> Here we are concerned with those who founded and organised it—who made it a possibility—and in this connection a word should be said of Herr Fritz Wärndorfer, who enabled the artist promoters to realise their ambition by investing the necessary capital to start the concern. From the very first Wärndorfer has been heart and soul in the movement, and to his untiring energy is due much of the success which has fallen to the Werkstätte.[95]

According to the foundation story of the Wiener Werkstätte, it was Waerndorfer's knowledge of the latest trends, his conversation skills, critique of local design, and enthusiasm about and commitment to the project that helped realize the dream: "One fine day, a visitor called Fritz Waerndorfer joined one of these heady talking sessions in the Café Heinrichshof, opposite the Opera, where young artists gathered round Hoffmann, and were usually also joined by Otto Wagner. This visitor had just returned from England, where he had spent some time with Mackintosh and his circle. He was able to provide many personal titbits about this artist and to discourse on William Morris's movement. His stories stimulated a lively conversation, conditions in Vienna were once again severely criticized, and there was no lack of daydreams spun and projects outlined."[96]

Waerndorfer envisioned the Wiener Werkstätte months before the discussion above took place—at a cultural event during the renovation of his house. Just as at Zuckerkandl's reported picnic at the Prater with Rodin and Klimt, when Klimt served as the flirtatious center of attention, Waerndorfer used a banquet in 1902 to arrange a small intimate brotherhood gathering in Klimt's honor. He also invited Bahr to his party.[97] For this occasion, Hoffmann designed a magnificent chair especially for Klimt, and Moser designed the tablecloth and the printed menu. Like Zuckerkandl, who published favorable reviews of Klimt, Waerndorfer celebrated Klimt's status as an authorial artistic binding force that would bolster his social gathering and encourage a new Gesamtkunstwerk design production. Klimt deserved this special tribute since he had supplied Waerndorfer with art for his newly renovated house. Furthermore, Klimt was an artist whose work changed with the semantics of the modern Austrian and secessionist applied arts. Carl Schorske has argued that Klimt's stylistic changes—from historicist (positivist) to individualist (psychological) and finally decorative (autistic, meaning noncommunicative) style—were prompted by his public victimization.[98] Klimt shared with his Jewish patrons the experience of being victimized (rejected, according to Bahr, as mentioned in the previous chapter). Waerndorfer had encouraged Bahr to write a book in defense of Klimt after Klimt's plans for decorating the ceiling of the staircase hall of Vienna University were harshly criticized in the media.[99] Bahr's book was published with the title *Gegen Klimt* (Against Klimt).[100] Similar to the case of Klimt's changing styles, the new modernist design served as a counterattack against the prejudice against and assault on Jews (and their "Jewish taste"). At the same time it replaced the required constraints of civilization (needed to show Jewish mastery of the European habitat) through decorative designs. The idealized victim role, the outsider status, and prominent Jews' conscious process of coming to terms with their "Jewishness" permeated the Viennese avant-garde rhetoric. Hevesi concluded his impressions of another afternoon entertainment at Waerndorfer's house by arguing that the new design offered a fantastic escape and bridged high cultural aspirations and [assimilated Jews'] existential conditions by erasing them both and prevailing through a dreamy, decorative fusion of art and life.[101] Waerndorfer did not erase his high cultural aspirations but combined them with the complexity of his experience as an assimilated Jewish patron by choosing to decorate his salon with scenes from Maeterlinck's play *The Seven Princesses*. Yet, Hevesi's conclusion does raise several questions. By providing Jewish clients with a new individualized setting, did the new Wiener Werkstätte design intend to offer them a shield against the growing antisemitic threat (at the time that the antisemitic Karl Lueger was mayor of Vienna)? Or did the overaestheticized setting trap them because it was so unique and different that they would never be able to escape the label of outsider?

The Austrians followed the example of English workshops and the ideologies of John Ruskin and William Morris,[102] yet the Wiener Werkstätte's program focused on the ideal of intercourse between people and objects of daily use: "Have we perhaps forgotten that the love with which a book has been printed, decorated and bound creates a completely different relationship between it and us, and that intercourse with beautiful things makes us beautiful?"[103]

The Wiener Werkstätte became Hoffmann's. He was the charismatic artistic director, and Waerndorfer was the one who believed enough in Hoffmann and in the project to provide the start-up funds. Waerndorfer gave the amount of 50,000 kronen.[104] The Wiener Werkstätte was registered in Vienna's Central Trade Registration on May 19, 1903. The firm was described as "Wiener Werkstätte, a manufacturing guild of craftsmen registered in Vienna with unlimited liability."[105] On June 9, 1903, a coda was added: "Josef Hoffmann, Koloman Moser, professors at the School of Applied Arts in Vienna will be directors, and Friederich Waerndorfer, factory owner in Vienna, treasurer."[106] Waerndorfer was granted the role of a treasurer, yet he also functioned as a public relations officer. It may have been Waerndorfer who encouraged the Wiener Werkstätte to represent a Jewish generational conflict drama in their decorative schemes: representing cultural difference through exoticism, as espoused by the older generation, while negating cultural representation through an emphasis on abstraction and geometric design, as espoused by the younger generation.

The original capital for the Wiener Werkstätte actually came from Waerndorfer's mother Bertha, née Neumann, who had proudly furnished her salon with historicist furniture.[107] She was a self-assured, tough client who wanted to receive full value for her money.[108] Bertha was sixty years old at this time, and she identified with the older generation of Jewish patrons such as Karl Wittgenstein. Moser integrated an Egyptian symbol of death into his design for her writing desk, which he created in 1903–4. Moser added the exotic reference to ancient Egyptian culture to cater to Bertha's taste; for her generation of Jewish patrons, the attractive visual reference to ancient Egypt was a reminder of their relationship to the diaspora in Egypt. Moser's design was a transitional piece, therefore, that represented the exotic Jewish identification of Waerndorfer's mother but also pushed forward, toward a more modernist aesthetic. Moser wished to transform the functional piece of furniture into a large beautiful box, which also evoked the impression of a large coffin. The only figural decoration on the upper part is a series of women dressed in black, their hands crossed in front of their chests in imitation of an ancient Egyptian mummy, recalling his series of women dancers at the back of the Secession House.

Moser's 1904 designs for a younger member of the family, Waerndorfer's twenty-four-year-old sister-in-law Margarethe Hellmann, expressed a more radical break with the past.[109] Moser designed Margarethe's furniture using maple stained black, with a partly polished glass inlay, and white metal for the handles. In contrast to the exotic decoration on Waerndorfer's mother's writing desk, Moser designed a solid modern piece for the patron's young sister-in-law. This design relied on a bold monochromatic effect, the front decorated with five vertical rectangular glass inlays, and a glass showcase on top with ovals enclosing rhombuses. The result was a new progressive minimalist acculturation "dress" projected onto furniture design. It is possible to identify the ethnic dress for Bertha's writing desk as an exotic historical exhibition piece, and the minimalist acculturation dress of Margarethe's showcase as a fashionable woman's dress.[110] The Wiener Werkstätte also created a mirror table for Margarethe made of lacquered light gray maple, with a delicate vertical ornament of a black-and-white checkered pattern at the sides of the table and white metal handles. The matching chair for the table was also lacquered light gray maple, a simplified variation of a classical round-back chair.[111] Moser's different designs for Bertha and Margarethe suggest that he took clients' tastes into consideration and designed the pieces according to the creative spaces they permitted him.[112] These in turn were defined by these patrons' different degrees of distance from their Jewish heritage, or the younger generation's desire to redefine themselves as Others in Viennese society not because of their exotic appeal but because of their self-mastery and distinction.

A similar conclusion concerning the Wiener Werkstätte's designers' awareness of different degrees of acculturation could be drawn by comparing the furniture with rich, exotic ornamentation in Karl Wittgenstein's Hochreit Hunting Lodge (1906–7) and the minimalist pieces in his daughter Margaret Stonborough-Wittgenstein's apartment in Berlin (1905).[113] The question of how much money was available to designers should also be considered as influential to the character of their design, and perhaps the younger generation was more limited in this regard.[114] Still, the older generation was identified with lavish and exotic projections and the younger, more acculturated, generation rejected the luxurious lifestyle and chose instead to identify with a more reserved, puritan, and minimalist lifestyle.[115] It is revealing to compare Margaret's reaction to the expected Wiener Werkstätte redesign of her father's hunting lodge with Waerndorfer's anticipation of her reaction. Both refer to different aspects of the design; she identifies it as "crazy" and Waerndorfer estimates that she will become crazy in the entrance hall. Margaret expressed her skepticism to her father after hearing of the Wiener Werkstätte changes in the hunting lodge, using the Yiddish word *meshuga*: "It sounds very *meshuga*, but perhaps it will turn out really beautiful, in any case I am extremely curious about the result. . . . There would have been plenty of room in Hochreit for us, but this way it will become really beautiful. The more baths and toilets, the more beautiful it will be."[116]

Waerndorfer wrote to Hoffmann after his visit to the hunting lodge: "The entrance room is a hit, up till the damned red that shoots through from the lodge across, but it is the most bright and lively that I know. The Stonborough will become simply crazy in the room."[117]

Waerndorfer also was fascinated by the possibility of marketing the new design's repetitive motifs, such as the checkered motif, and by identifying black and white as "national colors."[118] Both pattern and color choices would continue the secessionist ideal of design as regenerative. According to Leopold Rochowanski, Hoffmann's choice of black and white expressed both an aristocratic identification and a "tabula rasa."[119] How far Waerndorfer was willing to go in his pursuit of assimilation is further demonstrated in the following anecdote concerning the Wiener Werkstätte cutlery.

The need to replace the required constraints of civilization through a new decorative design became most evident in Hoffmann's experiment with artistic cutlery design for the Wiener Werkstätte. Waerndorfer suggested the idea of artistically arranging a table and used the above-mentioned occasion honoring Klimt in 1902 as an opportunity to ask Moser to arrange the table. This idea may have followed Waerndorfer's commissioning of Hoffmann to design artistic cutlery.

In the earliest version of the new cutlery design, the influence of Mackintosh's artistic semantics on Hoffmann is noticeable: Hoffmann adapted the rounded eye shape of Mackintosh's high-backed chair (exhibited in the eighth Secession exhibition) for the tablespoon in his flat model cutlery design.[120] The flattened handles of the artistic cutlery are also an adaptation of the flattened forms of Mackintosh's high-backed chairs in Waerndorfer's music salon. According to Hevesi, Waerndorfer was the only client who purchased Hoffmann's cutlery before 1906, and indeed the earliest surviving cutlery with the initials of its owners, dated March 1905, belonged to Lili and Fritz Waerndorfer.[121] Hevesi reported that the design of Waerndorfer's cutlery was completely different from what his generation remembered as children, and that the sauce spoon could serve as a subject for a lecture on logic.[122]

The Wiener Werkstätte exhibition titled *Arranged Table*, held in the autumn of 1906, presented different cutlery designs. Among them was Hoffmann's flat model cutlery, both the original model and the more practical variation bought by the Waerndorfers. Both models were decorated at the bottom with a series of four tiny balls horizontally attached to each other, which could have evoked the impression of ancient Assyrian earrings. Waerndorfer encouraged his designers to make artistic claims. To complete the magnificent impression at the exhibition of the arranged table with the cutlery, and to highlight the overall aesthetic, he may have suggested displaying Minne's *Kneeling Boy* on the middle of the artists' table—thus trying to make buyers believe that if they purchased the Wiener Werkstätte cutlery they would also purchase entrée to the old secessionist club or the new modernists' artistic community that he, Hoffmann, and Moll belonged to.[123] Waerndorfer's suggestion—or his acceptance of the idea—turned the casual event of dining into an erotic feast in which the young boy was being offered as a sacrificial object of attraction.[124] The viewer at the exhibition could imagine his or her guests eating from a delicate dinner service while admiring a statue of a naked boy. This was a variation on Waerndorfer's own experience in his dining room, only Minne's statues there were on stands at the end of the room and not on the table as part of the service. By using the statue of the boy to promote sales, however, Waerndorfer actually undermined Minne's artistic value for the sake of marketing modern design. And despite his efforts, visitors' reception of the work was less than enthusiastic. Two prominent Jewish critics—the editor of *Die Wage*, Rudolf Lothar, and the art critic of the *Neue Freie Presse*, Adalbert Franz Seligmann—criticized the cutlery. Lothar argued that geometric form rather than fantasy had served as a leading idea for the creation of the flat model and that the cutlery looked more like surgical instruments than instruments of pleasure.[125] Seligmann complained that the cutlery was more comfortable for cleaning than for eating.[126] Both critics noted that the cutlery design alienated the client from the utensils' actual purpose. The cutlery, like the sacrifice of the naked boy, failed to seduce these viewers and transformed the experience of design into an uncanny and estranging experience.

Waerndorfer's Body Reclamation II: Laughing at the Smart Student and Adoring the Pretty Dancer in Cabaret Fledermaus

Modern Jews' growing estrangement from Jewish heritage and the simultaneous transformation of modern design into an uncanny experience had to be discussed in public as part of a continuous culture of debate. Waerndorfer found a place to discuss it in his newly opened cabaret.[127] The idea for the Cabaret Fledermaus may have originated in a letter from Waerndorfer to Bahr in April 1906. Waerndorfer began his letter with the complaint that director Max Reinhardt did not ask Hoffmann to build his new theater and finished with the statement that he was sure Hoffmann's theater would be built, and he hoped it would be in Vienna.[128] Waerndorfer met Reinhardt at least once, since there is a photograph of Reinhardt at a garden party at the Waerndorfers' house,[129] and Waerndorfer may have been inspired by Reinhardt's theater production. It is also possible that Waerndorfer offered Hoffmann the commission because he wanted to compensate him for his missed opportunity with the notorious Reinhardt—Hoffmann would be able to prove his talents by building a small cabaret theater. The cabaret would also allow Waerndorfer and Hoffmann to advance their positions in the cultural scene. In much the same way as the patron Yella von Oppenheimer invited Hugo von Hofmannsthal to write the text and direct a series of tableaux vivants in her salon, Waerndorfer would use his cabaret to master his role as a producer of modern culture, gathering literary and artistic forces together in a lively and progressive Viennese creative discourse.[130] Hoffmann encouraged and engaged young artists and craftsmen to form a new working group to design the entrance hall to the cabaret. Hevesi stated that the colorful design of the cabaret served to entertain the "better people," offering them a new club where they could socialize with people of similar interests and at the same time develop their interests through engaging with the stage performances.[131] Integral to the cultural project was the rehearsal of new identification possibilities for Jewish patrons and intellectuals. While Sophie von Todesco and her daughter Yella had chosen young Hofmannsthal as their court poet, Waerndorfer chose Altenberg as his cabaret's court poet. These choices were not accidental. As noted in the first chapter, in his text accompanying the tableaux vivants, Hofmannsthal tried to expose the pretension behind the imitation of aristocratic court habits in the Oppenheimers' salon. Similarly, Altenberg and his Jewish colleagues, the authors Alfred Polgar (1873–1955) and Egon Friedell (1878–1938), exposed the pretension behind the new design aesthetics that Waerndorfer promoted. Like Oppenheimer, Waerndorfer needed public lambasting to come to terms with his Jewish identification and to assert his role as producer of culture.

As noted in the previous chapter, in her review of Cabaret Fledermaus's opening in October 1907, Zuckerkandl praised the new art culture for its aesthetic and its ethical creed of establishing a new shared cultural platform.[132] A month after her review was published, furious about Zuckerkandl's complimentary review of the cabaret, Kraus reacted in an article titled "Eine

Kulturtat" (A cultural offense), attacking both Zuckerkandl and Waerndorfer in a vicious manner. Kraus referred to Waerndorfer three times: first, as a man with the belief that money was the most precious thing in the world and that it was allowing the Viennese to flee from the correct view of history; second, as the ignorant host to whom Zuckerkandl attributed the responsibility for the crystallization of the art culture; and third, as the man whose money enabled the horrible taste of the Wiener Werkstätte to be realized in the cabaret. At the end of his review Kraus expressed his dreadful fear of strong women, especially strong Jewish women such as Zuckerkandl, by writing that "the snob" (Waerndorfer) who was "raised" by Zuckerkandl was "ready for the whip." Overlooking Kraus's personal antagonism against rich men (which Waerndorfer ironically also shared, in relation to rich Jewish men) and strong Jewish women, it is interesting to note that his description of the overbearing design produced the sadistic association of him holding a whip against the snob.[133] Nevertheless, with Cabaret Fledermaus, "the snob" Waerndorfer—blamed for strange Wiener Werkstätte designs—succeeded in providing an appropriate setting for new drama that would also symbolically raise the whip against assimilated Jews (specifically assimilated Jewish art lovers).[134]

In 1907 the idea of establishing a cabaret in Vienna was not new. Most earlier cabarets there had been inspired by French and German examples or Yiddish theaters in Vienna, the most prominent of which was the Budapester Orpheum Society, directed by the charismatic actor and a talented stand-up comedian Heinrich Eisenbach (1870–1923).[135] In November 1901 Felix Salten, a member of the Jung-Wien literary circle and an admirer of Eisenbach, had founded the Cabaret Jung-Wiener Theater zum lieben Augustin, for which Moser, then a member of the Vienna Secession, designed a poster.[136] Moser's poster showed an allegory, with a personification of theater dressed in a long robe decorated at the front opening and the bottom with a checkered pattern, holding two masks. Moser also designed the modern stage, and one of the critics described its curtain as having a black-and-white checked pattern.[137] Salten's cabaret was meant to represent the new literary and artistic generation and was favorably received by the critics Zuckerkandl and Hevesi.[138] According to Zuckerkandl's review of the first evening, among the performers were the sensational playwright Frank Wedekind and a dancer called Sartori. There was also an attempt to address a famous antisemitic legend with a performance of a shadow play called *Ahasver* (The Wandering Jew) with music by the French composer Georges Fragerolle.[139] Kraus immediately exposed the weak point in the new enterprise by making public the difficult

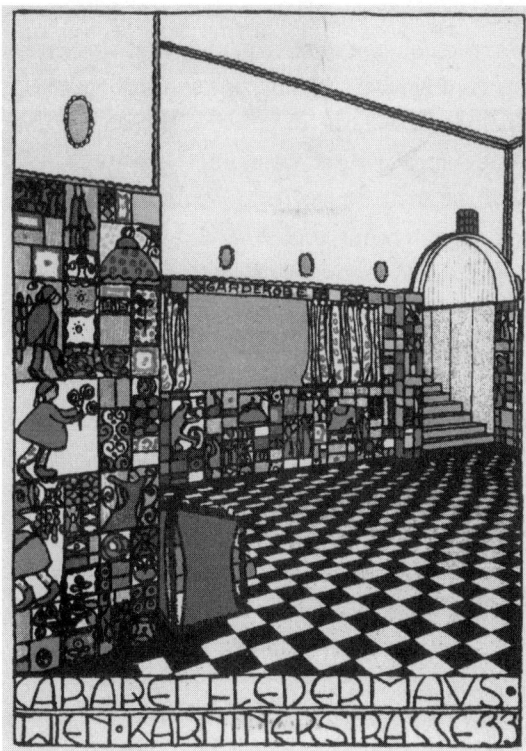

FIGURE 24. *Josef Hoffmann, barroom of the Fledermaus Cabaret, Wiener Werkstätte postcard no. 74, 1907*. Photo: © MAK–Austrian Museum of Applied Arts / Contemporary Art. KI 13748-4.

financial situation of its funder, Siefgried Löwy, and further criticized one of his favorite enemies, Hermann Bahr, who supported the cabaret.[140] In 1905, having been driven out of Munich, the gentiles Marc Henry and Marya Delvard founded the Cabaret Nachtlicht in Vienna, offering the original provocative Munich program; the artistic managers were Marc Henry and Hannes Ruch. The rough plastered walls were covered with caricatures and French posters, and a statue of Delvard was placed on a podium near a wall.[141] According to Altenberg's review, the original setting was designed by the architect Oskar Laske and the artist Karl Huck.[142]

Waerndorfer followed suit, hiring Hoffman to adapt and furnish Cabaret Fledermaus with the latest designs. Hoffmann's plans for the adaptation of the cellar were accepted in September 1907.[143] The cabaret would occupy the cellar of a new building at Kärntnerstrasse 33 in the inner city, two houses away from the new Telegraph Office of *Die Zeit*, with the entrance on Johannesgasse. The staircase hall, decorated with black-and-white marble stripes, led to a vestibule door and then to the entrance hall and bar (Fig. 24, Plate 11). This hall included a cloakroom, free-standing tables with square tops, and four chairs with rounded thin arms that were lacquered white.[144] There were three levels to the cabaret: the colorful entrance lobby and bar on the middle level, from where guests could either take the side stairs down to the lower and main level, which included the auditorium with its stage, or they could choose one of two side openings with stairs going up to the gallery of the auditorium with a view of the main stage. There were necessary side rooms such as the cloakroom, artists' dressing rooms, a kitchen, and toilets. The walls of the entrance lobby and bar were covered with seven thousand colored ceramic tiles up to head height. Lively colored ceramic tiles complemented the Wiener Werkstätte "national" black-and-white motif on the floor. The majority of these tiles were decorated with drawings, symbols, caricatures, portraits, and satiric anecdotes. The Wiener Keramik (Viennese ceramic), managed by Berthold Löffler and Michael Powolny, produced this "carnival dress."[145]

According to Hevesi, the auditorium, in contrast to the colorful lobby, was decorated in blue and white, though according to Eduard Sekler the colors were more like black (dark blue) and white. The upper gallery had eight boxes opposite the rounded stage, separated from each other only by a parapet. The gallery's back wall had vertical white plaster relief strips decorated with clusters of grapes, a possible reference to the Dionysian theater cult. The parapets were clad, like the back wall under the gallery, with dark gray veined marble. The floor was covered by a carpet with a dark and light gray checkered pattern. The Wiener Werkstätte's tables and the thin wooden chairs had playful small ball decorations and were lacquered white or black and upholstered with red covers. Illumination came from ball-shaped ceiling lamps and lamps dressed with umbrella-shaped lampshades on the gallery tables. Following up on the previous year's *Arranged Table* exhibition, the Wiener Werkstätte also designed the flower vases, dishes, and cutlery for the cabaret.[146] Only two reliefs decorated the auditorium, both on the gallery railing: Berthold Löffler's allegories of tragedy and comedy, represented as stylized ancient Greek female figures facing each other, one holding a mask next to her chest, and the other with a mask at the bottom right corner of the relief. Waerndorfer hired Jacob Kohn to do the catering.[147] Waerndorfer's aim was to invite many performers and lecturers to this dignified yet playful environment of black, white, and colorful tiles and lacquered lightweight furniture arrangements, to experience a modern mixture of music, song, dance, pantomime, and skits.

The Wiener Werkstätte interior was also a flattering setting for an important Jewish drama. Altenberg, as noted, became the theater poet, and his piece *Die Masken* (The masks) was performed on the cabaret's opening night in October 1907. The costumes for the three actresses in the show were designed by Carl Otto Czeschka, a colleague of Hoffmann at the School of Applied Arts, who had also cooperated with him on the design of Wittgenstein's hunting lodge. Referring to a review by Friedell in the Berlin journal *Die Schaubühne*, the German studies scholars Andrew Barker and Leo Lensing suggested that *Die Masken*, which consisted of hard-to-understand aphorisms recited on stage by three beautifully dressed women with "threatening" expressions—representing a "woman artist," a "coquette" and a "cosmopolitan woman"—was meant as an attack on the aestheticism of the Wiener Werkstätte.[148] It challenged the idea of a marriage of aesthetic design and cultural aspiration. It was disturbing to hear three beautifully dressed women speaking nonsense.[149] Altenberg's one-act piece exposed the incongruities between the new design and cultural aspirations. Malmberg recalls that Altenberg himself perceived this piece as "the highest point of idiocy" (he used the Yiddish word *Schmockerei*). However, he added: "But for the snobs it's good enough, exactly what they want."[150] Altenberg's statement that snobs can be satisfied with idiocy is reminiscent of Hofmannsthal's accusation delivered to the audience in Todesco's salon: "You have only life, they—they have style."[151]

The fruitful cooperation between Friedell and Polgar, both of whom were strongly involved in the cabaret's artistic productions between 1907 and 1910, is even more revealing of the Jewish drama taking place there. The German studies scholar Janet Stewart claims that the cabaret was a "reflection of its political and intellectual background" and suggests that the theater performances of the two authors reflected the growing German nationalism and promoted the superiority of German culture by ridiculing the codes of the liberal bourgeois civilization.[152] In contrast, I argue that in the plays of the two Jewish authors, there is irony and serious attempts to come to terms with the conflicts accompanying Jewish acculturation in Vienna. Among Friedell's and Polger's plays reviewed by Stewart is *Die Zehn Gerechten: Eine Kabarett-revue* (The ten righteous: A cabaret sketch), which Stewart analyzes as "an example of meta-theatre which provides commentary on the cabaret in the form of a cabaret sketch."[153] A central anecdote in the play provides a humorous commentary on the failure of Jewish assimilation. The anecdote is a parody of Jewish cultural conflict, one that Waerndorfer most likely experienced as well as his Jewish colleagues. The conflict is between Herr Taussig, a Jewish businessman, and Herr Staninski, an enthusiast of modern art. Taussig has been dragged to the cabaret by his wife and daughter and attends the show under protest. His wife is observing the performance through opera glasses, and his daughter shows her interest by holding the materials she needs to understand it (a program, text books, and notes).[154] In the direction notes, Taussig is requested to play with his pince-nez and do calculations in his notebook, suggesting his tenseness and inability to put aside his business concerns. When he does look at the stage, he expresses criticism by muttering "Meschugge" and "Like I say: craziness."[155] To the latter remark, his daughter replies: "But father, this is after all the Secession." When his neighbor, Herr Staninski—proving his engagement with the performance on stage by looking at it knowledgeably, laughing at the right places, and murmuring "Bravo"—identifies the show as "the temple of future art," Taussig reacts by identifying him as an antisemite.[156] The show thus reversed the balance of power that Waerndorfer experienced in real life. In the theater, the Jewish businessman felt threatened by the art lover, who appreciated what he, the businessman, could not understand. In reaction to his sense of being excluded, he saw the art lover as an antisemite. In reality, however, it was Waerndorfer the art lover who felt threatened by certain Jewish businessmen (his contemporaries) whom he needed to support his cultural projects yet who belittled his enthusiasm for modern art as ridiculous (though many were supportive).[157] Furthermore, Taussig twice attacks Altenberg by asking what he lives on and calling him a "meschugge," and blames his daughter who, because of her reading of his *Schmus* (flattery), has refused the advances of an accountant.[158] As Stewart correctly points out, Friedell and Polgar wanted to present the piece as a mirror image of their audience by including "two sections where there is action on the fictional stage and so the fictional audience sits in the darkened set, and two where the set is illuminated since there is no action on the fictional stage."[159] This mirror image, however, also included two references to the special Wiener Werkstätte design of the cabaret itself. When Frau Taussig asks her husband to behave, she says: "Moritz, I beg you, control yourself, [we are] in a room completely of marble!" Furthermore, other guests, who are concentrating more on the food being served than on the show, make remarks about the special design of the cabaret's silverware. Herr von Arthammer (a possible allusion to the gentile art patron Arthaber) says: "If only the program was as funny as the silverware."[160] Thus, the two authors not only mock the crowd but also question the value of the Wiener Werkstätte design. Just before the end, after another neighbor exposes the play by calling it idiotic, Herr Taussig stands up and says triumphantly to his wife: "Now, who said that we should go to the Budapester Orpheum? You or I?"[161] Thus, the authors declare their failure to compete with the Yiddish theater in entertaining the Jewish businessman. They indirectly recognize the Yiddish theater not only as an alternative entertainment but as integral to the public discourse that produced Viennese modernism.[162]

Waerndorfer could have identified with this critical reflection of his own role as an enthusiastic art lover admiring secessionist nonsense and even accepted the exposure of the Wiener Werkstätte design as an absurd alienating mask—his challenged trophy in the battle for social visibility among patrons. Yet even if Waerndorfer was pleased to see himself in this analogy, when he was confronted by the Jewish businessman as an antisemite, he could not have ignored the Jewish preference for Yiddish theater. He could not have dismissed the eventual comparison—and competition—with what was considered a representation of authentic Judaism.

As a teenager, Waerndorfer was a mischievous and idle student.[163] In the Jewish tradition, the student who is not smart enough is often excluded from discussions in class. Another cabaret sketch by Friedell and Polgar, titled *Goethe*, was a critical commentary on the praise of the smart student in the Jewish tradition and on a popular trend in the Jewish acculturation process of aspiring to know German culture better than the Germans. Friedell himself played the role of Goethe, who is asked by the unprepared student Züst to replace him in taking a test in German literature about Goethe's life; however, Goethe fails to pass. Instead, the knowledgeable student Kohn does superbly on the test.[164] The smart Jewish student emerges as the triumphant rival to Goethe on the subject of Goethe himself. The theater sketch became a huge success.[165] (Bourgeois Jewish Germans and Austrians revered Goethe.)[166] The choice of the name Kohn may be indirectly related to Kraus's ridicule of the Europeanization (plastic surgery) of the Jewish newsboy Kohn in the *Die Zeit* advertisements. Friedell exposes the ambitious young Kohn who succeeds—offering short correct answers spoken in a fast tempo—where Goethe fails. Standing nearby and hearing Kohn's demonstration of knowledge, Goethe is at first surprised but then enjoys the proceedings more and more, until finally his whole body shakes with laughter. It is not clear if Goethe approves of or dismisses Kohn's performance. Waerndorfer could be said to have identified with the figure of Goethe, who after failing a test about his own life compensates himself by ridiculing the victory of a Jewish student. Waerndorfer would also have identified with Kohn, noticing the gap between Kohn's wish, as the child of newcomers, to prove his knowledge of the history of Western civilization, thereby proving his successful acculturation, and the irony of alienating himself from that same history by inhabiting the role of the smart student in the Jewish tradition. The trap of the acculturated Jew was that whatever career he or she chose—successful businessman, knowledgeable student, and even art lover—he or she would always be perceived as an outsider or stranger, challenging the norm of the Christian consensus. Waerndorfer proved his lead in the battle over visibility in the Viennese art scene through the cabaret, as a setting also for contemporary Jewish debate about acculturation and integration. He insisted on embracing life as a modern theatrical artistic spectacle and exposed through his patronage the hypocrisy of bourgeois codes of respectability.

In addition to allowing authors to write about the friction between acculturated Jews and Christians and between acculturated Jews and traditional Jews, Waerndorfer also hoped to achieve in the cabaret what he failed to do in the interiors of his own house—namely, reclaim his body. He supported a public body reclamation ritual in his encouragement of reform dancers to perform on the cabaret's stage. Hofmannsthal asked Waerndorfer to allow the gentile Wiesenthal Sisters dance group to perform there, since it was appreciated as an experimental workshop for different theatrical performances.[167] Waerndorfer invited the three sisters to appear in mid-January 1908, and the first show took place before an audience that included Hofmannsthal, Hoffmann, Moser, and Klimt, as well as the dancer Ruth St. Denis. It was a great success for Wiesenthal and Waerndorfer. The performance of the three young dancers on the small cabaret stage evoked a strong reaction from one young viewer, the artist Kokoschka. According to his own report, Kokoschka was forced to come to terms with his awakening sexuality (his expressionist art would champion the Austrian modernist style).[168] Waerndorfer's stage allowed the Wiesenthals to become Viennese stars. Their historical relationship should be reconsidered in relation to Rhonda Garelick's thesis about how the dandy and the woman performer cast a "curious light on each other's performances." In this specific case, Waerndorfer's support of emancipated women's dance performances proves that the dancers "acted out" his own, and his club members,' fantasy of male bodily reclamation, according to Garelick: "I choose this particular couple (the dandy and the female performer) because both members wear their sexuality with such drama. Both indulge in self-conscious, highly theatrical gender play—the dandy in his sexually ambiguous social polish, the woman in her explicitly staged and painted erotic charms. Placed side by side so often in fin-de-siècle culture, these two figures cast a curious light on each other's performances, then ultimately fuse their roles, forming something beyond androgyny, giving birth to the concept of the 'star' as we know it today."[169]

Waerndorfer wore his sexuality through his identification with and exhibition of his love object, Klimt's femme fatale *Hope I*. His wearing of sexuality is further documented in his bookplate and in his keeping snakes as house pets. His displayed sexuality was part of his flirtation with the guests in his house, leading to his disclaiming of his body in his own home. Yet his promotion of the reform dance performances in his cabaret, as a form of shared body reclamation, had an immediate impact on his fashioning of Viennese modern style. It was, for example, picked up by the young expressionists Kokoschka and Egon Schiele and later projected onto their drawings and paintings.[170]

The Taming of the "Jew": Reading Richard Engländer (Peter Altenberg) in the Salon of Beer-Hofmann

The author Richard Beer-Hofmann also staged flirtatious dramas in his Biedermeier salon at the start of his career as a Viennese cultural producer. But, in contrast to Waerndorfer, his aim was not to come to terms with the Jewish tradition he had abandoned but to reconstruct it as an integral part of Viennese modern style.

In February 1894, during an evening gathering of the Jung-Wien literary circle at his salon, Beer-Hofmann asked his friend Hofmannsthal to read two poems by a newly discovered coffee house poet, Richard Engländer (who later changed his name to Peter Altenberg, as discussed in more detail in chapter 4)—"The Primitive" and "Don Juan."[171] According to Altenberg's report of the event to his friend Ännie Holitscher, the guests—who included Arthur Schnitzler and Felix Salten—were especially excited by the text of "Don Juan," which sketches the erotic relationship between a young author called Albert and his muse, a twelve-year-old girl who fancies him.[172] Deconstructing the inner world of his hero, Altenberg offered the listeners dream imagery, a chain of poetic associations—"the fragrant blossoming almond trees," "white acacias," "a white hand," a child's smile, and "a broken woman's soul"—as his entrée to their literary circle:

> Albert said: "the world is rich and beautiful—!"
> But it was his "inner world." Since the world around him was poor and banal.
> Is it also our "inner world," the fragrant blossoming almond trees and the white acacias?! And a white hand?! And the smile of a child?! And a broken woman's soul?! Also!![173]

In the process of cultural production, performing flirtation scenes in a close literary circle was liberating particularly for this group of Jewish authors whose sexuality was stigmatized by the majority of society. The reading performance literally granted them the possibility of transforming the stigma of their "Jewishness" into an elevated and shared artistic experience. Writing about the "sexualization of Viennese modernism," the sociological historian Franz X. Eder noted that sexuality also represented social relations, or an ensemble of social relations and interactions, in which the identity of the bourgeois man—namely, his sense of healthy normality—was defined in contrast to the sexuality of women, homosexuals, Jews, and blacks.[174] According to Eder, sexuality receives its meaning from sociohistorical reality. He suggests that through sexual practices people produce, as Robert Padgug has noted, "an ever-changing human world within nature and give order and meaning to it, just as they come to know and give meaning to, and to a degree, change, the realities of their own bodies, their physiology."[175] So could the reading of Altenberg's "Don Juan" shed light on the sexuality of the Jewish men present that evening, or does it shed light on their strategies of transforming "crime" into "vice"? According to Eder, Jews were identified as abnormal because of their different manners but also in relation to their questioning of the traditional gender division between man and woman. Moreover, the "sickness" of the Jewish man was contrasted with the "health" of the Aryan man.[176] This leads Eder to conclude that the sexuality of the Jews was perceived as a threat to society: "Jewish sexuality is regarded as especially dangerous to other sexualities because of its far more excessive disposition. It has the tendency to cross borders and tries in a cunning manner to infiltrate the bourgeois body."[177]

The art patron performing the role of the Jewish dandy challenged the traditional gender division. Altenberg championed this tendency to cross borders through reports of his (consummated or unconsummated) flirtations with young girls. In an attempt to explain why so much attention was paid to the "pathological Jewish sexual body," Eder suggests the breakdown of the monarchy, the challenging of bourgeois codes of respectability, and the "decadence" that was "everywhere."[178] He makes a further revealing reference to Jewish sexuality, which could also explain Beer-Hofmann's dandyism, through readings of Altenberg's flirtation texts at his salon—namely, the patron's sexuality conflated with his "Jewishness" but also tamed by experiencing the erotic as a shared (artistic) revelation.

"Jewishness" (underlined by an association of Slavic with Jewish) was identified with the threat of sensuality—the loss of control over the sexual drive. Supporting Eder's idea of projected "Jewishness" is a note by Hofmannsthal, written after a walk with Beer-Hofmann in 1894: "How strange that this is once more, that perhaps in Vienna we are the last thinking people, the very last people with complete souls at all [the last thinking souls], that perhaps a big barbarity, *a Slavic-Jewish, sensual world* is coming."[179]

Hofmannsthal imagines his friendship with Beer-Hofmann in terms of claiming themselves as the spiritual and heroic last men, while the rest of the world becomes barbaric, identified with Slavic-Jewish sensuality. Beer-Hofmann carefully fashioned himself as a Viennese dandy and later hired Hoffmann to design his grand hall as a classicist stage for his own performance of self-realization. Together they would create a cultural club like Todesco's, to serve as gathering place for cultivated Jews and gentiles. The creative partnership at the start of this new cultural community came about through the close friendship between Beer-Hofmann and Hofmannsthal. Did Altenberg help them tame the "Slavic-Jewish, sensual" part in them during the evening gathering described above while they were reading his texts? Beer-Hofmann consciously aimed to tame this "Slavic-Jewish, sensual" side, a process already witnessed in the short sketches read by Altenberg, to reconstruct a positive Jewish self-identification.

In contrast to Waerndorfer, Beer-Hofmman, viewed as a central figure in Jung-Wien both by colleagues at the beginning of the twentieth century and later by scholars, publicly celebrated his Jewish identification. He published his most famous poem, "Schlaflied für Miriam" (Lullaby to Miriam), first in the German literary journal *Pan* and later in an anthology, *Junge Harfen: Sammlung jungjuedischer Dichtung* (Youthful harps: A collection of young Jewish poetry; 1903).[180] The most revered phrase in his poem was "the blood of our fathers, fully tensed and proud. It is in *all* of us."[181] Beer-Hofmann, who may have known Waerndorfer through their mutual friends Bahr and Reinhardt, made a narcissistic confession similar to the one Waerndorfer had made in his letter to Hoffmann about his relationship to the secessionists. This was voiced in his breakthrough novel *Der Tod Georgs*, not as a self-belittling tactic but as an authorial claim: "in everything he searched only for himself and he found only himself in everything. His fate was the only thing that filled him up, and what happened apart from it happened at one remove from him, as if it was performed on stage, that what was said by others, appeared only to relate to him."[182]

Beer-Hofmann's hero, Paul, consciously decides to flirt with life so as not to be caught by its dictates—to "play with" it. Yet his flirtation is carefully orchestrated, motivated by the concrete program of reclaiming his Jewish identity. Triggered by the death of his friend Georg, Paul finds "his way back" to Judaism and finds his future in his dreams of his past.[183] In a short story published in the journal *Jugend* in September 1901 and discussed in the introduction of this book, Simmel tried to explain the subject of coquetry, meaning flirting. The seducer allows his or her victim to dangle, cleverly calculating the length of the rope so that it is stretched as far as it can go without breaking. The victim is enchanted by a promise that will not be fulfilled. Beer-Hofmann embraced artistic flirtation in his reclamation of his Jewish self-identification and further flirted with his guests and society in his modernist villa at Hasenauerstrasse 59, in Vienna's eighteenth district (the district where Waerndorfer also lived), where he took up residence in October 1906. He offered to share his positive Jewish identification with his guests, attracting them with words and symbols, keenly aware of their ambivalence toward Jewish culture. He needed Hoffmann to design his house as physical representation of this promise and at the same time to continue to attract Jewish and gentile guests and induce them to experience a positive, shared Jewish identification.

Beer-Hofmann and His Network of Opinion and Desire

Beer-Hofmann fashioned himself as a Jewish celebrity. As noted in the introduction, Garelick describes the dandy as securing his influence through a vast system of communication, creating a network of opinion and desire.[184] Beer-Hofmann came from an acculturated Jewish family, and he reconstructed his Judaism as a source of spiritual regeneration.[185] His uniqueness was his celebrity status as a proud, beautiful Jewish man and as a Viennese cultural producer. Models of Jewish masculinity were uncommon in the Viennese public space. The most striking appearance of this type was a group of four beautiful sculptures, almost naturalistic, that served as atlantes on the Palais Karl Goldschmidt façade (1879), designed by the proud Jewish architect Wilhelm Stiassny. The bearded prophets are striking in their erotic appeal, and they flirt with viewers through inviting poses, coquettish play with their garments, and the way they touch themselves. Goldschmidt bequeathed his palace to the Jewish community to manage his and his wife's charity foundation after their death. Grouped in pairs, the figure on the left is clearly Moses (following Michelangelo's version, without the horns), and the next younger figure may be King David; next to him could be King Solomon, and the older figure to the right may be Jeremiah.[186] Since Stiassny may have chosen the series of mature biblical Jewish men as a counter to Förster's and Hansen's caryatids (those proud representations of the historicist Jewish patrons' Hellenistic-Jewish heritage), the erotic display of these men could be a provocation: Who is more beautiful, your caryatids or our biblical heroes?

Beer-Hofmann was proud of his looks, and his beard was part of his self-fashioning as a beautiful Jewish man.

Kraus indicated Beer-Hofmann's authority by comparing him to a high priest (from the ancient temple) with his beard. It was his claimed role as "priest" that granted him prominence (visibility), according to Kraus, in the cultural scene: "The poet Beer-Hofmann must look like a high priest; or else he will be missing, since in the end he could have looked like the poet Beer-Hofmann."[187]

Indeed, Beer-Hofmann may have chosen to identify himself as Jewish through his beard, rather like Herzl and Freud. However, his stylish beard also identified him as bohemian like Bahr (whom Kraus, in the article quoted above, also attacked for falsely claiming the authority of a prophet through his beard). If Beer-Hofmann would become closely associated with a Jewish identification in his eventual role as patron, he first established his authority as a master of taste through his dandyism. Two early works of Beer-Hofmann addressed the topic of the dandy and his corruptive powers. In 1891, he wrote his first novella, "Camelias" (published in 1893) about the "beautiful Freddy," the "hero of the salon," who is fascinated by a young girl in white dress called Thea, whose photo he keeps on his desk.[188] He considers marrying Thea but rejects the idea. Instead he decides to keep his relationship with his long-time kept lover since he is afraid of aging and losing his potency. A year later Beer-Hofmann wrote a pantomime called "Pierrot Hypnotiseur," whose hero's ability to hypnotize the people around him, including his young maid, Colombine, whom he desires, leads eventually to her and his destruction.[189] In the first and the last scenes Pierrot requests Colombine to dance for him, revealing the ploy and eventually the tragic end of his seduction.[190] The destructive powers of Pierrot's hypnotizing diamond ring may have inspired Hofmannsthal's scene in the "The Student" of the father forcing his daughter with his magic ring to dance for him and his student against her wish (see chapter 2). Analyzing the construction of the dandy figure in both novella and pantomime, the German studies scholar Julia Bertschik points out how the symbolic play of colors in relation to Pierrot's dress in different scenes—changing from normal black and white to white wedding attire, then to black for death—discloses the uncanny theatrical metamorphoses of the dandyist subject. The dandy evokes both the hope of being satisfied (sexually and aesthetically) as well as the threat of being destroyed by him (his corruptive influence). The pantomime further integrated contemporary attempts to study the subject, by using either hypnosis or the methods of psychoanalysis.[191]

Introducing the dandy figure in her book *Mode und Moderne: Kleidung als*

Spiegel des Zeitgeistes in der deutschsprachigen Literatur (Fashion and modernity: Dress as mirror of the zeitgeist in German literature), Bertschik analyzes the experience of striptease in *Camelias*. As the dandy Freddy exposes himself physically and verbally, he gradually exposes the artificiality of his personality. This exposure reaches its climax when Freddy painfully frees himself from a skin-colored corselette, or bodice.[192] Beer-Hofmann does not shy from presenting his dandy as forcefully feminized. Bertschik points out that the ironic story of an aging dandy in a bodice implied the confusion of gender roles between the flirtatious theatrical woman and the hero of the salon.[193]

When Hofmannsthal orchestrated the tableaux vivants at the Todesco salon in 1893, mentioned in the first chapter, he asked Beer-Hofmann for historical accessories.[194] Beer-Hofmann was further asked to advise on costume as well as on the choice of book cover.[195] Beer-Hofmann also used his authority in matters of style among this literary brotherhood to project his, and their, positions as celebrities. In a letter he wrote to Schnitzler in September 1895, he attempted to set a code for his friends on how to be tourists in Italy.[196] Beer-Hofmann took several books by ancient Greeks rather than works of Italian authors to read during his Italian journey. Yet it was the German author Johann Wolfgang Goethe who inspired this vision: "We should be old men with beautiful pale eyes and smooth silky white hair, and *very* famous. So famous that women will boast of it if their mothers were once our lovers and young girls should make the effort to appear charming—and I mean 'charming' literally."[197]

The German studies scholar Konstanze Fliedl argues that it was a vacation at Lake Garda in northern Italy, at some distance from Vienna, that allowed Beer-Hofmann to fantasize about being part of a group of beautiful and famous men.[198] Fliedl further suggests that Goethe had established the role model of a beautiful, very famous, old German author, and it was his Italian journey that had set the literary ideal to which future generations aspired. In Beer-Hofmann's fantasy, his vision of future famous men was not only fabricated by his role as tourist in Italy but also by his role as a stranger in his own city, Vienna.

His declaration of uniqueness as a Jewish celebrity was grafted onto his house a decade later, when he chose the modern architect Hoffmann to design his villa at Hasenauerstrasse 59 (now destroyed) as an alternative to the Café Griensteidel in the center of the city, where he hosted his brotherhood of artistic (beautiful) men and confirmed his and their position in the Viennese art scene. The modern, yet classicist, stylized house (Fig. 25) was striking in the context of Hasenauerstrasse, as Hasenauer was an important Austrian

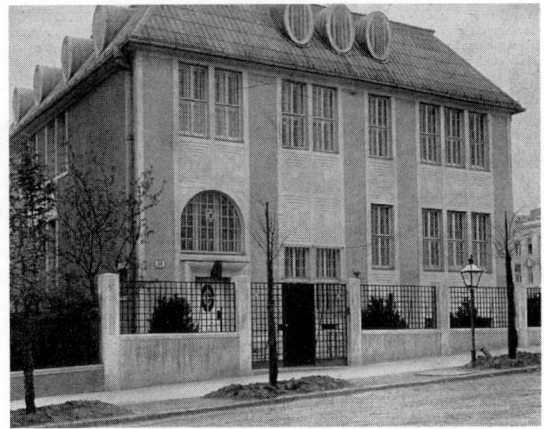

FIGURE 25. *Josef Hoffmann, Beer-Hofmann villa, 1906, reproduced in* Deutsche Kunst und Dekoration 25 *(1910): 389.*

historicist architect of the Ringstrasse. Moreover, Beer-Hofmann's insertion of a Star of David into the arched window above the entrance championed the patron's Jewish identification. Together with Hoffmann, Beer-Hofmann produced an architecture that witnessed a new art of socialization between beautiful Jewish men and their gentile colleagues and was in itself an emblem of blended modernist and classicist styles.

The Proud Jewish Dandy and His Modern Dress

It was Kraus who, in his early satire "Demolierte Literatur" (Demolished literature; 1897), offered the earliest detailed and critical portrayal of Beer-Hofmann as a true dandy in the tradition of the legendary British Beau Brummell. Kraus described Beer-Hofmann's careful investment in fine clothes down to the smallest detail, his supposed preference for associating with young men whose suits matched his own, and his careful fashioning of his environment to produce a beautiful and tasteful setting for a spiritual friendship club.[199] More than a decade later, Kraus challenged Beer-Hofmann's authority by hinting at his cooperation with Hoffmann in the design of his villa, and referring to his Jewish identification (represented in his poem "Lullaby to Miriam") as an "old shirt."[200] Yet Kraus was wrong. Beer-Hofmann's cooperation with Hoffmann did not undermine their modernism or Beer-Hofmann's Jewish identification.

Beer-Hofmann had proudly defined that identification early in his career in a letter to Theodor Herzl, after reading Herzl's *Der Judenstaat* (The Jewish state) in 1896: "What appealed to me more than everything in your book was what stood behind it: finally, again, a human being who doesn't bear his

Judaism like a burden or a misfortune, but rather is proud to be the legitimate heir of an ancient, distinguished civilization."[201] The later cooperation between author and architect in reviving classicist formalism—not as a direct historicist citation but as a way of abstracting (filtering) the classicist formal repertoire—did relate Beer-Hofmann's Jewish identification to the heritage of the Hellenist Jews, and specifically to the tradition of the Ringstrasse historicist patrons. But it was not regressive; rather, it served as stimulus to Hoffmann's stylistic progression from Jugendstil modernism to neoclassical modernism.[202]

It seems that Hoffmann felt inspired and eager to build Beer-Hofmann's private house. According to an anecdote reported by Sekler, the author and the architect discussed the future house in a café early one morning after a long party. Reinhardt had arranged a celebration in the Hotel Imperial on the Ringstrasse following the premiere of his production of Shakespeare's *Midsummer Night's Dream* at the Theater an der Wien. Many secessionists were present at this premiere. When the party finished, the group moved to a café next to the Stephansplatz, and it was here that Beer-Hofmann discussed with Hoffmann the idea of building his house. The architect immediately drew a first sketch for the villa on the marble tabletop. A year later, the construction was finished.[203] Perhaps it was also Bahr who encouraged them to cooperate on the project.[204] Among the prominent guests in the house were Shalom Asch, Peter Altenberg, Lou Andreas-Salomé, Hermann Bahr, Otto Brahm, Martin Buber, Richard Dehmel, Hugo von Hofmannsthal, Arthur Schnitzler, Thomas Mann, Fritz Mauthner, Emil Orlik, Max Reinhardt, Rainer Maria Rilke, Alfred Roller, Oskar Strnad, Richard Strauss, Jakob Wassermann, Franz Werfel, Berta Zuckerkandl, and Stefan and Arnold Zweig.[205]

The German studies scholar Abigail Gillman further develops the idea that Beer-Hofmann's aesthetics were related to Baudelaire's *flâneur*, while arguing that his dandyish inspiration and ideal labyrinth placement were Orientalist fantasies drawn from *One Thousand and One Nights*, the favorite book of the protagonist in *Der Tod Georgs*.[206] Yet Beer-Hofmann's fantasy of the Orient can also be understood as a critique of assimilation as well as of the secessionist style. Gillman quotes Beer-Hofmann's statement: "Their lives moved in winding and labyrinthine ways, peculiarly connected with other lives."[207] Beer-Hofmann came to terms with, or tamed, this labyrinth metaphor by projecting it as a decorative motif in the white coffers on the light beige façade of his modernist house and above the striped white wood paneling of its main hall. He and Hoffmann reworked the image of the labyrinth into its alternative, emphasizing instead a central square with five coffered frames around it, decorating the front and back façades of the house; similarly, a double coffered frame around a central square decorated the upper part of the public hall's wood paneling.[208] This presented the symbolic role of the house as a gathering place. The coffered decoration—also seen earlier in the wood paneling in the central room of the Villa Spitzer in the Hohe Warte—was identified as a classicist modernist element.[209] The coffered ceiling in the cupola of the Roman Pantheon (AD 126) would have been recognized as the primary classical source. It also had concrete ancient Egyptian sources, such as the sacral and royal furniture seen in the base of a pedestal in the Temple of Seti (Nineteenth Dynasty, circa 1300 BC) and in the cabinet of Psammetich II (Twenty-Sixth Dynasty, 590 BC) in the Kunsthistorisches Museum in Vienna.[210] Beer-Hofmann's critique of Orientalist aesthetics—namely, the artificiality of fake gold ornament on a white praying curtain[211]—was perhaps directed against the golden decoration on the Secession House's white walls. Hoffmann's choice to adapt an ancient geometric decorative motif was in accordance with Beer-Hofmann's reclamation of his Jewish identification (through the historicist link and the emancipation from exotic Orientalism of the secessionist group), supporting a stylistic transition from secessionism to classicist modernism.

In August 1906, two months before his family entered their new modernist house, Beer-Hofmann noted in a letter to his wife, Paula, his rejection of the ideal of the Gesamtkunstwerk. He did not like the performance of Richard Wagner's music, rejecting perhaps the artistic pretense in the Gesamtkunstwerk that he had witnessed in Bayreuth. He dismissed it as an artistic hypocrisy.[212] Beer-Hofmann did not necessarily distance himself from German romanticism, but he preferred to highlight the Jewish narrative. In 1895, he had married Paula Lissy. He was then twenty-nine, and she was sixteen. He was a loyal family man who regarded his wife and children as his valuable possessions. To describe his relationship to his children, he chose the metaphor of a large hall in a castle or a garden that stands empty, awaiting his return.[213] Beer-Hofmann traveled often enough to enjoy the reclamation of his possessions. He experienced his many returns to his family and to his house as a return to his Jerusalem. Interestingly, this way of describing his sense of attachment and return to a home, which echoed the return of the Jews, was visualized in the architectural design of his house—Beer-Hofmann claimed in a symbolic manner also his possession of Jerusalem.

Hoffmann designed the grand hall of the house, constructed as a middle level between basement and parterre (a raised ground floor), with a gallery. The gallery was decorated with four arches on the side leading to the

FIGURE 26a. *Beer-Hofmann villa, grand hall, interior facing arched gallery, 1905. Photo:* © *MAK–Austrian Museum of Applied Arts / Contemporary Art.* WWF103-143-1.

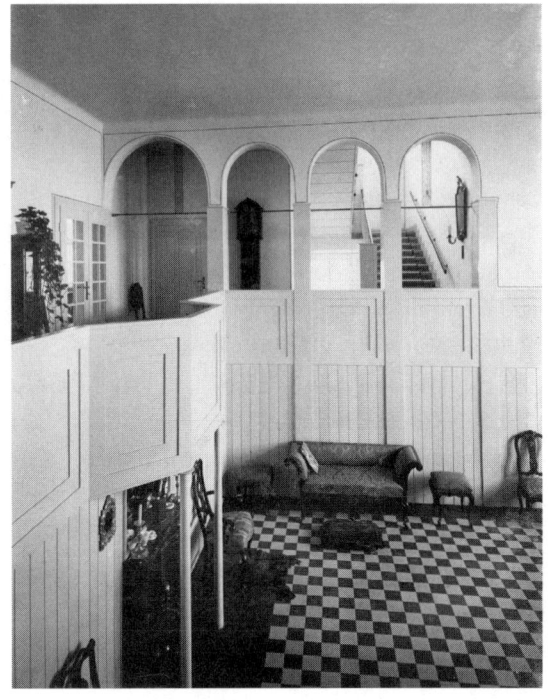

staircase. The design of the arches imitated a historicist model but also suggested the division in a synagogue—as seen, for example, in the Leopoldstadt Temple—that separated the men's place on the ground floor from the women's gallery (through which they were allowed to watch the happenings below).[214] The Star of David on the arched window above the entrance confirmed the house as a new culture center, in competition with the Secession House, though with a dramatic Jewish identification. Seen from the inside, the Star of David was meant to replace the ancient winged allegory of art in the round window of the Secession House's interior hall.[215] Beer-Hofmann's house represented his and his guests' Jerusalem in the Diaspora. The gallery arches might have been inspired by a drawing or photo of the Golden Gate in the Temple of Solomon in Jerusalem.[216] Yet Beer-Hofmann played with the associations and references. If the upper gallery imitated the experience of women in a synagogue looking down through the rails at the bimah and the holy shrine, Beer-Hofmann reconfigured expectations by arranging a descent through the arched openings to the main public hall that would lead one to look directly at not a Torah shrine, but a bourgeois shrine—a modernist glass showcase displaying porcelain plates and souvenirs he had collected on his trips (Fig. 26a–b).

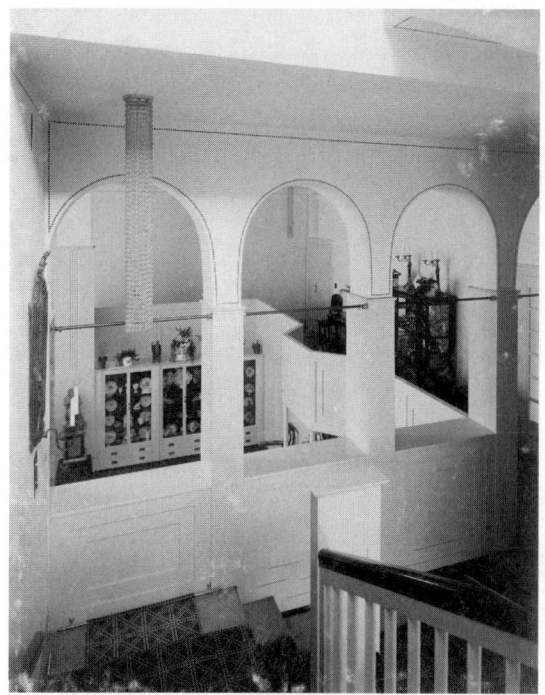

FIGURE 26b. *Beer-Hofmann villa, interior gallery facing glass cabinet in grand hall, 1905. Photo: © MAK–Austrian Museum of Applied Arts / Contemporary Art.* WWF 103-148-1.

The Beer-Hofmann house included a basement, parterre, first floor, and an attic covered with sheet metal. As noted above, it was the most striking modern house on the Hasenauerstrasse.[217] Yet the furniture inside was part of the author's inheritance.[218] The grand hall provided access into the rooms positioned along the external walls.[219] The relation between the modernist hall and the rooms further emphasized its role as a central gathering space. The center of the hall was empty, and the furniture was positioned along the wooden paneled walls to allow for free circulation. The floor was of white-and-black-checkered tiles. The main light came from large windows on the east side of the house. There was a creative tension between the simple geometric, checkered floor, the striped and coffered white paneling, the simple modern white glass cabinet in the corner next to the modernist framed fireplace, and the historicist furniture. The furniture included winged armchairs next to the staircase, two Chippendale chairs flanking the fireplace, and the Queen Anne–style chair next to the early-nineteenth-century Sheraton-style sofa, all of which demonstrated that Beer-Hofmann "saw nothing without ancestors," as he put it in *Der Tod Georgs*.[220] Beer-Hofmann and his guests experienced a new authentic drama, crossing frontiers and inhabiting the dialectic of past memories amid present social drama, between the personal conversation at the fringes and the collective happening at the center, between the wish to retreat and the wish to openly display oneself. A guest entering the house would pass the inner vestibule doors, enter the grand hall, and either pause to admire the hall's arrangement or continue up a short staircase to the blue salon, the music room. This music room received plenty of light through windows and, like the studio, opened to the terrace, where two staircases led down to the garden; one could find seating in the garden between these staircases.

In the public rooms on the parterre, Beer-Hofmann established his authority in relation to his designer Hoffmann through choosing wood parquet, Oriental carpets, and Biedermeier furniture. Yet he allowed Hoffmann to modernize a wood Biedermeier side table in the music room by staining it black. This use of a modern setting and modern color scheme helped Beer-Hofmann revitalize his own past (as in his play on the colors white and black, which he associated with marriage or death in *Pierrot Hypnotiseur*, mentioned above). He revitalized his inherited and purchased furniture—with which he constructed a historical narrative—by granting it a new artistic appearance. The Biedermeier furniture would be claimed for classicist eternity when the wooden side table was stained black and the music room chairs were upholstered with blue silk damask.[221] Beer-Hofmann displayed his mastery of stylizing his Jewish European past. The choice of black and blue also transformed his furniture into an artistic vision—a dreamed past: "He did not know any house that resembled the one of which he dreamed; and what was the estate where [he] spent spring at his grandparents? He did not even know his grandparents! And he himself was another person; or perhaps he knew himself better in the dream than in his waking state?"[222]

In the case of the inherited furniture, he needed his imagination and Hoffmann's cooperation to further stylize his Jewish identification. Beer-Hofmann's dandyism and self-invention can also be seen through Simmel's description of social play, or coquetry: "The social game has a deeper double meaning—that it is played not only *in* a society as its outward bearer but that *with* the society actually 'society' is played. Further, in the sociology of the sexes, eroticism has elaborated a form of play: coquetry, which finds in sociability its lightest, most playful, and yet its widest realization."[223] Beer-Hofmann the dandy wanted to prolong the time a guest would spend reflecting on the question of whether to leave or stay at the patron's home. This desire to toy with the guests' desire would be similar to the flirtation between a man and woman, where the game of consent or denial (satisfying or denying) is perpetuated.[224] Like Waerndorfer, Beer-Hofmann played

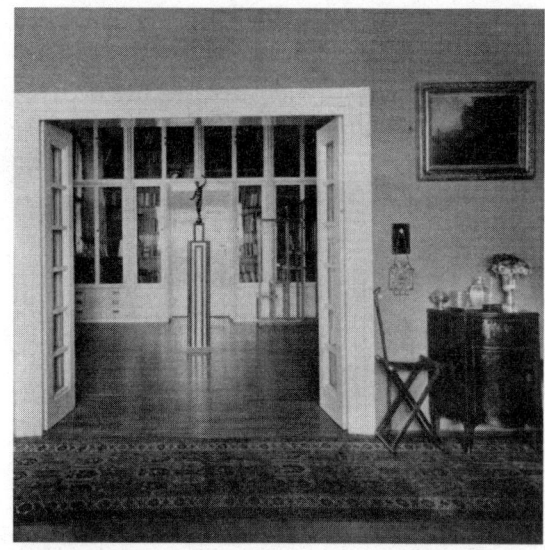

FIGURE 27. *Beer-Hofmann Villa, view of the library from the studio. Photo reproduced in Otto Schultze-Elberfeld, "Unsere Kunst, die Kunst unserer Zeit,"* Deutsche Kunst und Dekoration 22, no. 8 (1908): 75–85. Photo: © MAK–Austrian Museum of Applied Arts / Contemporary Art. BI 11983-1908-77.

both the role of the man watching and the woman tempting—or the woman watching from the gallery and the man acting in the main hall. This relationship was also reflected in the staging of his chosen artworks—allowing his guests to be on the verge of what they wanted to achieve while they allowed Beer-Hofmann to remain concentrated on himself. It was almost like a declaration that he was not seriously involved, as suggested by Simmel: "And this freedom from all the weight of firm content and residual reality gives coquetry that character of vacillation, of distance, of the ideal, which allows one to speak with some right of the 'art'—not of the 'arts' of coquetry."[225] Beer-Hofmann needed this flirtation strategy to prevent his constructed Jewish identification from being dirtied or challenged by his guests' possible prejudice or skepticism against it.

Beer-Hofmann chose quite different central sculptural attractions in his public rooms from what Friedrich Victor Spitzer had chosen in his collaboration with Hoffmann. In early photographs of Spitzer's Olbrich interiors, a striking bronze female figure, the *Water Carrier* (current location unknown), is seen in the music and dining rooms.[226] Later, she reappears at the corner of Spitzer's library, designed by Hoffmann.[227] Beer-Hofmann chose the figure of Fortuna (Fate; current location unknown) instead.[228] She stands on a regal modernist pedestal at the center of the author's library, with one leg on a ball and the second in mid-air (Fig. 27).[229] Hoffmann gave the Fortuna a white pedestal decorated with thin black frames to correspond to the library's book cabinet, which was enclosed with white-framed glass. Reflective of their different aesthetic spirits, Spitzer's servant woman had given way to Beer-Hofmann's naked allegory of fate. Walking through the library, one reached the dining room; both it and the studio could also be reached through the gallery passage overlooking the central hall. In the photograph showing the view from Beer-Hofmann's studio toward the library, where the sculpture of Fortuna is on its high pedestal, a silver Torah shield hangs next to the open doorway above a stool, positioned next to a cabinet beneath a landscape painting. An antique-looking walking cane leans against the frame of the doorway. While the walking cane can be identified as Beer-Hofmann's dandy signature, it is remarkable how nonchalantly the Torah shield (traditionally placed on Torah scrolls as decoration and symbolic protection) is integrated into the highly cultivated setting, indicating the importance of the owner's Jewish identification. The Torah shield, along with the Star of David in the arched glass window above the entrance door, were proud demonstrations of Jewish identification.

Beer-Hofmann's Hellenistic Jewish identification was further played out in a silent theater of imagery. In the music room he displayed terra cotta busts of Plato and Homer, and in his studio he had a wooden sculpture of King David in the baroque style.[230] These would be compatible with his self-identification. However, in the large hall, to ensure a sense of a shared cultural platform with his guests, he also displayed portraits of martyrs and angels and a bronze sculpture of a Japanese tea ceremony master on a wooden pedestal.[231] In the interiors and art objects of his home, Beer-Hofmann realized what Freud identified as the role of the Jewish father—to teach his children to cross frontiers,[232] allowing them (his children and his guests) to move from enjoying the large modernist space of the hall to enjoying the intimacy of the Biedermeier furniture at the periphery of the hall, as well as prompting them to move from Jewish cultural references to Christian ones. Beer-Hofmann's expansive cultural program led him from a fixation on Jewish identification to a more nuanced dialogue between Jewish culture and Western and Eastern cultures.[233] Through flirtation as a mode of aesthetics, the Jewish patron integrated his Jewish identification with cosmopolitan Viennese modernism.

At the beginning of *Der Tod Georgs*, Beer-Hofmann criticized secessionist aesthetics, specifically the golden Orientalist lure of the Secession House, and rejected the artificial temptations of the aesthete's labyrinth. Through his patronage Beer-Hofmann was the classicist dandy who had come to replace the secessionist aesthete. In his house, Beer-Hofmann collaborated with Hoffmann to transform the labyrinth idea into a coffered white decoration. Both façade and paneling were heightened in white, which manifested the

Jewish identification Beer-Hofmann presented in *Der Tod Georgs*—the image of a woman in a white dress.[234]

Gillman describes how, on his "way back" to reclaiming his Jewish identification, Beer-Hofmann's protagonist has a vision of the woman he loved who died, remembering her as the "woman in white." Here is Beer-Hofmann's poetic description: "She appeared almost without body; only her own white portrait, rising up in foreign lines from the blossoming and the confusion of stalks of the over-loaded narcissus wallpaper."[235] The "woman in white" in Beer-Hofman's book surfaced at the same time Klimt began his series of portraits of Jewish women in white.[236] The German studies scholar Karin Inderwisch offers an insightful comparison between Beer-Hofmann's and Klimt's female portraits, concentrating on Klimt's portrait of Margaret Stonborough-Wittgenstein (1905), discussed at the end of chapter 2. Inderwisch describes the modernists' dual experiences. She considers Klimt's representation of a sitter being trapped by outer conventions, represented through the disappearance of her body, the flattening of her appearance and being framed in the ornamental (Wiener Werkstätte) setting; at the same time Klimt represents his character's reclamation of spiritual independence through the framing of her head, with her facial expression meant to reveal her thoughts.[237] This dual experience is also demonstrated in Beer-Hofmann's metaphor of the woman in white. The disappearance of her body in a white dress allowed her spiritual freedom. Beer-Hofmann's romantic memory of the woman in a white dress, inviting him to rediscover his Jewish roots, may also have been inspired by the song mentioned in relation to Waerndorfer's presentation of the seven princesses in his music room, which welcomed the arrival of the sabbath: "Let's go my friend toward the bride, and receive the presence of Shabbat." Beer-Hofmann's literary metaphor of the woman in white, like the image of the seventh princess in Waerndorfer's salon, uses the experience of welcoming the Sabbath as a creative Jewish license to conceive modernism.

Sensuality played a role in Beer-Hofmann's Jewish identification as much as tamed, purified, and abstracted images did, as in the memory of a specter of a woman in a white dress. The white dress reflected in artworks also inspired the process of abstraction in architecture and design and in that sense became the symbol of the revolution of Viennese modernism.

In turn, Beer-Hofmann's vision of a woman in white emancipating herself from the decorative wallpaper could have served as an inspiration to the architect Adolf Loos, who is discussed next. In her interpretation of Loos's interior design for his and his wife's bedroom, the art historian Irene Nierhaus identifies Loos's bride's dress as a nonfigurative white dress (the white negated the bride's body form, specifically since the "dress" was both for her and for him). Furthermore, Nierhaus suggests that Loos's choice to reveal the female body underlying architectural structure, as he would do in baring the naked upper façade of the Goldman & Salatsch House across from the Hofburg at the center of Vienna, was an abstract interpretation of the traditional female dress; the abstraction having led to its absence.[238] Hevesi praised the lyrical tone of Loos's "snow white bedroom" design.[239] Beer-Hofmann's modernist vision of the woman in white replaced the Secession House's image of the woman in white, bejeweled with golden ornaments, and subverted prejudice against "Slavic-Jewish sensuality" into a reclamation of Jewish spirituality. The avant-garde continued to offer solutions for bridging the duality of existence of the Jewish dandies suspended between Jewish and gentile traditions. The following chapter explores how the dandy Altenberg encouraged the architect Loos to project a foreign and sensual environment onto his American Bar to attract men to enter and explore the compact space, while the tailor Leopold Goldman supported the architect's use of the white abstracted dress or nakedness as a seductive revelation to be grafted onto his Goldman & Salatsch House.

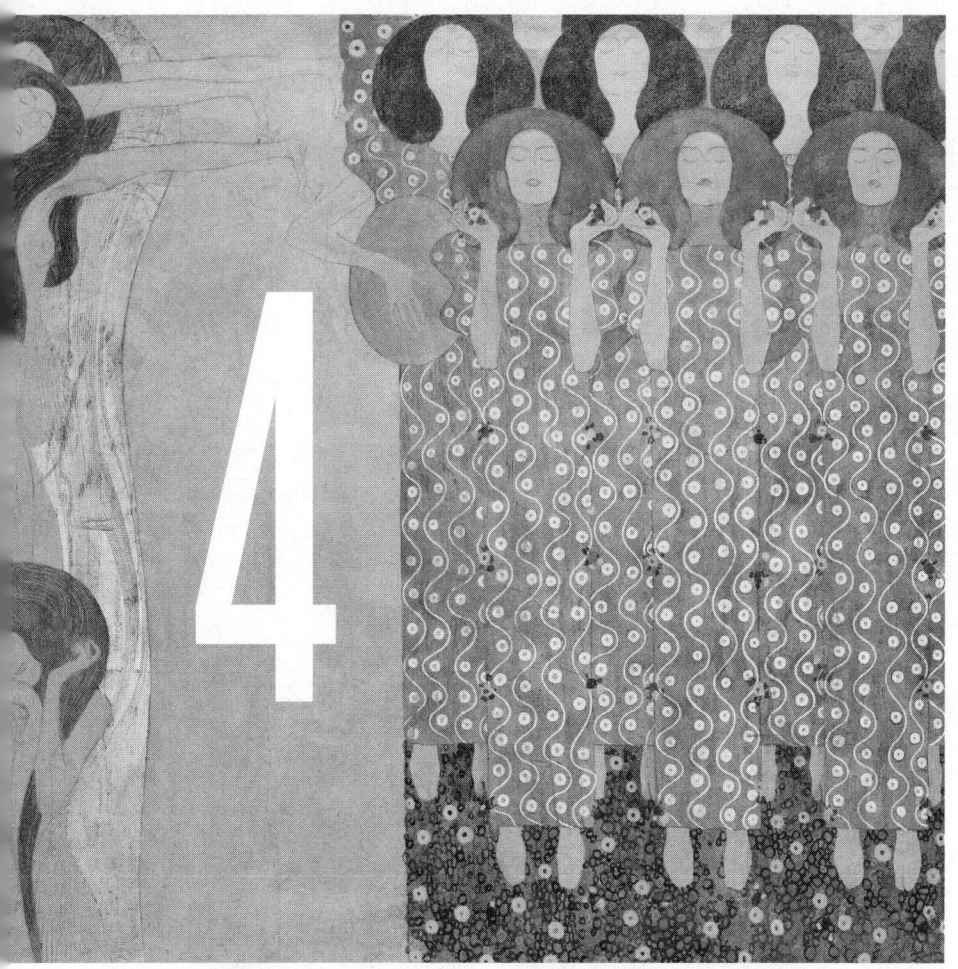

THE AVANT-GARDISTS
1908–11

*Peter Altenberg's Portrait in the
American Bar and Leopold Goldman
and the Goldman & Salatsch House*

Susan Sontag has written:

> Though I am speaking about sensibility only—and about a sensibility that, among other things, converts the serious into the frivolous—these are grave matters. Most people think of sensibility or taste as the realm of purely subjective preferences, those mysterious attractions, mainly sensual, that have not been brought under the sovereignty of reason. They *allow* that considerations of taste play a part in their reactions to people and to works of art. But this attitude is naïve. And even worse. To patronize the faculty of taste is to patronize oneself. For taste governs every free—as opposed to rote—human response. Nothing is more decisive. There is taste in people, visual taste, taste in emotion—and there is taste in acts, taste in morality. Intelligence, as well, is really a kind of taste: taste in ideas. (One of the facts to be reckoned with is that taste tends to develop very unevenly. It's rare that the same person has good visual taste and good taste in people *and* taste in ideas.)[1]

This chapter addresses how the architect Adolf Loos (1870–1933) succeeded in representing and elevating Jewish aesthetic sensibility not as a subjective preference but as a force to spur reaction in the Viennese public. It reexamines how, in opposition to the secessionists and Josef Hoffmann, Loos's modernist designs for the American Bar (1908) in the Kärntner passage and his Goldman & Salatsch House (1910–12) in Michaelerplatz allowed for a new performance of Jewish identification through conscious flirtatious acts between a performer (such as a tailor or guest of honor) and a client (or other guests and friends). The poet Peter Altenberg (1859–1919), whose portrait decorated the walls of the American Bar (Gustav Jagerspacher, portrait of Peter Altenberg, 1909, Wien Museum, Vienna), and the tailor Leopold Goldman (1875–1942), who cooperated with Loos in the design of his grand fashion house, helped Loos visualize flirtatious dramas in his architecture, provoking reflection not only on Jewish integration literally at the center of Viennese society but also on the relevance of taste to social interactions. Altenberg's and Goldman's subversion or use of prejudice against Jews would demonstrate cultural leadership in the battle for social visibility (Altenberg's bohemian brand and Goldman's tailoring brand) and serve as a creative stimulus for cultural progression. Altenberg's caricature at the American Bar was supposed to attract the poet's admirers and curious onlookers to the luxuriously furnished drinking establishment. A copy of the portrait hanging there today serves as testament to Vienna's fin de siècle heritage. Loos's naked design of the upper part of the Goldman & Salatsch House encouraged viewers to enter the house and get dressed in the tailor Goldman's elite fashion establishment. Each man's central role redefined the relationship between style and seduction; in the bar's exposé and in the fashion house's dressing, Altenberg and Goldman coproduced a new Viennese style. At first glance it appears the avant-gardists rejected immediate references to the Diaspora and its preference for an architecture that erased differences between Jewish and gentile culture, idealizing culture as a tabula rasa. Yet a second look at the new avant-garde style reveals it as a continuation of the modernist tendency toward abstraction and shows that it even returned to a concrete citation of historicism's classicist heritage, thus embracing a new ideal of making cultural difference a question of free choice.

Cultural Revolution: Jewish Emancipation, Modern Dress, and Vienna's Avant-Garde

In July 1898, Adolf Loos published an essay in *Ver Sacrum* titled "Die potemkinsche Stadt" (Potemkin City), supporting the secessionists' critique of the historicist style of the Ringstrasse and rejecting "pretentious" historicist fashion as false: "After all, should we be ashamed to live in a rental apartment in a building with many others who are our social equals? Should we be ashamed of the fact that there are materials that are too expensive for us to build with? Should we be ashamed to be nineteenth-century men and not men who want to live in a building whose architectural style belongs to an earlier age? If we ceased to be ashamed, you would see how quickly we would acquire an architecture suited to our own times."[2]

As a critical thinker who was aware that the choice of appropriate dress was crucial for Jewish integration into Viennese society,[3] Loos may have been criticizing the pretense of the historicist style for its failure to promote Jewish integration. In the October 1904 issue of *Ost und West* (East and West), a monthly journal for modern Judaism, the author Leo Winz explained the failure of assimilated Jews to attract the acceptance of the Christian majority.

Winz wrote that the Jews' new dress was a collection of foreign rags chosen at random to cover the shreds of their old clothes, and the more eager they were to get rid of the old dress, the more they appeared colorful and conspicuous.[4] It would be a big mistake, he wrote, to believe that this process of self-destruction, even if completely realized, would quicken or promote the process of assimilation. The opposite was true. Self-destruction, he argued, would provoke disgust in the simplest man, who would distance himself instinctively. Nevertheless, Winz acknowledged, "we have seen that the first condition for the social and physiological assimilation process is the 'appetizing' looks of the object who wants to assimilate."[5]

Winz's critical description of assimilation introduced his main message: that only if Jews fought assimilation and presented an independent and self-evident identity would the Christian majority accept the Jewish integration process. Loos may have thought himself to be (as Winz describes the smart man who witnesses the process of assimilation) "a thinking and thorough onlooker,"[6] but his observations yielded conclusions somewhat different from those of Winz. Loos offered his clients the possibility of presenting an independent and self-evident identity but supported the process of integration. He used his friend and colleague Kraus's critical rhetoric on proper Jewish acculturation for his own cultural agenda: fashioning the European Jew as a modern man. He regarded the Jewish man in a black caftan as a witness to failed Jewish emancipation. In an unpublished text titled "Jewish Emancipation," Loos reacted both to the 1898 performance of Theodor Herzl's play *Das neue Ghetto* (The new ghetto), about a young Jew's failed integration attempts, and to the secessionist Joseph Maria Olbrich's success at the Exposition Universelle in Paris in 1900. Loos criticized Jews for creating a new ghetto for themselves by comparing their choice of secessionist interiors in their homes to the habit of wearing the black caftan in public:

> Any friend of Jewish emancipation, any enemy of the ghetto, meaning any friend of our culture, must suffer when he sees how our Jews are creating a new ghetto. Jews who have given up the caftan a long time ago are happy now to take it up again. Since the secessionist interior furnishings are nothing but disguised caftans, like the names Gold and Silberstein, like the names Moritz and Siegfried.
>
> *One recognizes them through it.*
>
> For sure, there are also Aryan Moritzs and Siegfrieds, as there are Aryan owners of Hoffmann's interiors.
>
> They are the exceptions.

One recognizes them through it.

One should not misunderstand me.

I have nothing against a strong, energetic emphasis on Judaism. I will not oppose the man in the caftan. I respect the man who calls himself Moses or Samuel.

But I feel sorry for the man who wants to overcome the caftan and the Samuel and falls into an Olbrich or a Siegfried again.

Then we would again be in the old spot. *In the new ghetto.* And the poor people have believed that they could emancipate themselves from Judaism through an Olbrich or a Siegfried. Just eating ham is not enough.[7]

For Loos, the problematic of Jewish emancipation called for the creation of a new avant-garde style.[8] He may have agreed with Beer-Hofmann's key vision of a woman in white as a proper way of constructing modern Jewish self-identification, yet I argue that it was through his cooperation with two completely different characters, the bohemian poet Altenberg and the gentleman tailor Goldman, that Loos arrived at the new Viennese avant-garde style.

Possibly rephrasing Loos's critique of Olbrich's secessionist designs, but not noting it directly, the art historian Claude Cernuschi suggests: "For the anti-Semites, then, the ornamental and decorative aspects of the Secessionist style only reinforced the worst of stereotypes about affluent Jews: namely, that their cultural prestige was purchased by wealth rather than merit. In this sense, patronage of the Secession boomeranged: just as the Jews who sought to escape their Judaism by means of cultural achievement joined a predominantly Jewish rather than Gentile community, so did Jews who patronized the Secession make themselves more—rather than less—conspicuous Jews."[9] Far from supporting antisemitic ideology, Loos wanted to offer his Jewish clients a manifest design to allow them to choose between opting in and opting out of Viennese society. Moreover, he cleverly used tactics of flirtation, reminiscent of and yet different from those the secessionist Olbrich employed for Wittgenstein and Spitzer, and the modernist Hoffmann used for Waerndorfer and Beer-Hofmann, to offer a new Jewish acculturation ideal. How did Loos subvert secessionist rhetoric to advance a new avant-garde movement, and what key roles did Altenberg and Goldman play in his novel contribution to Viennese modernism?

In his theory of cultural production, the cultural sociologist Pierre Bourdieu differentiates between two kinds of capital. "Economic capital" refers to successful finance operations, and "symbolic capital" refers to "the degree of accumulated prestige, celebrity, consecration or honour and is founded on dialectic of knowledge (connaissance) and recognition (reconnaissance)."[10] He further argues that in the field of cultural production, artistic authority is established through the expression of a lack of interest in immediate monetary profit.[11] Yet cultural revolutions are always only partial: "This is why the strategy *par excellence* is the 'return to the sources' which is the basis of all heretical subversion and all aesthetic revolutions, because it enables the insurgents to turn against the establishment the arms which they use to justify their domination, in particular asceticism, daring, ardour, rigour and disinterestedness. The strategy of beating the dominant groups at their own game by demanding that they respect the fundamental law of the field, a denial of the 'economy,' can only work if it manifests exemplary sincerity in its own denial."[12]

Bourdieu's concluding argument concerns the denial of economic profit as part of avant-garde operative tactics. Both Altenberg and Goldman helped Loos achieve this "heretical subversion" of the secessionist movement, and the two architectural structures associated with them are evidence of symbolic capital's overriding economic capital. Loos's design of the American Bar was associated with Altenberg's fame (for asceticism, daring, devotion, and disinterestedness) in the art scene, and Loos's design of the Goldman & Salatsch House was associated with the tailor Goldman's ideological professionalism (above profit). Thus, the two places were the bastions of the new Viennese avant-garde.

Loos, Altenberg, and Goldman were the new avant-gardists in Vienna, supplanting the old avant-gardists of the secessionist movement. The 1898 founding of the Vienna Secession had been enthusiastically received by journalists, three of whom in particular—Hermann Bahr, Berta Zuckerkandl, and Ludwig Hevesi—secured the secessionists' political breakthrough in Viennese cultural production.[13] These critics formulated secessionist aims as a militant avant-garde program. For Hevesi, as noted in chapter 2, even the idea of a wall-painting having a "long nose" was provocative enough to demonstrate the movement's avant-garde character—since viewers were not used to it. In early 1897, Zuckerkandl had presented a new aggressive rhetoric for the applied arts in Vienna. In her article "Kunstindustrie" (Art industry) in the journal *Die Zeit*, she criticized the Christmas Industrial Exhibition, arguing in support of Austrian and artistic design but against industrial manufacture.[14] In contrast, Bahr was convinced that the moral regeneration of "the people" was possible only through the work of an aesthetically educated elite.[15] In his article introducing the Vienna Secession in the first issue of *Ver Sacrum*, he discussed the principle question behind its foundation: "Do we want business or art?"[16] While Zuckerkandl referred to the tension between industrial manufacture and artistic creation, Bahr promoted an avant-garde rhetoric opposed to capitalist profit. Kraus and Loos would later use similar rhetoric against cultural producers making profit.[17] Loos supposedly refused to show his works at the Vienna Secession until "the merchants are chased from the temple."[18] He used the antisemitic innuendo of the Christian narrative in which Christ threw the "merchants" out of the temple not necessarily to attach a Christian identification to his cultural agenda but rather to break from the secessionists and enter the battle for visibility and leadership in the Viennese avant-garde. Condemning the production of art for monetary profit had served the secessionists in their separation from the Künstlerhaus, and later it legitimized Loos's and his followers' critique against the secessionists and Hoffmann's architectural school. Following Bourdieu's theory of cultural revolution it is interesting to consider how Loos's coproducers and patrons —specifically Altenberg and Goldman—envisioned a return to their sources to establish a new avant-garde style.

The Unacculturated Jew and His Naked Sister, the Cultured Dress of Café Museum

Altenberg may have felt the conflict between the aesthetics of Catholicism and the ethics of Judaism in two postcards he possessed: Catholicism is represented by a photograph of the Cathedral in Maria-Zell covered with snow, and Judaism by a postcard of a painting by the Polish Jewish painter Wilhelm Wachtel titled *Friday Evening*. The second postcard depicts an elegantly dressed man holding his walking stick and top hat behind his back, standing outside a small house. Through a window he watches a woman cover her face as she blesses the Sabbath candles.[19] The cold of the church covered with snow in one postcard and the warmth of an interior lit by the Friday candles in the other may or may not have expressed Altenberg's romantic perception of Jewish nostalgia. The elegantly dressed man, standing in silent humility, represented the ideal of an acculturated Jew who chooses to remain outside the Jewish home; however, Altenberg deliberately defied this ideal in fashioning his revolutionary Jewish self-identification.

In many ways the concerns reflected in architecture and design echoed those portrayed in well-known literary examples. In 1908, the author and playwright Arthur Schnitzler confessed through Heinrich Bermann, the protagonist of his novel *The Road into the Open*, the embarrassment of being identified as a "Jew." Bermann describes his shame in witnessing a Jew ridiculing himself as akin to the humiliation that would accompany the sight of a sister undressing: "From our youth on we have been driven to see precisely Jewish characteristics as especially comical or repulsive characteristics, which is not the case with regard to the equally comical and repulsive characteristics of the others. And I won't conceal the fact that when a Jew behaves crudely or comically in my presence, sometimes such a painful feeling seizes me that I want to die, to sink into the earth. It's a sort of shame that is perhaps related somehow to the shame a brother feels if his sister undresses in front of him."[20]

Like the Jew Bermann describes, Altenberg often ridiculed himself publicly in cafés. Schnitzler was a prominent member of the early coffeehouse literary networks, and he could have had Altenberg in mind when he referred to the Jew behaving crudely in his presence. Vienna's cafés served as a club in which membership was bought for the price of a cheap cup of coffee.[21] The literature scholar Harold Segal described the Vienna coffeehouse as a miniature stage, with its leading players the artists and intellectuals: "Like the Cabaret, the fin-de-siècle literary coffeehouse was a miniature stage, but in the Viennese context some of its leading players were artists and intellectuals of Jewish background to whom verbal and mental showmanship could be aphrodisiacal."[22] Steven Beller further developed Segal's thesis in a lecture titled "The Jew Belongs in the Coffeehouse," which opened a conference accompanying the 2008 exhibition *Vienna Café 1900*. Beller identified the Viennese café as a "Jewish space" within the city and compared the café relationship to the city with the Jews' relationship to the Viennese, noting that coffee houses were at the heart of the city but outside its formal institutions, just as the Jews were prominent in the city (and were crucial in cultural productions) but were regarded as outsiders.[23] The art historian Tag Gronberg further notes the role newspapers played in Viennese coffeehouses in relation to identity performance: the printed word mirrored Austrian identification, and reading newspapers in the morning offered a new secular ritual that replaced religious prayers, so the "mass ceremony" of reading the newspaper helped fashion "a secular, historically clocked imagined community."[24] Gronberg further shows how the idea of a coffeehouse served as "a means of articulating selfhood and professional identity."[25] Through their lifestyles, Loos and Altenberg represented the bohemian idea of living on society's edge. Following Beller's comparison between the outsider position of the coffeehouse and the outsider position of the Jew in Viennese society, we can similarly consider how Loos's modern design and Altenberg's public performance and literary art transgressed ethnic, social, and cultural boundaries. Both Loos and Altenberg transgressed, and in some ways imitated one another, in the way they defined a new art of sociability.²⁶ For Loos and Altenberg sociability began with fashion. The two were against commercially motivated changes in fashion, yet they had strong notions of fashion's impact. While the architect Loos promoted the ideal of a man's suit, the poet Altenberg understood clothing as a "fine and artistic skin," as did the artist-designers at the time who supported "individual dress," such as Hoffmann.²⁷

Altenberg's ideal mixed simplicity and naturalness in opposition to artificiality. For him, this aesthetic ideal meant bodily hygiene and dietary and dress reform. It was not a lucrative or superficially fashionable pursuit, but one aimed at achieving an ideal of "spiritual nobility."²⁸ The white glove and white hand in his poetry evoked the same virginal effect—and were part of the programmatic connection between aesthetic and diet, linking physiology and spiritual principle, which offered a positive aesthetic of decadence²⁹ (idealizing "spiritual nobility" and offering aesthetic decadence can be considered as manifestations of artistic self-indulgent behavior). Describing the dress of young girls in his poems, Altenberg highlighted their sensuality and canonized them as a new fashion fetish. Ultimately, however, his wish to achieve "spiritual nobility" led to a denouncement of the body. Both Altenberg and Klimt focused on the sensuality of dress fabric, wallpaper, and furniture, sublimating the figure to interior settings and thereby achieving the dematerialization of the body.³⁰ This weaving the figure with the interior setting was Altenberg's art of self-stylization as a poet. He would further self-stylize himself in the décor of his private rooms in various hotels in his adult life.

Born Richard Engländer, he adopted the name Altenberg from the small Austrian town on the Danube. Peter was the nickname of a girl he knew and liked who was harassed by her brothers and forced to play the role of their servant boy. The fact that he adopted a boy's name given to a girl as a taunt suggests that he chose to repeat the inner experience of being taunted for supposedly belonging to another gender (instead of being taunted for belonging to another ethnicity). It has been assumed that Altenberg cultivated a feminine appearance and feminine handwriting—indeed, wearing a cape, sandals, and broad-brimmed hat challenged the norms of manly elegance at the time—yet he did not attempt to outright mimic women's fashion. He did not fit the bourgeois expectations of his father or even his colleagues, and he dropped out of his law and medicine studies to adopt a bohemian way of life. His bohemian style was demonstrated by his challenging standards of modesty by stating, for example, that he did not own underwear: "And if he was somewhat pretentious in acting the poet, who sees and experiences things differently from other people, it was perhaps his defense against a public which ridiculed him. For he was an unusual, somewhat ridiculous figure: bald, with an enormous moustache, always untidily dressed, and too poor to appear dignified. This is how he describes himself shortly before his death: 'On the 9th March, 1919, I shall be 60 years old. I go without a hat, with bare feet, which I never dry after a foot bath, in wooden sandals; I own neither underclothes nor night shirts.'"[31]

Bertschik describes Altenberg's bohemian dress as clownlike and a cross between a dandy and a lifestyle reformer (possibly adapting ideas from the back-to-nature social movement at the time, called *Lebensreform*). She further identifies his critique of fashion as a mixture of social rebellion against the rich, yet she notes that at the same time he used dress and accessories to seduce.[32] Altenberg drew attention to himself with an approach to fashion that was still a mixture of dandy and nature apostle. He wore a checked English suit, a sporty leather belt, a pince-nez tied to an overly wide string, and exposed his naked feet in sandals, wore a walrus moustache, and carried a club-shape walking stick. He spoke out against wearing costly jewelry, animal fur, or "disgusting expensive hats with plucked feathers from unfortunate animals." On the other hand, Bertschik notes, Altenberg poeticized himself—not only on paper—with elegant fantasy dress consisting of velvet, silk, flowing ostrich feathers, and antelope leather gloves.[33]

In 1896, after the publication of *Wie ich es sehe* (How I see it), Altenberg became a well-known personality in the Viennese art scene.[34] The interior of his small room at the Hotel Graben in the Dorotheerstrasse, where he lived during the last years of his life, was arranged as a large collage work (which can also be described as an art installation) of framed, inscribed photographs and postcards carefully hung on the walls. Altenberg's lifestyle, represented in his room, has been regarded as a "critique of, and resistance to, bourgeois society and culture."[35] His ideal model for identification was the "child-woman." Gronberg notes: "Altenberg presented himself not only as the friend and protector of childish femininity, but also as its masculine equivalent: naively innocent, receptive, capable of unerotic love—the male artist reverted to a pre-lapsarian, pre-Oedipal state."[36] Gronberg further offers interesting conclusions based on a comparison between the interiors of Altenberg's hotel room and the studio of the gentile artist Carl Moll, as depicted in his *Self-Portrait in the Studio* (circa 1906), which shows Minne's *Kneeling Boy*. The interiors served as artistic self-representation: "In advocating a different concept of synthesis between art and life, both interiors performed the role of artistic manifesto." The fetishlike presence of "youth" (Minne's *Kneeling Boy* and Altenberg's photographs of young girls) symbolized the interiors' utopian character.[37]

Altenberg further grafted a postmodern virtual socializing network onto his interior. He created his own type of Facebook world in his room to rehearse, master, and demonstrate his art of sociability with women—specifically young girls—and to eternalize his act of flirtation as a failed gesture of taking possession. In his first room in his brother's apartment, which he occupied from 1901 to 1904, he placed a photograph of Richard Wagner next to his bed. He positioned it between two women—one framed photograph of an elegantly dressed woman just above his raised head, and a second positioned next to Wagner, to the side of the bed.[38] In a brief text in his short-lived journal *Die Kunst* (1903), Altenberg, who described himself as an architect of the interior, noted the six faces he hung on a Japanese doormat: Wagner, Bismarck, Tolstoy, Annie Kalmar, Marie Renard, and a "noble dead eighteen-year-old young woman."[39] The last image of the dead young girl can be related to the dead virgin, the seventh princess in Waerndorfer's music salon, and to the image of Paul's dead ex-girlfriend dressed in white in Beer-Hofmann's *Der Tod Georgs*, suggesting the relevance of the visual metaphor in the contemporary network. The experience of mourning was closely associated with aesthetic communication and desire.[40] In his room in the Hotel London, where he stayed from 1904 to 1910, Altenberg positioned at the corner of his bed a collagelike arrangement of postcards and photographs of young women's faces together with drawings and photos of himself (Fig. 28) and a photo of an Ashanti woman with exposed breasts.[41] Here the young women served a similar purpose as the Minne sculpture placed in front of the mirror in Waerndorfer's studio: they were an artistic attempt to exchange and unite Altenberg's physical reflection with the image of his ideal. In his room in the Hotel Graben, where he stayed between 1913 and 1919, Altenberg arranged a collage of portraits of himself above his writing desk—five drawings and caricatures and a photo of himself—together with photographs of beautiful young women—as a more critical meeting of self and ideal.[42] In the corner of the room by the bed, next to his head, was a Christ on the cross, a photo of the dancer Grete Wiesenthal, an unidentified drawing, and two photographs—and a photograph of Richard Wagner (dated 1917/19).[43] How did Altenberg's orchestration of a postmodernist collage—a Gesamtkunstwerk or Facebook-style identity—or, essentially, his art of sociability projected onto his interiors, express his avant-gardist reclamation of his body and his achievement of Jewish emancipation? The positioning of the crucified Christ next to the photo of Wiesenthal, who performed at the Cabaret Fledermaus,

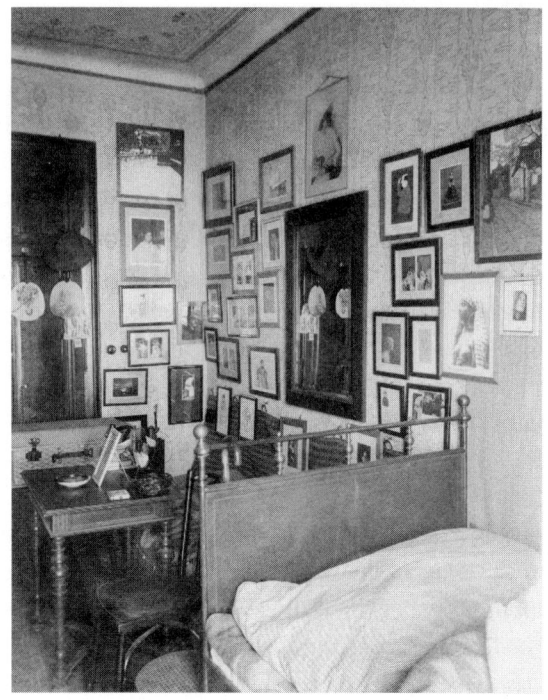

FIGURE 28. *Unsigned photograph of Peter Altenberg's room in the Hotel London, c. 1904–10. Wien Museum, Vienna. Inv. no. 94.832.*

is revealing inasmuch as Christ the man was forced to relinquish his body (and his sexuality) and Wiesenthal the woman enjoyed a public reclamation of hers.

Altenberg represented cultural difference and also made a claim integral to Viennese modernism, that of reclaiming the (Jewish male) body. Moreover, as seen in the reading of Engländer-Altenberg episode in Beer-Hofmann's salon discussed in a previous chapter, the poet also offered stimulus for flirtatious fantasies. As Schnitzler compared the shame of seeing another Jew ridiculing himself with a man's shame at seeing his sister's nudity, it seems that the fantasy of Jews being stripped of their clothes (to challenge their membership in Western culture) inspired Altenberg to fixate on the eroticism of the nude young girl. Altenberg's postcards of half-naked girls would replace the analogy of Schnitzler's naked sister—except that Altenberg championed this kind of dangerous revelation and rejected the acculturation mode that would cringe at the removal of clothes.[44]

For his part, Loos identified clothing—namely, proper suits—with the claim of professional and artistic authority. As a young man in his late twenties, Loos, who had studied architecture but did not complete his studies and earn a degree, wrote an article titled "Die Herrenmode" (Men's fashion), which was published in the *Neue Freie Presse* in May 1898: "Somewhere an American philosopher says, 'A young man can count himself rich if he has a brain in his head and a decent suit in his wardrobe.' That is a philosopher who knows the world. He knows people. What use is a brain if one doesn't have the decent clothes to set it off?"[45]

In 1893, Loos decided to embark on a journey to America.[46] Little is known about his stay in America but, presumably, his main motivation was to visit the Chicago World's Fair. While in America, he did not work as an architect but found employment at various short-term jobs, such as dishwasher and journalist.[47] Yet his journey made an irrevocable impression on him. In mid-1896, he returned to Vienna with a new sense of pride and a fresh perspective on the culture of everyday life. In his tribute to Loos in Kraus's *Die Fackel* (1909), Robert Scheu identified Loos as representing "the cosmopolitan" in Vienna.[48]

In his 1907 article on Loos, Hevesi compared Loos's interiors to his tailored suits, claiming that both represented geometric elegance.[49] Yet Loos's definition of the ethics of men's fashion in "Die Herrenmode" and in "Die Kleidung" (Clothing), published in *Das Andere* in 1903, was borrowed from others. In the opening passage of "Die Herrenmode," he argued that the number of citizens in a state who allowed themselves to imitate the dress of the king served as an important measure of the progress of culture.[50] Furthermore, in "Die Kleidung" he argued that the goal of men's fashion was not to draw attention to oneself in public: "To be dressed in the modern way is not to stand out at as the center of culture on a certain occasion in the BEST society."[51] Several scholars in the 1980s and 1990s compared Loos's arguments to the cultural heritage and sartorial principles of the British dandy. The architect and curator Burkhardt Rukschcio and the architect and author Roland Schachel identified Loos's fashion ideal as the legendary English dandy Beau Brummell.[52] In his article "Adolf Loos and the English Dandy," Jules Lubbock outlined the social ideology implicit in Loos's ideas about style.[53] Lubbock introduced more evidence that Beau Brummell served as a role model for Loos on the cultural criteria for style, noting the Englishman's renowned statement that a gentleman's worst crime was to draw attention to himself. Perceived as a heroic figure, Brummell was a social climber who offered lessons that could be applied to everything in life.[54] In "Undressing Architecture: Fashion, Gender, and Modernity," Mary McLeod refers to Lubbock's article and also mentions Beau Brummell as Loos's ideal. She points out, however, that the fashion psychologist John Carl Flügel described Brummell's reform of men's dress around 1800 as the beginning of the great renunciation of men's dress.⁵⁵ In "White Out: Fashioning the Modern," Mark Wigley introduced the notion of Loos's explicit rejection of fashion, especially women's fashion. Furthermore, Wigley pointed out Loos's preference for the relative standardization of men's clothes over the variety in women's clothes, referring to Loos's article titled "Architecture" (1910) about the quiet and anonymous production of twentieth-century style by tailors and other craftsmen.⁵⁶ Wigley acknowledged that Loos looked to the evolution of the man's suit in England as a clothing model.⁵⁷ Loos critiqued female fashion as beholden to the coquette's fancies, while men's fashions were established by the gentleman. In this dichotomy, Loos attempted to preserve a social structure divided along gender lines. In *White Walls, Designer Dresses*, Wigley observed that Loos viewed fashion as the "only means of maintaining identity," and that, along those lines, Loos's writings were "nothing more than the attempt to discipline fashion."⁵⁸ Loos's view on fashion would evolve, however, to suggest that man no longer needed to express his individuality through clothes—or maintain an identity in that sense—and that clothes could instead be used as a mask.⁵⁹ Loos's views on fashion would extend to his appraisal of architecture as being a form of dress. Beatriz Colomina argues in "On Adolf Loos and Josef Hoffmann" that Loos's blank building façades were used as a social mask.⁶⁰ Loos's promise to match the ethics of men's fashion with architectural design raises a further question: did he see architecture as a tool with which to influence new trends and become, by extension, as prominent in the etiquette of socialization as clothing? Could his architecture—for example, the coffeehouse—direct a certain kind of sociability? According to Loos, the ideal of men wearing similar conservative suits could be compared to the above-mentioned allure of the shared reading of newspapers in cafés. Both served as forces to bind the members of a new progressive society together, guaranteeing the outsider both the security of the insider and the cultural lead over those he criticized for being wrong and those who rejected him.

In 1899, Loos designed the interior and façade of the Café Museum located at Friedrichstrasse 6 (on the corner of Friedrichstrasse and Operngasse) owned by Ludwig Frisch.⁶¹ Through his somewhat bare interior design, Loos expressed opposition to opulent late historicism and to Jugendstil café interiors. Inside the Biedermeier L-shaped, two-hall arrangement, where the cashier's seat and display counter were opposite the café's main entrance, low mahogany paneling complemented velour British wallpaper with a light green stripe.⁶² Loos settled the problem of the two wings' unequal length by using a partition wall with mirrors and a series of pictures depicting traditional male activities such as horse racing and hunting (similar to the pic-

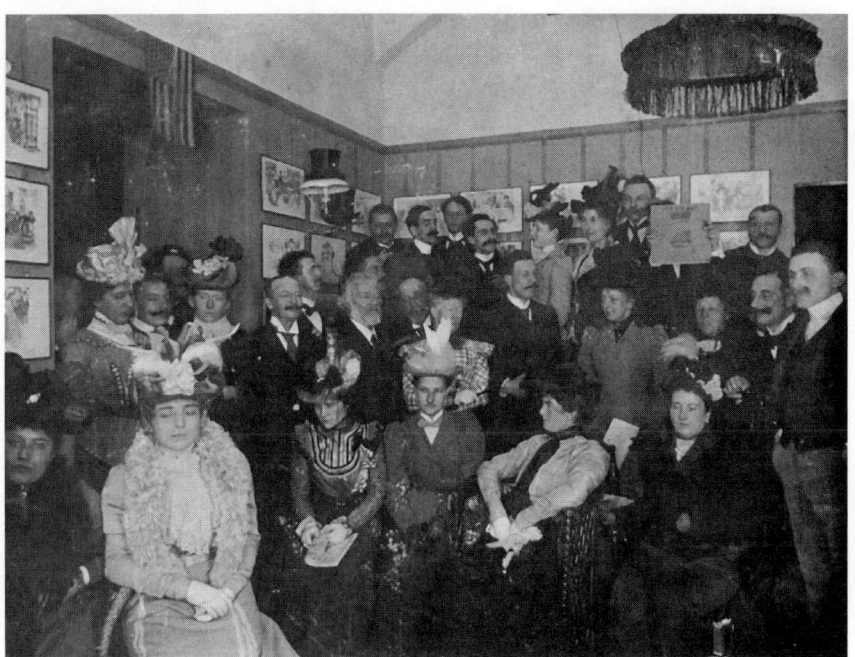

FIGURE 29. *Adolf Loos, Gibson Room, Café Museum, April 1899. Courtesy of Burkhardt Rukschcio.*

tures he would hang in the Kniže men's fashion store more than a decade later), creating an intimate room fashioned to resemble a men's club.[63] At the other end of the café was the Gibson Room, also known as the ladies' room (Fig. 29).[64] On the back wall of this room Loos placed twenty-seven drawings by the American artist Charles Dana Gibson, divided into three rows of nine drawings. The immediate impression of Gibson's drawings is that they flatter a male perspective on the world, offering a light entertainment show, but in addition to this Loos chose the drawings to relate his design to modern sports fashion for both men and women. Loos may have been inspired by his fellow writer and future client, the biology professor Theodor Beer, of Jewish origin, and an article of Beer's in May 1896 in the journal *Die Zeit* praising the American artist. Beer complimented the elegant and correct clothing of men and women in Gibson's drawings, suggesting that this could serve to counteract inner character defects.[65] The idea of clothing counteracting inner character defects could have appealed to the Jewish guests in the coffeehouse, who were worried about prejudice against them.

Just before he started designing the Café Museum, Loos went with Altenberg to visit the art salon Artaria in Vienna's Kohlmarkt. Altenberg explained their shared enthusiasm for Gibson's album of drawings at the gallery as an expression of the merits of Anglo-Saxon culture.[66] Indeed, at the celebration for the opening of the Café Museum, the Gibson room was decorated with an American flag above the door.[67] Loos applied his own demand for modern dress and Beer's praise of correct clothing in the Café Museum's lightweight interior. Round white marble tabletops surrounded by bentwood chairs stained light red created a charming, flowery impression. Hevesi suggested in his review of the café that Loos's rather simple design was "almost nihilistic."[68] It was nihilistic in that it challenged traditional values. yet it was also a carefully planned discursive space appropriate for hosting and promoting contemporary intellectual discourse. The lightweight red chairs enabled a dynamic interaction inside the space, since they could be moved easily from one table to another and guests could move easily from one discussion circle to the next.[69] Furthermore, Loos's choice of a smooth white stucco façade with blue window frames, and the golden letters spelling CAFÉ MUSEUM,[70] countered not only the upper part of the 1880s historicist corner house but also the exotic aesthetics of the Secession House a block away. The café served as a distinguished business card that reflected Loos's correct self-presentation.[71] The simple color harmonies of striking white, blue, and gold outside and soft green, light red, and white inside were a creative and chic achievement of modernist formal and spatial articulations. To offset the dynamic movement around the three heavy billiard tables in the main space, Loos arranged electric lamp fittings on the ceiling and on the walls in a monotonous rhythm to produce a calming effect.[72] He further used the fashion dictates of the time for his modernist choreography: while women wearing heavy decorated dresses would not have felt comfortable sitting on the lightweight chairs, men in solemn black suits may have felt elevated to the position of masters of the cheerful setting.[73] In an early photograph of Café Museum there is a top hat on a high shelf, harking back to the Victorian period. The shiny silk top hat offered a sensual contradiction to the nihilistic café interior—an anachronistic symbol of royal status also associated with the marketing campaign of Loos's favorite fashion salon, Goldman & Salatsch.[74] The owner of the café, the photographer, or Loos may have placed it there to refer to the anonymous gentleman customer who forgot his top hat, thereby giving the place a British status symbol, similar to the attitude claimed by Goldman & Salatsch. Through its façade with golden letters resembling a business card, the Café Museum's aristocratic and business flair offered the client in black suit—as the elegant man in Altenberg's postcard representing "Judaism" appears, with top hat in hand—to feel mobile and respected, a master of the situation.

The Café Museum gave modernist patrons a place to reclaim their cultural authority. When, in 1903, the patron Fritz Waerndorfer met the critic Hermann Bahr at the Café Museum to discuss their book defending Klimt,[75] Loos's cheerful Biedermeier-like setting served as the backdrop. It was on this stage that Waerndorfer gave Bahr the newspaper clippings attacking Klimt, so that Bahr could formulate his defense. The café was also certainly Loos's claim to architectural authority. It was situated not only near the Secession House but also close to Vienna's Technical University and the Academy of Fine Arts, and Loos would sit in the café criticizing both the secessionists and the current design education in front of a group of architectural students from both schools. His influence was strong enough to motivate a leading professor at the Technical University, the Jewish architect Carl König, to forbid his students from attending Loos's gatherings.[76] The Café Museum was fashioned like a *gemütlich* (cozy) yet modern club to promote shared intellectual discourse and, in the Gibson room, it was also Loos's tribute to his friend Altenberg with whom he shared an admiration for Gibson's work. The setting was not meant to tame the Otherness of Altenberg's unacculturated appearance but to grant the poet a home in the Gibson room.

The Voyeur Altenberg and the Drama of Seduction in the American Bar

In contrast to Café Museum, which encouraged sociability and *Gemütlichkeit* (coziness), the American Bar (Fig. 30a), matched sociability with the *unheimlich* (uncanny) through its luxurious setting and the caricature portrait of Altenberg (Fig. 30b, Plate 12).[77] Loos's design of the American Bar, the first bar in Vienna, used an intensified sensual play of muted lighting and luxurious materials—marble, onyx, milk glass, mahogany, and polished metal fittings and mirrors—all of which heightened the experience of visual ecstasy, giving the stranger Altenberg a stage for a flirtatious drama (without women). Altenberg wrote that the American Bar was "of unprecedented richness and at the same time, not overdone, but, rather with the appearance of serenity like the most precious treasures of nature itself."[78] His words ("the most precious treasures of nature") were similar to those he used for girls he felt attracted to. But what role did Altenberg play in fashioning this cultural setting, this compact men's club?[79] The bar's compact size may have reflected Altenberg's self-perception as an avant-garde artist, as he stated at the end of a letter to Arthur Schnitzler in July 1894: "Thus I am and remain a writer of 'worthless samples' and the finished product [*Ware*, meaning merchandise]

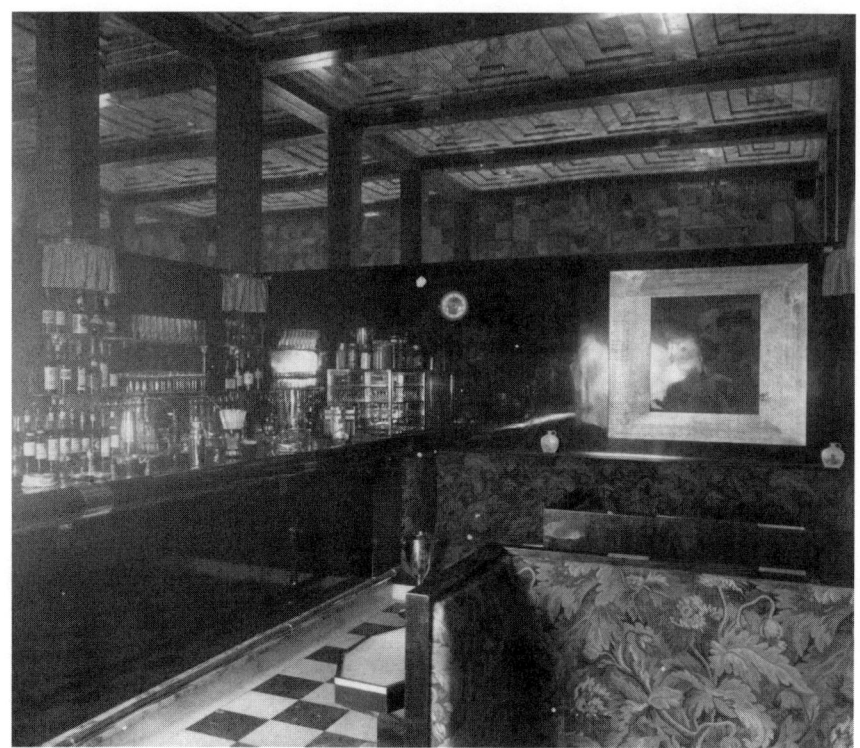

FIGURE 30a. *Adolf Loos, American Bar, early photo of the interior, with Gustav Jagerspacher's portrait of Peter Altenberg, 1909. Photo: Bundesdenkmalamt, Vienna.*

never appears. A kind of a little pocket mirror, powder mirror, no world mirror."[80] Loos's luxurious and regal small mirror setting framed the caricature portrait of the poet Altenberg. The luxurious setting (which could also be compared to the luxurious Wiener Werkstätte interiors in Wittgenstein's hunting lodge in its use of expensive materials and their colorful interplay) at the same time grants a sense of belonging to an exclusive club.

During an evening at the Beer-Hofmann salon in February 1894 (described in the previous chapter), Hofmannsthal read Altenberg's "The Primitive." It begins with a flirtation scene in a coffeehouse, in which a young man offers to protect a young woman who claims she is going to be beaten by another man in the café. He takes her to his small room. Altenberg describes a painting of the Last Supper in the room and a golden coin with the portrait of the Jewish philosopher Baruch Spinoza covering the face of Judas. The girl asks for the golden coin, and after she kisses him goodbye the young man is exposed as Judas. It is her kiss that makes him feel like the Judas—the Jew

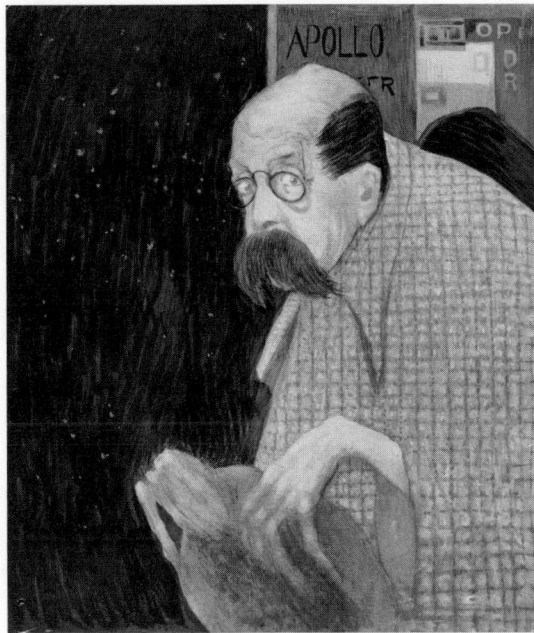

FIGURE 30b. *Gustav Jagerspacher, portrait of Peter Altenberg, 1909. Wien Museum, Vienna. Inv. no. 094-715-001.*

—who betrayed Christ. In the original biblical scene it was Judas who kissed Christ, but here, the man—identifying himself as Judas—receives the kiss. The lesson is that money corrupts. In the scene that takes place before her departure, the young woman is sitting naked next to the fireplace, while he sits at the table opposite her in his small room, which Altenberg describes as possessing "individuality." Looking at her, the gallant young man writes in his notebook:

> De pudore. Modesty! Perhaps it is the perception of the gulf between what we should and could be physically, and what we still are. We fret over our own ego, which in the stress of life becomes stunted. This worry is called "modesty." Don't look at me the way I am! We feel ashamed because of everything that destroys our ego and obstructs its development. It is the anxiety that we are still not the "last." The "God-like"—
>
> But what do you conceal when you have become your own ideal, when you are radiant in the "idea become deed"?! Then you are in paradise, as you were once, and you show yourself naked! *The "beautiful" kills "shame"*![81]

Altenberg exposes his hero's motivation: his indulgent observation of the girl's beauty. For Altenberg beauty was a way not only of attaining his ideal but also of killing shame (in relation to the experience that money corrupts and also perhaps to the betrayal of Judas's kiss). In a brochure used to solicit donations for the Viennese Journalists and Authors Association's Concordia Ball in April 1899, the secessionist-like journal published a text by Altenberg referring to him as "*Seelengucker*" (souls' watcher). The previous page bore Hans Schliessman's drawing of Altenberg standing on a heart shape in the sky. Wearing a stylish beret and a cape as an overcoat, Altenberg holds a flower in his right hand and a telescope in his left that is directed at a naked young woman surfacing from smoke given off by burning straw above the heart. Altenberg is shown as a romantic voyeur.[82] The idea of inviting a male gaze to watch beautiful women was part of the Viennese avant-garde rhetoric. During construction of the Secession House, Loos was also embedding the male gaze into the interior design of the apartment of Eugen Stössler (1899; the dining room furniture is in the Hofmobiliendepot Collection, in Vienna). He inserted a reproduction of Edward Burne-Jones's painting *Golden Stairs* (1876–80), of beautiful women in white descending stairs, into the simply designed dining room cabinet. In Burne-Jones's painting, the women have bare feet, and some are holding musical instruments. Altenberg had referred to Burne-Jones's ideal of otherworldly ladies standing on tiptoes in his story "Der Freund" (The friend), and this may have inspired Loos to use the Burne-Jones reproduction. Altenberg also noted the evocation of a sense of place not through presence but through the consumer's experience. In his text a woman who waits each month for her issue of the British journal *The Studio* feels "Ich bin in England" (I am in England) after she receives it.[83] Loos perhaps intended to transmit experience similarly, inviting the male gaze to enjoy beautiful women by accessing reproductions of women rather than actual women—by placing the Gibson drawings in the Café Museum and inserting the Burne-Jones reproduction in the cabinet in Stössler's apartment. However, in hanging Altenberg's portrait in the American Bar, Loos meant to reverse the situation and place the guests in the bar under Altenberg's gaze. Guests adopted the role of beautiful women, becoming the subjects of Altenberg's uncanny gaze. Yet this gaze, as suggested in "The Primitive," is loaded with protest (against the clients that money corrupts) and with shame (about Judas's betrayal).

Another aspect of the *unheimlich* is related to the sense of displacement in the bar. Loos designed the interior and façade for the American Bar in Kärntner Passage 10 in 1908. Above the door was a colored glass canopy with an American flag design, placed on a slant and lit from the inside. The bar's name was spelled with colored glass lettering in a mosaiclike pattern. Below the American flag four red Skyros marble pillars gave the façade a complementary classical identification. The American flag concluded a process that had begun with the hanging of the American flag in the Gibson Room at the Café Museum's opening, and continued with the placement of the American flag beside the English flag at the upper window of the Goldman & Salatsch store. Goldman's courage in placing the American flag above his entrance showed that he supported Loos's wish to mark pioneering American settlements on the Viennese map.[84]

The American flag, a visual reference to Anglo-Saxon culture, drew on Loos's desire to realize a new diasporic position for himself, Altenberg, and possibly other clients entering the American Bar, promoting not a return to Jerusalem, but a relocation to another place: the United States or England.[85] Like Altenberg, Freud also idealized England, but as a place where Jews could win respect in contrast to their discrimination in Austria, as he noted in a letter to his fiancée, Martha, in 1882: "I am aching for independence, so as to follow my own wishes. The thought of England surges up before me, with its sober industriousness, its generous devotion to the public will, the stubbornness and sensitive feeling for justice of its inhabitants, the running fire of general interest that can strike sparks in the newspapers—all the ineffaceable impressions of my journey of seven years ago, one that had a decisive influence on my whole life, have been awakened in their full vividness. . . . Must we stay here, Martha? If possible let us seek a home where human worth is more respected."[86]

In 1906, aware of the Jewish romantic identification with British culture, Hevesi published a humorous piece on the absurd theory that Englishmen actually originated from the lost ten tribes of Israel.[87] Regardless of these diversions, Loos did address Jewish romantic identification with England and Jewish collective memory through his structures as firm rejections of the Ghetto and in their historical relationship to ancient Egypt.[88]

Rhonda Garelick has noted that the match between style and seduction was tolerated only if it was performed by a celebrity and in a group of believers. Thus, Loos encouraged his Jewish friends and colleagues to see him as a dandy and as one who also secured their dandyism through subtle confirmation of their uniqueness in being strangers (as the title of his short-lived journal *Das Andere* suggests).

Loos dressed the modest interior space in the American Bar with noble materials and used optical tricks to evoke a grand impression. The art historians Ludwig Münz and Gustav Künstler noted the interior's extraordinary distinction and its demand for a certain attitude from the visitor. Furthermore, they observed that Loos used mirrors to offset the impression of a small space

—one also experiences the silky smooth mahogany wooden panels on the lower walls as confining—in a discreet choreography that relies on the moving deployment of a twofold beauty of regulated form and noble material. Concerning the gentle light that fills the room, Münz and Künstler described it as warm and intense: "and it is not without influence on the visitor who silently allows himself unconsciously and without reservation to surrender to the visual experience."[89]

Loos used traditional black-and-white marble for the bar's checkered floor and mahogany cladding for the lower half of the walls, which would also have been suitable for a man's studio or an elegant dining room.[90] The upper part, stretching far above the heads of the guests, was covered with mirrors. These gave the illusion of expanded space and denied an immediate narcissistic gratification. This delayed pleasure principle, in the form of a cultured interior outfit, may have been the architect's way of encouraging the visitor to aspire to higher aesthetic and intellectual gratification.[91] To emphasize the poetic atmosphere, Loos used soft lighting coming from the milk-glass windows above the glass entrance doors, which were themselves covered with curtains. Additional light came from the electric lights attached to the pillars, and from the modern-looking tables illuminated from within. Elsie Altmann, Loos's second wife, claimed that in Loosian spatial design, light acts as an independent material, to be handled like any other material: "The appropriate lamps mounted on the pilasters are covered with curtains, while those lamps which light the table-tops from underneath achieve a subdued effect through the frosted glass."[92]

If it is not difficult to see the bar as Loos's tribute to Altenberg, aspects of the design can also be said to pay tribute, though less directly, to Kraus, another friend in the coffeehouse literary circle. The flowery William Morris fabric for the original upholstery of the benches around the tables[93] remind one of the curtains in Kraus's study.[94] This subtle reference to his friend through a design element would have allowed Kraus to feel at home. Furthermore, for Loos and his clients the reference to Kraus's study may have reflected the intellectual and ethical pursuits in the distinguished men's club.[95] Loos's aim was ambitious, as noted in his review of Arthur von Scala's 1897 Christmas exhibition at the Austrian Museum: "It is the task of modern artists to raise the taste of the multitude in its various characteristic class gradations; in doing so they are fulfilling the needs of the intellectual aristocracy at any given time."[96]

Kraus supported Loos's career both by promoting his architecture in his journal *Die Fackel* and securing clients for him. It is not clear when Loos met his loyal friend and colleague. Scholars are divided, some arguing that he met Kraus in the company of Altenberg as early as 1897, and others claiming that, as the first surviving postcard from Loos to *Die Fackel* would testify, they met only in early 1900.[97] The first family member of Kraus to address Loos with a request to redesign her apartment was his sister Mary Turnowsky (1900). Following her example, Kraus's brothers Alfred, a jurist and industrialist, and Rudolf, a factory owner and codirector of the firm Julius Meinl, asked Loos to design their apartments in 1905 and 1907, respectively. Through Alfred Kraus, Loos had the opportunity to set foot in the city of Pilsen (Plzen) in Bohemia. Loos's first client in Pilsen, Wilhelm Hirsch, an owner of a wire-grating factory, may have been a relative of Rosa Hirsch, whom Alfred Kraus married in 1900.[98] Hirsch hired Loos to design his apartment after touring the apartments of the Kraus brothers.[99] Loos obtained numerous design commissions through Kraus's networks. The Jewish architect Paul Engelmann—who as a young man worked as a secretary at Kraus's journal and who later became a student of Loos—described Kraus, Loos, and Ludwig Wittgenstein as "creative separators."[100] Engelmann also cooperated with Ludwig Wittgenstein on the Wittgenstein House (1928), as discussed in chapter 2. Engelmann described the three men's separation of essence from the subsidiary (the significant from the insignificant) in culture and argued that their authorial acts claimed this distinction by taking the opposition—that is, a separated role in society. They challenged the existing stylistic efforts (historicist, secessionist, and modernist) to overcome division in all fields, and with their harsh critiques they provoked the rise of a fresh foundation for society.[101] The American Bar was also meant to provoke questions about the role of the Jewish artist in society.

The William Morris fabric that echoed Kraus's study had been a substitute for Loos's first choice, however, which carried its own interesting associations. According to Hevesi, Loos originally wanted to upholster the benches with the light green leather generally used for car seats.[102] As the Goldman & Salatsch men's fashion salon (an important patron of his) delivered uniforms to the first automobile club, Loos wanted to give the guests in his compact pub the illusion of sitting in a car. Loos may also have wanted to offer a place of refuge for Goldman's clients (the bar as an advertisement complementing those of the salon: uniforms and an American pub for automobile drivers). However, this plan failed since the requisite amount of leather for the upholstery was not available, and the solution was found with the William Morris flowery textile, so closely identified with British culture. Loos fashioned the perfect Western site of difference for Altenberg's staged appearance in his pub.¹⁰³ Feeling comfortable in their seats, the guests would have looked up to the ceiling to discover the designed landscape—and would have been confronted with the gaze of the night wanderer Altenberg. The caricature by Gustav Jagerspacher (Fig. 30b, Plate 12) evokes the impression of a modern wandering Jew—his back is bent forward, he appears to have just stopped walking to look at his viewer, and instead of a walking cane he holds his hat with bony fingers.¹⁰⁴ It shows how skillfully Loos promoted Jewish narrative as part of Viennese high culture.¹⁰⁵

Decorating the wall opposite the entrance, Altenberg's portrait with its broad, gilded frame was the only painting in the miniature elitist men's club. In his review of the American Bar, Altenberg noted that "in this locale only men are allowed in" and concluded with this praise: "It is luxuriously original and simple at the same time. The acknowledgment of the nobility of the material which nature produces, begins with us, and slowly wins more awareness!"¹⁰⁶ The salon and the club gave also Jewish dandies the legitimacy to display themselves and champion a celebrity status. Yet the bar also presented the temptation to drunkenness and destruction of the communication system that made a "network of opinion and desire"¹⁰⁷ possible and granted celebrity status. Jagerspacher's caricature of Altenberg shows him scurrying across the city at night—only his head and hands revealed outside a tent-like checkered cape, as he looks fearfully to one side, while his elongated hands appear old and fragile. His head is framed by a striking red poster advertising the Apollo variety theater on the Gumpendorferstrasse, as though he has just left the place. The Apollo poster documents Altenberg's journalistic work between 1905 and 1909, when he reviewed variety and cabaret shows for the *Wiener Allgemeine Zeitung*.¹⁰⁸ Because these less desirable associations could be made with Altenberg, his presence provoked different reactions in Viennese members of the coffeehouse and bar set.

Oskar Kokoschka's 1909 portrait of Peter Altenberg with shapeless dress, dirty hands, and a helpless look seems to support the prejudice against the tortured, assimilated Jew as voiced by Bahr in his above-mentioned review of Herzl's play *Das neue Ghetto*.¹⁰⁹ Kokoschka painted Altenberg in a coffeehouse, appearing surprised and emotionally shaken. The intense physical experience that is depicted is said to be the result of Altenberg's anger at being asked to produce a text (to entertain) on the spot by a guest who was supposed to buy him a drink. Perhaps Altenberg was already drunk, or perhaps he was taken by surprise by the request and further enraged because of his dependency on the charity of others.¹¹⁰ Contemporaries identified the outsider element in Kokoschka's portrait, describing it as "half coffeehouse

Jesus, half cab driver of eternity" and a "study of expression of the Ahasver [wandering Jew] of modern poetry of the soul."[111] Altenberg was an ideal subject since he rejected the bourgeois lifestyle and offered the exotic appeal of a homeless poet. Kokoschka used a psychological representation to expose the relationship between the poet's artistic persona and his psychology. But why did Jagerspracher's caricature and Kokoschka's painting make Altenberg look ugly? In the photographs Altenberg chose to accompany his publications he looks rather charming. In Kokoschka's portrait his eyes are protruding, his moustache hangs down sadly, and his neck appears creased and wrinkled.[112] The murky background color further reflects the poet's inner turbulence. Could it be that Kokoschka was frightened by Altenberg's drunkenness? Or did Kokoschka use Altenberg's state to expose an inner conflict at the heart of the Jewish acculturation process—the threat of being exposed as a Jew? This exposure of a Jew who seeks acceptance by Christian society was already represented in an exaggerated and vicious manner in a short novella by Oskar Panizza, another German author, before Altenberg was discovered.

Panizza's 1893 *The Operated Jew* is about the Jew Itizig Faitel who suffers from the same horrible "Jewish looks" as his father and grandfather and wants to become a gentleman goy and rid himself of everything "Jewish."[113] The scandalous and antisemitic Panizza published articles about sex and degeneration in the *Wiener Rundschau* between 1897 and 1901. This was a progressive liberal journal that published prominent Jewish authors such as Kraus, Altenberg, Hofmannsthal, Zuckerkandl, Hugo Haberfeld (an art historian and a client of Loos), and Ludwig Abels.[114] The son of the patron Jacob Rappaport, who bought Palais Schey and who helped Wittgenstein in his career, also worked as the editor of the *Wiener Rundschau* during these years. Panizza's novella was radical in its visualization of the transformation of the "ugly Jew" into a "Gentile dandy." Faitel's ambition was not only to change his looks but also to belong to Gentile society:[115] "Faitel's ambition mounted even higher.' Faiteles! Such a bootiful yid, such a fine yid! Such a elegant yid!'—This is the way Faitel frequently spoke to himself when he stood in front of a mirror, but only in his thoughts.—'So you tink now you're a Chreesten, witt no drop Jewishness? You tink you could go whereever you want wot you should take a seat wit de fine people wot everyone should think: dat's one of us!'"[116]

Faitel, who goes through a painful process of acquiring a "Christian mask," finally reveals his true identity after getting completely drunk.[117] The German studies scholar Sander Gilman suggests that the story's moral: is that "Jews become their true selves when constraints of civilization are removed."[118] In other words, Jews depended more than gentiles on constraints of civilization

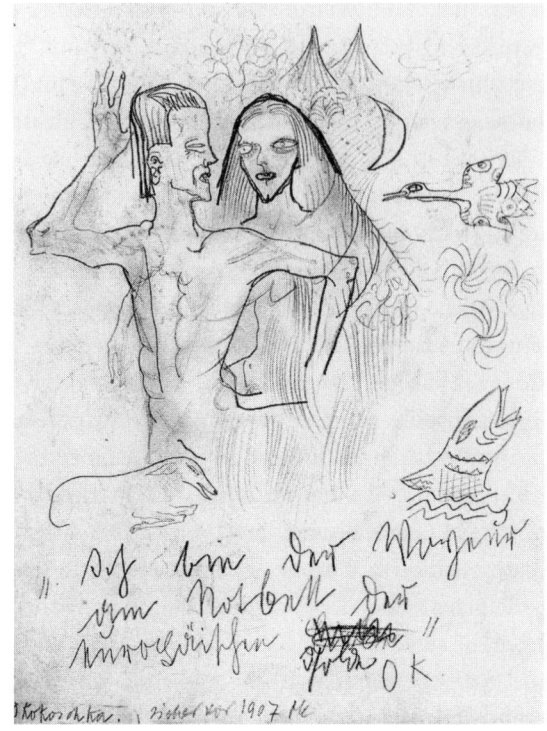

FIGURE 31. *Oskar Kokoschka*, Ich bin der Voyeur am Notbett der europäischen Isolde, December 1909. Black crayon, pencil, stumped, on white vellum paper (private collection). © 2015 Fondation Oskar Kokoschka / Artists Rights Society (ARS), New York / ProLitteris, Zürich.

or a cultured setting to be acceptable. Loos thought that secessionist decorative design could not guarantee Jewish clients the necessary setting of required restraint. It was his outfitting of houses and interiors that would provide the required constraints of civilization. Moreover, the new style, offering civilizing constraints in the form of fashionable or cultured dress, compensated for their owners' feelings of shame for supposedly being ugly by allowing them to emerge as celebrity dandies—new beautiful men. In the beautiful, sensual, and luxurious setting of the American Bar, Altenberg appeared less poor, yet still threatening. This provocation associated with Altenberg would again be picked up by the young Kokoschka in the American Bar, though in another instance, in the form of a drawing that acknowledged the idea of a flirtatious drama without a woman as the addressee.

In December 1909, Kokoschka drew a self-portrait with a woman in a landscape titled *Ich bin der Voyeur am Notbett der europäischen Isolde* (I am the voyeur in the needy bed of the European Isolde; Fig. 31). Kokoschka wrote originally, "I am the voyeur in the needy bed of the European love," but he erased the "love" and wrote "Isolde" underneath, referring to the famous medieval legend of Tristan and Isolde, also known in Vienna through Wagner's opera of the same name. (As noted in chapter 2, the first piece Alexander von Zemlinsky played on the piano for Alma Schindler in Spitzer's music salon was "Tristan.") Kokoschka drew his voyeur on a piece of paper from the American Bar guest book, as the signature on the back of this drawing —"American-Bar 15.XII 1909"—proves.[119] Did Altenberg's portrait, looming above him in the bar, provoke Kokoschka's foreigner's voyeuristic gaze at the European Isolde? Did Kokoschka choose to adopt Altenberg's outsider position (flirting, even without women around)? In Kokoschka's portrayal of Altenberg in his piece "The Viennese and the Artist," written on the occasion of the reopening of the Altenberg room in Otto Kallir's Neue Galerie in Vienna in 1934,[120] he placed "Altenberg's early and original appreciation of black African culture at the center of his literary description of him."[121] Leo Lensing argues that Kokoschka may have promoted Altenberg's championing of Ashanti culture as a "primitive" culture against the claim of "educated society."[122] Since the article was written during the fascist era, and given the threat of Nazi Germany's racial laws, Lensing suggests that the clash between black primitive culture and the new educated society could have also been a cover for the clash between the Jewish culture and the new Germanic culture.[123] For Kokoschka, Altenberg's gaze in the American Bar was that of the stranger looking at European Isoldes.

The secessionist circle and its opponents competed for Altenberg's portrait as a prestigious art object to promote their cultural club (Altenberg appeared on illustrations for Cabaret Fledermaus as well) or drinking establishment (his portrait in American Bar), respectively. Given this avant-gardist battle, Altenberg's inscription on the recto of Jagerspacher's portrait five years after it was finished is crucial to understanding the avant-gardist battle to visualize the ideal in relation to an aspired nature: "Are we not all caricatures of God's actual plans made for the 'ideal and aspired nature'?!?"[124] It was the gazing, primitive, Jewish Altenberg looking not at Isolde but at Kokoschka himself, sitting and drawing in the American Bar, that inspired Kokoschka to direct the foreigner's gaze at the European Isolde in his drawing.[125] Kokoschka used Altenberg as a role model to challenge cultural taboos, and Loos claimed Altenberg's portrait at the American Bar as a form of patronage of his design.

The match between the unnatural image of the night wanderer Altenberg and the superb cultivation of beautiful, natural material (marble and wood) in a luxurious setting transformed prejudice against "Jewishness" into a triumphant expression of Viennese decadence.[126] Loos highlighted Altenberg's seductive pose with the decadent dress of the bar's furnishings to celebrate Altenberg as a leading avant-gardist poet and adopt him as patron to claim the highest cultural prestige in the Viennese art scene.[127] Klimt also provides an example of an artist who transformed negative associations with "Jewishness" into a positive association with artistic luxury. Klimt's portrait of the art patron Adele Bloch-Bauer (1907, Collection Neue Galerie, New York) is dramatic, with its daring, tight golden dress, golden robe, shining necklace, and armbands. Bloch-Bauer is seated majestically on a luxurious golden armchair against an opulent golden background. The erotic symbols such as triangles, eggs, and eyes in her flowing gown may suggest that she is dressed up for flirting with her viewer. At the same time, the symbols mirror the viewer's voyeuristic gaze. Klimt crowned Adele as a new Jewish queen, transferring the prejudice identifying Jews with the power of wealth to a timeless mythological sphere.[128] Yet she also represents a new type of modern woman. Her entrapment by convention is represented in her body's disappearance behind the overwhelming ornamental setting of the Wiener Werkstätte interior, yet Klimt acknowledges her spiritual independence by encircling her head and focusing on her facial expression. At the center of the composition, her naked hands clasp each other in a romantic gesture. Similarly, Loos designed the interior of American Bar as a luxurious dress setting for the golden-framed portrait of Altenberg, transferring the prejudice identifying Jews as the eternal wanderers into a timeless, opulent, and delightful sphere.

Dressing and Undressing: The Art of Flirtation in a Viennese Men's Fashion Salon

> Which style is the building? The Viennese style of the year 1910. But people do not understand that. They search for strange models in far-off lands, just as they looked for American models for the Café Museum. And here, as I did with the café, I collected elements from the old Viennese coffeehouses and building façades to find the modern, the truly modern style.[129]

There was less American exoticism and more Austrian dandyism in Loos's façade for the Goldman & Salatsch men's fashion salon in Michaelerplatz (1909–11). Michael Goldman (1843–1909) and his son Leopold, together with Loos, would fashion a new elitist notion of the Viennese dandy with their building. Yet this notion of the dandy, as it was ultimately grafted onto the new Goldman & Salatsch house, should be reconsidered in relation to older Viennese architectural traditions and Viennese fantasies and fears about undressing men or women—specifically Jewish men—as in Schnitzler's confession in *The Road into the Open*.

In a September 1898 article titled "Wäsche" (Underwear), Loos praised the high standard of innovative products that Goldman & Salatsch offered their clients. Furthermore, he claimed that they had introduced the idea of the gentleman's outfitter to Vienna. Explaining the outfitter's task of selecting distinguished articles for men's wardrobes, he argued that there was enough spiritual work in it to fill a man's soul. He emphasized, however, the critical decision making involved a great deal: "An outfitter keeps in stock everything belonging to menswear. Not an easy task. For every article he sells he is responsible to the buyer for its correctness. In a well-run gentleman's outfitters one can expect to be able to choose an item completely at random and not end up with something not in good taste, i.e. not correct."[130]

Loos supported Michael Goldman's aspiration to promote a lucrative and individual business image. More than a month later, in the evening edition of *Neue Freie Presse*, an advertisement appeared: "*Outfitters. Complete outfits for men, in a distinguished style, Vienna, I Graben 20, ground floor and mezzanine. Goldman & Salatsch.*"[131] When Loos compared the outfitter to an art dealer in "Wäsche," he directly expressed his wish that the tailor would rise above the calculation of a simple retailer—meaning mere financial gain—and turn into a producer of culture. Like Waerndorfer, who wanted to exchange his reputation as a partner in his family's textile factories for that of a noble art patron, young Leopold Goldman was also enchanted by the idea of becoming a cultural producer through supporting Loos's cultural reform program. With an ambitious plan to build a modern building across from the Hofburg, Goldman made his largest cultural investment in his Goldman & Salatsch fashion firm.[132]

Leopold's father, Michael, belonged to Karl Wittgenstein's generation, though unlike Wittgenstein, Michael was not raised in a wealthy family, nor did he earn a great fortune.[133] Goldman was a self-made man from a lower-middle-class background who reached a respectable social position through his skilled catering to the dressing needs of Viennese bourgeois and aristocratic men.[134] Like Wittgenstein, who was introduced to the Viennese cultural scene through his mother Fanny (née Figdor), Michael Goldman looked to his younger brother Sigmund Goldmann (1852–1916)—who owned a lucrative book and art store, later turned into an art gallery—and to the young and inexperienced architect Loos to be his mentors in the Viennese cultural scene. In contrast to both Wittgenstein and Sigmund Goldmann, Michael was not interested in the fine arts. Yet Michael and Sigmund understood the necessity of a defense tactic against the growing antisemitism at the end of the 1890s (reflected in the rise in popularity of the antisemitic Karl Lueger, Vienna's future mayor), and this gave rise to their desire to influence the cultural scene.[135] Michael's son, Leopold, was seven years younger than Fritz Waerndorfer. Like Waerndorfer, he entered his father's family business after a year's apprenticeship in the textile industry in England, but in contrast to Waerndorfer, Leopold Goldman identified with his profession and found a creative way to get further involved in the family business by courting new clients and contributing different patented instruments to the salon's lucrative fashion production. It is assumed that Leopold also joined the Freemasons, again like Waerndorfer, perhaps wishing to rise above the inherited frictions in Viennese society.[136]

Dressing

In early January 1898, Michael Goldman, then sole owner of Goldman & Salatsch, asked Loos to design him a store adjacent to his tailoring workshop in Graben Street.[137] Loos had just finished his first commissioned assignment, which was only a few houses away from Goldman's shop at Kohlmarkt 5. The client in that case, Ernst Ebenstein, a highly respected gentile court tailor, had commissioned Loos at the end of 1897 to redesign the interior of his men's fashion salon in the mezzanine and to design a modest American-style wooden façade (Wittgenstein would welcome this striking visual reference to American culture when he bought the building at the beginning of the twentieth century).[138]

A decade earlier, Goldman had moved from Schottenring 18, in the Textilviertel (Textile quarter) on the Ringstrasse, to the central address of Graben 20, mezzanine, stairway Naglergasse 1.[139] The new address expressed Goldman's acknowledged need to locate his workshop in an impressive looking house, strategically connecting the three most important shopping streets in Vienna—Kohlmarkt, Graben, and Tuchlauben—and placing his store on the European map of international elite stores. The shop was located in a grand historicist house that had been designed by Ferdinand Fellner the Elder and built in 1855–58.[140] The entrance façade of this magnificent house was decorated with half-naked caryatids (these forms would later reappear in the connotation of the half-dressed avant-gardist Goldman & Salatsch House). With the historicist façade Goldman could claim the same noble bearing for his store that the Jewish bankers and industrialists claimed through their historicist rental apartment palaces on the Ringstrasse. But in contrast to those patrons, Goldman did not pretend to imitate the snobbish habits of the aristocracy.[141] On his building's top floor he placed a large business sign, which could be seen almost from the beginning of the street, and which became an integral part of the landscape of the center of Vienna.[142] Loos could have learned about Goldman & Salatsch's subscription system for clothes from advertisements in the *Neue Freie Presse*, such as the following: "Goldman & Salatsch Tailors, Vienna Graben 20, English Men's Suits, Hunting, Sport and Riding Clothes. Subscription-System for the Distinguished Men's World."[143] In November 1896, Goldman placed his first advertisement in the prestigious journal *Der Salon, Oesterreichisches Adelsblatt* (The salon, Austrian Aristocracy Gazette). The advertisement was in the form of a visiting card with the upper right corner folded down.[144] Given the growing popularity in Vienna of the newly elected Mayor Lueger, the new partnership between the Goldmans and Loos in 1898 was a brave public statement to prove to the Viennese, but also to the European community, that Jews and gentiles could have equal entrée into Western society.

Loos designed Goldman's store on Graben for an elite clientele. To maintain the store's high standards, he wanted his design to make the client feel as if he were in an elegant store rather than in a tailor's studio, with perhaps only the textile samples as a reminder that clothes could be ordered.[145] The director of a well-funded store would never do the tailoring himself but would instead concentrate on salesmanship and representation of his business in front of his clients. The management of the workshop would be handed over to the tailor, who was also responsible for the workmanship.[146] The ideal relationship between the salon owner and his client was formal and confidential at the same time: the client would be invited in writing to try on the suit he had ordered. He would be led into a specially designed fitting room and never allowed to the workshops. The store's reputation rested on the elegance of the suit, fitted to the individual's measurements. The owner's promise to his client was that his product would guarantee his integration in the best Viennese society. Michael Goldman, a small blond man with blue eyes, fit the distinguished image of his store.

In a 1901 article titled "Ein Wiener Herrenmodesalon" (A Viennese men's fashion salon), Ludwig Abels, the editor of the monthly journal *Das Interieur*, praised Loos's design for the Goldman & Salatsch store in Graben, referring not to the façade but to the interior. He acknowledged the debt of Viennese men's fashion to the English model and recognized Loos's aspiration to achieve English elegance without disclosing any specific source.[147] Indeed, the author continued: "Smooth, reflective surfaces, concise forms, bare metal—these are the main elements, from which such a perfect fashionable shop is created."[148] He identified the first hall he entered from the street, a narrow selling room for lingerie and accessories, as the "outfitting department."[149] The closets to the left of the entrance displayed ties, hats, and walking sticks seen through faceted glass as if through a window shop. The walls were dressed with transparent glass closets with subtle, linear frames of dark wood. Abels praised the choice of snakewood, a hard and beautifully colored veined wood. The handles were made from shining brass. On the right side and the back wall were mirrors, which—according to Abels—served the double function of reflecting the client's image as he tried on clothes and enlarging the impression of the narrow hall.[150] But this was not the only interior element with a double function. Two showcases with sliding doors in the middle of the selling room served as counters or desks as well. Rukschcio granted these showcases a third, psychological, function—that of "orientation"—in that they formed a narrow path that encouraged the client to continue walking forward to the next room.[151] Special lighting heightened the elegant impression. Underneath the ceiling, a row of small, cagelike showcases produced a striking light effect; brass-housed electric lights framed small, square, faceted glass panes. The vaulted ceiling magnified the effect with its rough white plaster.[152] Abels further noticed that Loos used brass as a repetitive motif for the base of the built-in closets and the showcases, the handles of the upholstered stools, and the bars for the office partition at the end of the hall. From this office, the director or the accountant could observe the whole room through a blind lens, without being seen.[153] He could maintain control through the reflection in his observing mirror. Abels concluded his impressions of the first hall by saying that everything was practical, worked efficiently, and was of the highest quality.

Encouraged to move forward, the visitor reached a spiral staircase, leading him to the tailoring department on the first floor. Turning to the left, he found the accounting office and waiting room. The office desks were enclosed with glass panes, especially designed to serve as standing counters as well. The accountant's privacy was preserved through the bars surrounding three sides of his desk. The spiral lamps hanging from the ceiling reminded Abels of an elastic spring. Walking through the office, the visitor reached the waiting room, a small, windowed niche that imitated the coziness of an English salon. Two facing pairs of elegant armchairs with square tables between them were placed near the curtained window; two benches flanked the gas fireplace framed with bricks and with a mirror placed diagonally above it, contributing to the atmosphere of a private salon. To give an original touch to the cozy arrangement Loos added another spiral lamp hanging from the ceiling. From the waiting room, the visitor was called to the dressing room. For the discreet dressing room doors, Loos creatively adapted the idea of a

Japanese screen.[154] The walls of free-standing cabinets, made of white lacquered wood with square panes of blue Tiffany glass, evoked an intimate atmosphere, making the client feel comfortable about undressing and being measured for a suit, as well as to return a week later for a fitting. Loos not only designed an elegant and practical elite fashion salon, but he also presented the tailoring profession with an idealized self-representation. His interior design realized the professionalism of the progressive tailor. In the entrance hall (outfitting department), he transformed the spatial plan and the walls' surface into a geometric chart by using rectangular mirrors, cabinets, and drawers, as well as high sale counters. The geometric mapping of space reflected what came to be regarded during the nineteenth century as the tailor's positivist Weltanschauung, which relied on mathematical calculations to arrive at a perfect fit for the client. If the positivist ideal was that science could improve the human condition, the modern tailor's ideal was that mathematical measuring systems could remedy the imperfections of the human body. Loos's design represented the ideal of self-mastery—the client should feel that he was in control of his movements and his thoughts and that the fashioning of his suit was a master's choice. The reorganization of familiar elements resulted in a new, meaningful configuration that allowed the client and salesman to influence each other. Loos encouraged a kind of creative adjustment by allowing both to search for ideal clothing, while at the same time maintaining alertness through multiple mirrors. He further matched different design elements creatively so that, for example, in the office and waiting room the severity of the geometrical forms and striped patterning were lightened by the Oriental carpet and the armchairs upholstered in flowery material. Decorative elements literally lightened up the atmosphere, such as the spiral lamps, whose feminine, spiral qualities lightened the masculine striped furniture in the office and waiting room. These aesthetic matches reflected the design of a proto-unisex outfit.[155] In the dressing room Loos further contrasted a traditional Oriental carpet with the modern cubical grid of the cabinets, developing these aesthetic elements in awareness of their different gender representations and geography as a unified outfit, thereby producing the appropriate atmosphere for fruitful interaction between owner and client. Goldman's store in Graben (1898; further façade renovation, 1901) was supposedly Loos's last "total design,"[156] yet his design of their new store in the Goldman & Salatsch House, created more than a decade later, was a more developed example of the Gesamtkunstwerk. The distinguished and innovative character of its interior design reflected the successful character of the fashion firm.

Loos's design of a rational positivist representation and a club setting for the Goldman & Salatsch store was not accidental: at that time, it was fashionable to recreate an elegant bourgeois salon setting for the waiting rooms in elite fashion stores. However, Loos rejected the usual historicist salon in favor of the English salon, adapting it to the new zeitgeist. Referring to the German art critics Wilhelm Bode and Julius Meier-Graefe, who described a program with no name, the architectural historian Stanford Anderson identified the desired direction as follows: "generation of form from necessity, practicality, simplicity, artlessness, evident mathematical formal systems, and the avoidance of ornament while preserving something of fantasy or atmosphere. This is not architectural functionalism but a playing out of architectural invention for a social purpose within—and with respect for—the constraints of the material world."[157]

The German critics—who promoted concepts such as form generated from need, health considerations, materials, and construction—also based their arguments on the rejection of historicism and art nouveau (secessionism). They advocated artlessness and the elimination of ornament, favoring function and aim. But even though they appreciated engineering as pure *Sachlichkeit* (functionality or objectivity), they asked for something more that could be identified as encouraging "sociability": "something that was not the ideal hovering over the real but rather the interplay of invention, or convention, with the material world in facilitating our ability to linger with our friends in a creatively evolving cultural setting—[Richard] Streiter's character and milieu, [Julius] Meier-Graefe's milieu and atmosphere."[158]

Loos's intention was also to provide Goldman with the cultural authority to cater to a progressive and exclusive milieu. Goldman & Salatsch's clients were members of the Viennese and the European elite. In 1893, fifteen years after the foundation of the firm, Michael Goldman's promotion campaign was crowned with a new contract to deliver the uniforms for the Austro-Hungarian Imperial Yacht Squadron, the firm's first major achievement, which secured their access to aristocratic clients.[159] In 1899, Goldman received the title of court tailor from the court of the Austro-Hungarian Empire. This did not necessarily mean that Goldman was delivering clothing directly to members of the imperial household, but it was a mark of prestige and a recognized stamp of professionalism.[160] In June 1900, in the firm's front-page ad in a sports journal, the text accompanying an illustration of ankle boots, a walking stick, and a top hat, read: "From Head to Foot. Tailors and Outfitters, Goldman & Salatsch, K. u. K. Court-Deliverers, I Graben 20."[161]

Proud of his professional self-image, in particular as it was represented

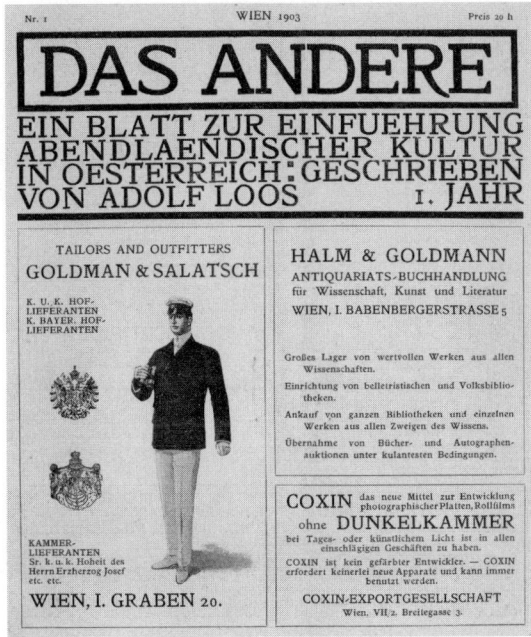

FIGURE 32. *Adolf Loos, Das Andere, no. 1 (1903)*: front page with a Goldman & Salatsch ad. Photo: © MAK– Austrian Museum of Applied Arts / Contemporary Art / Georg Mayer. Bl-71871-1.

through Loos's distinguished design, Goldman was successful in his campaign to win over the court: a year later his ads in the sports journal stated that the firm was the kaiser's court deliverer (meaning that the firm had the right to deliver goods to the court, a prestigious position) as well as the Archduke Josef's chamber deliverer (supplier of clothes to the royal household).[162] In March 1902, Goldman received the title of court deliverer to the Bavarian court,[163] and both additional titles appeared in his ad at the Viennese directory in 1903.[164] The cooperation between Goldman and Loos was criticized by Loos's close friends, possibly out of jealousy. In a 1903 letter to Kraus, Altenberg accused Loos of pushing his way into his journal *Die Kunst* by promising his publisher advertisements from first-class businesses.[165] Goldman & Salatsch was one of the firms, with two large advertisements in the only two issues of Loos's *Das Andere* that year (Fig. 32). The façade of the first store on Graben (1898) and later Loos's journal (1903) became shared visiting cards for the tailor Goldman and the architect Loos.[166] After the new design of his store was completed, and possibly honoring a rqeuest from Loos, Goldman hung American and British flags in the window above his entrance.[167] In doing so, Goldman both acknowledged Loos's design achievement and stated his preference for American and English ways of dressing and living. Goldman not only expressed his support of Loos's cultural program,[168] but

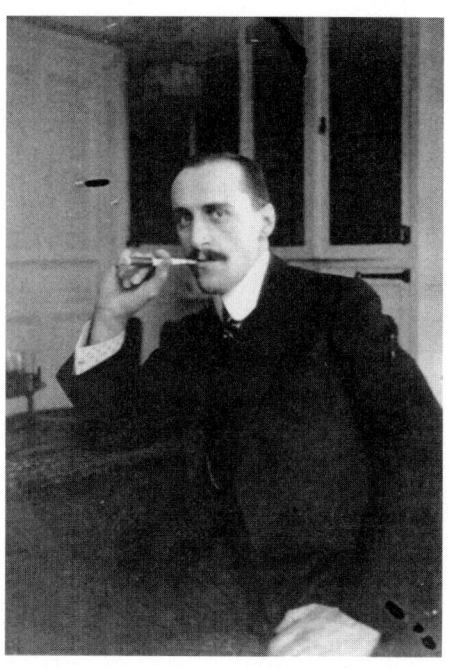

FIGURE 33. *Unsigned photograph of Leopold Goldman, 1909. Courtesy of the late Kitty Goldmann, Santiago, Chile.*

he made his store an active participant in a pioneering cultural campaign on behalf of the Other.[169]

Leopold Goldman supported his father's patronage of Loos. Leopold was a handsome man of medium height, well built with light brown hair and brown eyes. On May 31, 1908, at the age of thirty-two, he married Lilly Beligradeanu, who came from a wealthy Romanian Sephardic Jewish family. While visiting his close school friend Alfred Pincas, Leopold saw a photograph of Lilly and her two sisters, one of whom, Irene, was Pincas's wife. According to the story told by his daughter Kitty, Goldman immediately fell in love with the woman in the photograph and invited Lilly to visit Vienna, where they were married in the Sephardic synagogue.[170] In a photograph taken a year after their marriage, Goldman is unmistakably proud. An elegantly dressed man with a mustache, his hair smoothly brushed back, and with a gracious stance, Leopold was ready to embark on an ambitious and revolutionary cultural production (Fig. 33).

Goldman identified himself and was identified by others as a Viennese gentleman who claimed the authority of an outfitter. His professional approach to fashion design served as a role model for Loos. The psychological advantage of Loos's architectural designs was based on observations of the outfitter's practice in the production of a personally fitted suit, which involved a dialogue between tailor and client intended to establish familiarity. The tailor would first measure the client. Then he would ask a few questions, the answers to which would provide indications about his client's personal habits: how many pockets he would need; whether he needed a pocket in his shirt for his glasses (the pocket would be stitched to the required length); where he usually placed his keys (this pocket would need a double lining), and so on. Sometimes to help communicate his needs, the client would be asked to empty his pockets so he could demonstrate how he prepared himself for the day. Finally, while the client tried on the finished suit, the outfitter and client would together examine the end result, and if necessary make further corrections to length or width.[171] In 1900, after winning a second major client, the first Austrian Automobile Club, Leopold Goldman invented different luxury products to accommodate the specific needs of this niche market. For example, at the end of April 1900, he submitted one of his inventions to the Austrian patent office: "a Blanket with a Foot-Muff" was registered in November 1901.[172] The invention offered passengers in a carriage or automobile a comfortable way to cover their legs and at the same time to keep their feet warm by placing them inside a pocket in the blanket. Dressing oneself also meant dressing warmly. At the end of March 1906, Goldman submitted another original idea to the Austrian patent office: "A Glass Bottle with a Closure Serving as a Drinking Glass," registered in September 1907,[173] offered a useful way to carry a bottle whose lid functioned as a drinking glass. Furthermore, the part of the glass that covered the neck of the bottle served as a measuring unit for mixing liquids. Goldman's inventions expressed his awareness of the needs of car drivers and passengers, supplying them with an original and hygienic container for a drink during long rides. Goldman's inventions paralleled his creative outfitting methods.

In his above-mentioned lecture "Modern Architecture," on the occasion of his inauguration, Otto Wagner had issued a battle cry against historicism (as noted in chapter 2), demanding that architects fit the looks of their buildings to modern clothing. This was replaced by Beer-Hofmann's modernist vision of the white dress challenging the decorated white walls of the Secession House. In the Goldman & Salatsch House, the white dress was transformed into a sensational avant-garde male suit. According to Rebecca Houze, "the Secessionists' interest in fashionable design was largely informed by their place within a culture of 'dressing up,' which they were able to convert into a modern, visual language of creative, therapeutic transformation."[174] Houze adds a different, more mundane, source for Vienna's interest in fashion—namely, "the important textile and tailoring industries that developed in

Central Europe in the mid-nineteenth century. Vienna became the terminus for many Bohemian Jewish immigrants, who were able to establish profitable careers in the urban textile trade."[175] According to Houze, however, the historical context of a textile tradition did not factor into the different attitudes of the two leading Viennese architects at the time, Loos and Hoffmann, who relied heavily on Gottfried Semper's "dressing principle" and how clothing was used to produce "style" in this regard.[176]

To counter Houze, however, it appears that the professionalism of the Jewish tailor Goldman from Moravia, and later the professionalism of his son, did contribute to Loos's new timeless, and at the same time transformative, avant-gardist style. Loos respected the professionalism of Michael Goldman, the migrant from Moravia, and believed that his tailored suits played a role in determining modern aesthetics. Loos claimed, for example, that Josef Hoffmann changed his style after his visit to the Goldman & Salatsch store.[177] In his essay "On Fashion," Georg Simmel presented the simultaneous modern desire to both stand out (opt out) and fit in (opt in)—these different approaches were supposedly represented in both Hoffmann and Loos.[178] I argue that Hoffmann and Loos offered their Jewish clients designs that imitated the mode of self-exclusion in the lifestyle of the—in the case of Hoffmann, perhaps aristocratic, and in the case of Loos, bourgeois—gentleman: While Hoffmann relied on the decorative program as an aesthetic way of establishing uniqueness, encouraging the client to erase his or her personal history, Loos relied on the British model as a cultural form, allowing the client freedom to choose between "opting in" and "opting out."[179]

Loos offered a setting as a cultured dress that allowed clients to choose independently whether to opt in or opt out of Viennese society. As noted in the case of Waerndorfer's dining room and studio, Hoffman grafted an uprooted, elitist aesthetic, which would have confirmed prejudice specifically against Jewish patrons, and trapped his client in an exotic pose. According to Leila Kinney, both Simmel in "On Fashion" and Thorstein Veblen in *The Theory of the Leisure Class* (1899) understood that fashion "is construed both as an arena for the construction of identity and as a conceptual metaphor that explains the incompleteness of contingency of that effort."[180] The only thing that fashion may have contributed to was the question of connectedness versus competition, formulated as a modernist cliché of the male suit versus the female dress.[181] Loos's offer of a distinct experience of connectedness with British outfits for his clients' interiors and anonymous façades resulted from a shared vision in a new art of Jewish sociability; this vision could be summarized in the exclusivity of a fashion piece, the frock coat.

The frock coat, characterized by a knee-length cut, was a popular man's coat during the mid- to late nineteenth century. In 1907, Hevesi reviewed Loos's interiors and quoted him explaining his interiors as different variations of a frock coat: "And when he furnishes an apartment, he guarantees: 'It is always the same. Like a frock coat, it could not look differently. The lining naturally will be different and the pockets are varied according to the need, but a frock coat is a frock coat. This is my sideboard, this is my desk. And still each room looks completely different. The variety is infinite.'"[182]

Loos evoked a mature and sensual man's "body image" in his architectural designs, perhaps by choosing the "silk smoking jacket," as the architectural historian Mary McLeod has suggested, or by visualizing in his interiors the fine needlework of a frock coat's silk lining, as he himself admitted.[183] He wanted to grant his clients a sense of belonging to an elite intellectual and aesthetic club. Early in his career he recognized correctly that the frock coat was a classic and representative article of clothing that would slowly be removed from the market.[184] Loos marketed his interiors as variations on a frock coat to claim a distinguished and classical trademark. Did he expect that his frock coat interior design could serve as an alternative modern dress to the caftan secessionist interior design—as he promised in his text on "Jewish Emancipation," quoted above in this chapter? This question is critical, given Loos's claim of mastering the subtleties of men's fashion. At the beginning of his above-mentioned review, Hevesi compared Loos's interiors to his tailored suits and claimed that both represented geometric elegance.[185]

The German studies scholar Mark Anderson noted that for the acculturated Jewish aesthetes and writers who followed French and English dandy role models, "the dialectic of distinguishing oneself without being noticed inevitably had a different political meaning," and he describes how their choice of "dressing up" reflected conflict with their fathers and their repositioning in the society: "Their parents and relatives, often enough professionals in the clothing business, stood out as Jews, looked and dressed 'like Jews' in the eyes of an anti-Semitic public; at the same time, however, they were in the process of giving up their religious beliefs and trying to assimilate into German society. The sons (for the question of female clothing is entirely different for social and historical reasons) fled from this unhappy combination into a more refined, aristocratic, less visibly 'Jewish' elegance."[186]

Loos's choice of replacing the caftan with the frock coat echoed the wish of the Jewish sons for an invented aristocratic father (or a father who was a public official) dressed in a frock coat; the model of the frock coat was a demonstration of their rejection of the historical memory of—and, supposedly, prejudice against—the Jewish caftan of their forefathers. Leopold Goldman's father Michael definitely did not wear a caftan. It was Loos most likely who chose to transform the frock coat into a farewell tribute to him. In July 1909, Michael Goldman was buried in the Jewish section of Vienna's Central Cemetery. His headstone is a narrow, rectangular black marble slab on which his name and dates are inscribed.[187] The black marble gravestone appeared as an abstraction of the frock coat: Michael was buried symbolically in his eternal elegant black suit. (Loos may have conceived of this minimalist elegant design on his own).[188] In the middle of the grand triangular staircase in the Goldman & Salatsch House, a relief portrait of Michael Goldman was placed as another direct tribute to his memory, illuminated from above with natural light.[189]

The professionalism of both Goldman and Loos, which contributed to their unique lead in the avant-garde movement, depended not on originality but rather on a continuous improvement of an existing, high-quality product. For Loos, the quality product was also part of the Hellenistic European heritage.[190] Goldman and Loos offered concrete, shared cultural forms including those of the noble classical tradition and the respect for high-quality material. Hoffmann's later critique of the Goldman & Salatsch House was that the "classical columns and window surrounds were hardly consistent with our ideas."[191] Hoffmann himself relied on classicist forms in his reformation of modern style, as witnessed in the Beer-Hofmann villa, but here he critiqued the dominance of the façade's Tuscan columns. Just as the new Hellenistic Jews used references to the classical past to create a shared cultural platform for rapprochement, Loos and Goldman applied similar tactics to opt in, keeping the royal reputation of Michaelerplatz. The Goldman & Salatsch House was smartly positioned across from the new north gate of the kaiser's palace (1893), between the noble Josef Count Heberstein Palace, designed by Carl König (1896–99),[192] and the neoclassical façade of the Church of St. Michael (1792). The Tuscan columns echoed the church's frontal columns, and the rounded windows at the entrance mirrored the rounded north gate of the kaiser's palace. Two other eighteenth-century houses on the left side of the fashion house were a nostalgic remnant of a past era.

Monumental classical columns emphasized the masculine authority of men's suits in fashion at the end of the nineteenth century.[193] Loos's Tuscan columns adorning the entrance of the men's fashion salon were a clear reference to the ideal male suit and the virile impression of neoclassical architecture. Referring to the origins of the male suit and its artistic background around 1800, the historian Anne Hollander notes a desire in both fashion and architecture to redefine male sexuality: "The strong simple forms of modern design, as they were first conceived for Neoclassic architecture, were perceived as naturally masculine. Esthetic theory at the time is full of words like 'virile' and 'muscular' to describe the proper character of buildings created with the new simplicity of form based on ancient prototypes."[194]

After the opening of the store in 1912, a Goldman & Salatsch advertisement in Adolph Lehmann's address book for Vienna presented an image of the entrance with the four Tuscan columns and bay windows.[195] The columns were Leopold Goldman's demonstration of triumph and would act as the Goldman visiting card; for Loos the columns were the way to translate the business interests of his clients into a cultured dress. With the radical separation of the public commercial area, with the columns, set off from the private area above, with its smooth stucco façade, Loos ennobled the commercial interests of Goldman & Salatsch.[196] He fashioned a neoclassical and modern house, with the monumental Tuscan columns serving as emblems of this new style and replacing the caryatids that decorated the building at the corner of Graben and Kohlmarkt, where the old Goldman & Salatsch store was located.

Loos offered Leopold Goldman a distinguished outfit with transformative power, and Goldman, then, in his profession, offered his clients their own distinguished outfits with transformative power. Even though the intent of elite, culturally prestigious fashion salons was not necessarily to be democratic, the formal criteria that determined the elegance of men's tailored clothing and the rituals staged in the salons contributed to a leveling process in society. Subtly orchestrated by Loos's design, the ceremony of purchasing a chic fashion article, sports outfit, or tailored suit should have further granted the client the authority of a man of taste.[197] A saleswoman in the large hall would ask a client entering the Goldman & Salatsch fashion house about his special interests. If he was searching for the latest sports outfit, he would be directed to walk down or take the elevator to the sports department in the basement. Beneath the basement was a subbasement for storage. A private elevator that connected the sports department, the ground floor, and the mezzanine also went to the upper floors to the roof level, where the professional tailoring school was located.[198]

A close look at a particular aspect of the client's experience at the Goldman & Salatsch House reveals the intricate plays that the architect Loos contrived. They began with the customer entering the grand hall, paneled with mahogany, where ready-made clothes and articles were sold (Fig. 34). If the client announced that he would like to purchase a bespoke suit, he would be encouraged to continue a few steps forward in a straight line, reaching a single

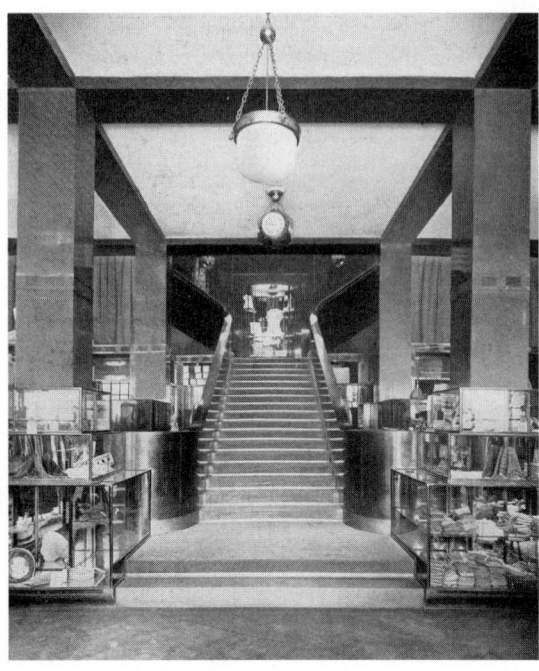

FIGURE 34. *Adolf Loos, entrance hall, Goldman & Salatsch House, 1911.* Heinrich Kulka, Adolf Loos: Das Werk des Architekten (Vienna: Schroll, 1931).

flight of stairs that separated into two lateral branches, like the staircases in a Viennese baroque palace. Climbing up the stairs he would reach the outfitting department on the mezzanine. He would pass the bookkeeping office, where an employee would direct him to the waiting corner on an upper level of the mezzanine. On a higher level, with lower ceilings, the waiting corner was an intimate setting. There, the customer would be invited to sit in a leather club chair next to the bay windows with a framed, plain glass panel set within small square panes of glass, and would look across the Michaelerplatz to the Hofburg.[199] Here the client was symbolically positioned near the father of the Austro-Hungarian Empire, and furthermore, the plain glass openings in the bay windows allowed the clients to peep at the kaiser's private quarters. The mere possibility of walking around the waiting room and looking through the openings stimulated an imaginary social game of looking, appraising, appreciating—and at the same time possibly being watched by pedestrians on the square or by the kaiser himself across the street. The aristocratic art of sociability, this exchange of looks, was performed at a secure distance. The waiting corner's aristocratic claim was further supported by a painting hanging on a side wall—a copy of Giovanni Battista Moroni's masterpiece *The Tailor* (circa 1570; the National Gallery, London)—which also represented Leopold Goldman's pride in the history of his profession. Loos and Goldman's choice to hang this portrait further demonstrated that this fashion salon was part of a respectable European cultural history. Parallel to securing an illusion of hierarchy, however, the master tailors contributed to a quiet revolution that would redefine the distinguished class. They granted bourgeois citizens with no aristocratic ties and bourgeois Jews an entrée to the elitist men's club—a club whose members could afford to buy excellent tailored suits and to dress like the king of England—so they could position themselves literally among the best representatives of Western society.

The bourgeois newcomers achieved cultural authority through their distinct taste and propriety.[200] Furthermore, they gained their superior stance by being aware of and open to subtle innovations in fashion. But how did Loos transform the old-fashioned frock coat into modern Western dress? Did he indeed offer his Jewish clients an alternative to the secessionist (Eastern) caftan or the outdated historicist classicist design? Given the ceremony involved in purchasing an article of clothing, one wonders whether Goldman and Loos intended to achieve a break from the past. Celebrating its new prominence, Goldman & Salatsch opened an additional sales counter on the top floor of the renowned and newly renovated Grand Hotel on the Ringstrasse.[201] With that gesture, Leopold Goldman, like Karl Wittgenstein, returned and joined the historicist patrons on the Ringstrasse (the Grand Hotel is few steps away from the Palais Gomperz). This raises the question: What revolutionary contribution did the new Goldman & Salatsch House in fact make to Viennese cultural production, specifically to strategies of dress and socializing?

Undressing

Knowing Goldman's appreciation of quality fabric, Loos traveled to Greece and Italy in search of suitable materials for dressing not only the façade and front entrance but also the side entrance to the building.[202] At the beginning of March 1910, Loos traveled to Algeria, Morocco, and Greece in search of marble. In April, he bought the green Cipollino marble intended for the façade of the business area and purchased the four columns in Euboea in Corinth. The site had only been discovered six years before, and Loos took pride in the idea that the house would be the first major building to be dressed in it.[203] On the northern Aegean island of Skyros, he chose speckled red Skyros marble to dress the side entrance hall for the residents of the house. He continued to Carrara in Tuscany, where he ordered the white marble for the colonnaded front entrance hall floor, the side entrance hall floor, and the walls of the side staircase leading to the first floor.

By 1906 the Goldman & Salatsch fashion firm was widely renowned.[204] Yet at the end of 1909, when Loos and the Jewish master builder Ernst Epstein presented the model of the future building to friends and clients, the gentile author Richard Schaukal, an admirer of Loos, issued a warning that the naked upper parts would prove controversial and that Loos would face a bitter fight with public opinion.[205] If Loos and Goldman had wanted to give the Goldman & Salatsch House a new classicist dress to ennoble its commercial character and rise to the royal occasion, what did they want to claim through undressing the upper part? Loos and Goldman were aware from the outset that they were building a house that might force them into open confrontation with the Viennese public. Goldman was even risking his good reputation. One of their critics argued that the modernist outfit of the façade, with its combination of sober roof and upper floors and colored marble clothing on the lower store area and columns, exhibited a contradiction similar to that of a lady wearing an automobile cap, an English jacket, fancy skirt, and dancing shoes.[206] The critic was challenging Goldman & Salatsch's reputation as a first-class men's fashion salon, whose main clientele comprised members of different sports clubs and the Austrian Automobile Club. The new house was further described in a critical review as a naked building, yet assembled from the finest materials (free of the baroque mayonnaise, the rococo hairnet, and the modernist squares of the Wiener Werkstätte).[207] Other critics such as Otto Stoessl, Karl Kraus, and Herwarth Walden felt flattered by the mere association with this new object of attraction.[208] Yet this object also provoked disgust. Altenberg blamed Loos in a letter to Lilly Steiner—the wife of Hugo Steiner, one of Loos's most loyal Jewish clients—for focusing on self-promotion: "I can stand Loos only in his better moments, but his toothpaste-Barnum and Bayley [sic] advertising campaign for his own personal cause was Jewish, inartistic, and disgusts me."[209] Through their careful choice of dress for the store area, Goldman and Loos opted in, but they also consciously opted out. How did Goldman and Loos use dress—while also using the scandalous idea of undress in public—to achieve a lead in the battle for social visibility in the Viennese art scene?

Pierre Bourdieu argued there can be no "artistic magic" without the "magic group" or a group of believers. The magic act "would be nothing without the whole tradition leading up to her [the artist's] gesture, and without the universe of celebrants and believers who give it meaning and value in terms of that tradition."[210] Goldman and Loos were critically aware of the process of dressing and undressing—and promoted Jewish emancipation by using dress as a key to the process of Jewish acculturation or culturation. Their house was received accordingly by their "network of opinion and desire,"[211] supported by Kraus's *Die Fackel*. Kraus furthered the relevance of the undressed Goldman & Salatsch House within the acculturation process.

The fear of arousing shame through undress played a central role in Jewish acculturation. In an 1870 caricature in *Der Floh*, which drew attention to Sophie von Todesco's staging of tableaux vivants in the Todesco salon for philanthropic causes, the salon lady is dressed in a transparent dress, with one breast revealed and the second covered by a transparent scarf. She asks her female escort: "Don't you think Comiesse that my dress is a bit too low cut?" "Mon Chér [sic], Baronesse [answers her escort]—what should we do? It is for the good of the poor."—"Bon [answers the Baronesse]. In order to dress the poor—we must—do the opposite."[212] The dialectic of dressing and undressing was central to the question of attaining the highest social visibility in Viennese society. Simmel was a direct point of reference for Loos. Simmel's October 1895 essay in the liberal journal *Die Zeit*, "Zur Psychologie der Mode: Sociologische Studie" (On the psychology of fashion: A sociological study), influenced Otto Wagner and Loos's idea of basing the modernization of architecture on the ideal character of fashion—identified as contemporary women's fashion for Wagner and as timeless men's fashion for Loos.[213] In his above-mentioned essay "On Fashion," Simmel explained the role of shame in relation to choices of dress that avoid personal interaction and allow one to disappear within a group. The threat of stepping into the center and making oneself conspicuous is manifested as "a painful oscillation between emphasis upon and withdrawal of the sense of the self."[214] Fashion solves this by granting the individual a sense of being part of a mass experience and a sense of belonging. But even more, it grants the individual the possibility of releasing himself from shame by elevating him (his body) through generalization and neutralization into a work of art.[215] Yet the fear of being stripped of their clothes and the wish to become a distinct work of art was realized in Loos's actual refusal to dress the modern Goldman & Salatsch House (Fig. 35). With Goldman's support, Loos waited for weeks for the arrival of the Cipollino marble for the lower façade while the city officials, the public, and the media questioned the legitimacy of the naked façade, pretending that he needed to see the lower part's dress to determine a fitting color and possible décor for the upper parts of his building. Loos enjoyed the attention given to the public dressing up and the threat of leaving naked a building owned by Jewish patrons in the center of the city opposite the Hofburg. Ultimately, the naked upper part caused a public scandal that lasted for almost two years; to Loos and Goldman the provocation only asserted their singular authority.

FIGURE 35. *Adolf Loos, Goldman & Salatsch House façade, 1911.* © *Albertina, Vienna.* ALA 2408.

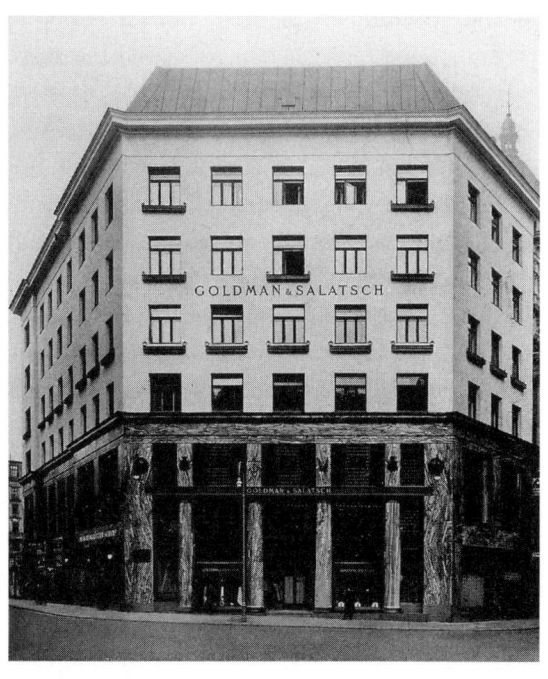

In the concept of a work in progress, either in an outfitter's ideal matching of the appropriate shirt to trousers and so on, or in a building's construction, Goldman and Loos shared an enthusiasm for the creative process in which the final product had to be of first-class quality. To evoke the sensual experience needed to lure clients to their building, and to further ensure the masculine and independent status of the architectural form, the façade's elegant four-part outfit offered a colorful delight. The Goldman & Salatsch House was ultimately "dressed" with gray granite as a base line,[216] watery green Cipollino marble for the main business area, light gray plaster for the apartment area, and a green copper roof above a jutting cornice (the green copper would eventually turn black, like a hat with a trim). Loos's unusual outfit for the Goldman & Salatsch House is certainly a deviation from the formal language of men's fashion: a combination of green marble trousers (the Tuscan columns) with a white (immediately changed to off-white or light gray)[217] shirt (the flat upper part). The colorful combination challenged the firm's sober reputation, which had been achieved through advocating the man's black suit. A possible explanation for the deviation is that Loos was expressing his provocative interpretation of progressive development in men's fashion and the need to lighten up, also endorsed in the Goldman & Salatsch House. In 1907 Lux concluded his article titled "Correct Clothing" in the journal of the

Viennese Master Tailors for Male Clients organization with the following recommendation: "There are conventions like all customs, and the wisdom to observe them is a sign of upbringing. It does not necessarily imply strain, but easy and taken-for-granted practice and habit rule constraint practiced with the freedom of naturalness. Also naturalness is a pose, and after Oscar Wilde certainly the most difficult one."[218]

The inspiration to lighten up the Goldman & Salatsch House was indeed the dandy's pose of naturalness. Yet the need for lightening up men's fashion had also been prompted by the growing popularity of sports two-piece suits at the time. Sport suits in general allowed men to brighten their dress with new colors.[219] For the Goldman & Salatsch House, Loos chose a natural, high-quality material for below (Cipollino marble) and a neutral complementary color for above (light gray painted stucco), thus completing a revolutionary, yet elegant, house suitable for modern dandies. His architectural design represented a new masculine ease that allowed a greater corporeal and spiritual elegance for the house and its owner.

However, for the acculturated European Jew, this new sense of ease also meant a negation of past heritage—the illusion of life as a tabula rasa. The smoothly shaved upper portions symbolized for Kraus, Loos's loyal supporter in the public debate, the act of shaving a beard. In his essay "Der Löwenkopf oder Die Gefahren der Technik" (The lion's head or the dangers of technology) in October 1913, Kraus attacked the historicist and secessionist styles by ridiculing the dwellers in Vienna's second district (Leopoldstadt) who complained that heavy buses would cause their houses to shake and consequently endanger the decorative fixtures on their buildings. By identifying these fixtures and ornaments as "beards" that should be shaved, Kraus may have promoted Loos's plain façade, modernist architecture as a positive representation befitting modern Jews (those living outside the Mazzesinsel, the nickname of the second district).[220] In his essay, Kraus referred to three prominent personalities who used their beards to express false pretensions: the secessionist Hermann Bahr; the pro-German Jewish historian Heinrich Freidjung; and the Jung-Wien author, Zionist, and client of Hoffmann, Beer-Hofmann. Kraus concluded his essay: "I can make a tabula rasa. I sweep the streets, I loosen the beards, I shave the ornaments."[221] Kraus's mention of the phrase "tabula rasa" refers to his earlier praise of the façade of the Goldman & Salatsch House: "The selfless defenders of the past, who would rather be buried under the ruins of houses that are falling apart, are as upset as the artistic art masons who see a missed opportunity for babbled invasions and for the first time experience what it is to stare at life as tabula rasa."[222] The

Jewish shaved beard was part of Goldman and Loos's aesthetic fight to claim the lead in the battle for social visibility among acculturated Jews in Vienna, yet the shaved beard also transformed the building into a manifestation of a new avant-garde ideal of eternal youth, replacing earlier cultural icons such as Minne's *Kneeling Boy* and Klimt's androgynous half-naked women.

Loos's wish to claim the stance of eternal youth actually continued the *ver sacrum* (sacred spring) ideology, representing the independence claims of a rebellious younger generation, and furthered the regenerative cultural program of the secessionist movement.[223] As mentioned above, Simmel had addressed the subject of coquetry, meaning flirting, in the journal *Jugend* as early as 1901.[224] *Jugend* played an important role in the creation of modern Viennese styles.[225] Simmel concluded his story with the message that flirting is actually valuable since it reflects the essence of object relations not only between man and woman but also between man and material object: it tempts you to desire something you will never possess. The relationship between style and possession is crucial for understanding the contribution of Jewish patrons to modern architecture and design in Vienna. Goldman was willing to give up money to prove that he had an authorial lead and to assert ownership over his house as an avant-gardist cultural production.[226] To advance the new fashion building, Goldman had made a financial sacrifice and denied himself immediate profit, as recognized in the concluding passage of a review in support of the house in *Wiener Allgemeine Zeitung*.[227] And Goldman was aware that he was offering a new provocation—challenging the historicist style—through the naked upper façade. Moreover, the feminized masculine appeal of the new house, as reported in the media, fit Otto Weininger's critique of the secessionists' ideal "new woman" as a "tall lanky woman with a flat chest and narrow hips."[228] As Cernuschi pointed out, Weininger connected it to the following phenomenon: "The enormous recent increase in a kind of dandified homosexuality may be due to the increasing effeminacy of the age."[229] Loos transformed this prejudice against "the increasing effeminacy of the age"—or the threat of Judaization, as described in the introduction to this book—into his and Goldman's triumphal architectural statement.

The novel mix of plain stucco and green marble caused a moral provocation in the media that could be compared to the scandal accompanying Klimt's presentation of androgynous female exotica—for example, the half-naked young female in his painting *Water Serpents* of 1904–7 (originally in the collection of Karl Wittgenstein, today this is in the Belvedere, Vienna). Loos may indeed have been inspired by Klimt when he matched naked stucco with luxurious marble, which was interpreted by a number of critics as an erotic effect. In February 1911, Engelmann—Loos's future student—attempted to defend the façade of the Goldman & Salatsch House, comparing its two parts to two types of women, the upper part soft and virginal (so that you would like to kiss it), and the lower, marble part naïve and lustful (like a lascivious woman).[230] The flat-chested upper part was also identified with the androgyny of a girl's body. Peter Haiko has argued that "here, eros is defined as love of the female body in its early, childish, pubescent stage. The Loos house thus becomes the architectural incarnation of still innocent, preadolescent nakedness, a stage of development that, as we know, fascinated not only Adolf Loos, but also Peter Altenberg and Egon Schiele—as it did, indeed, all of fin-de-siècle society."[231] Haiko also quotes the statement Loos had made in an article on women's fashion: "The child-woman came into fashion. One yearned for immaturity."[232] In his article, Loos had mentioned his friend Altenberg in connection with the phenomenon of admiring young girls. Altenberg's creative authority was thus also projected onto the youthful image of the house. Possibly influenced by Altenberg's admiration of Klimt—in contrast to Kraus, who had dismissed Klimt's paintings as an expression of Jewish taste—in 1908 Loos toyed with the idea of calling his Kärntnerstrasse bar the Klimt Bar[233] before naming it the American Bar. Nonetheless, with his androgynous, seemingly half-naked façade for the Goldman & Salatsch House, Loos attempted to prove to the public that he was a better secessionist than Klimt—and demonstrated that he could better represent the flirtatious relationship between the Jewish patron and the Viennese public.

With the support of his tailor and loyal client Goldman, Loos fulfilled the promises made by the founders of the secessionist movement: to display a new image of physical youth; to refuse to yield to public demands; and to demonstrate, in the name of true art, an indifference to immediate profit. Furthermore, if we compare the secessionist buildings by Wagner—for example, the Majolica House (1898–99) at Linke Wienzeile 40, possibly inspired by a flowery shirt seen on the back of the journal *Wiener Mode* on July 1, 1898—to Loos's Goldman & Salatsch House, we recognize Loos and Goldman's victorious moment in the chronicles of Viennese modernism. The façade's progression from a decorative dress toward a geometric abstraction in architecture marked Loos's progress in succeeding the secessionist avant-garde. As mentioned above, Hevesi described Loos's style in relation to his suits as representative of (his tailor's) geometric elegance. Loos and Goldman had the effrontery to combine the fin de siècle ideal of female youth with the ideal of geometrically elegant men's fashion, reinventing the ethos of men's fashion through avant-garde architecture. They were the culmination of an evolutionary process that had begun with the ideal of not standing out in public and led to the secessionist ideal of eternal youth. Loos furthermore subverted the negative expectations of Goldman as a Jewish client—that he would have no style and a bad moral influence—and creatively redefined along with his client the culture of men's fashion. The tailored façade of the central fashion house opposite the Hofburg exemplified the modern in the androgyny of its unisex outfit and reflected acculturated Jews' and liberal gentiles' identity desires.

The new avant-garde style of the Goldman & Salatsch House further promised the cultural regeneration of both Jewish and Viennese traditions. Loos's choice of watery, patterned trousers for the lower area could be associated with the idea of the fountain of youth, illustrated through the light blue coloring in an early drawing of the façade. The idea of recovering youthful vitality through entering the fountain of youth is deeply rooted in German culture and celebrated in a masterpiece by Lucas Cranach the Elder, *Der Jungbrunnen* (The fountain of youth; 1546). This romantic idea also served to celebrate and promote the match between a reformed lifestyle and modern architecture. The collage façade of the Goldman & Salatsch House, with the flowing water of the marble and the more reserved mathematical motif (the bay windows), further classifies the design as an avant-garde unisex outfit. Loos applied patterns independent of the original male or female dress items with which they were typically associated. Another projection of unisex dress onto the house is the neutral light color of the upper floors, which expressed not only virginal female nudity[234] but also male secrecy (it seemed to reflect a silent pose).[235] The references to the shaved beard and water, the ultimate avant-garde statement of eternal youth, would have supported the house's claim to have surpassed the secessionists' designs, and in exchange would have granted the owner and coproducer—Leopold Goldman—the title of the most elegant Viennese gentleman.

The Lost Honor of Leopold Goldman

In 1911, Loos recognized Goldman's important contribution to his architectural achievement in his famous lecture "Mein Haus am Michaelerplatz" (My house at Michaelerplatz): "Here I must acknowledge the great contribution one of the clients, Herr Leopold Goldman, made to working out the ground plan. It is thanks to his collaboration, thanks to his brilliant ideas, thanks to his business knowledge, which repeatedly crystallized in genuine innovations[,] that the ground plan developed as it did. And there is one other thing I must thank him for. He stood by me, unwaveringly, when people were saying 'The whole of Vienna has good taste, apart from Loos.'"[236]

Buildings played a special role in Jewish self-styling and hope for eternal fame, around which the "magic group" of one's orbit could be concentrated.[237] Freud was not a patron of modern art and architecture, yet tellingly he expressed the public figure's ambition of associating his achievements with specific buildings. In June 1900, in a letter to his friend and colleague Wilhelm Fliess in Berlin, Freud asked if he thought that a marble tablet would one day be placed on the spa hotel Belle Vue in Vienna's nineteenth district with the text: "In this house on 24 July 1895, the Secret of Dreams was revealed by Dr. Sigmund Freud."[238] Freud wanted to identify the hotel as an architectural witness to his achievements. Like Beer-Hofmann, who through his house wanted to erect a monument to the achievements of his literary group (destroyed following a decision by Viennese city officials), Goldman wanted to erect a monument to his creative professional achievements and to his fashion salon's group of clients.

Goldman's other investment in a Loos design, a less striking historicist apartment building (1909) in Vienna's nineteenth district, also had a smooth upper part but was less provocative. This design included Goldman's grand family apartment, a private cultivated garden, and a swimming pool. Goldman, who considered himself a Viennese gentleman, decorated the walls of the lobby in his apartment with four maps showing Vienna, Austria, Europe, and the world. It is possible that Loos recommended this décor, giving the lobby the double identity of a family gathering place and an English gentleman's studio,[239] but it represented Goldman's wish to position himself as a gentleman with a cosmopolitan outlook. While his private house secured this identification, his business house would grant him fame as a Viennese celebrity. Goldman closely followed media coverage of the purchase and construction of the house, and even after the scandal of the undecorated upper façade erupted, he continued to collect articles on his architect and his house.[240] Goldman found in this media coverage a confirmation of the production's achievement. His house was his contribution to the Europeanization and modernization of Vienna's landscape and a symbol of his fame as a Viennese producer of culture.

However, Goldman's fame as identified with an elite fashion firm's building, and the reference to gold in his name, would be held against him.[241] Leopold; his wife, Lilly; his oldest son, Fred; and his partner Emanuel Aufricht died in the Holocaust.²⁴² The Viennese preference for associating his fame not with merit but with money reveals the twofold heritage of Jewish patrons of style and seduction. For years Goldman's seduction of money was irrationally associated with the threatening power of Jewish money, and his essential contribution to the fashioning of a new Viennese avant-garde style went unacknowledged.

CONCLUSION

The patrons and architects discussed in this book understood the stylized self-image, projected onto façades, interiors, and design objects, as granting them emancipation. Fashioning new styles was a most challenging and creative task for Jewish patrons since—as the sociologist Zygmunt Bauman has noted—"the foreigner" is "the carrier and the personification of *incongruity*."[1] Grafting onto Viennese high culture their Jewish micronarratives as strangers who came to stay opened new dimensions of thinking and thus created change.[2] The Jewish patrons discussed in this book were caught in a larger Viennese social and political dynamic that constantly challenged their achievements due to misunderstanding, jealousy and small-mindedness, and they were ultimately perceived as threats to local tradition. Integral to their achievement, nonetheless, was their wish to prove their belonging to Vienna, their support of Vienna's and Austria's modernization, and their ability to acknowledge and transform prejudice against them into gestures of cultural triumph.

The Jewish patrons Eduard von Todesco, Gustav von Epstein, Ludwig Hevesi, Karl Wittgenstein, Friedrich Viktor Spitzer, Isidor Singer, Fritz Waerndorfer, Richard Beer-Hofmann, Peter Altenberg, and Leopold Goldman fashioned their personas as Jewish dandies and Viennese celebrities in different manners according to their heritage, social networks, and specific cultural ambitions. Yet while celebrated dandies during this period such as Oscar Wilde and Charles Baudelaire did not present—and even negated—moral claims, the Jewish patrons presented here had concrete agendas concerning their families' survival and the preservation of Jewish culture. In confronting the rise of antisemitism and recognizing the merits of secularization, Jewish patrons preferred acculturation (which implies promoting new aesthetic codes for social bonding between Jews and gentiles, while renewing Jewish cultural forms) rather than assimilation (which implies a total absorption and disappearance of Jewish cultural forms). The patrons Hevesi, Wittgenstein, Waerndorfer, and Altenberg were assimilated or chose the assimilation path on a personal level, yet they engaged with the subject of Jewish cultural difference and consequently contributed to the renewal of Jewish culture in the public sphere. Integral to their ambition was the devising of new styles to guarantee Jewish emancipation. In May 1897, Theodor Herzl, the leader of the new Zionist movement, wrote to the architect Oskar Marmorek: "Dear Friend, I will happily speak with you a few more times about Jewish style. Please come to my place again at 5 pm. I think that this style should express the feeling of liberation. Serenity (serenitas). I lack the knowledge to describe it, what I think about it."[3] Herzl, who was confronted with instances of antisemitism, represented his wish for liberation and serenity in his idea of "Jewish style." For him "Jewish style" was an expression of Jewish emancipation. Like Herzl, leading Jewish patrons used the Western European dandy pose in their interpretation of style and in so doing claimed authority as Viennese cultural producers;[4] furthermore, they used their authority as cultural producers to secure their Jewish identification. In contrast to Herzl's Zionist writings, their efforts were to advance integration in Viennese society by creating and promoting shared cultural platforms. Their goal was to teach their children and fellow Jews a survival strategy, showing them both sides (meaning both Jewish and gentile cultures), and enabling them to cross frontiers in the European Diaspora.

Jews' and Christians' newly gained familiarity with each other in the public and private arenas in the nineteenth century created vulnerability and provoked a shock of nearness. This shock—or, as Simmel referred to it, "a slight aversion, a mutual strangeness and repulsion, which will break into hatred and conflict at the moment of a closer contact"[5]—was not only between Jews and Christians: a certain physical distance was kept between social classes, generations, genders, and even neighbors. Yet the new proximity between Jews and Christians led to a heightened tension and—with the Jewish patron's persistent need to prove, share, and flirt—may have aroused strong emotions of hate (including self-hate). These can be said to have been documented in Otto Weininger's *Geschlecht und Charakter* (Sex and character; 1903), mentioned in the introduction; in Arthur Schnitzler's *The Road into the Open* (1908), mentioned in chapter 4; and Schnitzler's scandalous play *Professor Bernhardi*, describing an antisemitic conflict in a hospital (1912). Sigmund Freud made a critical observation of this experience of shock accompanying physical proximity, particularly in the reconsideration of the dependency of Jews on gentiles, and described the Jewish perspective on it in his groundbreaking book *The Interpretation of Dreams* (1900). In the beginning of his analysis of his dream "My son, the Myops," Freud wrote: "The Jewish problem, concern about the future of one's children, to whom one cannot give a country of their own, concern about educating them in such a way that they can move freely across frontiers."[6]

Freud's dream was provoked by Theodor Herzl's play *Das neue Ghetto* and the work's handling of the subject of failed Jewish integration into Viennese society (Herzl's play is discussed in chapters 2–4. Freud's reaction to Herzl's play, which pointed out the threat of Jews not having a place of their own, was to embrace the threat of no territory as an intellectual blessing. To understand the principles of secular Jewish survival and the new direction of art patronage that several Jewish businessmen and intellectuals at the end of the nineteenth century were developing, it is important to cite the whole dream:

> On account of certain events which had occurred in the city of Rome, it had become necessary to remove the children to safety, and this was done. The scene was then in front of a gateway, double doors in the ancient style (the "*Porta Romana*" at Siena, as I was aware during the dream itself). I was sitting on the edge of a fountain and was greatly depressed and almost in tears. A female figure—an attendant or nun—brought two boys out and handed them over to their father, who was not myself. The elder of the two was clearly my eldest son; I did not see the other one's face. The woman who brought out the boy asked him to kiss her good-bye. She was noticeable for having a red nose. The boy refused to kiss her, but holding out his hand in farewell, said "Auf Geseres" to her, and then "Auf Ungeseres" to the two of us (or to one of us). I had a notion that this last phrase denoted a preference.[7]

The first threat in the dream is expressed through the need to remove the children to safety from Rome. However, it is Siena where Freud finds himself waiting, "almost in tears." His state of being almost in tears is connected to his sitting at the edge of the fountain. The fountain is the association that motivated Freud to replace Rome with Siena. However, the fountain, the sadness, and his state of being almost in tears relates to a Jew's sadness in the Babylon Diaspora, longing for Jerusalem. This idea is evoked in the quote, "By the waters of Babylon we sat down and wept."[8] Freud is not weeping but is almost in tears. He can still identify with the Jewish experience (here, the regret over the loss of Jerusalem), but he holds himself back from weeping. Still, it is nostalgia that introduces the concept of geographical displacement for Freud: Rome, Siena, and Babylon are names of different places that recall the experience of Jews in the Diaspora. The second threat is a recognition that the gentile woman responsible for taking care of his son is drunk (her nose is red). While the idea of the red nose ruining a portrait was a metaphor suggested by an architect when he confronted his client for ruining his design—the anecdote told by an art historian to challenge Todesco's patronage—here Freud's description of the gentile woman with a red nose supports his suspicion that she is a danger to his son. In his dream Freud witnesses how his eldest son demonstrates the lesson of survival, the lesson of negation. His son reverses his farewell, "Auf geseres," his address to the gentile attendant or nun, into a salutation, "Auf Ungeseres," addressed to Freud. The negation expressed in his farewell represents a defense against the threat presumably posed by the gentile's hatred of him. Freud explains "geseres" as "a genuine Hebrew word derived from the verb "goiser," and it is best translated by "imposed sufferings" or "doom."[9] This threat may be related to the religious rhetoric of the punished Jews (originating in the wish to punish Jews for rejecting Christ as the messiah), since the geseres (imposed sufferings) were motivated and legitimized by hate rhetoric. Furthermore, the negation of the threat is made possible through a Yiddish-like match between a German particle (un) with a Hebrew word (geseres). This match could suggest a paradox because even if the Hebrew word resurfaces as an act of self-defense, it is the addition of the German particle that enables the actual reversal of the threat. In addition, the negation of the word "geseres" is perceived as a binding experience between son and father, and it is through the evocation of their historical heritage and the negation of a threat projected onto the gentile attendant that one will be able to cross frontiers.[10] Interpreting the message of his own dream, Freud concludes that he will educate his son to see both sides so he will be able to cross frontiers.

From the early 1860s, after Jews received the right to settle and own land in Vienna, and following their reception of equal rights in 1867, Jewish patrons fashioned new houses or houses as gathering places together with their architects as expressions of their belonging to the city. Their designs exhibited the dialectical process of representing themselves in Vienna and demonstrated their ability to cross frontiers as a survival tactic in the Diaspora. The structures they built also expressed their European (Western or romantic Eastern) Jewish identification in a creative manner that also allowed them and their children to continue crossing frontiers. There were different frontiers to cross to secure survival: those related to geography, language, culture, and careers. Liberal Jews created and supported new designs that contributed to the modernization of Vienna and further helped fashion new styles. The dialectical process of placement in Vienna, as well as expressions of displacement to other places in Europe, the United States, or the Near East, served as sources of inspiration to both patrons and architects. The question may be whether Jewish patrons mastered this dialectic better than gentile patrons. The new styles that Viennese Jewish patrons fashioned can be seen in Todesco's stylized Renaissance Italian public rooms (designed at a time when Jews in Italian cities were still forced to live in ghettos) or in Waerndorfer's modern Scottish music room (which offered an artistic pilgrimage place for European visitors to Vienna). Still, there were distinctions of attitude among the different Jewish patrons.

If Todesco requested in the interior design of his dining room (1864) a decorative setting referring to the Medici to reaffirm his relationship to grand European history, Waerndorfer ordered a Mackintosh interior design for his music salon (1902) to befit a modern Austrian-European tradition. Furthermore, while Todesco chose prominent Greek symbols like caryatids to decorate the top floor of his façade or paintings of the Trojan war in his dining room to fashion an avant-gardist Jewish self-identification, defined in relation to Hellenistic Jewish ancestry but with the additional intention of creating a shared cultural platform for Jews and gentiles, Waerndorfer chose a modernist European playwright's fairy-tale narrative, that of the Seven Princesses, to express personal nostalgia for the Friday night ceremony, thereby integrating a Jewish religious custom into an avowedly bohemian setting. Both Todesco and Waerndorfer aimed to enable their children to continue to cross frontiers. In pursuing this goal, the historicist Todesco and the modernist Waerndorfer claimed active roles as Austrian cultural producers despite prejudice against them as Jewish patrons. Both were ridiculed: Todesco as an ignoramus and Waerndorfer as a snob. As a single young man, Todesco had already set an example by joining Biedermeier literary clubs that were established to promote sociability between gentiles and Jews and between prominent and less-known businessmen and authors or journalists. His design choices for the public rooms in his historicist palace were related to this progressive literary club tradition, and even Todesco's humor, challenging cultural sacred cows, was part of it. In an early letter, Waerndorfer suggested to Hermann Bahr his wish to renew Austrian applied arts, and he would later help the secessionists recruit British and Scottish designers to their eighth exhibition. He invited both Austrians and Scots to cooperate not only in the exhibition halls but also in his private house. Three years after offering Bahr different possible ways to renew Austrian applied arts, Waerndorfer (together with his mother) secured the large investment necessary to found the Wiener Werkstätte. In

1906, the exhibition of the Wiener Werkstätte in London helped define Austrian cultural identity in modern Europe.[11] In 1909, Waerndorfer reported proudly to Bahr on the Wiener Werkstätte's achievements after it was praised by the wives of two American museum directors.[12] For Waerndorfer the test for the success of the Wiener Werkstätte's modern style (and for its financial security) was in the modern style's ability to cross frontiers.

The historicist banker and patron Epstein and the secessionist cultural critic and author Hevesi used their reputations as experts in matters of taste to leave eternal marks on the city and its culture. Epstein also secured his fame through purchasing old masters to upgrade the artistic value of his magnificent city palace (1872), and Hevesi presented his invaluable testimony and insight in two books that still serve today as among the most important source books for Viennese modern culture, *Acht Jahre Sezession* (1906) and *Altkunst—Neukunst, Wien, 1894 bis 1908* (1909). Both Epstein and Hevesi secured their belonging to Vienna by using their patronage to claim membership in exclusive clubs: Epstein to the elitist Ringstrasse society and Hevesi to the Vienna Secession. Moreover, perhaps sensing or admiring the model set by the dandy Disraeli (as mentioned in the introduction), both used their membership in elites to transform their supposedly Jewish crime into a celebrated artistic vice. In the process of transforming crime into vice, the role of the mirror and the notion of reflection in fashioning authority was crucial to these cultural producers. Epstein's motto "Be who you appear to be" appeared on his coat of arms, and he acted as a true Viennese Jewish gentleman even after his financial ruin. Hevesi took a risk as a Jewish critic in describing art as a mirror and as a reflection of his and his readers' shared self-image. He used his reviews to fashion readers' expectations of the new secessionist movement and idealized the Secession House as a place also for Jews on the cultural stage. In other words, he presented to his readers secessionist art as a mirror to their ideal self-identification.

The modernist patron and author Beer-Hofmann and the avant-gardist patron and poet Altenberg secured position as dandies through careful construction of networks of desire and opinion. Both men were acknowledged as Viennese celebrities. While Beer-Hofmann positioned himself in the Viennese art scene, choosing symbols that represented his proud Jewish identification, Altenberg chose a bohemian lifestyle that reworked the negative aspects of "Jewishness." Beer-Hofmann demonstratively defined his villa as a Jewish home by placing the Star of David in the arched glass window above the entrance door. He also placed a silver Torah shield next to the doorway to his studio to show a dandylike, nonchalant, and creative integration of a

Jewish liturgical object in his villa's interior. Altenberg lived in hotels and was eternalized as a night wanderer in a caricature portrait hung at the American Bar (1908). He created his own spaces for enticement, such as his hotel rooms, where he hung a photo of Richard Wagner as part of his collection in a sort of precursor to Facebook. If Beer-Hofmann and Altenberg claimed authority as Viennese dandies, they were also challenged. Beer-Hofmann was criticized for his Jewish beard, and Altenberg similarly singled out for his hysterical outbursts. Moreover, their ability as patrons to encourage emotional engagement between seduction and style—namely, in how they seduced audiences with narcissistic poses while presenting sensitive and psychological portraits of their inner lives—was simultaneously hailed as modern and rejected as uncanny.

The industrialist and secessionist patron Spitzer and the journalists and modernist patrons Singer and Kanner redefined the Jewish acculturation process by challenging conservative codes of respectability or notions about appropriate behavior and manners of communication. Yet in so doing they may have confirmed stereotypical characterizations of Jewish difference.[13] If the historicist patron Todesco provoked with the intention of challenging the acculturation process, Spitzer challenged the host's role in a different manner. Spitzer exposed a voyeuristic inclination through his art of sociability and used the architect Joseph Maria Olbrich's original secessionist setting (1899) in his apartment (and later in his villa) to encourage flirtation scenes: his apartment became a performance space for the young Alma Schindler (later Alma Mahler) to flirt with Olbrich and later for her love affair with his protégée, the composer Alexander von Zemlinsky. Yet there was a dark motivation to his watching Alma's flirtations in his music salon and in how he ruled himself out from the flirtation scenes by playing the eunuch. In an anecdote from this period (discussed above), Alma reported that Spitzer had been chased away from the main dinner table at the house of her stepfather, Carl Moll, after the opening of the Secession House in 1898; the young Alma initiated the chase of the "black-moor" Spitzer, framing him as the outsider (and not only because Spitzer was a single man, since Klimt—who was also chasing Spitzer—was single as well).[14] Spitzer used his setting to be included in the secessionist club, but his inclusion as a Viennese celebrity was conditional, since as a Jewish dandy he was still dependent on being accepted by others.

Choosing a modernist style to secure inclusion was transformative for the Jewish patrons, but the new style at times further exposed their fundamental exclusion. When the modernist patrons Singer and Kanner invited Bahr to join their journal *Die Zeit* as the editor of the art section, they backed a winning horse in the race to acculturate Jewish media entrepreneurs and modernize Vienna. Choosing the architect Otto Wagner to design the prominently positioned Telegraph Office and art gallery for their newly founded newspaper *Die Zeit* in 1902 was supposed to be another winning choice. Indeed, Wagner's groundbreaking design for Singer demonstrates the architect's stylistic development and his move from Jugendstil to modernism, championing a new formal language. Yet despite Singer and Kanner's use of new modernist designs, the language they used in opposition to the political regime led to the dismissal of their newspaper as expression of "loud communication," showing no respect for the Europeanization ideal of restrained and moderate language, and further led to their humiliating, public framing as Eastern Jews. Singer and Kanner's attempts to reclaim authority after Kraus exposed the newsboy on their advertisement as looking too Jewish—as discussed above—by changing him to a boy who looked gentile and thus forcing on him symbolic plastic surgery, reveal that their new style did not erase stereotypical differentiation between Jews and gentiles but rather championed it. In retrospect, this historical anecdote exposes the weakness in their ambitious project for progress in Austrian culture.

The industrialist and secessionist patron Wittgenstein was a baptized Protestant and a second-generation assimilated Jew. In 1898, he was fifty-five and one of the richest and most prominent public figures in the Austro-Hungarian Empire. Wittgenstein had retired from all his enterprises and decided to reinvest his fortune mainly in real estate and in secured investments outside Austria, independent of the well-being of the monarchy. The Jewish patron Leopold Goldman was thirty-five in 1910. The avant-gardist patron and tailor Goldman was a secular, or—as he later defined himself—free-thinking—Jew. Along with his partner and brother-in-law, Emanuel Aufricht, he had gained control of the elite men's fashion salon that his father Michael Goldman had established. Furthermore, he had recently received the honorary title of court deliverer. In contrast to Wittgenstein, Goldman depended on the well-being of the monarchy, since his main clients were European aristocrats and bureaucrats. Wittgenstein was a self-made millionaire and an uncompromising patriarch who used a few ugly tricks in the process of expanding his business into the largest steel cartel in the empire. The wealthy Goldman, the son of a self-made man, was a good-natured gentleman who worked hard to maintain the good reputation of his elite men's fashion salon. These two different personalities financed two modern houses central to the chronicles of Viennese modern architecture and design. The iconography of both houses, the Secession House and the Goldman & Salatsch House, reflect the double identity of Jewish patrons in Vienna as Western Jews whose cultural roots were in the Near East.[15] Both the Secession House and the Goldman & Salatsch House provoked public scandals, yet both houses connected Vienna to different European traditions and to Near Eastern architecture, consequently marketing the city as cosmopolitan. The Secession House was designed as an ostentatious Jugendstil temple for lovers of modern art, manifesting a daring match between sacral Orientalism, with specific reference to historicist Moorish synagogues, and—according to Olbrich—the architecture of Doric temples. The Goldman & Salatsch House is an essential example of an alternative pioneering modern architecture and a refined composite of neoclassical, British, and Mediterranean style, highlighted through the smooth surface of the upper architectural elements. The choice of the secessionist Wittgenstein and the avant-gardist Goldman to support architectural hybrids with Hellenist and Oriental elements reveals a trend of Jewish patrons going back to their roots. Therefore, these houses can also be regarded as leading a new Jewish avant-garde. In this manner, Wittgenstein and Goldman, like their predecessors, offered new Jewish narrative representations as integral to Viennese high culture before World War I.

Jewish patrons fashioned their dandy personas to strike out in public, inspiring heated debates in the media and provoking at times public scandals as they constructed networks of opinion. The facts that Waerndorfer sat with Bahr in the Café Museum, collecting articles for a book to defend Klimt's reputation after the scandal concerning Klimt's university panels and that Goldman supported Adolf Loos throughout the public scandal over his design for the flat upper part of his building's façade demonstrate that Jewish patrons were willing to risk their reputations (and their fortunes) to prove their loyalty to and belief in the cause of fashioning new Viennese styles. The process of artistic reclamation for these Jewish patrons took place alongside their acknowledgment that their seduction of viewers would be seen as a threat. Koloman Moser's booklet for Waerndorfer, with its figure of the temptress Salomé (1903), and the criticism and praise of Goldman & Salatsch House as a pornographic public exhibit further document the projection of this prejudice onto the Jewish patrons. If their authorial intent as patrons was to use the architectural environment to demonstrate their belonging to Vienna, creating constructive shared cultural platforms for Jews and gentiles, then their wish to use negative aspects of "Jewishness" to assert creative freedom and their wish to subvert the prejudice against Jews for overt sexuality and low morals resulted in the reversal of the architectural message. The critical

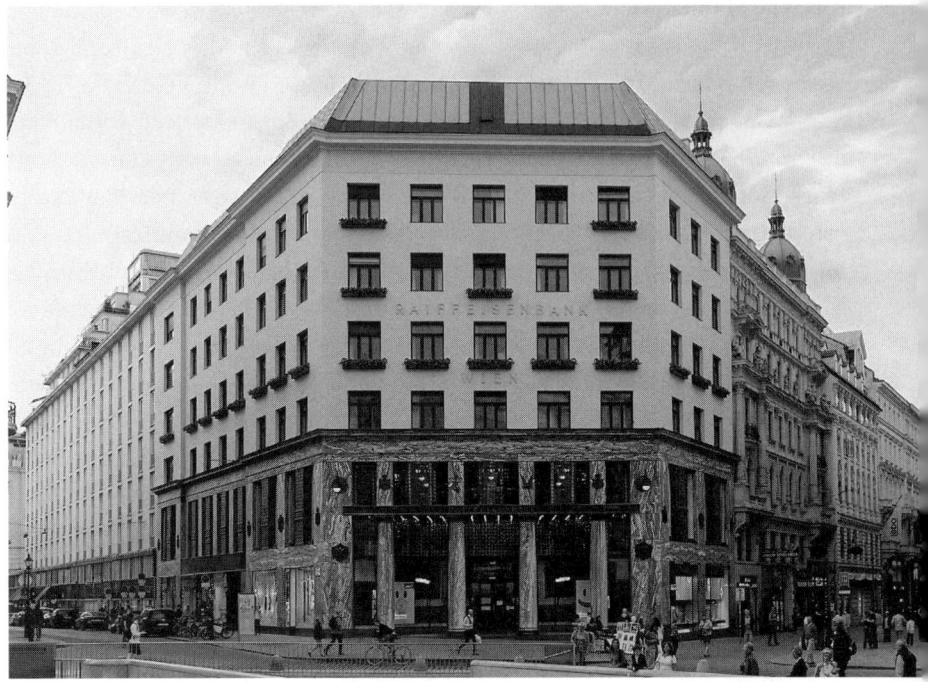

FIGURE 36. *Adolf Loos, Goldman & Salatsch House, 1911.*
Photo: © 2015, Benjamin von Radom.

contribution of the patrons Todesco, Epstein, Hevesi, Wittgenstein, Spitzer, Singer, Kanner, Waerndorfer, Beer-Hofmann, Altenberg, and Goldman to Viennese modernism is exemplified in the interiors of their homes and their objects of daily use, which offered open confrontations to a Viennese public. They attempted to reconstruct what was rejected as seductive Jewish flirtation and experienced as uncanny.

Given these open confrontations or cultural clashes, we can reconsider how the Jewish patrons and their architects grafted a survival strategy onto Viennese style. Hugo von Hofmannsthal's statement "You have only life, they —they have style" in the text accompanying his series of twelve tableaux vivants,[16] addressed to his patrons on the Ringstrasse, can be contextualized as part of the Jewish patrons' creative tactic of exposure and concealment in shaping new Viennese styles. Loos's claim for cosmopolitanism (following the British model) fit this tactic of exposure and concealment to create a shared identity between Jews and gentiles while acknowledging the Jewish experience of cultural difference. According to the German studies scholar Daniel Purdy, "if nationalism arises from the belief that another group has stolen the mythic pleasure of community, then Loosian internationalism entails the reverse: the admission that another group will always remain superior, more progressive, more elegant."[17] Since Jewish patrons supposedly did not have style and supposedly did not belong to the community of the Catholic majority (or even—though they tried—to the national German community), the avant-gardists projected a supra-international claim to assert a leading role by fashioning the Viennese style as progressive. The new avant-garde style succeeded in integrating cultural difference as part of a reformist Viennese style. The reference to the British gentleman allowed the patron and his architect to challenge prejudice against Jews as Easterners. Accessing the British template for style facilitated Goldman and Loos's project to advance revolutionary Viennese avant-garde style (Fig. 36, Plate 13). The two subverted prejudice against a Jewish lack of style and Jews' bad moral influence on Viennese society into a gesture of shared emancipation.

Jewish patrons of modern architecture and design freed themselves from conservative and reactionary fashion and design dictates and created shared cultural platforms that promoted public debate. They engaged audiences and challenged them to cross, eliminate, or reestablish boundaries between Jewish culture and Christian culture in Vienna, to secure distance between them. While their efforts were underscored by poses of flirtation, the discursive process of representing new Jewish identification and flexible frames of self-imaging were the core of Viennese modern style.

NOTES

Introduction

1. This follows Paul Ricoeur's hermeneutic method of grafting historical explanation onto narrative comprehension ("On Interpretation," in Ricoeur, *From Text to Action*, 1–20).

2. For example, there is no mention of patronage in Ludwig Münz's 1936 public appeal, published in the *Wiener Zeitung*, to preserve the "Loos-Haus" (referred to in this book as the Goldman & Salatsch House) as a historical monument: "Das Loos-Haus muß das bleiben, was es ist: ein Denkmal seiner Zeit und seines großen Schöpfers" ("Die Gefährdung des Loos-Hauses auf dem Michaelerplatz").

3. Beller, "Who Made Vienna 1900 a Capital of Modern Culture," 177.

4. Ernst Gombrich, *The Visual Arts in Vienna Circa 1900*, 5 (my emphasis).

5. See McGuinness, "Wittgenstein und das Judentum," 70 and 76.

6. Patrons discussed in this book made a distinct contribution to Viennese modern architecture and design, coming to terms with their Jewish heritage and creating their own Jewish identification. The terms "acculturated" and "assimilated" can be understood as referring to two different processes. Contemporaries understood assimilation as the process of Jewish acculturation, yet more specifically it meant Jewish integration through conversion to Christianity. In turn, Jewish acculturation in Vienna—before and after Jews were granted equal rights in 1867—has been identified as the cultural process of integration into Christian society (see Rozenblit, *The Jews of Vienna*, 3).

7. Schorske, a cultural historian, downplays the Jewish identities of central protagonists, instead arguing that the crisis of liberalism led to the sons' rebellion against their liberal fathers (*Fin-de-Siècle Vienna*, 6). Le Rider, a German studies scholar, notes that their painful acknowledgement of their failure to assimilate forced intellectual Jews to find original answers to the "Jewish question" (*Modernity and Crises of Identity*, 5).

8. Blom, "Rebelling in a World of Façades"; Colomina, "Sex, Lies and Decoration"; Huey, "Das Ästhetisierte Individuum"; Natter and Frodl, *Klimt und die Frauen*.

9. Topp, *Architecture and Truth in Fin-de-Siècle Vienna*.

10. Bedoire, *The Jewish Contribution to Modern Architecture*.

11. Shapira, "Imaging the Jew."

12. The contribution of three Jewish architects—the historicist Wilhelm Stiassny, the secessionist Oskar Marmorek, and the modernist Paul Engelmann—are briefly examined below. All three engaged with the Jewish national ideology of Zionism.

13. For a discussion of evaluating cosmopolitanism as the "quality of relations," see Humphrey and Skvirskaja, introduction.

14. Zweig writes: "When I attempt to find a simple formula for the period in which

I grew up, prior to the First World War, I hope that I convey its fullness by calling it the Golden Age of Security" (*The World of Yesterday*, 1).

15. Jewish patrons and journalists immediately recognized the threat of Lueger's antisemitic campaign (Editorial).

16. The art historian Martin Powers argues: "What we call 'style' is an important means whereby social groups project their constructed identities and stake their claims in the world" (Powers, "Art and History," 384).

17. Hevesi and Waerndorfer converted to Protestantism, Wittgenstein was a second-generation Christian (his Jewish parents had converted to Protestantism), and Spitzer and Altenberg left the Jewish religion. No documents regarding Altenberg's conversion were found, but he was buried in a Christian ceremony. I analyze these personalities as Jewish patrons through their active roles in Jewish networks and to the extent that they used symbols of Jewish culture and were received as Jews by Viennese society.

18. See Erving Goffman's theory about the presentation and performance of self with respect to public validation (*The Presentation of Self in Everyday Life*).

19. Pollak, "Cultural Innovation and Social Identity," 67.

20. Regarding the questioning of "identity" as an analytical category and using "identification" as an alternative, see Brubaker and Cooper, "Beyond 'Identity,'" especially 14–15 and 18–19.

21. Simmel became part of the Viennese public discourse, especially after the publication of his influential essays in leading Viennese newspapers and journals (which occurred at the same time as the creation of the central architectural and design works analyzed in this book). For a discussion of his influence, see Frisby, *Georg Simmel in Wien*.

22. Simmel, "The Problem of Style" in Simmel, *Simmel on Culture*, 216. The art critic Zuckerkandl and the architect Loos also published in *Dekorative Kunst*.

23. When "Jewishness" appears with quotation marks in this book, which is most of the time, the quotation marks are meant to emphasize that it is a coded reference to a biased or bigoted understanding of what Jewishness could be.

24. I am grateful to Benjamin von Radom for his discovery of these two caryatids as part of his research on caryatids in Vienna's first district.

25. On the transformation of the iconography of Judith in the nineteenth century from a devout woman who saved her nation to a temptress who killed a man, see Friedman, "The Metamorphosis of Judith," 244–46. See also Lathers, "Posing the 'Belle Juive,'" 27.

26. The dismissal of modern art and design as representing Jewish taste is discussed in chapter 2.

27. Garelick, *Rising Star*, 11.

28. Quoted in Arendt, "The Jews and Society," in Arendt, *The Origins of Totalitarianism*, 69. The third book in the trilogy "Young England," *Tancred* is concerned with reconciling Judaism with Christianity and the relevance of this in the British Empire (see Diniejko, "Benjamin Disraeli and the Two Nation Divide").

29. Crime attributed to Jews in the Christian rhetoric was projected onto two stories of Jewish conspiracy: the betrayal of Judas Iscariot, which was responsible for Christ's crucifixion, and the refusal of Ahasver (the wandering Jew) to recognize Christ as the messiah. These narratives of religious hate rhetoric were sustained through other accusations against Jews, in blood-libel stories or fantasies about Jewish conspiracies to take

over the world. The identification of "Jewishness" with horrifying crimes was further promoted by the press and performed in the law courts in Vienna around the end of the nineteenth century (see Vyleta, *Crime, Jews and News*).

30. Simmel, "The Metropolis and the Mental Life," in Simmel, *Simmel on Culture*, 175. See also the discussion of Simmel's text in Donald, *Imagining the Modern City*, 10.

31. Donald, *Imagining the Modern City*, 11. The quote by Simmel also appears (in a slightly different translation) in Simmel, *Simmel on Culture*, 181. Unless otherwise stated all translations are mine.

32. Shapira, "Gaze and Spectacle in the Calibration of Class and Gender."

33. Replacing the caftan with a Westernized jacket was integral to Eastern European Jews' integration in Vienna. Theodor Gomperz, a prominent Jewish scholar who referred to religious conversion as a way to protect his children from persecution, identified it in several private letters as "Costümwechsel" (change of dress) (quoted in Kann, *Theodor Gomperz*, 186–87).

34. Simmel, "Koketterie." The journal *Jugend*, in which this item appeared, played an important role in the creation of Viennese modern styles, as discussed in the following chapters. In this story, Simmel's characters muse on the nature of flirtation as a game of satisfaction and denial, the rules and parameters of which the Jewish patrons of Vienna would have known as well.

35. Ibid., 672

36. Wagner's inauguration lecture was published as a book in 1896.

37. Dankl, *Die "Moderne" in Österreich*, 61.

38. Förster, "Plan der Bauzeitung und Aufforderung an Männer von Fache." See also Höhle, "Vom Glacis zur Ringstrasse," 31.

39. This parallel extrapolates on Friedrich Achleitner's notion of style as language; different styles applied in the Ringstrasse reflected a "linguistic confusion" (*Wiener Architektur*, 16).

40. Sina was a friend and business partner of leading Jewish patrons. In his book on Viennese society, Paul Vasili identifies members of the families of Rothschild, Todesco, Königswarter, Wiener von Welten, Springer, and of few other Jewish families, and the gentile Sina as "finance barons" (*Die Wiener Gesellschaft*, 356–99).

41. Niemann and Feldegg, *Theophilos Hansen und seine Werke*, 55.

42. Baroni and D'Auria, *Josef Hoffmann und die Wiener Werkstätte*, 23.

43. Ibid., 28–29 and 42.

44. Ibid., 41–42.

45. Waerndorfer is identified as the founder of the Wiener Werkstätte and as a Viennese artist and merchant in the title of his photo with the fashion designer Paul Poiret in New York in 1929 (Scapin, "Vally Wieselthier und Paul Poiret in New York").

46. Lux, "Sanatorium," 407.

47. Long, *The Looshaus*, 70–71.

48. Dumba invited the decorative artists' team, Ernst Matsch and Gustav Klimt, to complete the decoration of the interiors in his public rooms. His patronage resulted in a celebrated masterpiece, Klimt's *Schubert at the Piano* (1899; now destroyed). See Franz, "'A True Memorial to the Viennese Flamboyant Style.'"

49. I argue that Jewish patronage was constructed as an existential strategy in defense

against antisemitism and was necessary to secure social position and claim cultural authority. With respect to patronage strategies in general and the aim to ennoble oneself through cultural claims, see Roeck, "Kunstpatronage in Vergangenheit und Gegenwart," 7–8.

50. Zuckerkandl, "Die Linie."

51. Mayreder hired Loos to design the Viennese Women's Club. Loos's interiors were praised for their comfort and modernity in St., "Wiener Frauen-Club," 295. See also Rukschcio and Schachel, *Adolf Loos*, 72.

52. Rose, *Jewish Women in Fin de Siècle Vienna*, 3.

53. Ibid.

54. Ibid.

55. Weininger, *Geschlecht und Charakter*.

56. Labanyi, "'Die Gefahr des Körpers.'"See also Hoberman, "Otto Weininger and the Critique of Jewish Masculinity."

57. B. Anderson, *Imagined Communities*, 6. Barbara Kirschenblatt-Gimblett and Jonathan Karp note how the "arts—and the debates they engendered—give sound, shape, and dramatic form to such imaginings in all their local and historical specificity" (introduction, 2).

1. The Historicists, 1860s–70s

1. These palais, as they are called, were built as rental apartment palaces. The model of rental apartment palaces (*Zinspalast*) accommodated the desire of the rich bourgeoisie to own luxurious houses and to secure profit through offering rental apartments on the houses' upper floors. The demarcation between landlord and renters was demonstrated through the decorative emphasis of the first floor (*bel étage*) where the landlord resided and a separate grand staircase leading to his apartment (Haiko and Stekl, "Architektur in der industriellen Gesellschaft," 284.)

2. This term refers to the Jewish populations affected by Alexander the Great's colonization of the Middle East. Between the third and the second century BC, Hellenistic Jews adopted Hellenistic cultural customs yet continued to believe in monotheism.

3. For more on Soupiritum and an earlier notable circle called Ludlamshöhle (Ludlam's cave), see Lasher-Schlitt, "Grillparzer's Attitude towards the Jews," 18; Sichrovsky, *Mein Urahn, der Bahnbrecher*, 125 and 131. Harry Sichrovsky was a business colleague and later a relative of Eduard Todesco by marriage.

4. Todesco intervened in politics even before Jews received equal rights. For a reference to Todesco as the host of social gatherings that were also clearly political, see Bauernfeld, *Erinnerungen aus Alt-Wien*, 293–94.

5. Julius von Gomperz, *Jugend-Erinnerungen*, Brünn: Verlag des Verfasser, 1902, 35–36. See also Sichrovsky, *Mein Urahn, der Bahnbrecher*, 145.

6. The painting refers to Psalm 137:1: "By the waters of Babylon, there we sat down and wept, when we remembered Zion." For a discussion of the evening event, see Rossbacher, *Literatur und Bürgertum*, 135.

7. There are five books, presumably written c. 400–100 BC, which are read on five main Jewish festivals: Ruth, Song of Songs, Ecclesiastes, Lamentations, and Esther.

8. L. Sp. [Ludwig Speidel], "Feuilleton."

9. T. Gomperz, *Traumdeutung und Zauberei*, 32. Gomperz's lecture was on Artemidorus of Ephesus and his work in clarifying myths. See also Rossbacher, *Literatur und Bürgertum*, 248.

10. T. Gomperz, "Der Zionismus," in T. Gomperz, *Essays und Erinnerungen*, 198.

11. On the relationship of Gomperz, Todesco, Wertheimstein, and Lieben to Grillparzer, see Hock, "Lebensbild," 1:cx–cxli.

12. For more on Fanny von Arnstein and her influence on the cultural and political climate in Vienna see Spiel, *Fanny von Arnstein oder die Emanzipation*, 106. Also see Elana Shapira, "Kunst und Repräsentation," 11–16.

13. Sophie von Todesco and her sister were recognized patrons of Grillparzer, and Sophie was lauded for organizing the celebration of his eightieth birthday. For example, see letters to Sophie Todesco from Johann Prince Schwarzenberg, Schloß Frauenberg, December 28, 1870, and Dr. Lex, secret advisor to King George of Hannover, Gmunden, December 28, 1870, in "Kallir-Konvolut," edited by Ernst Kobau, 38, Todesco Archiv der Villa Wertheimstein, Archiv des Bezirksmuseum Döbling, Vienna.

14. Notable at the time was the blood-libel trial in Hungary in April 1882 of Aaron Scharf and several other Jews for supposedly killing Esther Sólymossy, a Christian girl. Theodor Gomperz wrote about it in a letter: "The affair haunts me like a bad dream [original in English], von dem man immer glaubt, er müsse im nächsten Augenblick verschwinden. Aber man erwacht und man schläft ein, und der Spuk will immer nicht von uns weichen" (quoted in Kann, *Theodor Gomperz*, 132).

15. In 1856 Ignaz Ephrussi arrived in Vienna with his father Charles Joachim Ephrussi (1792–1864) In the same year Ignaz founded the bank Ephrussi & Co. in Vienna with his brothers, who owned the M. Ephrussi and Co. and Ephrussi and Porges banks in Paris and London, respectively. The facts that Ignaz settled in Vienna only in the second half of the nineteenth century and that his banking transactions were mostly in Eastern Europe and mainly with Russia may explain why he was not included in reports on Viennese Jewish businessmen or reports on Jewish art patrons at the time. Only around 1900 were the prominent roles of Ignaz von Ephrussi's son Viktor (1860–1945) and his wife as cultural producers reported in liberal newspapers.

16. Wagner-Rieger and Reissberger, *Theophil von Hansen* 235. The chapters on Hansen's private clients are by Reissberger.

17. Bloch, *Hellenistische Bestandtheile im biblischen Schriftthum*, 67–69.

18. Ibid., 8–14.

19. Simmel, "The Stranger," in Simmel, *The Sociology of Georg Simmel*, 402 (my emphasis).

20. Uhl, "Die Gesellschaft," 532–3. Jews had received permission to own land and build houses in 1860, receiving equal rights with gentiles seven years later.

21. "Feuilleton: Ueber die Neugestaltung Wien."

22. Schorske, *Fin-de-Siècle Vienna*, 36–37.

23. Ibid. 36.

24. Ibid., 38.

25. Jellinek is quoted in Wolfgang Häusler, "'Orthodoxie' und 'Reform' im Wiener Judenthum in der Epoche des Hochliberalismus," 42.

26. For the background and reception of the German synagogue, see Nikolaus Vielmetti, "Die Bedeutung des Tempels in der Seitenstettengasse für die jüdische Gemeinde in Wien."

27. Heidrich-Blaha, "Josef Kornhäusels Synagoge in Wien," 132.

28. The Jewish community was not officially recognized until 1852.

29. Since the plans analyzed here follow European usage, in which the first floor is identified as the ground floor, the second floor as the first floor, and so on, I will also follow that usage in this book.

30. Quoted in Heidrich-Blaha, "Josef Kornhäusels Synagoge in Wien," 136.

31. Kohlbauer and Krohn, *Beste aller Frauen*, 19 and 55 (with a reproduction of the Torah curtain Hermann Todesco donated to the City Temple, made from the wedding dress of his daughter).

32. The Gomperz family had already worked with Förster (J. von Gomperz, *Jugend-Erinnerungen*, 46.) Förster was also responsible for the second Ashkenazi synagogue, the monumental and Moorish style Leopoldstadt Temple in Vienna's second district (1858).

33. Salomon Mayer von Rothschild had bought the house at Renngasse 3 on November 15, 1844. In 1853 he gave it to his son Anselm Salomon von Rothschild (Harrer, "Wien," 701.) For more on the Rothschilds' properties, see Köstlin, "Das Neue Wien," 2. See also A. Nierhaus, "Vor-Bild Frankreich."

34. The memorial book is in Vienna's Jewish Museum (Inv. no. 4051). For a reproduction of the illustration, see Shapira, "Todesco, Förster, Hansen, and the New Hellenistic Jews on Vienna's Ringstrasse," 281.

35. Assmann, "Opting In und Opting Out," 140.

36. Romano and Schwendenwein were favored by both Jewish and gentile patrons who built on and near the Ringstrasse. Their prestigious projects included the Palais Metternich in 1846–48 and the grand Jewish Temple in Brünn (now Brno) in 1855.

37. L. T. [Ludwig Tischler?], "Die Neubauten der Ringstrasse in Wien," 171, 173.

38. The Todesco, Springer, Wiener, Gomperz, Königswarter, and Kann families created a modern high-class ghetto here, confirming their sense of belonging. A few years later this tendency to cluster tightly together relaxed: Eduard Wiener von Welten moved away and built a new palace in Schwarzenbergplatz (1869), across from another Jew, Viktor von Ofenheim (1868), and Gustav von Epstein built next to the Parliament (1871).

39. Todesco's younger sister Amalie married Springer in May 1840. After divorcing him, she married Karl Löwenstein and remained in Eduard's neighborhood, first at Heinrichshof on Opernring and then at Walfischgasse 10 (Lehmann, *Allgemeiner Wohnungs-Anzeiger*, 1881, 599).

40. Förster, "Wohnhäuser in Wien, Ecke der Ringstrasse, am Ausgange der Kärntnerstrasse links," 27. For Springer's purchase of Klein's lot with Förster's plan, see his letter of ownership in the Baupolizei Akt (municipal building inspection) documents (MA 8 EZ 727, Wiener Stadt- und Landesarchiv, Vienna).

41. Bammer, *Architektur als Erinnerung*, 16. I am grateful to the architect and architectural critic Otto Kapfinger for the reference to Bammer's book.

42. I thank Benjamin von Radom for sharing with me the close-up photos of the caryatids of the Palais Todesco as well as his detailed descriptions of them.

43. *Israelitischer-Frauen-Wohlthätigkeit-Verein, 100, Vereinsjahr Jubiläums-, und Jahres-Bericht für das Jahr 1915,* 1–3.

44. Several variations on the Greek caryatids on the Erectheion could be seen in the first Ringstrasse houses of the early 1860s—for example, in the façade at the entrance of the house of Ferdinand Fellner the elder at Operngasse 2 (1863). These caryatids did not demonstrate cultural identification so much as popular decoration.

45. See the façade plan for Palais Todesco from May 1861 in MA 37 EZ 607/I, Baupolizei—Magistrat der Stadt Wien—Zentrale, Vienna. Förster's decoration of the upper floor with a series of caryatids may have been influenced by Carl Tietz's caryatid decoration on the Palais Schlick in the ninth district, at Türkenstrasse 25. Förster's younger colleague Hansen had also included caryatid decorations on the balcony of the *bel étage* in the redesigned Palais Sina at Hohen Markt 8–9 (1858), near the center of the Jewish community in Seitenstettengasse.

46. Förster explained this in relation to his building for the gentile patron Franz Klein in Brno ("Das Wohnhaus des Herrn Franz Klein in Brünn," 46–47).

47. Todesco's influence on the stock exchange was crucial. When news arrived that the Habsburg monarchy was losing the war against Prussia in Königgrätz, fears of a stock market crash abounded. But Todesco started buying stocks, and everyone followed his example. This is reported in Benedikt, *Die wirtschaftliche Entwicklung in der Franz-Joseph-Zeit,* 73. For another reference to the event, see Wagner-Rieger and Reissberger, *Theophil von Hansen,* 296, note 55.

48. The Hercules motif is recurrent in the palace of Prince Eugen in Himmelpfortgasse 8, built 1697–1723 or 1724, and is featured in its ceiling paintings and reliefs. The palace was occupied by the finance ministry beginning in 1848. Todesco must have been in regular contact with the ministry since his bank dealt mostly with government bonds (Wagner-Rieger and Reissberger, *Theophil von Hansen,* 241 and 294, note 51).

49. Spitzer, "Wiener Spaziergänge." Spitzer appears to be criticizing the discrepancy between the pretension of the chosen Greek style of the Parliament building and the dress of the members of Parliament.

50. Burckhardt, *Briefe an Einen Architekten,* 15–16, quoted in Mattiolo, *Jacob Burckhardt und die Grenzen der Humanität,* 27. In the summer of 1875, Burckhardt wrote to the Swiss architect Max Alioth, criticizing Jewish palaces in Frankfurt. He complained that rich Jews build with caryatids that could never appear at all beautiful due to the Jews' own "ugly" appearance. Burckhardt was well known and highly appreciated in Vienna. For more on his prejudiced views on Jews, see ibid., 30.

51. For more on "opting in" or "opting out" of a given group and as strategies of style, with a value function, see Assmann, "Opting In und Opting Out," 128.

52. Garelick, *Rising Star,* 11.

53. "Family resemblance" refers here to Ludwig Wittgenstein's idea of a "complex network of similarities overlapping and criss-crossing" rather than one common feature (quoted in Sluga, "Family Resemblance," 1). The choice of caryatids for the façades of the Todesco, Epstein, and Ephrussi palaces would be another "family resemblance."

54. Inv. no. 20163 6/110, Library of the Academy of Fine Arts, Vienna (Archiv und Kupferstichkabinett der Akademie der bildenden Künste Wien).

55. Wagner-Rieger and Reissberger, *Theophil von Hansen,* 278, note 50.

56. Ibid., note 49.

57. Ibid., 276, note 44.

58. The nine wall paintings were described as: "Herophile weissagt Trojas Untergang durch Paris [Herophile, the priestess of Apollo, warns of the fall of Troy through Paris] / Hirten finden den ausgesetzten Knaben von einer Bärin gesäugt [A herdsman finds the rejected boy suckled by a female bear] / Paris Liebesbund mit Oenonen [Paris's loving bond with the nymph Oenone, who was skilled in the art of prophecy and medicine] / Paris beschützt Hirten und Herden gegen Räuber [Paris defends herdsmen and their herds against thieves] / Cassandra erkennt in Paris ihren Bruder [Cassandra recognizes Paris as her brother] / Helenas Entführung durch Paris [Paris's abduction of Helen] / Achill wird auf Apollos Geheiß von Paris getötet [Paris kills Achilles with the help of Apollo's arrow] / Paris wird von Philoctet in der Schlacht verwundet [Philoctetes mortally wounds Paris] / Oenone verflucht den um Rettung flehenden Paris [Oenone curses Paris who pleads for help]" (ibid., 276).

59. Grün, *Glückliches Wien!*, 136. Reissberger quotes this in Wagner-Rieger and Reissberger, *Theophil von Hansen*, ibid, 276. For a further nuance related to the assessment of Jewish patrons, see another reference to Grün in which his description of Todesco is less flattering and more aligned with stereotypes of Jewish stinginess (ibid., 278, note 50). See also Rossbacher, *Literatur und Bürgertum*, 128.

60. Wagner-Rieger and Reissberger, *Theophil von Hansen*, 276, note 45.

61. Uhl wrote: "Hansen und Carl Rahl schmückten einen Prachtsaal im Palais Todesco, der bis heute noch kaum übertroffen worden ist, mit goldenen Decken- und prachtvollen Wandgemälden" ("Die Gesellschaft," 532).

62. Wagner-Rieger and Reissberger, *Theophil von Hansen*, 232. Austrian rule over the Venice from 1797 to 1866 may also explain the inspiration.

63. Ibid., 278, note 48.

64. Frimmel, "Aus der Sammlung Todesco," 149.

65. Ibid.; Lillie, *Was einmal War*, 806.

66. Frimmel, "Aus der Sammlung Todesco," 149–51.

67. Ibid., 149. For more information about Oppenheimer's collection, see Lillie, *Was einmal War*, 798.

68. Frimmel, "Aus der Sammlung Todesco," 150. Theodor Frimmel actually saw Oppenheimer's collection in Palais Todesco. See also Lillie, *Was einmal War*, 801.

69. Todesco paid 250 florins for the painting (Johnson, *The Memory Factory*, 282, note 38).

70. Saar, *Seligmann Hirsch*, 22.

71. Ibid., 24.

72. Ibid., 102 (letter from Saar to Louise Auspitz-Gomperz, December 4, 1888.) Saar also corresponded with other members of the Gomperz, Lieben, and Wertheimstein families about his book.

73. Ibid., 98–115. The edition of the novel contained a discussion of reviews of the book.

74. It was clear to Todesco's friends in his literary club that he was a proud Jew and that he rejected the idea of conversion (Bauernfeld, "Alfred der Große, Szenen aus dem Jenseits," in Bauernfeld, *Erinnerungen aus Alt-Wien*, 332).

75. Jews' pride and accomplishment in speaking other European languages was viewed negatively by antisemites (Jankowitsch, "Mode in Wien, 1870 bis 1890," 65).

76. Vasili, *Die Wiener Gesellschaft*, 382.

77. Gurlitt (1850–1938) was an art historian and architect. It is possible that he was invited to Todesco's palace because of his relationship to the son of Förster, with whom he had opened an architects' studio. Gurlitt became a Nazi sympathizer though he never received recognition for his support of the Nazis since he was identified as a half-Jew. It remains an open question whether Gurlitt's report on the events in Todesco's apartment reflected his ambivalent attitude toward his Jewish origins.

78. Gurlitt, *Im Bürgerhause*, 56. See also Wagner-Rieger and Reissberger, *Theophil von Hansen*, 277. Aniline is a chemically produced dye.

79. Fürst, *Das Palais Todesco*, 16.

80. A. Loos, "Vom armen reichen Mann."

81. In an antisemitic caricature titled "Moderne Judenverfolgung" (Modern persecution of Jews) in *Der Floh* (January 1, 1869, 3), a badly dressed Jewish patron with checked trousers and a striking red nose is holding his open wallet and standing between two women who are flirting with him and different representatives of society, including an artist showing his painting, asking him for money.

82. Simmel, "The Sociology of Sociability," in Simmel, *Simmel on Culture*, 125.

83. Ibid.

84. Letter from Joseph Wertheimer, Dr. Engel, Gu. [Gustav] Epstein, Frankl, and Dr. Leopold Kompert, members of the board of the association for caring for the needy orphans of the Jewish community to Eduard and Sophie Todesco, April 4, 1868, Inv. no. 4055, Sammlung Jüdisches Museum Wien, Vienna. I am grateful to Ernst Kobau for sharing with me his transcript of this letter.

85. Frauberger, "Gustav Ritter von Epstein," 4:9. Epstein was ennobled as Gustav Ritter von Epstein in 1866 (Gaugusch, *Wer einmal war*, 576).

86. Frauberger, "Gustav Ritter von Epstein," 4:11; "Palais Epstein," 51. There are no traces of the Latin text in the cupola today.

87. "Palais Epstein," 49.

88. Höhle, "Vom Glacis zur Ringstrasse," 40.

89. Dahm, "Die Baugeschichte des Palais Epstein," 51).

90. The façade plan signed by Hansen was drawn on July 28, 1868, and submitted to the Viennese authorities on November 9, 1868 (MA 37 EZ 168, Baupolizei—Magistrat der Stadt Wien—Zentrale, Vienna).

91. Frauberger, "Gustav Ritter von Epstein," 8.

92. Vincenti, *Wiener Kunst-Renaissance*, 58. The sculpture is reproduced in Wagner-Rieger, *Die Wiener Ringstrasse*, vol. 1, *Das Kunstwerk im Bild*, Fig. 86c.

93. Epstein went bankrupt in 1873. His oldest son was very sick at the time, and the family stayed in the palace until after the son's death in 1876.

94. Dahm, "Die Baugeschichte des Palais Epstein," 53.

95. *Oesterreichische Schachzeitung*, September 1873, 268. Steinitz was a Jewish Austrian chess champion who came from a poor background.

96. Several similarities between the interiors of the Palais Epstein and the Parliament building suggest that Hansen may have used the Palais Epstein as a model for his ambi-

tious ideas for Parliament—a decision to create a family resemblance between the private and the public houses. I thank Günther Schefbeck, head of the Austrian Parliament archive, for this observation.

97. Hamann, "Der Bauherr Gustav Ritter von Epstein," 42.

98. Mayer, *Die Wiener Juden*, 294.

99. Lehmann, *Allgemeiner Wohnungs-Anzeiger*, 1864, 151. Lazar Epstein was the registered owner of a cotton factory in Prague, a wholesale trader, and a money exchanger.

100. Hamann, "Der Bauherr Gustav Ritter von Epstein," 44.

101. Ibid.

102. Frauberger, "Gustav Ritter von Epstein," 10. See also Wagner-Rieger and Reissberger, *Theophil von Hansen*, 302.

103. Frauberger, "Gustav Ritter von Epstein," 10.

104. Dahm, "Die Baugeschichte des Palais Epstein," 59–61.

105. Vincenti, *Wiener Kunst-Renaissance*, 58. Lustro is imitation marble, produced through an expensive process of mixing stucco and color.

106. Ibid., 59.

107. Ranzoni, *Wiener Bauten*, 72.

108. Wagner-Rieger and Reissberger, *Theophil von Hansen*, 227.

109. Vincenti, *Wiener Kunst-Renaissance*, 60.

110. Wagner-Rieger and Reissberger, *Theophil von Hansen*, 251 and 319, note 28.

111. Frauberger, "Gustav Ritter von Epstein," 12.

112. Ibid.

113. Reissberger argues that the arrangement of fountain and faun—and the use of marble—were meant to demonstrate control over nature, a dynamic that lost its charm in the interior (Wagner-Rieger and Reissberger, *Theophil von Hansen*, 234).

114. Vincenti, *Wiener Kunst-Renaissance*, 60–61.

115. Ranzoni, *Wiener Bauten*, 72. However, it was in the Louvre according to Frauberger ("Gustav Ritter von Epstein").

116. Frauberger, "Gustav Ritter von Epstein," 11.

117. Wagner-Rieger and Reissberger, *Theophil von Hansen*, 243.

118. For a detailed description of the Todesco allegories, see ibid., 240–43.

119. Ibid., 249.

120. Vincenti, *Wiener Kunst-Renaissance*, 59.

121. During the late eighteenth century, the criterion of symmetry and pedantic neoclassicism prevailed. See Praz, *An Illustrated History of Interior Decoration*, 170–73.

122. Ranzoni, *Wiener Bauten*, 73.

123. Wagner-Rieger and Reissberger, *Theophil von Hansen*, 287, note 78.

124. Simmel, "The Stranger," in Simmel, *The Sociology of Georg Simmel*, 403.

125. Wagner-Rieger and Reissberger, *Theophil von Hansen*, 249–52.

126. Frauberger, "Gustav Ritter von Epstein," 12.

127. Inventory of the library of the MAK–Austrian Museum of Applied Arts / Contemporary Art, Inv. no. BI 521 to BI 528, and BI 563; MAK–Bibliothek und Kunstblättersammlung / Archiv.

128. Reissberger refers to the escapist element in the ballroom—the narcissistic closed

environment created through the mirrors (Wagner-Rieger and Reissberger, *Theophil von Hansen*, 233).

129. Ranzoni, *Wiener Bauten*, 73. See also Vincenti, *Wiener Kunst-Renaissance*, 60.

130. Wagner-Rieger and Reissberger, *Theophil von Hansen*, 284, note 55.

131. For more on the contents of the studio, see Frauberger, "Gustav Ritter von Epstein," 11.

132. Reissberger refers to Hansen and Rahl's explanation of the program: "besingt die Macht und den Triumph Amors über das Götter- und Menschengeschlecht" (quoted in Wagner-Rieger and Reissberger, *Theophil von Hansen*, 285, note 59).

133. For a quotation from Hansen and Rahl's explanation, see ibid., note 60.

134. After his visit to the public rooms, Ranzoni visited the tasteful reception room and boudoir of the lady of the house and was allowed to look at the Pompeii bathroom (*Wiener Bauten*, 74.)

135. This question was raised by other scholars researching Epstein interiors. Copies of the letters between the Grand Duke and Epstein were even requested. Yet the heirs of the Grand Duke turned down the request (discussion with Schefbeck at the Palais Epstein on June 30, 2011).

136. Wagner-Rieger and Reissberger, *Theophil von Hansen*, 251.

137. Ibid.

138. Ibid.

139. Ibid., 304, note 103. See also Hamann, "'Von der Magie des historischen Ortes,'" 303.

140. The striped marble pattern, identified with the Oriental style, decorated the lower part of the wall cladding of the Palais Epstein staircase. Hansen chose a pattern of narrow brown stripes on a pink marble background for the private staircase, an example of a polychrome character common to his designs.

141. His second building was at Börseplatz 3, on the corner at the back of the future stock exchange building. Epstein and Hansen received permission for the building at the end of 1871 (MA 37, EZ I/146, Baupolizei—Magistrat der Stadt Wien—Zentrale, Vienna).

142. Frauberger, "Gustav Ritter von Epstein," 12.

143. Hamann, "Der Bauherr Gustav Ritter von Epstein," 45.

144. Lichtblau, *Als hätten wir dazu gehört: Österreichisch-jüdische Lebensgeschichten aus der Habsburgermonarchie*, quoting Moritz Güdemann's memoirs ("Aus meinem Leben," 1899–1918, Vienna).

145. The orthodox community wanted a building that would compete with Förster's monumental Moorish style temple built for the reform community in the 1850s. For more on Epstein's access to both Wagner and important members in the orthodox community, see I. Müller, *Die Otto Wagner-Synagoge in Budapest*, 42.

146. Ibid., 43.

147. For Epstein's influence on the development of Wagner's Jugendstil design for his houses, see Shapira, "Assimilating with Style," 121–28.

148. The Epstein family remained in its palace with the help of mortgages until the oldest son, Friedrich, died in 1876. Epstein spent the last three years of his life in Vienna's fourth district, in a rented apartment owned by the Lower Austria Trade Association,

where for many years he had been a prominent official (Hamann, "'Von der Magie des historischen Ortes,'" 305–7).

149. Quoted in Rossbacher, *Literatur und Bürgertum*, 137. Rossbacher suggests that Hofmannsthal's text points out the tension between appearance (*Schein*) and reality (*Sein*) (ibid., 136–38). Hofmannsthal's quote also appears in Wagner-Rieger and Reissberger, *Theophil von Hansen*, 281, note 53. Reissberger explains it as a reference to the impossible contradiction between the life of the "second society," meaning the rich new aristocrats, and their ideal image of their lives. Yet Reissberger also notes that by producing tableaux vivants, this society succeeded in imitating an aristocratic custom.

150. Quoted in Reissberger, "Zum Problem künstlerischer Selbstdarstellung in der zweiten Hälfte des 19. Jahrhunderts," unnumbered page.

151. Quoted in ibid., 767. The last lines read: "They don't know confusion, the spell / Of the dark frightening life not / It [the spell] that runs with your blood in your pulse / Nor what surrounds you with enigmatic chaos: / And what blows along in them, you never understand it: / Eternal quietness, great harmony" (ibid.). Reissberger explains the quote as documenting how life and art reflect the gap between the harmonious ideal and the frightened reality.

152. Ibid., 744. Adrienne Hakim was the niece of Ignaz von Ephrussi's wife, Emilie, née Porges.

2. The Secessionists, 1897–1902

1. Lothar, "Von der Secession," 813. Interestingly, an early reader of *Die Wage* was Theodor Gomperz, Sophie Todesco's brother, who followed the journal's articles on the situation of the Jews in Eastern Europe (Kann, *Theodor Gomperz*, 297).

2. In 1900, Kraus challenged the great success of Klimt and the secessionists at the Paris Exposition Universelle (World Exhibition) by noting that the Parisians had dismissed them as representing "Jewish taste" (Kraus, "Was einem der feingefühligsten Kunstgelehrten . . . ," 22). He would make this argument again, questioning the identification of the Vienna Secession style as an "Austrian style" ("Ganz wider den Willen der Natur," 9).

3. For a historical review of the expression "Judaization" as negative, from Richard Wagner's usage to the ultimate Nazi hate rhetoric, see Aschheim, "'The Jew Within.'"

4. Quoted in Koss, *Modernism after Wagner*, 1.

5. Koss, *Modernism after Wagner*, xiii.

6. Wittels, *Der Taufjude*, 38. An early caricature titled "Das Judenthum in der Musik, wie es dem Richard Wagner willkommen ist" (Judaism in music, how Richard Wagner is [being] welcomed), depicts Jews in the audience during a Wagner concert in *Kikeriki*, May 12, 1872, 4. Emile Zuckerkandl, Berta Zuckerkandl's grandson, vividly recalled the first time he attended a performance of an opera by Wagner (*Tannhäuser*) with his grandmother (telephone interview, November 26, 2003).

7. Zuckerkandl, "Kunst und Kultur, Das Kabarett 'Fledermaus.'"

8. Szeps-Zuckerkandl, *Ich erlebte fünfzig Jahre Weltgeschichte*, 179.

9. Bahr, "Die Vierte Ausstellung, Klimt, Engelhart, Andrei, Fräulein Ries," 122–24; Mahler-Werfel, *Tagebuch-Suiten, 1898–1902*, 143). See also Natter, "Fürstinnen ohne Geschichte?," 67; Gronberg, *Vienna*, 79–81.

10. Aichelburg, *Das Wiener Künstlerhaus*, 129. Eugen Felix served as president of the Künstlerhaus in 1874–76, 1888–90, and 1896–98.

11. Shedel, *Art and Society*, 20.

12. Clark, "Olbrich and Vienna," 7:37.

13. Ibid., note 70. The temporary exhibition building was built to display paintings depicting the Oriental journey of Crown Prince Rudolf in 1890.

14. Ibid., 7:38.

15. Hevesi, "Die Wiener 'Sezession,'" in Hevesi, *Acht Jahre Sezesson*, 1–4.

16. Kapfinger and Krischanitz, *Die Wiener Secession*, 15.

17. Clark, "Olbrich and Vienna," 7:38.

18. Natter, *Isidor Kaufmann 1853–1921*, 350.

19. Wilhelm, "Künstlerhaus," 394.

20. G. Fliedl, *Gustav Klimt, 1862–1918*, 62. For Hevesi's positive reception of the Munich secessionists' exhibition in Vienna, see "Moderne Malerei," in Hevesi, *Acht Jahre Sezession*, 525–32.

21. The pessimistic symbolism in Klimt's paintings can be traced back to Hevesi's complimentary analysis of the Munich secessionists' paintings (Hevesi, "Moderne Malerei," 525–26).

22. In 1893, Klimt and his partner Franz Matsch were hired to decorate two rooms in the historicist rental apartment palace of Nicolaus Dumba. The patron accepted Klimt's *Schubert at the Piano* (1899), reflecting the artist's change of style from historicism to impressionism. See *Die Welt von Klimt, Schiele und Kokoschka*, 22.

23. Hevesi, "Die Wiener Sezession," in Hevesi, *Acht Jahre Sezession*, 3–4.

24. Regarding the new location, see Clark, "Olbrich and Vienna," 7:39.

25. Olin, "Nationalism, the Jews, and Art History," 463–64.

26. Strzygowski, *Die bildende Kunst der Gegenwart*, 15.

27. See Shapira, "Assimilating with Style," 126.

28. O. Wagner, *Moderne Architektur*, 33.

29. Wagner-Rieger and Reissberger, *Theophil von Hansen*, 304, note 103.

30. I. Müller, *Die Otto Wagner-Synagoge in Budapest*, 42–43.

31. Ibid., 186.

32. Ibid., 94. See also Moravánszky, "Byzantinismus in der Baukunst Otto Wagner als Motiv seiner Wirkung östlich von Wien," 41.

33. Alofsin, *When Buildings Speak*, 51.

34. Ibid.

35. I. Müller, *Die Otto Wagner-Synagoge in Budapest*, 12.

36. Hevesi, "Otto Wagner," in Hevesi, *Acht Jahre Sezession*, 277–78.

37. Ibid., 276.

38. Hevesi, "Wie soll man den Leopoldstädter Tempel bauen?," *Pester Lloyd*, April 8, 1899.

39. Ibid.

40. I. Müller, *Die Otto Wagner-Synagoge in Budapest*, 88–90.

41. Moravánszky, "Byzantinismus in der Baukunst Otto Wagner als Motiv seiner Wirkung östlich von Wien," 42.

42. Ibid., 41.

43. I. Müller, *Die Otto Wagner-Synagoge in Budapest*, 91.

44. Hanak-Lettner, "Quasi una fantasia," 23. An earlier version of lyrics for the famous waltz by the Jewish Viennese journalist, translator and librarian Josef Weyl (Joseph Aloys Peter Weil), c. 1869.

45. I thank the historian Louise Hecht for noting the author's distinction between "us" and "them."

46. Clark, "Olbrich and Vienna," 7:31.

47. Ibid., 7:32.

48. Ibid. The court pavilion was a railway station built near the Habsburg summer residence of Schönbrunn for exclusive use of the imperial court. I suggest that a synagogue may have served Wagner and Olbrich as the model for this court pavilion. A possible inspiration for the combination of a cubic architectural form with a modest cupola may have been Viala du Sorbier's great synagogue in Algier (1865).

49. Ibid., 7:38.

50. Ibid.

51. Ibid.

52. Ibid.

53. Ibid., 7:38–39.

54. Ibid., 7:39.

55. Ibid., 7:40.

56. Ibid.

57. Ibid.

58. Ibid.

59. Hevesi, "Das Haus der Sezession," in Hevesi, *Acht Jahre Sezession*, 63–68.

60. Hevesi, "Weiteres vom Hause der Sezession," in Hevesi, *Acht Jahre Sezession*, 70.

61. Ibid., 71. The house's expected additions were not built either. Hevesi's detailed knowledge of the plan documents how closely he was involved in the construction of the house (ibid, 70–74).

62. Arnold, "Der Wiener Styl."

63. Quoted in Kann, *Theodor Gomperz*, 284, note 301.

64. This angel-like personification was identified by an anonymous contemporary critic as an Egyptian Isis ("Die Secession im eigenen Hause").

65. Quoted in Bisanz-Prakken, "The Beethoven Exhibition of the Secession and the Younger Viennese Tradition of the Gesamtkunstwerk," 142.

66. Bahr, "Die Secession."

67. For an extended examination of Bahr's promotion of avant-garde art and literature in *Die Zeit*, see Tielsch, "Die Wochenschrift 'Die Zeit,' als Spiegel literarischen und kulturellen Lebens in Wien um die Jahrhundertwende."

68. Bahr, *Der Antisemitismus*, unnumbered title page. Bahr collected essays on antisemitism from prominent personalities such as Theodor Mommsen, James Arthur Balfour, Ernst Häckel, Annie Besant, and Henrik Ibsen and published them in his book. Before his marriage to the Jewish actress Rosa Jokl, he left the Catholic church and she the Jewish religion (M. Müller, "Heirat mit Rosa Jokl").

69. Auspitzer was involved in the production of different cultural events. In 1897 he also founded the Urania Institute as a center for popular education, related to the planned

imperial anniversary exhibition and following the example of the Berlin Institute for Popular Education. Österreichischer Gewerbeverein Interessensvertretung für Industrie, . . . Chronology of the Austrian Trade Union at http://gewerbeverein.at.dedi787.your-server.de/de/zeittafel_1815–1938/1815_-_1938, Accessed August 1, 2014.

70. M. Müller, "Emil Auspitzer." Auspitzer expected Bahr to write about what Auspitzer was interested in, which led Bahr to resign. In contrast, Kanner and Singer allowed Bahr to express his ideas freely in *Die Zeit* (Schülz, "Hermann Bahr als Publizist in Berlin," 131).

71. Bahr, introduction, 2–3.

72. Ibid., 3.

73. Ibid., 4.

74. Tielsch, "Die Wochenschrift 'Die Zeit,' als Spiegel literarischen und kulturellen Lebens in Wien um die Jahrhundertwende," 101–3.

75. Kraus, "Darmstadt," 12.

76. Olbrich, "Das Haus der Secession," 5.

77. Bahr, *Das Hermann Bahr Buch*, 87.

78. Kornberg, *Theodor Herzl from Assimilation to Zionism*, 50–53.

79. Herzl, *Das neue Ghetto*. First published in the Zionist newspaper *Die Welt* in 1897, the play was performed in early January 1898.

80. Bahr, "Das neue Ghetto," 28.

81. Ibid. This quotation from Bahr refers directly to the monologue of Jakob Samuel, the young lawyer in the play.

82. Bahr, "Vereinigung bildender Künstler Österreichs," 10, 13 (my emphasis)

83. Shedel, *Art and Society*, 28.

84. Quoted in Le Rider, *Modernity and Crises of Identity*, 148.

85. Olbrich, "Das Haus der Secession," 5. Olbrich was referring to the Greek temple of Segesta in Sicily, a recognized place of pilgrimage, as the inspiration for his temple, which would match Doric temple structures with an Oriental dome. The reference to the temple was not accidental.

86. Johnson, "Athena Goes to the Prater," 56.

87. The figure is identified as Hofmannsthal because of the references to Narcissus, but does not resemble photos of Hofmannsthal.

88. Quoted in Goldschmidt, *Quer Sacrum*, 51.

89. Lang, "Das Secessionsgebäude," 940.

90. To show that the Vienna Secession was also committed to the classicist heritage, Klimt's poster promoting the secessionists' first exhibition depicted Theseus fighting the Minotaur, with the goddess Pallas Athena as Theseus's protector. Theseus's nudity expressed the purity of the younger generation, and the Minotaur was identified with their fathers and old institutions. The exposed male sexual organs, however, caused a scandal, and three phallic tree trunks were used to cover them.

91. Many of *Der Floh*'s former writers were acculturated Jews: Hevesi, Herzl, Karl Emil Franzos, and Julius Bauer ("Unsere einstigen Mitarbeiter," *Der Floh*, December 31, 1893, 66).

92. "Die Secession," *Der Floh*, November 27, 1898, 5. In the original German, the caption reads: "Was, Du bist auch ä Kunstfreund geworden?" "Nu, wenn die ganze Welt schreit 'Seht's es on, seht's es on,' will ich es mir auch onseh'n."

93. "Bei Fregoli," *Der Floh*, January 1, 1899, 4.

94. "Die Secession zu Hause," *Der Floh*, January 29, 1899, 6. The pointillist technique of the 1890s generated a veiled but shimmering and vibrating surface.

95. Hevesi, "Ver Sacrum," in Hevesi, *Acht Jahre Sezession*, 10. Hevesi defended Koloman Moser's colorful prints and demonstrated the new aesthetic by comparing the striking colors to wallpaper with a long nose. Perhaps Hevesi was reacting to the well-known Gurlitt anecdote about Todesco's salon, in which the owner's addition of red tablecloth was compared with a striking red nose in a portrait, which may have been a coded reference to Jewish influence on modern aesthetics.

96. Speidel, "Feuilleton: Wohlthätigkeits-Vorstellung."

97. Hevesi, "Feuilleton: Der Aristopath," The reference to the word psychopath may have originated in Richard Krafft-Ebing's book *Psychopathia Sexualis* (1886).

98. The heroic Judith's story is related to the celebration of Hanukkah; it tells of the beautiful Judith's act of intoxicating and then killing Holofernes, the Assyrian general, to save her city, Bethulia.

99. Shedel, *Art and Society*, 68.

100. Quoted in Hevesi, "Die Ausstellung der Sezession," in Hevesi, *Acht Jahre Sezession*, 12.

101. Hevesi, "Die erste Ausstellung der Vereinigung bildender Künstler Österreichs," in Hevesi, *Acht Jahre Sezession*, 39.

102. Ibid., 40–41.

103. He registered with the police as a resident in Wallfischgasse in Vienna, on September 25, 1876 (Hevesi's police registration, Meldezettel Archiv, Wiener Stadt- und Landesarchiv).

104. Verlassenschaftsakt nach Ludwig Hevesi (A IV 22/10), Wiener Stadt- und Landesarchiv. Less than a year later, in November 1891, Hevesi wrote his first will (ibid.).

105. In 1910, Hevesi indicated "Mosaisch" (Jewish) as his religion in his police registration. See Kohut, *Berühmte israelitische Männer und Frauen in der Kulturgeschichte der Menschheit*, 2:9–11. (Hevesi's name appears immediately after Herzl's). See also Patai, "Ludwig Hevesi," 2:1586 (which gives the wrong death date for Hevesi).

106. Hevesi, "Wie soll man den Leopoldstädter Tempel bauen?," *Pester Lloyd*, April 8, 1899.

107. Quoted in Bisanz-Prakken, "The Beethoven Exhibition of the Secession and the Younger Viennese Tradition of the Gesamtkunstwerk," 143. In the original German, the quote reads: "Lehren wollen wir euch, mit uns vereint fest zu werden, wie ein Thurm von Erz, als Erkennende, Wissende, Verstehende, als Adepten, als Herrscher über die Geister!"

108. Hevesi, "Weiteres vom Hause der Sezessionin Hevesi, *Acht Jahre Sezession*, 72.

109. For more on the development of the golden cupola, see Kapfinger and Krischanitz, *Die Wiener Secession*, 51 and illustrations 52a–e.

110. Clark, "Olbrich and Vienna," 7:40.

111. Hevesi, who published in the *Fremden-Blatt* regularly, may have recommended Olbrich as the designer for Klarwill's gravestone. See Clark, "Olbrich and Vienna," 7:45; Olbrich, "Grabmal für die Familie v. Klarwill auf dem Dornbacher Friedhofe," 6.

112. It is also a symbol of the people of Israel and the individual Jew, and of the

Torah. See Karolina Koziura, "Jewish Cemetery of Chernivtsi," http://www.academia.edu/5444863/Jewish_cemetery_of_chernivts, accessed October 1, 2015.

113. Clark, "Olbrich and Vienna," 7:41.

114. In his book on Austrian art in the nineteenth century, Hevesi notes that his quote was placed on the "forehead" of the Secession House as a serious warning to the public (*Österreichische Kunst im 19. Jahrhundert*, 284).

115. Hatvany, "Ludwig Hevesi."

116. Hevesi, "Das Haus der Sezession," in Hevesi, *Acht Jahre Sezession*, 69.

117. I thank Otto Kapfinger for this reference. According to him, the ambassador of the United States, Ronald Lauder, paid for the costs of regilding the cupola during renovation on the house (my conversation with Kapfinger).

118. On the relationship between modern architecture and contemporary fashion, see O. Wagner, *Moderne Architektur*, 33. Yet the Secession House is a further development of Wagner's principle of clothing, as noted above in relation to his design of the synagogue in Pest.

119. Hevesi, "Die Wiener 'Sezession'" in Hevesi, *Acht Jahre Sezession*, 4.

120. Hevesi, "Weiteres vom Hause der Sezession," in Hevesi, *Acht Jahre Sezession*, 70; Hevesi, "Arthur Strasser," in ibid., 90–91.

121. Hevesi was also a generation older than his colleagues who supported the secessionist movement, Zuckerkandl and Bahr.

122. Olbrich, *Ideen von Olbrich, Text von Ludwig Hevesi*.

123. Hevesi, "Einleitung zu Olbrichs 'Ideen,'" in Hevesi, *Acht Jahre Sezession*, 211.

124. According to Hermine Wittgenstein, Karl's oldest daughter, beyond the figural imagery, it was a certain serenity in the composition—the emphasis on horizontal and vertical—that she regarded as granting "ethical" quality to pictures in their collection. H. Wittgenstein, *Familienerinnerungen*, 112.

125. For a reference to an imagined Jew in the historical and cultural context of Viennese modernism, see Le Rider, *Modernity and Crises of Identity*, 4–5.

126. Until then, Wittgenstein and his close business associates, identified as the "Wittgenstein group," handled their financial affairs through a provincial bank, the Lower Austria Eskompte-Gesellschaft, which was managed by the German Jew Max Feilchenfeld. See Gaugusch, "Österreichs Industrie gewidmet," 152.

127. "Wittgenstein's Abschied," *Die Wage*.

128. Hermine Wittgenstein would balance her father's approach to money against the Christian message of charity for the poor: "K[arl] W[ittgenstein] sagt: Wer kein Kleid hat erwerbe Eines, das ist der wahre Socialismus. Reichtum ist keine Schande. Grenze?" (quoted in Mathias Iven [ed.,] *"Ludwig Sagt . . .": Die Aufzeichnungen der Hermine Wittgenstein*, Berlin: ParErga, 2006, 62).

129. In *Die Fackel* in early February 1900, Karl Kraus attacked the patronage of the Rothschild, Gutmann, and Wittgenstein families, claiming their good will was a coverup for an ugly exploitation of the coal miners. Kraus, "Seit Wochen stehen in Norden." The Wittgensteins and the Gutmanns worked together for charitable causes. The Gutmanns generously contributed to the Verein gegen Armut und Betteleі (Association against Poverty and Begging), founded in 1879. Karl Wittengenstein's mother, Fanny, was one of the

founders of this association, and his brother, Ludwig, served as its chairman for many years (Prokop, *Margaret Stonborough-Wittgenstein*, 139 and 206.)

130. McGuinness, *Wittgenstein, a Life*, 1. The portrait of the couple from around 1802 shows both with impressively self-assured expressions and dressed in a Western manner. It is reproduced in Waugh, *The House of Wittgenstein*, at the top of the page facing 180.

131. Günther, "Karl Wittgenstein und seine Bedeutung für den Aufbau und die Entwicklung der österreichischen Volkswirtschaft," 156.

132. Bramann and Moran, "Karl Wittgenstein, Business Tycoon and Art Patron," 108.

133. Ibid. Leopoldine Kallmus's father was Jewish. However, she was baptized and raised Catholic.

134. Wessel's central role in the Todesco and Wertheimstein families can be seen in the frequent mentions in the correspondence of the Gomperz family (in Kann, *Briefe an, von und um Josephine von Wertheimstein*). For more about Wessel's work as tutor to the Wittgensteins, see McGuinness, *Wittgenstein, a Life*, 10. See also Gaugusch, "Die Familien Wittgenstein und Salzer und ihr Genealogisches Umfeld," 120. As Gaugusch points out, among the families who signed the death notice, only the Wittgenstein family had converted to Christianity at this time.

135. Assmann, "Opting In und Opting Out," 140.

136. Hermann was thirty-seven and Fanny was twenty-five when they married (Gaugusch, "Die Familien Wittgenstein und Salzer und ihr Genealogisches Umfeld," 123). Herman was identified as a merchant and Fanny as the daughter of Wihelm Figdor, a partner in a retail business (ibid.). See also McGuinness, *Wittgenstein, a Life*, 3.

137. Rappaport's significant position in the financial scene of the Austro-Hungarian Empire was attacked in an antisemitic caricature by Fritz Georg Grätz titled "Jacob Rappaport, der Wunderrabbi vom Kolowratring" (Jacob Rappaport, the wonder rabbi from Kolowratring) on the front cover of *Die Bombe*, January 29, 1882.

138. A rare review of Rappaport's career, published in his obituary in the *Boston Evening Transcript* on August 13, 1886, documents the circles of influence that were part of Rappaport's world, with mention of various European nobles and aristocrats as well as remarks on his own business acumen ("Recent Deaths"). In another report on his death, the *London Times* identified Rappaport, who was born in Lemberg, in Galicia, as a "Polish Jew" (obituary of Jakob Rappaport).

139. Bramann and Moran, "Karl Wittgenstein, Business Tycoon and Art Patron," 110.

140. Günther, "Karl Wittgenstein und seine Bedeutung für den Aufbau und die Entwicklung der österreichischen Volkswirtschaft," 160. Günther mistakenly states that Max von Gomperz was president of the Credit-Anstalt bank at the time, but Eduard von Wiener was.

141. It is possible that Rappaport was a central stockholder of this company, or that he represented Rothschild and Gutmann as stockholders in this company, but that is not clear.

142. Following the stock exchange crash in 1873, Rappaport bought the St. Egyder steel factory in Lower Austria. Rappaport owned the majority of the factory's stock. He invested money to improve the condition of the Alpine Montangesellschaft, to which he added his purchase of the St. Egyder factory. In 1887, after Rappaport died, Wittgenstein bought his stock in the factory from his heirs and other stock from his friends, acquiring

the majority of the shares. Wittgenstein reorganized and improved the steel production and concentrated on the factory's finances (Mathis, *Big Business in Österreich*, 250).

143. Simmel, "The Stranger," in Simmel, *The Sociology of Georg Simmel*, 406.

144. "Karl Wittgenstein als Kunstfreund."

145. Vasili, *Die Wiener Gesellschaft*, 386.

146. Prokop, *Margaret Stonborough-Wittgenstein*, 28–30. The Wittgenstein family lived in the Alleegasse historicist palace for almost six decades. The house was destroyed after World War II.

147. Figdor was considered the greatest private collector in Europe. See Sjörgen, "Die Familie," 99.

148. Weixlgärtner, *Führer durch die Dr. Albert Figdor-Stiftung*, 4.

149. Prokop, "Zum Umgang mit Kunst und Ästhetik in der Familie Wittgenstein." I thank Ursula Prokop for a copy of her lecture.

150. H. Wittgenstein, *Familienerinnerungen*, 18–20. As the secretary of Vienna's Jewish community, Ludwig August Frankl also knew Gustav Epstein, who was a member of the board of the Jewish community. Both names appear in a thank-you to the Todescos.

151. Fanny's mother, Amalia, was buried in February 1863, and her father, Wilhelm, was buried in April 1873 (Gaugusch, "Die Familien Wittgenstein und Salzer und ihr genealogisches Umfeld," 124). Hermine noted that the ancestors of the Figdor family lived in Kittsee, Burgenland, in Austria (Hungary until 1920–21) and that few of them were subscribers to a historical work that was published in the Hebrew language, which she believed indicated that spiritual interest had always been in the family. Kittsse is one of the seven Jewish communities that existed in Burgenland between 1670 and 1938 (H. Wittgenstein, *Familienerinnerungen*, 20).

152. Aichelburg, *Das Wiener Kunstlerhaus*, 64. Fanny donated 300 florins in May 1881 to the Kunstlerhaus. For her support of young musicians, see H. Wittgenstein, *Familienerinnerungen*, 37.

153. Fanny seems to have tried to interfere in Karl's marriage. For her recommendations to Leopoldine Kallmus, then Karl's fiancée, see Nyíri and McGuinness, introduction, xxv.

154. Rappaport's heirs sold the Palais Schey to someone named Benda in 1899. Wittgenstein used the two well-lit rooms that he rented in this palace to inspect new paintings for his city house. See Karl Wittgenstein to the secretary of the Vienna Secession, January 22, 1902, 44.3.15, Secession Archiv, Vienna.

155. H. Wittgenstein, *Familienerinnerungen*, 19–20. Hecht, ed. *Ludwig August Frankl*, 15. Jacob Rappaport's father, Moritz, recorded his admiration of Frankl in a poem of his own, *An Ludwig August Frankl, zum 70. Geburtstag*.

156. Leuenberger, *Schrift-Raum Jerusalem*, 32–34.

157. For more on his view of the Orient, see Hecht, *Ludwig August Frankl*.

158. Kraševac, "Ivan Meštrović und sein Wiener Mäzen Karl Wittgenstein," 140–42.

159. Zaunschirm, *Gustav Klimt, Margarethe Stonborough-Wittgenstein*, 51–53.

160. "Fremde Gäste in der Secession." See also Arnold, "Die Ausstellung der Secession." The church condemned Klinger's painting as not Christian.

161. H. Wittgenstein, *Familienerinnerungen*, 111.

162. Villari, *Giovanni Segantini*, 183.

163. Ibid. See also Hirsch, "Codes of Consumption," 160; Fred [Alfred Wechsler], *Giovanni Segantini*.

164. Günther, "Karl Wittgenstein und seine Bedeutung für den Aufbau und Entwicklung der österreichischen Volkswirtschaft," 163.

165. Shedel, *Art and Society*, 57.

166. H. Wittgenstein, *Familienerinnerungen*. See also Kapfinger and Krischanitz, *Die Wiener Secession*, 20. See also ibid., 138, notes 21–23.

167. Hilger, "Geschichte der 'Vereinigung bildender Künstler Österreichs,' Secession 1897–1918," 16–18.

168. "Karl Wittgenstein als Kunstfreund."

169. The experience of financing the Secession House may have inspired Wittgenstein to experiment in planning modern houses. See Waldhuber and Kruse, *Aristokratischer Chic auf der Insel Brioni, 1893–1919*, 15–16.

170. Kapfinger and Krischanitz, *Die Wiener Secession*, 138, note 22.

171. K. Wittgenstein, "Auf einer Weltreise," in K. Wittgenstein, *Karl Wittgenstein*, 12–21.

172. A photo of Wittgenstein taken during his trip at an archaeological site in Egypt is revealing: dressed in a white suit, smiling after have climbed to a higher level, he leans on a stone carved with ancient Egyptian hieroglyphics and looks down, possibly at the unseen photographer, while his wife, Leopoldine, standing on the ground, looks up at him. Wittgenstein's conqueror pose further reveals his relationship to the historical place. The photo is reproduced in Sjörgen, "Die Familie," 102.

173. The Secession House would not have been the only place where colonial desires were evoked. See Priddis, "Ashantee and the Colonial Gaze," 3.

174. A possible inspiration for the Secession House's laurel leaf golden cupola may have been Charles Chipiez's 1887 reconstruction of the Temple in Jerusalem, with two lotus-shaped trees framing the gateway to the Southern Court of Israel (Chipiez and Perrot, *Le Temple de Jérusalem*, plate 4). See also Kravtsov, "Reconstruction of the Temple by Charles Chipiez and Its Applications in Architecture," 27.

175. Hevesi, "Weiteres vom Hause der Sezession," in Hevesi, *Acht Jahre Sezession*, 70.

176. New Protestants, even after converting to Christianity the Wittgenstein family remained outsiders in the Catholic capital of the Habsburg monarchy (McGuinness, *Wittgenstein, a Life*, 2–4). Some of Karl's siblings married Catholics, which made their Protestant identification less clear. Moreover, Karl allowed his wife to raise their children as Catholics. Yet the newcomer perspective may have been a motivation for Wittgenstein. In 1902, he commissioned Hoffmann to design a Protestant church in St. Aegyd in lower Austria. Its façade had no figural imagery and the interior contained only a few painted saints (Sekler, *Josef Hoffmann*, 64 and 280–81). Wittgenstein's idea of building a church for his workers followed Gutmann and Rothschild's similar act for the workers at the Witkowitz Mill (Arnbom, *Friedmann, Gutmann, Lieben, Mandl, Strakosch*, 70–72). While Gutmann and Rothschild built a progressive workers' colony, arranged around the church, Wittgenstein made his mark with a modern Protestant church in a town with a Catholic majority.

177. Bisanz-Prakken, "The Beethoven Exhibition of the Secession and the Younger Viennese Tradition of the Gesamtkunstwerk," 142.

178. Photos of the Beethoven sculpture in the music salon and the red salon are reproduced in Sjörgen, "Die Familie," 107 and 115. There is also a photo of it on top of the grand staircase.

179. For example, he wrote a letter to Carl von Wiener, the president of the Academic Association for Literature and Music in Vienna, confirming the donation of 3,000 kronen to start a new musical journal (Karl Wittgenstein to Carl von Wiener, October 14, 1909, Leontine Donath Estate 546/72–1, Handschriften- Autographen- und Nachlass-Sammlung, Österreichische Nationalbibliothek, Vienna).

180. Quoted in "Der Stadtrath gegen Klinger 'Beethoven.'"

181. Wittgenstein was criticized for organizing, with the Gutmann family in Bohemia, a steel cartel to fix prices (Rudolf, *Banking and Industrialization in Austria-Hungary*, 97–99 and 248, notes).

182. Karl Wittgenstein to the secretary of the Secession, September 16, 1902, 44.3.16, Secession Archiv, Vienna.

183. B. Walter, *Theme and Variations*, 152–54.

184. Natter, *Die Welt von Klimt, Schiele und Kokoschka*, 44. See also Zaunschirm, *Gustav Klimt, Margarethe Stonborough-Wittgenstein*, 51.

185. Wittgenstein had hired the architect Eduard Frauenfeld Jr. to build a hunting lodge for him in Hochreit, Rohr am Gebirge, in Lower Austria in 1888. In 1906, Hoffmann redesigned the interiors of two rooms in a modernist style. See Sekler, *Josef Hoffmann* 75–77.

186. Windisch-Graetz, "Das Jagdhaus Hochreith," 30–32.

187. Kraševac, "Ivan Meštrović und sein Wiener Mäzen Karl Wittgenstein," 136.

188. Mahler-Werfel, *Tagebuch-Suiten, 1898–1902*, 607. This entry in the diary of Alma Schindler, who became Mahler through her marriage with the composer and conductor Gustav Mahler and later became Werfel through her marriage with the author Franz Werfel, is from December 27, 1900.

189. In November 1869 Berl founded the wholesale firm D. Berl in Vienna, with branches in Aussig, Prague, Budapest, and Brno. He bought coal mines—specifically those that produced brown coal (lignite)—in Bohemia, Hungary, and Croatia and participated in other industries. Many of Olbrich's early clients were either assimilated Jews or of Jewish origin: Berl; his brother-in-law, Friedrich Victor Spitzer, a sugar factory owner; Max Friedmann, a machine factory owner; the consul Ladislaus von Dirsztay; and the newspaper publisher Isidor von Klarwill.

190. Quoted in Gronberg, "The Inner Man," 87. Kraus, "Die diesmalige Ausstellung," 19. The banker Wilhelm Zierer was the father-in-law of Oscar Berl, the son and heir of David Berl. For more on familial connections between prominent Jewish families, see Mahler-Werfel, *Tagebuch-Suiten 1898–1902*, 348, note 8.

191. Kodek, *Unsere Bausteine sind die Menschen*, 26.

192. Johann Auspitzer was the brother of the author and editor Wilhelm Auspitzer mentioned above. The German title of the lecture is "Was ist modern und was ist in der Mode?" See Kodek, *Zwischen Verboten und Erlaubt*, 128.

193. "Venice in Vienna" reproduced a small Venice in the Prater, which was divided into a large nature park and amusement and exhibition areas. Marmorek's design included replicas of Venetian palaces, canals, piazzas, bridges, houses, boulevards, and even a small

convent. There were restaurants, bars, halls for theatrical and musical performances, exhibition halls, sports clubs, travel agents, and even a post office—all housed in the Venetian buildings and on Venetian squares. Marmorek also designed residential buildings. In 1898, Marmorek designed the Nestroyhof for his father-in-law Julius Schwarz as a fashionable art nouveau building decorated with beautiful female faces. In 1902, Marmorek designed the Rüdigerhof for Else Weiss as a modernist building, with a colorful façade of minimalist Oriental and Greek classicist style (Kristan, *Oskar Marmorek*, 232–35).

194. Kodek, *Unsere Bausteine sind die Menschen*, 226.

195. Kodek, *Zwischen Verboten und Erlaubt*, 143.

196. Membership in the secessionist club also did not object to German national identification, as Oskar Berl who married Flora Zierer in 1899) proved through his cofounding of the Deutsches Volkstheater in Vienna. This theater promoted German nationalism and opposed the multiethnic character of the Austro-Hungarian Empire: Mahler-Werfel, *Tagebuch-Suiten, 1898–1902*, 764.

197. Bing, "L'Art Nouveau," in Bing, *Artistic America, Tiffany Glass, and Art Nouveau*, 228–29.

198. Abels, "Joseph Maria Olbrich," 162.

199. Lehmann, *Allgemeiner Wohnungs-Anzeiger*, 1898, 2:1114 (Friedrich Victor Spitzer, Ph Dr. Grillparzerstr. 7, I); 1899, 2:1235 (Grillparzerstr. 7, I); 1900, 2:1151 (Schleifmühlgasse 7 [sic] IV/1); 1901, 2:1171 (Schleifmühlgasse 4 IV/1); 1902, 2:1183 (Schleifmühlgasse 4 IV/1); 1903, 2:1205 (Steinfeldtgasse 4 XIX).

200. Borsi and Godolo, *Wiener Bauten der Jahrhundertwende*, 321.

201. *Neue Freie Presse*, November 13, 1895.

202. Starl, *Lexikon zur Fotografie in Österreich*, 459–61.

203. Mahler-Werfel, *Tagebuch-Suiten, 1898–1902*, 398.

204. Ibid.

205. Ibid.398–400.

206. Ibid., 149. The entry is from November 24, 1898.

207. Folnesics, "Das moderne Wiener Kunstgewerbe," 256.

208. Clark, "Olbrich and Vienna," 7:47.

209. A. Loos, "Das Heim," 9. English translation by Michael Scuffil.

210. A positive review of the collaboration by Julius Korngold appeared in *Neue Freie Presse* on March 10, 1903 (Fenzl, "Alexander Zemlinsky," 27–29).

211. Simmel, "The Problem of Style," in Simmel, *Simmel on Culture*, 216.

212. Alexander Zemlinsky's father, Adolf, converted to Judaism to marry Clara Semo, who came from a rich Sephardic family. Adolf helped edit a book on the Sephardic Jewish community in Vienna (*Geschichte der türkisch-israelitischen Gemeinde zu Wien*, 1888.)

213. Zemlinsky's ugliness (which was "notorious," according to Alma's stepfather) was used to mock Alma by guests at a lunch at the Zuckerkandls, where Gustav Mahler courted her for the first time (Kristan, *Josef Hoffmann*, 22–24).

214. Mahler-Werfel, *Tagebuch-Suiten, 1898–1902*, 463. The entry is from February 26, 1900. In his apartment Spitzer tried matching Orientalism with modernist secessionist design (the Turkish smoking room was fashionable in the second half of the nineteenth century, as evidenced by the Turkish room ordered by Crown Prince Rudolf in 1888).

215. Mahler-Werfel, *Tagebuch-Suiten, 1898–1902*, 471. The entry is from March 14, 1900.
216. Ibid., 483–85. The entry is from March 28, 1900.
217. Ibid., 634. The entry is from March 8, 1901 and is also quoted in Fenzl, "Alexander Zemlinsky," 64.
218. Mahler-Werfel, *Tagebuch-Suiten, 1898–1902*, 723.
219. Sekler, *Josef Hoffmann*, 266–270 and 273–75.
220. Ibid., 49. The quote also appears in Kristan, *Josef Hoffmann*, 21.
221. Hevesi, *Altkunst—Neukunst, Wien*, 217–18. The essay is dated November 8, 1905.
222. Lux, "Villenkolonie Hohe Warte, erbaut von Prof. Joseph Hoffmann," 153–55.
223. McGuinness, *Wittgenstein, a Life*, 2 (my emphasis).
224. Hofmannsthal, "Der Schüler." Concerning the original version of the pantomime, see Gillman, *Viennese Jewish Modernism*, 57–58.
225. In the published version, the rabbi became a learned alchemist, Bochur became a student, and the daughter kept the name Taube (Hofmannsthal, "Der Schüler").
226. Gillman, *Viennese Jewish Modernism*, 63.
227. Hofmannsthal, "Der Schüler," 1207.
228. Ibid., 1208. The ugly Jew and beautiful Jewess were not conflicting perceptions of stereotypical "Jewishness"; rather, they were both representations of degenerate nature, as the pantomime's conclusion shows when the daughter is killed. See Stögner, "Antisemitisch-misogyne Repräsentationen und die Krise der Geschlechtsidentität in Fin de Siècle," 236.
229. Gillman, *Viennese Jewish Modernism*, 59–61.
230. The story's Jewish elements resurface through body language and in the conclusion (Gillman, "Hofmannsthal's Jewish Pantomime," 440–42).
231. Prokop, *Margaret Stonborough-Wittgenstein*, 51. The marriage ceremony took place at the evangelical church in the inner city.
232. Prokop, *Margaret Stonborough-Wittgenstein*, 99.
233. I refer to the idea of "Jewishness" and the possibilities it offered to promote self-marketing presented by Janis Bergman-Carton ("Negotiating the Categories," 60).
234. Quoted in McGuinness, Ascher, and Pfersmann, *Wittgenstein Familienbriefe*, 73 (my emphasis).
235. The biographer of Ludwig Wittgenstein argues that a Jewish background was a hindrance to him only in very special situations, such as when Ludwig wanted to join a German national sports club and was rejected (McGuinness, "Wittgenstein und das Judentum," 60).
236. Wijdeveld, *Ludwig Wittgenstein, Architect*, 51–53.
237. For Engelmann's ideas about and attention to the idea of a Jewish state and his emigrating to Palestine, as well as Ludwig Wittgenstein's interest in this, see U. Schneider, "Vom 'Wittgensteinhaus' zum 'Café Techelet,'" 115–16. Engelmann eventually emigrated in 1934 (Wijdeveld, *Ludwig Wittgenstein, Architect*, 48 and 57). Both Hermine and Margaret refer in letters and diary entries to their discussions about ethics with Engelmann; Margaret expressed in her diary in 1918 her wish to come to terms with her Jewish identification (Prokop, *Margaret Stonborough-Wittgenstein*, 99).
238. Regarding Wittgenstein's alterations of Engelmann's plan and the new design as

representing well-controlled movement, see Wijdeveld, *Ludwig Wittgenstein, Architect*, 159 and 165.

239. Simmel, "The Problem of Style," in Simmel, *Simmel on Culture*, 216.

3. The Modernists, 1902–7

1. Regarding Singer's socialist publications before he published the journal *Die Zeit*, see E. Walter, "Die Funktion journalistischer Opposition," 13–15.

2. The journal's advocacy of the latest modern movement in Europe was praised by Hugo von Hofmannsthal (Moser and Zand, "Die Zeit, ein 'Wiener Posten der guten Europäer," 247).

3. Rebhann, "Die Zeit," 20–21. See also E. Walter, "Die Funktion journalistischer Opposition," 58.

4. Ibid.

5. Gaugusch, *Wer einmal war*, 903.

6. Rebhann, "Die Zeit," 12.

7. Ibid., 15–16. See also E. Walter, "Die Funktion journalistischer Opposition," 26–28. Singer bought Fischhof's estate and asked one of his colleagues to publish a collection of his unpublished works.

8. For more on Fischhof's views on integrating federal states and his recognition of Austria as a German state historically, politically, and culturally, see E. Walter, "Die Funktion journalistischer Opposition," 27.

9. H. Schweiger, "Shaw's Contributions to *Fin-de-Siècle* Vienna," 137. Notably, the English professor and Zionist Leon Kellner has been mentioned as introducing the Fabian Society to Viennese readers. The Viennese Fabian Society was dissolved in 1901.

10. Ibid. 138.

11. Ibid., 139.

12. Ibid.

13. E. Walter, "Die Funktion journalistischer Opposition," 69.

14. The journal's art critic, Richard Muther; the architect Otto Wagner; and Isidor Singer were the three members of the committee that chose the winning design. Wagner was chosen as artistic advisor, perhaps to substantiate the newspaper's modern reputation (ibid., 68). The members were not satisfied with the entries but selected the design of a student of Otto Wagner, the Austrian architect Hans Mayr.

15. Ibid., 72–73.

16. The newspaper's aims were published in Kanner and Singer's editorial, "Unser Blatt," on September 27, 1902. See E. Walter, "Die Funktion journalistischer Opposition," 21.

17. O. Wagner, *Moderne Architektur*, 102.

18. Ibid., 33.

19. Houze, "Fashion, Disguise, and Transformation," 38.

20. For more on the commercial aspect of Wagner's early seductive architecture, as in two houses on the Linke Wienzeile, see Shapira, "Assimilating with Style," 129–31.

21. "Unser Depeschensaal."

22. Photographs of the Telegraph Office and art gallery interiors are reproduced in Lux, "Der Depeschen-Saal der 'Zeit' in Wien."

23. Varnedoe, *Wien 1900*, 37.

24. Singer and Kanner supported the government's commission of modern architects for the Postal Savings Bank, echoing their hiring of Wagner: "A Postal Savings Bank, as an institution that has emerged from our modern life-demands in architectural terms a completely contemporary, that is functional-formal, design" (quoted in Topp, *Architecture and Truth in Fin-de-Siècle Vienna*, 106).

25. Rebhann, "Die Zeit," 16. Singer "war etwas bohemienhaft veranlagt. Eine fesselnde Erscheinung an sich, verstand er es durch Geist und Witz seine Gesprächspartner zu faszinieren. Bei Frauen machte er grossen Eindruck."

26. Quoted in E. Walter, "Die Funktion journalistischer Opposition," 76. Kraus played on the prejudice against Eastern European Jews, for example identifying Singer's style as "Schmock style."

27. Quoted in ibid., 79.

28. Kraus describes the Jewish boy as "mit riesigen Ohren, der Krummnase und den feuchten Glotzaugen" and the gentile boy as "die Ohren kurzgeschnitten, der Höcker auf der Nase wegrasiert, die wulstigen Lippen verschmälert, das schwere Augenlied hinaufgeschoben." ("'Zeit'—Genosse," 22–23, and "Die Europäisierung der 'Zeit' oder 'Der kleine Kohn ist weg!,'" 17).

29. In 1895, Carl Moll had supported Waerndorfer's admission to the Künstlerhaus. It is possible that Moll later encouraged him to switch his allegiance to the secessionist movement (Aichelburg, "Künstlerhaus, Mitgliederverzeichnisse, Freunde und Mitarbeiter").

30. For more on Waerndorfer's contribution and British influences, see Fritz Wärndorfer, telegraph to Josef Hoffmann, June 27, 1900, 43.4.6, Secession Archiv, Vienna.

31. "George Minne," 38. Documents show that *Kneeling Boy* played a large role in secessionist salons, influencing Moll (*Self-Portrait*), Hoffmann (see the photograph of Hoffmann's apartment in Neulinggasse 24, published in Lux, *Die moderne Wohnung und ihre Ausstattung*, 190), and Waerndorfer (see Fig. 21). Oskar Kokoschka would challenge the notion of the pious boy in *Die träumenden Knaben*, published by the Wiener Werkstätte in 1908.

32. "George Minne," 35.

33. Bahr, "Das neue Ghetto," 8.

34. Malmberg, *Widerhall des Herzens*, 28. Malmberg also referred to the art patron Emil Franzos's "dark color," further suggesting that this alludes to Jewish identity (ibid., 44).

35. The letterhead is reproduced in Shapira, "Modernism and Jewish Identity in Early Twentieth Century Vienna," 58.

36. With antisemitic associations, the artist portrayed a small old man with a semitic nose and white beard clasping his hands with satisfaction; another depicted a male profile with a semitic nose and pointed ears (caricatures reproduced in *Ver Sacrum*, 1900, 350 and 354).

37. The animal-like profiles of the female members of the audience in Aubrey Beardsley's "The Wagnerites," published in 1894 in the *Yellow Book*, might have inspired Behmer's caricature.

38. König's caricatures are reproduced in Bisanz-Prakken, *Heiliger Frühling*, 143.

39. Regarding Kafka and the "traffic of clothes"—the need to wear proper dress to

travel and associate with other people in public, see M. Anderson, *Kafka's Clothes*, 123–44, especially 131–35.

40. According to Sander Gilman, the Jewish man's dark skin "marked it as both sexually perverse and racially degenerate" (quoted in Davison, "The 'Jew' as Homme/Femme-Fatale," 87).

41. Farkas, *Hermann Bahr, Prophet der Moderne*, 67. Bahr left the editorial board of *Die Zeit* in autumn 1899.

42. Fritz Wärndorfer (in 1902 Wärndorfer changed his name to Waerndorfer) to Hermann Bahr, May 29, 1900, A25001 BaM, Autographen und Nachlässe Sammlung, Österreichisches Theatermuseum, Vienna (hereafter OT).

43. Vergo, "Fritz Waerndorfer as Collector," 33.

44. Fritz Wärndorfer to Hermann Bahr, May 6, 1898, A25032 BaM, OT.

45. The eighteenth is also known as the cottage district.

46. Fritz and Lili Waerndorfer had three children: Helene (1897–1938), Carl Richard (1899–1983), and Herbert Gustav (1905–24).

47. I thank Heidrun Weiss and Wolf-Erich Eckstein of Vienna's Jewish Community Archive for the biographical dates and other information on Fritz and Lili Waerndorfer.

48. For anecdotes on Lili and her linguistic abilities, see Waerndorfer, "Eleonora Duse und Josef Hoffmann," 44.

49. The redesign of his public rooms probably began with Hoffmann's design for Waerndorfer's studio on the first floor in early 1902. Meanwhile, in April of the same year Fritz and Lili Waerndorfer converted to Protestantism. By the end of that year, Mackintosh's design of the music room on the ground floor would conclude the redesign of the public rooms, and the patron would also change his name from the German Wärndorfer to the Anglicized Waerndorfer.

50. The reference to modern Viennese interiors as theatrical artistic spectacle was noted in the introduction. See Baroni and D'Auria, *Josef Hoffmann und die Wiener Werkstätte*, 40.

51. Fritz Waerndorfer to Eduard Josef Wimmer-Wisgrill, August 9, 1924, 11.214 Aut 24, Kunstsammlung und Archiv, Universität für angewandte Kunst Wien, Vienna (hereafter UAK).

52. In "Das individuelle Kleid" (Individual dress; 252), Hoffmann argued that clothing must fit the wearer's character. Like the architect Adolf Loos, Hoffmann also associated dress design with interior design.

53. Quoted in Schweiger, *Wiener Werkstaette*, 43.

54. Wagner-Rieger and Reissberger, *Theophil von Hansen*, 240–42.

55. The triple mirror arrangement above the fireplace was not necessarily meant to show off Minne's sculpture. In an earlier published photograph a nonfigurative sculpture and two flanking flower vases were placed on the fireplace (reproduced in *Innen Dekoration*, May 1902, 136).

56. See Gronberg, "The Inner Man," 80–82.

57. For information on Waerndorfer's purchase of the sculpture, see Natter, *Die Welt von Klimt, Schiele und Kokoschka*, 58. A comparison of Behmer's caricature of the hybrid animal in Waerndorfer's letterhead and Minne's *Kneeling Boy* raises the question of whether Waerndorfer had a poor self-image in relation to his ideal self-representation.

58. The critic Hevesi likened looking at Klimt's paintings to the enjoyment of champagne—they satisfied sophisticated tastes ("Haus Wärndorfer," in Hevesi, *Altkunst—Neukunst, Wien*, 223). Minne's sculpture could be associated with the narcissistic enjoyment of drinking water from the fountain of youth.

59. Weidinger, *Oskar Kokoschka, Dreaming Boy, Enfant Terrible*, 47.

60. Shapira, "An Early Expressionist Masterpiece."

61. Kokoschka, *Die träumenden Knaben*, 5. See also Shapira, "The Pioneers."

62. The canard that Jewish men lacked honor was expressed in Vienna through the German national fraternities' ban on challenging Jews to duels. The disparaged honor of Jewish men reached throughout Europe during France's Dreyfus affair, 1894–1902. See Davison, "'The Jew' as Homme/Femme-Fatale," 77–81. The assimilated Jewish author and pseudoscientist Otto Weininger adopted the antisemitic prejudice against Jewish men and argued that both Jews and women lacked "self-respect" (Weininger, *Geschlecht und Charakter*, 412). Weininger's book became a bestseller and a fashionable topic among Jewish patrons. A few patrons even sent a copy of the book to their favorite artists.

63. Simmel, "The Stranger," in Simmel, *The Sociology of Georg Simmel*, 406. See also Kernmayer, *Judentum im Wiener Feuilleton (1848–1903)*, 77–79.

64. Fritz Wärndorfer to Josef Hoffmann, December 23, 1902, 3996/3, UAK.

65. For more on Waerndorfer's distancing himself from the cultural preferences and tastes of prominent Jewish families, see Fritz Waerndorfer to Hermann Bahr, June 3, 1903, A 25010 BaM, OT.

66. Hevesi, "Haus Wärndorfer," in Hevesi, *Altkunst—Neukunst, Wien*, 222. See also Hevesi, "Ein moderner Nachmittag," in Hevesi, *Flagranti und andere Heiterkeiten*, 167.

67. Voglhuber, "Die Kunst des Wiener Jugendstiles und seine ägyptischen Formulierungen bei Fassaden- und Innenraumgestaltungen," 115. Voglhuber indicates the decoration of false doors in ancient Egyptian graves (ibid., illustrations 13a and 13b, 152 and 153).

68. Simmel, "The Stranger, in in Simmel, *The Sociology of Georg Simmel*, 406.

69. This is similar to the Jewish dandy critically described by Hannah Arendt, as discussed in the introduction.

70. Cixous and Clément, *The Newly Born Woman*.

71. The terms appear throughout Dijkstra, *Idols of Perversity*, 376–401. For another critical perspective on the antisemitic views on the Jewish body, see Gilman, *The Jew's Body*.

72. E. Fuchs, *Die Juden in der Karikatur*.

73. Fritz Wärndorfer to Josef Hoffmann, December 23, 1902, 3996/3, UAK.

74. Robertson, "Margaret Macdonald Mackintosh," 56.

75. A photograph showing the grand piano in this room is reproduced in ibid., 36.

76. In the sixteenth century Rabbi Shlomo Halevi Alkabetz from Safed wrote the liturgical song *Lecha Dodi* recited on Friday as part of the *Kabbalat Shabbat* (welcome of the sabbath) ceremony. Its refrain is "Let's go my friend toward the bride, and receive the presence of Shabbat," ending with: "Come, O Bride! Shabbat Queen!" A further important German reference is the well-known poem by Heinrich Heine, "Princess Shabbat."

77. Fritz Waerndorfer to Eduard Josef Wimmer-Wisgrill, October 4, 1924, 11.214 Aut 25, UAK.

78. Robertson, "Margaret Macdonald Mackintosh," 54.

79. Hevesi, "Ein moderner Nachmittag," in Hevesi, *Flagranti und andere Heiterkeiten*, 174.

80. Quoted in Vergo, "The Vanished Frieze," 15.

81. Hevesi, "Haus Wärndorfer," in Hevesi, *Altkunst—Neukunst, Wien*, 222. The story of the seventh princess was not a naïve fairy tale but related to a grown-up erotic fantasy. The curtains separating the music room and the dining room were decorated at the top with four appliqué panels designed by Frances MacNair (circa 1903). Two of the four panels depicted an intimate erotic engagement between two women, and the other two each showed a woman, one lifting her head and the other lowering her head as if for a kiss. A photograph of all four panels is reproduced in Vergo, "The Vanished Frieze," 73.

82. Wagner-Rieger and Reissberger, *Theophil von Hansen*, 251.

83. Pincus-Witten, "The Iconography of Symbolist Painting," 60.

84. Fritz Waerndorfer to Eduard Josef Wimmer-Wisgrill August 5, 1926, 11.214 Aut 42, UAK.

85. Fritz Waerndorfer to Eduard Josef Wimmer-Wisgrill, September 20, 1923, 11.214 Aut 7, UAK. It is not clear when Waerndorfer first joined the Freemasons. It is documented, however, that in April 1912 he joined the "Treue" (Loyalty) Freemasons' lodge. He was recommended by one of his loyal partners in the Wiener Werkstätte, the publisher Sigmund Rosenbaum (Kodek, *Unsere Bausteine sind die Menschen*, 371).

86. Le Rider, *Modernity and Crises of Identity*, 262–64. On the concept of the Jewish *homme fatal*, see the discussion below about the music room and gallery in Waerndorfer's house.

87. Kraus, "Salomé," 8–10.

88. Houze, "Fashion, Disguise, and Transformation," 212.

89. Simmel referred to the wish to avoid serious discussion ("The Sociology of Sociability," in Simmel, *Simmel on Culture*, 126.).

90. Malmberg, *Widerhall des Herzens*, 103.

91. Ibid., 105.

92. Fritz Wärndorfer to Hanke, May 29, 1900, 43.4.6, Secession Archiv, Vienna. Schnitzler's *Reigen* includes ten dialogues between a man and a woman, in some cases from different social classes and in other cases from the same class. The dialogues were meant to undermine traditional habits by flirting with male sexual fantasies and exposing Viennese social hypocrisies.

93. Quoted in Farkas, *Hermann Bahr, Prophet der Moderne*, 137.

94. Hevesi, "Haus Wärndorfer," in Hevesi, *Altkunst—Neukunst, Wien*, 223.

95. Levetus, "The 'Wiener Werkstätte,' Vienna," 196. Waerndorfer also first received acknowledgment for his patronage in the chronicles of the Wiener Moderne by British art historian Peter Vergo, "Fritz Waerndorfer as Collector," in *Alte und Moderne Kunst*, 1981, Issue 177.)

96. Quoted in W. Schweiger, *Wiener Werkstaette*, 30. Starting modestly with two rooms and one cabinet at Heumühlgasse 4, in the fourth district, in October 1903, the firm (most likely with Waerndorfer's investment) eventually purchased a three-floor factory building at Neustiftgasse 32 in the seventh district (ibid., 30 and 33).

97. Fritz Wärndorfer to Hermann Bahr, May 6, 1902, A25005 BaM, OT.

98. Schorske, *Fin-de-Siècle Vienna*, 246.

99. Farkas, *Hermann Bahr, Prophet der Moderne*, 149–51. Zuckerkandl later encouraged Klimt to repurchase his painting for the university panels (1905) from the Education Ministry (*Zeitkunst Wien 1901–1907*, 167).

100. Bahr, *Gegen Klimt*. See Fritz Waerndorfer to Hermann Bahr, September 17 and 19, 1903, A25000 BaM and A24994 BaM, OT. It was Koloman Moser's idea, but the production of the book was a collaborative work between Waerndorfer and Bahr.

101. Hevesi, "Ein moderner Nachmittag," in Hevesi, *Flagranti und andere Heiterkeiten* 176–78.

102. Shapira, "Assimilating with Style," 210–12.

103. Quoted in W. Schweiger, *Wiener Werkstaette*, 43.

104. Ibid., 30 and 33.

105. Quoted in ibid., 27.

106. Quoted in ibid. The original German is "Josef Hoffmann, Koloman Moser, k. k. Professoren der Kunstgewerbeschule in Wien werden als Directoren und Friedrich Waerndorfer, Fabrikant in Wien, als Cassirer."

107. Rochowanski, *Josef Hoffmann*, 26–27.

108. Bertha Waerndorfer to Franz Hanke, June 13, 1902 43.4.7, Secession Archiv, Vienna.

109. For a reference to Waerndorfer's commission for his sister-in-law, see Rennhofer, *Koloman Moser*, 85–87. Margarethe Hellmann left the Jewish religion, possibly in connection with her planned marriage to Ladislaus Rémy, in 1904 (Austritt-Kartei, 1904, Israelitische Kultusgemeinde Wien, Matrikenamt, Vienna).

110. The similarity between the showcase designed for Hellmann and one designed for the Floge sisters' salon (Rennhofer, *Koloman Moser*, 90, Fig. 147) reinforces the connection between Jewish assimilation and new designs in the Viennese fashion scene.

111. Daniele Baroni and Antonio D'Auria originally attributed Hellmann's set of bedroom furniture to Josef Hoffmann (*Josef Hoffmann und die Wiener Werkstätte*, 96–97).

112. Moser explained his 1906 departure from the Wiener Werkstätte as due to its too-varied activity and its reliance on clients' tastes (W. Schweiger, *Wiener Werkstaette*, 69).

113. Here I compare specific choices of furniture decoration. For example, Hoffman designed a game table for Karl Wittgenstein with reliefs by Carl Otto Czeschka and carved figures of American Indian tribal chiefs; this can be compared to Hoffmann's design of a low salon table for Margaret Stonborough-Wittgenstein, with the embellishment consisting solely of four simple, solid, square elongated legs.

114. In the case of Margaret Stonborough-Wittgenstein, the Wiener Werkstätte's commission came from her father.

115. Zaunschirm, *Gustav Klimt, Margarethe Stonborough-Wittgenstein*, 72.

116. Quoted in Prokop, *Margaret Stonborough-Wittgenstein*, 59.

117. Quoted in ibid.

118. In a 1906 review of the dance performance of Maud Allan in Vienna, Hevesi quotes Otto Wagner describing the dancer as a slender figure in white and black. Hevesi added to Wagner's observation that these were the "national colors" of the Wiener Werkstätte (Hevesi, "Miß Maud Allan," in Hevesi, *Altkunst—Neukunst, Wien*, 281).

119. Rochowanski, *Josef Hoffmann*, 34. The color play of black and white appears al-

ready in the arrangement of the corner of the fireplace in Waerndorfer's studio (for a photo of Waerndorfer's studio corner, see *Innen Dekoration*, May 1902, 136).

120. Hoffmann's experimental design for the decorated spoons and forks (1905) is evidence of how Mackintosh's furniture inspired him. See examples in Neuwirth, *Josef Hoffmann*, 160–97.

121. Ibid., 23. Hevesi noted that Waerndorfer was the only client who purchased the cutlery, and Neuwirth notes the date of purchase (*Josef Hoffmann*, 33).

122. Hevesi, "Haus Wärndorfer," in Hevesi, *Altkunst—Neukunst, Wien*, 221–23.

123. A photograph of the artists' table at the exhibition is reproduced in W. Schweiger, *Wiener Werkstaette*, 57.

124. Waerndorfer may have been inspired by a Joseph Englehart screen inlaid with wood that showed a naked youth lying on a table playing with a garland. The first panel of the screen shows the boy lying on his back, and the fourth shows him lying on his stomach. It was reproduced in *Ver Sacrum* (1898, no. 9, 7).

125. Quoted in Neuwirth, *Josef Hoffmann*, 31.

126. Ibid., 31–33.

127. Waerndorfer was eager to participate in the Viennese culture of debate, as seen in his encouragement that Bahr write a defense of Klimt, mentioned above.

128. Fritz Waerndorfer to Hermann Bahr, April 11, 1906, A25024 BaM, OT.

129. The photograph, probably taken in early 1906, documents the presence of Hoffmann, Reinhardt, Klimt, Moser and Alfred Roller. MAK–Austrian Museum of Applied Arts / Contemporary Art: MAK–Wiener Werkstätte Archiv, Inv. no. K.I 13740b).

130. Hoffmann praised Waerndorfer for founding Cabaret Fledermaus and described in detail how Waerndorfer successfully gathered together leading Viennese authors, artists, and dancers and discovered new talents to perform in his cabaret (Hodin, *Bekenntnis zu Kokoschka*, 67–69).

131. Hevesi, "Kabaret Fledermaus," in Hevesi, *Altkunst—Neukunst, Wien*, 241 and 244.

132. Zuckerkandl, "Kunst und Kultur, Das Kabarett 'Fledermaus.'"

133. Kraus, "Eine Kulturtat," 9. Kraus may have reversed Nietzsche's recommendation to a man who is going to meet a woman not to leave the whip at home.

134. Wiener Werkstätte, "Das Ästhetische Programm: Eine Schrift der Wiener Werkstätte zur Eröffnung der 'Fledermaus,'" 163.

135. For further information about Heinrich Eisenbach, see Hans Veigl, *Lachen im Keller*, 9–14. The first Jewish theaters in Vienna were established in the 1890s. But the Parisian cabaret Le Chat Noir, founded in 1881, served as the original model for the cosmopolitan and provocative cabarets in Germany and Austria.

136. Salten, "Eisenbach," in Salten, *Geister der Zeit*, 171.

137. Veigl, *Lachen im Keller*, 16.

138. Ibid., 16–18.

139. Ibid., 17.

140. Ibid., 18–20.

141. Ibid., 24.

142. Ibid., 25.

143. Sekler, *Josef Hoffmann*, 318.

144. The Cabaret Fledermaus furniture was produced by the firm Jacob and Josef Kohn. See Pichler, "Das Kabarett Fledermaus," 58.

145. Sekler, *Josef Hoffmann*, 318.

146. Ibid., 319.

147. Gewerbe-Register Fritz Wärndorfer, Registration no. 2866/1, Zentral Gewerbe Register der Stadt Wien, Vienna.

148. Barker and Lensing, *Peter Altenberg*, 124. See Friedell's text on Cabaret Fledermaus in Segal, *The Vienna Coffeehouse Wits*, 215.

149. Malmberg, *Widerhall des Herzens*, 77.

150. Ibid. In German, Altenberg said "der Höhepunkt der Schmockerei" and "Aber für die Snobs ist es gut genug, gerade das, was sie wollen." Kraus had criticized Zuckerkandl and Waerndorfer as snobs, and Malmberg also recalled Altenberg's dismissal of Macdonald's frieze in Waerndorfer's salon as "Höhepunkt der Schmockerei" (ibid., 104).

151. Quoted in Rossbacher, *Literatur und Bürgertum*, 137.

152. Stewart, "Egon Friedell and Alfred Polgar," 156; see also 164–66.

153. Ibid., 160.

154. Friedell and Polgar, "Die zehn Gerechten," 67.

155. Ibid., 68. The original German is "Wie ich sag: a Narrentum."

156. Ibid., 69. In the original German, the daughter says, "Aber Papa, das ist doch Sezession," and Staninski says, "ein Tempel der kommenden Kunst."

157. In his letters to Bahr describing his search for further financial support for the Vienna Secession and the Wiener Werkstätte, Waerndorfer documented this resentment.

158. Friedell and Polgar, "Die zehn Gerechten," 70–72.

159. Stewart, "Egon Friedell and Alfred Polgar," 161.

160. Friedell and Polgar, "Die zehn Gerechten," 70. In the original German, Frau Taussig says, "Moritz, ich bitt Dich, moderier Dich, in a Zimmer ganz aus Marmor!" and Herr von Arthammer says, "Wenn's Programm so lustig wär,' wie's Besteck."

161. Ibid., 72.

162. Polgar's respect for the Budapester Orpheum is expressed in his "Heinrich Eisenbach."

163. Shapira, "Assimilating with Style," 173.

164. Friedell and Alfred Polgar, *Goethe, Eine Szene*.

165. Malmberg, *Widerhall des Herzens*, 78.

166. Wilfried Barner, "Jüdische Goethe Verehrung vor 1933." Barner presents mainly examples from German literature. See also M. Anderson, *Kafka's Clothes*, 60. Waerndorfer's letters to Wimmer-Wisgrill from the 1920s are full of quotes from Goethe.

167. Kalina, "Hugo von Hofmannsthal und der Tanz," 144. See also Malmberg, *Widerhall des Herzens*, 81–87.

168. Kokoschka, *Letters, 1905–1976*, 17.

169. Garelick, *Rising Star*, 3.

170. Werkner, "Kokoschkas frühe Gebärdensprache und ihre Verwurzelung im Tanz."

171. Both were published in Altenberg, *Wie ich es sehe*. "The Primitive" was the second part of a larger text, "The Revolutionary," whose first part was "The Greek" and whose third part was "Dialogue." "The Primitive" is about a young girl with a pale face and white

hands who searches for the protection of a young man, who takes her home and adores her as if she was his queen.

172. Schnitzler's diary entry on this evening and Altenberg's letter to Holitscher are quoted in Lunzer and Lunzer-Talos, *Peter Altenberg*, 73. For more on the early network of Beer-Hofmann, Hofmannsthal, Schnitzler, and Salten, see Scherer, *Richard Beer-Hofmann und die Wiener Moderne*, 3. The age of consent in the Austro-Hungarian Empire at this time was fourteen.

173. Altenberg, *Wie ich es sehe*, 60.

174. Eder, "Diese Theorie ist sehr delikat," 168.

175. Quoted in ibid., 166.

176. Ibid., 172. Eder's sources are Weininger, *Geschlecht und Charakter*, 417, and Mosse, *Nationalismus und Sexualität*, 170–72.

177. Eder, "Diese Theorie ist sehr delikat," 173. Later Eder quotes Sander Gilman's note that Jews represented "a specific type of perverse sexuality" (Gilman, *Sexuality*, 274).

178. Eder, 173–75.

179. Quoted in Eder, 175–76 (my emphasis).

180. Gelber, "Interfaces between Young Vienna and the Young Jewish Poetic Movement," 64–66.

181. Cohn, "Richard Beer-Hofmann," 22. The original German is "Blut unserer Väter, Voll Unruh und Stolz. In uns sind *alle*."

182. Beer-Hofmann, *Der Tod Georgs*, 106.

183. Ibid., 99–101.

184. Garelick, *Rising Star*, 11.

185. Beer-Hofmann's reconstruction of his Judaism can be compared to that of Martin Buber, who rejected the prejudice of Jewish Orientalism as material Orientalism by offering a new agenda of spiritual Orientalism (Judaism as spiritual source). Beer-Hofmann referred to biblical sources and Zionist revivalism. For a discussion of the popularity of Buber's teachings, see Mendes-Flohr, *Divided Passions*, 83–85. For more on the relations between the authors, see Krechting, *Richard Beer-Hofmanns jüdisches Denken*, 28, note 54.

186. The biblical prophets are without attributes. The sculptor, as yet unidentified, drew on a number of Renaissance prototypes.

187. Kraus, "Der Löwenkopf oder Die Gefahren der Technik," 7.

188. Beer-Hofmann, "Camelias," 88 and 104. The first mention of the nickname "beautiful Freddy" comes at a party when the young Thea relaxes his fears and tells him that he is still "young and beautiful, the beautiful Freddy" (ibid., 88). Concerning Freddy's fascination with Thea, see also ibid. 93–94 and 96.

189. Beer-Hofmann, "Pierrot Hypnotiseur."

190. Ibid., 70–71 and 114–15.

191. Bertschik, *Mode und Moderne*, 167.

192. Ibid., 133. Bertschik notes that this feminine and therefore sexually coded corset-like underwear was also used by men who wore clothes that fit close to the waist, beginning in the Biedermeier period. *Camelias* consists of the reflections of the decadent dandy, Freddy, and treats his infatuations, his misgivings about social norms, and his existential fears.

193. Bertschik, *Mode und Moderne*, 133.

194. This event is carefully analyzed in the first chapter of this book. See also Hiebler, *Hugo von Hofmannsthal und die Medienkultur der Moderne*, 317; Reissberger, "Zum Problem künstlerischer Selbstdarstellung in der zweiten Hälfte des 19. Jahrhunderts," 750.

195. K. Fliedl, "Arthur Schnitzler und Italien," 132. Stefan Scherer points out Beer-Hofmann's authorial position in Vienna's literary scene even before he published his own texts (*Richard Beer-Hofmann und die Wiener Moderne*, 2–4).

196. K. Fliedl, "Arthur Schnitzler und Italien," 132.

197. Quoted in ibid.

198. Ibid., 133.

199. Quoted in K. Fliedl, "Gedächtniskunst," 116.

200. Karl Kraus, "Ein ältere Firma," 9. The original German is "Auch die Moderne war in Programm reich und gut vertreten. Das 'Schlaflied für Miriam' von Beer und Hoffmann.... Aber das trägt man doch wirklich nicht mehr!"

201. Quoted in Gillman, *Viennese Jewish Modernism*, 151.

202. Sekler, *Josef Hoffmann*, 110.

203. Ibid., 106. The source is a letter from Miriam Beer-Hofmann-Lens to Sekler dated April 8, 1967. The details of this anecdote are not completely clear, and there are conflicting accounts. In any case, the anecdote reveals both Hoffmann's eagerness (in promptly drawing a sketch) and the setting of their bohemian artistic network.

204. Beer-Hofmann trusted Bahr's judgment and appreciated his literary works, as documented in his letters to Bahr (Beer-Hofmann, *Briefe: 1895–1945*, 14–21).

205. Sekler, *Josef Hoffmann*, 508, note 8. The source is a letter from Miriam Beer-Hofmann-Lens to Sekler dated April 8, 1967. For a letter about Beer-Hofmann's art of sociability and charisma from the German Jewish author Rudolf Borchardt to the lawyer and later cultural historian Otto Deneke dated March 18, 1902, see Scherer, *Richard Beer-Hofmann und die Wiener Moderne*, 4. Borchardt describes Beer-Hofmann as surprisingly strong, healthy, and beautiful, and an extremely smart man.

206. Gillman, *Viennese Jewish Modernism*, 83–85.

207. Quoted in ibid., 84.

208. The façade and back of Beer-Hofmann's villa are reproduced in *Deutsche Kunst und Dekoration*, 1910, 388–90.

209. Sekler identified the house as more classicist than any of Hoffmann's previous buildings. (*Josef Hoffmann*, 106). The design can refer to the Lycian graves discovered in the nineteenth century and the Temple of Paestum (Voglhuber, "Die Kunst des Wiener Jugendstiles und seine ägyptischen Formulierungen bei Fassaden- und Innenraumgestaltungen," 65).

210. Voglhuber, "Die Kunst des Wiener Jugendstiles und seine ägyptischen Formulierungen bei Fassaden- und Innenraumgestaltungen," 69, illustrations 122 and 123. Hoffmann's application of the antique and primary form of multiple frames, specifically in relation to the Star of David and the arcades in the gallery discussed below, granted the façade and the setting of the public hall of Beer-Hofmann's house a monumental appearance with concrete ancient Egyptian sacral references. See Hoffmann's sketch for a monumental pavilion (1903) and the sketch for a mausoleum (1905–6) in Voglhuber, "Die Kunst des Wiener Jugendstiles und seine ägyptischen Formulierungen bei Fassaden- und Innenraumgestaltungen," illustrations 154 and 156).

211. Beer-Hofmann, *Der Tod Georgs*, 13. This is in contrast to scholars identifying Beer-Hofmann's writing style in his book as impressionistic and ornamental Jugendstil. See K. Fliedl, "Gedächtniskunst," 125, note 8, for interpretations of Beer-Hofmann's style as Jugendstil.

212. Beer-Hofmann, *Der Briefwechsel mit Paula*, supplement 2, letter 180, 90.

213. Ibid., 95.

214. Beer-Hofmann wrote: "So sah er den Tempel; und nicht den Tempel bloß. Denn allen Dingen, von denen er wußte, *hatte er Leben gegeben*" (This is how he saw the Temple; and not only the Temple. Because of all the things, of which he knew he had given life) (*Der Tod Georgs*, 33). My emphasis of the last words is to stress Beer-Hofmann's granting to his house, the "old temple," new life (a new synagogue).

215. For a photo of Beer-Hofmann's entrance hall, see MAK–Austrian Museum of Applied Arts / Contemporary Art: MAK–Wiener Werkstätte Archiv, Inv. no. WWF 103–142–1.

216. An image that supposedly appeared in Louis Felicien Joseph Caignart de Saulcy, *Voyage autour de la Mer Morte et dans le terres bibliques* (1853), is reproduced next to the title page in Bedoire, *The Jewish Contribution to Modern Architecture*. The French author reports on his journey to Palestine in 1850–51. His book was published in Paris in 1853, and a copy could be found in the Austrian National Library.

217. See Beer-Hofmann villa, circa 1905, in Grüner, *Moderne Villen in Meisteraquarellen*, plate 39.

218. He also searched antique shops, such as Fischer's shop in the Führichgasse in Vienna's first district, for old furniture (Beer-Hofmann, *Briefe*, 20).

219. Sekler, *Josef Hoffmann*, 298.

220. Quoted in Gilmann, *Viennese Jewish Modernism*, 82.

221. Heimann-Jelinek, "Die Welt des Richard Beer-Hofmannn," 32.

222. Beer-Hofmann, *Der Tod Georgs*, 54.

223. Simmel, *Simmel on Culture*, 125.

224. Ibid.

225. Ibid.

226. A possible attribution of this sculpture can be made to Austrian artist Hans Müller through a comparison with Müller's "Magd mit Waserkübel (Maid with water bucket.) For photos of Spitzer's dining room and music room, see *Interieur* 2 (1901): 100, 104, 105, and 108.

227. Lux, "Villenkolonie Hohe Warte, erbaut von Prof. Joseph Hoffmann," 166.

228. Lillie, *Was einmal War*, 156. In Aryanization documents it was dated as having been made at the end of the eighteenth century and described as lead, though it was most likely bronze.

229. Photographs of Beer-Hofmann's interiors showing the importance of *Fortuna* in the library were reproduced in *Deutsche Kunst und Dekoration* (1908): 76–78. See also Lilie, *Was einmal War*, 156. Sekler identifies the sculptor as Giambologna (Giovanni Bologna [1529–1608]) (*Josef Hoffmann*, 299), and the work may indeed have been a copy of Giambologna's *Fortuna*. Beer-Hofmann's collection included the works of two late-nineteenth-century modernist landscape painters, the Jewish artist Tina Blau and the gentile artist Theodor von Hörmann.

230. Lillie, *Was einmal War*, 155–56.
231. Ibid., 154.
232. Freud, *The Interpretation of Dreams*, 478.
233. My formulation on transitions in space and time and from fixation to nuance refers to Gillman's explanation of Beer-Hofmann's renunciation of the aesthetic impulse in favor of transcendence, "providing a 'way back' from space into time, from fixation to a more nuanced knowledge of the past" (*Viennese Jewish Modernism*, 89). In contrast to Gillman, I do not think Beer-Hofmann renounced his aesthetic impulse but used it to modernize his Jewish identification.
234. The vision of the woman in white dress may have inspired Hoffmann's design of Paula's room, which was decorated completely in white, with a bay window overlooking the garden. The room is reproduced in *Deutsche Kunst und Dekoration* (1908): 79 and Sekler, *Josef Hoffmann*, 299. The white bedroom was a personalized adaptation of the white public hall at the center of the house.
235. Beer-Hofmann, *Der Tod Georgs*, 16. The original German is "Fast körperlos schien sie; nur ihr eigenes weißes Bild, das sich in fremden Linien von den Blüten und Stengelgewirr der narzissenübersäten Tapete hob."
236. Shapira, "Gaze and Spectacle in the Calibration of Class and Gender," 160.
237. Inderwisch, *Augen-Blicke bei Richard Beer-Hofmann*, 21–30, especially 30.
238. I. Nierhaus, *Arch6*, 128–30. I return to the analysis of Loos's Goldman & Salatsch House at the end of this book.
239. Hevesi, *Altkunst—Neukunst, Wien*, 287.

4. The Avant-Gardists, 1908–11

1. Sontag, "Notes on 'Camp.'"
2. A. Loos, *Spoken into the Void*, 96.
3. A. Loos, "Briefkasten," 8.
4. Winz, "Assimilation," columns 644–46.
5. Ibid.
6. Ibid., column 644.
7. Quoted in Rukschcio and Schachel, *Adolf Loos*, 70 (my emphasis).
8. These arguments are developed from my previous essays. See Shapira, "Tailored Authorship" and "Adolf Loos and the Fashioning of 'the Other.'"
9. Cernuschi, *Re/Casting Kokoschka*, 132. Cernuschi refers to Loos's unpublished text only few pages later (ibid., 138).
10. Bourdieu, *The Field of Cultural Production*, 7–9.
11. Ibid., 15–17.
12. Ibid., 83–85.
13. See Dankl, *Die 'Moderne' in Österreich*, 50.
14. Zuckerkandl, "Kunstindustrie," 26. See also Dankl, *Die 'Moderne' in Österreich*, 58.
15. Farkas, *Hermann Bahr, Prophet der Moderne*, 63.
16. Bahr, "Vereinigung bildender Künstler Österreichs," 9–11.
17. Hevesi was the only one who was not blinded by this rhetoric and who continued to review exhibitions at the Künstlerhaus objectively (Hevesi, "Jef Lambeaux im Künstler-

hause," 864–66). In his review of Cabaret Fledermaus's opening, Kraus criticized Waerndorfer's preoccupation with money ("Eine Kulturtat," 1–9).

18. A. Loos, "Keramika," 369. The original German is "Man hat mich aufgefordert in der Sezession auszustellen. Ich werde es thun, wenn die Händler aus dem Tempel vertrieben sind. Händler? Nein. Die Prostituierter der Kunst."

19. The postcard "Das Judentum!" (Judaism) is reproduced in Barker and Lensing, *Peter Altenberg*, 34; and "Der Katholizismus!" (Catholicism) is reproduced in ibid., 35.

20. Schnitzler, *The Road into the Open*, 114.

21. Zweig, *The World of Yesterday*, 39.

22. Segal, *The Vienna Coffeehouse Wits*, 12.

23. Beller, "'The Jew Belongs in the Coffeehouse,'" 53–56.

24. Gronberg, "The Viennese Coffeehouse," 66–67.

25. Ibid., 67.

26. This follows Susan Henderson's general observation in "Bachelor Culture in the Work of Adolf Loos," 126. Henderson offers a few interesting observations, but unfortunately there are factual mistakes in her article. I also refer to Daniel Purdy's argument that Loos rejected ornament as an expression of ethnicity ("The Cosmopolitan Geography of Adolf Loos," 49).

27. Bertschik, *Mode und Moderne*, 103.

28. Ibid.

29. Ibid., 106.

30. Ibid., 109. For a further comparison of how Klimt and Altenberg exoticized Jewish female bodies, see Kelley, "Perception of Jewish Female Bodies through Gustav Klimt and Peter Altenberg."

31. E. Hoffmann, *Kokoschka*, 92.

32. Bertschik, *Mode und Moderne*, 102.

33. Ibid.

34. *Wie ich es sehe* was followed by *Ashantee* in 1897, *Was der Tag mit zuträgt: Fünfundfünfzig neue Studien* in 1901, *Prodromos* in 1906, and *Märchen des Lebens* and *Die Auswahl aus meinen Büchern* in 1908, all published by Samuel Fischer in Berlin. *Bilderbögen des kleinen Lebens* was published by Reiss in Berlin in 1909.

35. Gronberg, "The Inner Man," 74–76.

36. Ibid., 83.

37. Ibid., 86.

38. See the photograph reproduced in Lunzer and Lunzer-Talos, *Peter Altenberg*, 162.

39. Quoted in ibid., 163. Just before he was hospitalized in a mental clinic in the winter of 1909, Altenberg published an essay called "Hysterie" (Hysteria) describing a young woman in a sanatorium left alone but surrounded by photographs of those who "educated her": Beethoven, Wagner, Maeterlinck, and Bismarck. Her doctor describes her sickness as "Krebs der Frauenseele" (cancer of women's soul) ("Hysterie," 111–13).

40. Riou, "Aesthetic Imagination as Network?," 235–37. Riou's argument concerning gentile and Jewish authors' use of visual metaphors to secure the construction of a social network around the end of the nineteenth century also supports this book's argument about patrons' wish to secure a Jewish self-styling through architecture and design and the critical relationships between modern design and the patrons' art.

41. See the photograph reproduced in Lunzer, and Lunzer-Talos, *Peter Altenberg*, 165.
42. See the photograph reproduced in ibid., 166.
43. See the photograph reproduced in ibid., 167.
44. For a further reference to the dependency of Jewish authority on proper dress, see Freud, *The Interpretation of Dreams*, 272. Altenberg felt comfortable with his body. A photograph of him at the Lido in Venice, circa 1900, has the inscription: "Show me how you are built, and I will tell you who you are! Peter Altenberg" ("Zeige mir, wie Du 'gebaut' bist, und ich werde Dir sagen, *Wer* du bis! Peter Altenberg") (Inv. no. 13.239, Wien Museum, Vienna).
45. Quoted in Stewart, *Fashioning Vienna*, 45. Loos's statement refers directly to a January 9, 1897, *Die Zeit* review of Emerson, titled "Emerson's Use of Jokes and Humor" (Stewart, *Fashioning Vienna*, 45).
46. Altmann-Loos, *Adolf Loos der Mensch*, 20.
47. Rukschcio and Schachel, *Adolf Loos*, 23–31. See also: Altmann-Loos, *Adolf Loos der Mensch*, 22–23.
48. Scheu, "Adolf Loos." Loos's third wife, Claire, quotes her husband as saying: "I am a cosmopolitan, like any other true European" (C. Loos, *Loos Privat*, 77).
49. Hevesi, "Adolf Loos," in Hevesi, *Altkunst—Neukunst, Wien*, 285.
50. A. Loos, "Die Herrenmode."
51. A. Loos, "Die Kleidung," 8.
52. Rukschcio and Schachel suggested that Beau Brummell served as model for Loos (*Adolf Loos*, 61).
53. Lubbock, "Adolf Loos and the English Dandy," 44–46.
54. Ibid.
55. McLeod, "Undressing Architecture, 60. McLeod refers to John Carl Flügel's famous *The Psychology of Clothes*, published in London in 1930.
56. Wigley, "White Out," 207–9.
57. Ibid., 209.
58. Wigley, *White Walls, Designer Dresses*, 172.
59. A. Loos, "Ornament und Verbrechen," (1908), in A. Loos, *Trotzdem*, 88.
60. Colomina, "On Adolf Loos and Josef Hoffmann," 66–68. Colomina refers here to a famous citation from Loos's 1914 "Heimatkunst": "The house does not have to tell anything to the exterior; instead, all its richness must be manifest in the interior" (quoted in Colomina, "On Adolf Loos and Josef Hoffmann," 66).
61. Ludwig Frisch is noted as the *cafétier* (coffee shop owner) in an advertisement for the opening of Café Museum placed in the *Neue Freie Presse* on April 19, 1899. I thank Markus Kristan for this reference. It is not clear if Ludwig was related to Moritz Frisch, the assimilated Jewish publisher of Karl Kraus's early publications, including the latter's pamphlet against Zionism, *Eine Krone für Zion*, in 1899.
62. Rukschcio and Schachel, "Adolf Loos und das Kaffeehaus," 27. See also Gronberg, *Vienna*, 74–76.
63. I further develop here Tag Gronberg's argument about Loos evoking a sense of masculinity in his café, reclaiming the Biedermeier ethics of clothing (and low-key arrangement) and the idea of a gentleman's club with the presence of billiard tables and newspapers (*Vienna*, 74–76).

64. See Rukschcio's reconstruction plan in Rukschcio and Schachel, *Adolf Loos*, 418.

65. Beer, "Gibsons Zeichnungen," 107.

66. Altenberg, "Zwei anglo-saxonische Künstler."

67. See the photograph reproduced in Ruschckio and Schachel, *Adolf Loos*, 68, Illustration 61. A British flag decorated the room's ceiling (ibid., 69, Illustration 62.) See also Gronberg's discussion about the ideal of the thin woman and modernity and Loos's wish to relate his café to his admiration of American culture (Gronberg, *Vienna*, 84 and 86).

68. Hevesi, "Kunst auf der Straße." See also Hevesi, "Moderne Kaffeehäuser."

69. Loos wrote: "Der Drawing room aber, unser Salon, wird seiner Bestimmung gemäß leichte, also leicht transportable Sessel aufweisen. Auch sind diese nicht zum Ausruhen da, sondern um bei leichter, anregender Conversation die Sitzgelegenheit zu bieten. Auf kleinen, kapriziösen Sesseln plaudert sich's besser als im Großvaterstuhl" (But the drawing room, in accordance with its purpose, will have light chairs, that is, chairs that can be easily moved). "Das Sitzmöbel," translation from Loos, *Ornament and Crime*, 65.

70. "Ein neues Kaffeehaus." See also Rukschcio and Schachel, *Adolf Loos*, 420.

71. A. Loos, "Briefkasten," 8–10.

72. Loos's color play between the green cover of the billiard tables and the light green striped wallpaper would have been another calming effect.

73. Loos did not necessarily express gender bias in his choice of chair design as much as try to encourage women to change their heavy dresses for practical two-part suits. Four years later the cultural critic Joseph August Lux confirmed Loos's logic in choosing a chair that would support the sitter's wish to appear elegant (Lux, "Biedermeier als Erzieher," 150.)

74. In February 1903, Goldman & Salatsch advertised that they were the Viennese agents for the Henry Heath firm, located at 105 Oxford Street, London, which manufactured hats for the king (*Allgemeine Sport-Zeitung*, February 1, 1903, 104).

75. See Fritz Waerndorfer to Hermann Bahr, September, 17 and 19, 1903, A25000 BaM and A24994 BaM, Österreichisches Theatermuseum, Vienna).

76. Long, *The Looshaus*, 40.

77. It is unknown who commissioned Loos to design the American Bar and who owned it the first few years. Loos's early sketch was drawn on a receipt from the Café Amerika, located in Vienna's second district (at Praterstraße 50) and owned by Adolph Loewenson. The current owner of the American Bar is Marianne Kohn.

78. Quoted in Long, *The Looshaus*, 38. Another translation of Altenberg's statement appears below.

79. Kenneth Frampton refers to the classical clubroom elegance of the bar's interior (*Modern Architecture*, 92).

80. Quoted in Friedell, *Das Altenbergbuch*, 81. The original German is "Deshalb bin und bleibe ich doch nur ein Schreiber von 'Muster ohne Wert,' und die Ware kommt alleweil nicht. Ich bin so ein kleiner Handspiegel, Toilettespiegel, kein Welten-Spiegel."

81. Quoted in Segal, *The Vienna Coffeehouse Wits*, 150 (my emphasis).

82. Quoted in Lunzer and Lunzer-Talos, *Peter Altenberg*, 89. The illustration is reproduced on the same page.

83. Altenberg, "Der Freund," 15.

84. Loos's American sites may have been inspired as both a contrast and a comple-

ment to the inner city's pilgrimage places. Gronberg has considered whether Loos's Gibson Room in the Café Museum was "a kind of 'Amerika in Wien,' as an exoticism of the modern rather than of the past" (*Vienna*, 86–88.). According to Andrew Barker, Altenberg did not share Loos's infatuation with things American, "but this did not stop Loos from wishing to dedicate the interior of his American Bar to Altenberg" (*Telegrams from the Soul*, 99).

85. Purdy, "The Cosmopolitan Geography of Adolf Loos," 61. This particular diasporic claim should be reconsidered in socioeconomic terms, as an elitist identification. Regarding American-Anglo influences in the Viennese social sphere, see Costello, "Adolf Loos's Kärntner Bar"; Máčel, "American Bar. 1907–8," 141.

86. Quoted in Le Rider, *Modernity and Crises of Identity*, 224.

87. Hevesi, "Sind die Engländer Juden?"

88. For a more detailed discussion of Loos's conscious reference to Jewish memories in his interiors, see Shapira, "Adolf Loos and the Fashioning of 'the Other.'"

89. Münz and Künstler, *Der Architekt Adolf Loos*, 40. Loos used mirrors in the grand staircase in the Goldman & Salatsch House to merge the reflection of the visitor with the grand space. In the American Bar mirrors were used to reflect the luxurious setting.

90. The floor could have been inspired by Loos's dining room in Villa Karma (1903–6), or it could have been a reaction to the entrance hall of Hoffmann and Wiener Werkstätte's Cabaret Fledermaus (1907).

91. The delayed pleasure principle prevented customers observing their own reflections; their first order of business was to acclimatize themselves to the new cultured dress of the place itself.

92. Quoted in Spindler, "Zur Affinität von Interieur und Mode: Eine analysierende Gegenüberstellung theoretischer und praktischer Konzepte von Adolf Loos und der Wiener Werkstätte," 18.

93. See the photo reproduced in Rukschcio and Schachel, *Adolf Loos*, 457, illustration 486.

94. See the photograph in Lunzer, Lunzer-Talos, and Patka, "*Was wir umbringen*," 74. It is not known if Loos recommended this fabric to Kraus for his studio after designing his bar, or whether he remembered the fabric from Kraus's studio when he needed something to cover the bar benches.

95. Loos's reference to Kraus's working space can also be related to the social ideals associated with Morris.

96. A. Loos, "Weihnachtsausstellung im Öst. Museum." The English translation is from A. Loos, *Spoken into the Void*, 94.

97. The early date is introduced in Rukschcio and Schachel, *Adolf Loos*, 37. The later date is suggested in Lunzer, Lunzer-Talos, and Patka, "*Was wir umbringen*," 176.

98. Lunzer, Lunzer-Talos, and Patka, "*Was wir umbringen*," 187.

99. Loos consciously avoided publishing photographs of his interiors in journals after 1903; Loos's new clients therefore would typically have seen his work in person, through social networks.

100. Quoted in Barnouw, "Loos, Kraus, Wittgenstein, and the Problem of Authenticity," 265–66.

101. Ibid., 266.

102. Hevesi, "Eine American Bar," 215.

103. See the photograph reproduced in Rukschcio and Schachel, *Adolf Loos*, 457, illustration 486.

104. Altenberg's Jewish self-identification is also related to the identification of Jews as prone to hysteria ("Brief aus Wien," 20).

105. Shapira, "Adolf Loos and the Fashioning of 'the Other,'" 2:229–31.

106. Quoted in Altmann-Loos, *Mein Leben mit Adolf Loos*, 261–3. In his review Altenberg noted the need for higher footstools in all sitting locations to motivate new and freer dressing habits.

107. Garelick, *Rising Star*, 11.

108. Costello, "Adolf Loos's Kärntner Bar," 151.

109. Bahr, "Das neue Ghetto," 28.

110. Kokoschka, *My Life*, 40–42. For different accounts of the painting's background story, see Lensing, "Scribbling Squids and the Giant Octopus," 196–98.

111. Quoted in Lensing, "Scribbling Squids and the Giant Octopus," 207.

112. Altenberg was not ideally handsome, yet he took care that his photographs showed him in a charming light. His lover, Helga Malmberg, described her disappointment in his looks at their first meeting (*Widerhall des Herzens*, 31).

113. Panizza, "Der operierte Jud."

114. In February 1899 Loos and Zuckerkandl published articles in this journal: Loos on "English Art on the School Bench" and Zuckerkandl on the Pointillist art movement. I assume that these authors were aware of Panizza's antisemitic story, but if they were, how did they come to terms with it?

115. "Ever since his pointed chin stopped drilling into the breast-plated tie, he had made the firm decision 'to become such a fine gentilman just like a goymenera and to geeve up all fizonomie of Jewishness'" (Panizza, *The Operated Jew*, 68.)

116. Ibid., 70.

117. Gilman, *The Case of Sigmund Freud*, 39. Panizza's antisemitic story is certainly a projection of his own deranged fears about "the Other" (ibid., 41–43). Yet this projection was hailed as a slander against assimilated Jews. Those fed up with the constant suspicion that they were hiding their true body underneath a borrowed "Christian mask" decided to search for a new mask more appropriate to their identity.

118. Ibid., 39.

119. The drawing is reproduced in Strobl, "Kokoschka, der Klimttöter," 22–24.

120. Lensing, "Scribbling Squids and the Giant Octopus," 196.

121. Ibid., 198.

122. Ibid., 199.

123. Ibid., 202.

124. Quoted in Lunzer and Lunzer-Talos, *Peter Altenberg,* 129.

125. In an early autobiographical sketch, Altenberg notes the primacy of visual experience, "the Eye, the Eye, the Rothschild fortune of every human being" (quoted in Lensing, "Scribbling Squids and the Giant Octopus," 202).

126. For a critique of "Jewishness" as lacking naturalness and authenticity, see Stögner, "Antisemitsch-misogyne Repräsentationen und die Krise der Geschlechtsidentität in Fin de Siècle," 239.

127. For a perceptive description of their relationship, see Safran, "Adolf Loos: Our Contemporary," 59.

128. For an extended interpretation of the portrait of Adele Bloch-Bauer, see Shapira, "Imaging the Jew," 161.

129. A. Loos, "My Building on Michaelerplatz," in A. Loos, *On Architecture*, 155. Loos indirectly distanced himself from the American claim he made on fashion stores and on the American Bar façade to defend the Goldman & Salatsch house's modernist design.

130. A. Loos, "Wäsche," in Loos, *Ornament and Crime*, 116.

131. *Neue Freie Presse*, November 3, 1898.

132. Given the modest inheritance Michael Goldman left his heirs (Michael Goldman, A118/9, Wiener Stadt- und Landesarchiv) and despite the firm's presumed large yearly profit, I suggest that Leopold Goldman and his partner and brother-in-law, Emanuel Aufricht, decided to spend more than they could prudently afford on their new building to obtain symbolic capital.

133. Michael was born on January 12, 1843, to Wolf and Louise (née Husserl) Goldmann in the Jewish community of Austerlitz in Moravia. After serving in the army of the Austro-Hungarian Empire, he migrated to Vienna around 1868 and in 1878 founded the men's fashion firm Goldman & Salatsch with the tailor Josef Salatsch (1840–1907), a Catholic migrant from Bohemia (Shapira, "Assimilating with Style," 235–36).

134. "Michael Goldman."

135. Michael's advertisements for Goldman & Salatsch appeared in *Freies Blatt, Organ zu Abwehr des Antisemitismus* (Free paper, organ of the Association to Ward off Antisemitism) between 1894 and 1896.

136. It is not confirmed that Goldman joined the Freemasons, but Aufricht was a confirmed member of a Viennese lodge (Rukschcio, "Die Bedeutung der Bauherren für Adolf Loos," 9).

137. See Goldman's letter of request for the title of court tailor (OmeA 1899 rub 12/G/5 Zl. no. 835: January 25, 1898. Haus-, Hof- und Staatsarchiv, Vienna). For an early review praising Loos's design, see Abels, "Ein Wiener Herrenmodesalon." Michael Goldman and Salatsch had a successful partnership until 1895, Vienna's municipal election year. Perhaps fearing Karl Lueger's antisemitic campaign calling a boycott of Jewish stores, Salatsch left the firm in 1896, before Loos became a regular client.

138. For the façade design, see Rukschcio and Schachel, *Adolf Loos*, 41. The building where Ebenstein's salon was located was built in 1896. Paul Wittgenstein (Karl's son?) and Leopoldine Wittgenstein bought it in 1903. The house included sixteen stores and nine apartments. While Loos was supported by both Goldman and Ebestein, the former did not fear public exposure, while the latter preserved an elitist reputation and avoided public exposure.

139. *Allgemeine Sport-Zeitung*, February 17, 1889, front page. The salon remained at Graben 20 for more than twenty years.

140. Ferdinand Fellner is known for his design of theaters. He also built the houses at Tuchlauben 17 (1857) and at the corner of Operngasse and Hanuschgasse (1865). Stylistically he belonged the school of romantic historicism, with other prominent architects such as August Sicard von Siccardsburg, Eduars Van der Nüll, Theophil Hansen, and Anton Ritter von Ötzelt (Wagner-Rieger, *Wiens Architektur im 19. Jahrhundert*, 141).

141. The old gentile business families who settled at the central streets—Kohlmarkt, Graben, and Tuchlauben—in the nineteenth century included the Artarias (art dealers), Ebensteins (tailors), Arthabers (textile manufacturers) and Hornbostels (textile manufacturer). The successors of Dominik Artaria and Franz Ebenstein would initiate the architectural modernization of Kohlmarkt.

142. See three photographs of Graben circa 1900 reproduced in Winkler, *Blickfänge*, 17.

143. *Neue Freie Presse*, September 4, 1896, 3. The subscription system was apparently imported, following an English model. An advertisement in *Allgemeine Sport-Zeitung* noted: "The English System: Men's clothing purchased in the way of subscription is favored by *all social circles* for its practicality, cheapness, but especially through solid and highly elegant execution of the requested [clothing]. . . . Goldman & Salatsch" (on January 12, 1890, 44).

144. *Der Salon, Oesterreichisches Adelsblatt*, Vienna, 1 November 1896, 7. The same advertisement appeared regularly until the end of December 1896.

145. Leiter, "Die Männerkleider-Erzeugung in Wien," 509.

146. Ibid.509–10.

147. Abels, "Ein Wiener Herrenmodesalon," 145.

148. Ibid.

149. Abels, "Ein Wiener Herrenmodesalon," 149. In his first reconstruction of the ground floor, Rukschcio estimated the dimensions of the small entrance that served as a short passage to the selling room itself ("Studien zu Entwürfen, Projekten, Ausgeführten Bauten von Adolf Loos," PhD diss., Vienna University, 1973, 18. See the reconstruction plan in Rukschcio and Schachel, *Adolf Loos*, 415.

150. Rukschcio observed four uses for the mirror: to reflect the objects inside, to reflect the client, to expand the client's range of vision, and to appear to enlarge the space—as in baroque interiors (Rukschcio, "Wien, Adolf Loos und das Haus am Michaelerplatz," 424).

151. Rukschcio, "Studien zu Entwürfen, Projekten, Ausgeführten Bauten von Adolf Loos," 18.

152. Abels, "Ein Wiener Herrenmodesalon," 149.

153. Ibid.

154. Rukschcio, "Wien, Adolf Loos und das Haus am Michaelerplatz," 424.

155. It was common to find a mixture of stripes and flowers in women's dresses at this time. Loos also suggested striped wallpaper for the Café Museum and the Viennese Women's Club interior in 1900 (ALA 2644, Adolf Loos Archiv, Albertina, Vienna).

156. Rukschcio and Schachel, *Adolf Loos*, 415.

157. S. Anderson, "Sachlichkeit and Modernity, or Realist Architecture," 338.

158. Ibid., 339.

159. At its height before World War I, the international Austro-Hungarian Imperial Yacht Squadron Yacht Club included members from Germany, Hungary, Italy, the United States, and other countries, most of whom were very wealthy aristocrats and a few of whom belonged to the high bourgeoisie. See Bilzer, *Das K.u.K. Yachtgeschwader*, 8–11.

160. Haslinger, *Kunde*, 19.

161. *Allgemeine Sport-Zeitung*, June 6, 1900, 552.

162. *Allgemeine Sport-Zeitung*, June 7, 1901, 783.

163. As made public in the Bavarian court journal that publicized royal laws and regulations in the name of his majesty the king of Bavaria: "Hoftitel-Verleihungen," *Gesetz- und Verordnungs-Blatt für das Königreich Bayern*, no. 12, Munich, March 12, 1902, 120.

164. Lehmann, *Allgemeiner Wohnungs-Anzeiger*, 1903, 1:1053.

165. Barker and Lensing, *Peter Altenberg*, 231.

166. Loos expressed his respect for Goldman's fashion firm in "Die Herrenmode."

167. See the photograph reproduced in Sterne, "Automobilistische Wiener Firmen," 7.

168. In 1903, the cultural critic Alfred Wechsler introduced Loos as "der aus Amerika eine Freude an der Logik mitgebracht hat" (Fred, *Die Wohnung und ihre Ausstattung*, 120). In 1907, Hevesi presented a similar argument in "Adolf Loos" (Hevesi, *Altkunst—Neukunst, Wien*, 285).

169. Goldman also ventured into new sports games: In December 1900, ping pong achieved world-wide fame following a grand competition in London, and within months Goldman offered the "tennis table" in his store (*Allgemeine Sport-Zeitung*, September 21, 1901, 1079.)

170. Trauungs-Protokol der Türkisch Israelitischen Gemeinde in Wien, 1884–1938, Reg. No. 280, Israelitische Kultusgemeinde Wien, Matrikenamt, Vienna. Kitty Hedda Goldmann was born on June 9, 1918 (Geburts-Buch für die israelitische Kultusgemeinde in Wien, 1918, Reg. no. 896, ibid.).

171. I am grateful to the late Peter Kniže, son of Fritz Wolff-Kniže, Loos's patron and tailor, for this explanation. See also the report by one of Loos's students in Richard Neutra, *Survival through Design*, 300. Also see ibid., 387.

172. Leopold Goldman registered the patent with the Austrian Patent Office: Österreichisches Patentamt, Patentschrift No. 5948, issued on November 25, 1901. There are no registration numbers in the Austrian Patent Office for patents issued before 1910. Six patent submissions by Leopold Goldmann (under that name, instead of the Anglicized Goldman) were accepted and are registered with the Austrian patent office. Several interesting patents by Robert Goldmann—Leopold's brother, who was an engineer—were also accepted and are registered.

173. As described the invention was described in Leopold Goldman's patent registration with the Austrian Patent Office: Österreichisches Patentamt, Patentschrift No. 30068, issued on September 25, 1907. There are no registration numbers in the Austrian Patent Office for patents issued before 1910.

174. Houze, "Fashion, Disguise, and Transformation," 19.

175. Ibid., 24.

176. Ibid., 32.

177. Loos invited Hoffmann and Moser to visit the interiors of a new apartment he had designed for Stössler. Shortly after that, Hoffmann went to the Goldman & Salatsch store and became a client. Loos concludes the anecdote by saying that since then, the date for which can be found in the client books of Goldman & Salatsch, Hoffmann has dressed as a European, and the straight line became the characteristic of the secessionist movement (Rukschcio and Schachel, *Adolf Loos*, 62).

178. Simmel, "On Fashion," in Simmel, *Simmel on Culture*. See also Houze, "Fashion, Disguise, and Transformation," 33.

179. Shapira, "Adolf Loos and the Fashioning of 'the Other,'" 2:229.
180. Kinney, "Fashion and Fabrication in Modern Architecture," 479.
181. Ibid., 476–78.
182. Quoted in Hevesi, "Adolf Loos," in Hevesi, Hevesi, *Altkunst—Neukunst, Wien*, 285.
183. McLeod, "Undressing Architecture," 65–66.
184. Shapira, "Tailored Authorship," 56–58.
185. Hevesi, "Adolf Loos," in Hevesi, Hevesi, *Altkunst—Neukunst, Wien*, 285.
186. M. Anderson, *Kafka's Clothes*, 218.
187. He is buried in grave number 047, line 012, group 052A, section T1 of the Vienna Central Cemetery.
188. This refers to a suggestion made by Rukschcio during a conversation with me in early 2000 after inspecting a photograph of the gravestone. It is also in accordance with Loos's choice of black marble for the bath in the Beer Villa in Montreux, Switzerland (1903) and for the future façade of the Kniže store (1913), as well as with his preference for minimalist form, as in the cubic form for his future private houses.
189. I am grateful to Burkhardt Rukschcio for this information. He conducted extensive interviews with workers in the salon and with Kitty Goldmann, Michael's granddaughter.
190. As early as October 1898, possibly after finishing Goldman's store, Loos claimed that future design should be a continuation of classical heritage (*Spoken into the Void*, 104).
191. Quoted in Long, *The Looshaus*, 145.
192. Kristan, *Carl König*, 84.
193. See, for example, the advertisement for the Merchant Tailor in *Internationale Modenzeitung*, October 1895 (unnumbered page).
194. Hollander, *Sex and Suits*, 7.
195. Lehmann, *Allgemeiner Wohnungs-Anzeiger*, 1913, 1:22. The Lehmann directories were produced irregularly from 1859 to 1870. From 1870 on they were produced annually until 1942, with the exception of a single edition for 1921–22. From 1893 on each edition was divided into two volumes.
196. Loos's daring separation was further supported by the mismatched axes of the lower and upper parts.
197. The Goldman & Salatsch salon had mainly male clients and was subtly orchestrated to promote the ideal of social mobility.
198. Rukschcio, "Wien, Adolf Loos und das Haus am Michaelerplatz," 431.
199. A similar play of framed plain glass in the middle of checked window glass is found in Robert Örley's Sanatorium Luitlen, in Vienna's eighth district, at Auersperg Straße 9, 1907–8. In terms of carefully mediated visibility, Örley's arrangement in the context of a private hospital treating skin diseases may be contrasted to Loos's window arrangement as a construct tempting the client to look out as well as invite the look in. For another reference to Örley's influence on Loos's design, see Long, *The Looshaus*, 76–78.
200. Chenoune, *A History of Men's Fashion*, 17.
201. According to the salon's visiting cards, this new business cooperation was established around 1911. In 1911, the Grand Hotel purchased two adjoining buildings, Kärntnerring 11–13, adding approximately 100 rooms to the old wing (Andreas Augustin, *The Most Famous Hotels in the World: Ana Grand Hotel Wien*, London, 1994, 110.)

202. The two shared a great appreciation for quality material as documented in the following anecdotes: Goldman's last patent submission, "A Soap-body and an Arrangement for Its Storage When It's Not in Use," was registered in the Austrian patent office on March 25, 1921 (Patentschrift No. 83416, Registration no. A3854/18, Österreichisches Patentamt). Goldman thought about different options for storing soap that would prevent waste and make it easy to handle at the same time. His solution was an additional substance outside the soap (not in the center) held between two holders on a bowl. Years later, Loos's third and last wife, Claire Loos (née Beck), whom he married in 1929, wrote in her memoirs the following anecdote titled "A Reason for Divorce": "Loos enters the bathroom. His face is red from anger. 'You want to be my wife?' he shouts, 'You, who have no respect for material? Allowing it to be senselessly wasted, to be dissolved to nothing? You waster, you! Do you know that throughout my life I have fought against senselessness, against ornament, against squandering? And you, my wife, you dare to leave excellent soap to senselessly dissolve in water?" (C. Loos, *Loos Privat*, 30).

203. Rukschcio and Schachel, *Adolf Loos*, 148. For a reference to Loos's defense of his house, see "Die beanstandete Fassade des Baues am Michaelerplatz."

204. In 1906 Goldman & Salatsch was registered in the *Jahrbuch der österreichischen Textil-Industrie* as employing seventy workers, specializing in automobile clothing, and exporting goods to Germany, Russia, France, China, Japan, Australia, and South America (Hanel, *Jahrbuch der österreichischen Textil-Industrie*, 164).

205. Schaukal, "Ein Haus und seine Zeit," 183. See also Long, *The Looshaus*, 80. Schaukal issued a supportive review during the controversy, so it could be that this warning was meant to prepare Loos for it. Still, it must have occurred to Loos and Goldman that the radical, naked upper façade would be provocative.

206. Czech and Mistelbauer, *Das Looshaus*, 86.

207. "Vandalismus in Wien," 138.

208. Indeed, in a letter to Walden, as Christopher Long pointed out, Kraus mentioned his pleasure in being noted in the review (*The Looshaus*, 145 and 218, endnote 17).

209. Quoted in Long, *The Looshaus*, 172.

210. Bourdieu, *The Field of Cultural Production*, 81.

211. Garelick, *Rising Star*, 11.

212. "Lebende Bilder," caricature in *Der Floh*, April 10, 1870.

213. Simmel, *Georg Simmel in Wien*, 25 For more on the intricate relationship between modern architecture and fashion, establishing the origin and questioning the idealization of white walls, see Wigley, *White Walls, Designer Dresses*, 156.

214. Simmel, "On Fashion," in Simmel, *Simmel on Culture*, 199.

215. Ibid., 204.

216. The ground on which the house was built was slightly uneven; Ludwig Münz and Gustav Künstler praise Loos's solution of placing the columns on the same ground level, raised on one side through steps (*Der Architekt Adolf Loos*, 98).

217. Czech and Mistelbauer, *Das Looshaus*, 43.

218. Lux, "Korrekte Kleidung," 29. It should be noted that Leopold Goldman was on the board of this association (see "Vereinigung der Herrenkundenschneidermeister Wien," 12).

219. As early as 1896 the German architecture critic Richard Streiter observed the

revitalization of men's fashion through English sports suits ("Das deutsche Kunstgewerbe und die englisch-amerikanische Bewegung," 107).

220. For an insightful analysis of the second district, the Leopoldstadt, as a Jewish space, see Silverman, *Becoming Austrians*, 119–24.

221. Kraus, "Der Löwenkopf oder Die Gefahren der Technik," 7. On the idea of a clean-shaven house as possible statement against Jewish particularism, see Werkner, "The Child-Woman and Hysteria," 138, note 18.

222. Kraus, "Das Haus auf dem Michaelerplatz," 5.

223. Ver sacrum (the phrase was the title of the secessionist movement's journal and inscribed on the Secession House) referred to a religious practice in ancient Rome in which a group of youngsters would be expelled from society and expected to build their own new settlement.

224. Simmel, "Koketterie," 672.

225. The secessionist Klimt found plenty of sources for his handling of erotic subjects in *Jugend*, and in his early works the expressionist Kokoschka found there inspiration for his portrayal of children and erotic themes.

226. For a detailed description of Goldman's authorial intent to defend Loos's design, see Goldman's correspondence with city authorities in Pogacnik, *Adolf Loos und Wien*, 196–215, specifically 197–99 and 202.

227. "Der Neubau auf dem Michaelerplatz."

228. Quoted in Cernuschi, *Re/Casting Kokoschka*, 97.

229. Quoted in ibid.

230. Engelmann, "Das Haus auf dem Michaelerplatz." See also Stoessl, "Das Haus auf dem Michaelerplatz"; Haiko, "The 'Obscene' in Viennese Architecture of the Early Twentieth Century," 93.

231. Haiko, "The 'Obscene' in Viennese Architecture of the Early Twentieth Century," 93.

232. Quoted in ibid.

233. ALA 260, Adolf Loos Archiv, Albertina, Vienna. The different titles suggested were Marble Bar, Klimt Bar, and Kärntner Bar. These were placed above a sketch of the entrance façade of the bar. Loos's interest in using Klimt's name can remind us of Waerndorfer's event at his house as a tribute to the celebrity artist Klimt.

234. Haiko, "The 'Obscene' in Viennese Architecture of the Early Twentieth Century," 93.

235. Friedrich Achleitner observed that the Loos House provoked criticism and even aggressive reactions mainly because of the silent stance of the upper floors. This, he further suggests, was especially noted in comparison with the talkative stance of the historicist palaces. The Loos House was silent about the "truth" it expressed (*Wiener Architektur*, 42).

236. A. Loos, "Mein Haus am Michaelerplatz," II–III.

237. Bourdieu, *The Field of Cultural Production*, 81.

238. Quoted in Gronberg, *Vienna*, 15. The spa hotel was located between Grinzing and Cobenzl, an area characterized by hills and forests. Gronberg points out the element of performativity and Freud's awareness that he was playing a specifically modern role within the Austro-Hungarian *Residenzstadt*—namely, Vienna—as well as on a wider international stage (ibid., 15 and 34).

239. Kerr, *The Gentleman's House*, chapter 10.

240. Leopold Goldman's album collection of articles on the Goldman & Salatsch Building or the Looshaus 1909–1938 (Adolf Loos Archiv, Albertina, Vienna).

241. The late Kitty Goldmann, daughter of Leopold, remembered encountering jokes targeting the firm's reputation, for example: "A guy tells his friend 'I bought a Salatsch & Goldman,' and his friend inquires, 'How come? I thought the name was Goldman & Salatsch.' 'No,' says the guy, 'I decided I wanted the Salatsch on the inside and the gold on the outside'" (interview with Kitty Goldmann in Santiago, Chile, February 17, 2001).

242. On the fate of the Goldman family and Aufricht, Goldman's partner, in the Holocaust, see Shapira, "Assimilating with Style," 353–55.

Conclusion

1. Bauman, *Moderne und Ambivalenz*, 82. See also Kernmayer, *Judentum im Wiener Feuilleton (1848–1903)*, 76–78.

2. Kernmayer, *Judentum im Wiener Feuilleton (1848–1903)*, 78.

3. Quoted in Kristan, *Oskar Marmorek*, 28. The original German is "Lieber Freund, gern plauderte ich mit Ihnen noch ein paarmal über jüdischen Styl. Kommen Sie doch wieder gegen 5 Uhr NM. zu mir. Ich denke mir, daß dieser Styl das Gefühl der Befreiung ausdrücken soll. Eine gelassene Heiterkeit (serenitas). Ich bin zu unwissend, um das auszuschreiben, was ich mir darüber denke."

4. Burri, "Theodor Herzl and Richard von Schaukal." Schaukal, the liberal gentile author mentioned in chapter 4, was an admirer and follower of Adolf Loos.

5. Quoted in Donald, *Imagining the Modern City*, 11.

6. Freud, *The Interpretation of Dreams*, 478. Reference to this quote is made in chapter 3 in relation to the analysis of the design of Beer-Hofmann's villa.

7. Ibid., 477–78.

8. Ibid., 478.

9. Ibid. In the history of the Viennese Jewish community there were two *gezerot* that led to the destruction of two Jewish communities: the first was ordered by Albrecht V in 1421, and the second was ordered by Leopold I in 1670.

10. See Le Rider, *Modernity and Crises of Identity*, 221–23.

11. Referring to Hermann Heller's report on the Austrian exhibition in London in 1906, the design historian Heather Hess concludes that the "emphasis on culture helped Austria forge an identity distinct from German," recalling Heller's complains that for too long "Austria had been mistaken for Australia, or worse, considered a German province." The role of the decorative arts in promoting the national position of Austria had already been noted by the director of the Austria Museum of Art and Industry ("The Wiener Werkstätte and the Reform Impulse," 119).

12. Fritz Waerndorfer to Hermann Bahr, July 11, 1909, A25033 BaM, A24994 BaM, Autographen und Nachlässe Sammlung, Österreichisches Theatermuseum, Vienna). Waerndorfer wrote: "'Und wissen sie, wo wir heute halten?' Da kommen 2 Amerikanerinnen zu uns, Gattinnen von Amerikanischen Museumsdirektoren, pflanzten sich vor Hoffmann und: 'Wir wollen Ihnen nur mittheilen, dass es heute schon keine einzige kleinste Stadt in Amerika gibt ohne Hoffmann—und WW—Spuren, und dass wir in Amerika

wissen, *dass sie hier in der WW den Styl für die ganze Welt und die nächsten hundert Jahre machen!'*—Fein!!—Noch ein Paar Jahre aushalten, und wir drücken thatsächlich der ganzen Welt unsern WW—Stempel auf!"

13. For a further discussion on identifying the operational frameworks encouraging and enforcing the performance of "Jewish difference," see Silverman, *Becoming Austrians*, 7–8.

14. Mahler-Werfel, *Tagebuch-Suiten, 1898–1902*, 149.

15. This dual character was represented in the debate over the choice of style for synagogues in Central Europe. The architecture of the new temples reflected a painstaking process of defining Jewish self-representation (I. Müller, *Die Otto Wagner-Synagoge in Budapest*, 15–16.

16. Quoted in Rossbacher, *Literatur und Bürgertum*, 137.

17. Purdy, "The Cosmopolitan Geography of Adolf Loos," 61–63.

BIBLIOGRAPHY

Archives (all in Vienna)

Academy of Fine Arts Vienna, Kupferstichkabinett (Graphic Collection)
Adolf Loos Archiv, Albertina
Baupolizei—Magistrat der Stadt Wien—Zentrale
Dokumentationsarchiv des österreichischen Widerstandes: Project "Namentliche Erfassung der Opfer der Shoa"
Israelitische Kultusgemeinde Wien, Matrikenamt
Kunstsammlung und Archiv, Universität für angewandte Kunst Wien
Landesinnung Wien der Kleidermacher, Alte Kartei
MAK–Austrian Museum of Applied Arts / Contemporary Art (Österreichisches Museum für angewandte Kunst / Gegenwartskunst): MAK–Bibliothek und Kunstblättersammlung (Library, registration books)
MAK–Austrian Museum of Applied Arts / Contemporary Art (Österreichisches Museum für angewandte Kunst / Gegenwartskunst): MAK–Wiener Werkstätte Archiv
Österreichisches Patentamt
Österreichisches Staatsarchiv: Haus-, Hof- und Staatsarchiv
Österreichisches Staatsarchiv: Kriegsarchiv
Österreichisches Theatermuseum
Sammlung Jüdisches Museum Wien
Secession Archiv
Todesco Archiv, Villa Wertheimstein, Archiv des Bezirksmuseum Döbling
Wiener Stadt- und Landesarchiv
Zentral Gewerbe Register der Stadt Wien

Interviews with Relatives of Jewish Patrons

Goldmann, Kitty, interview February 16–21, 2001, Santiago, Chile
Kniže, Peter, interview October 2, 2000, Vienna
Zuckerkandl, Emile, telephone interview November 26, 2003

Primary Sources (Originally Published before 1930)

Abels, Ludwig. "Ein Wiener Herrenmodesalon." *Das Interieur* 2 (1901): 145–51.
———. "Joseph Maria Olbrich." *Das Interieur* 2 (1901): 162.
Altenberg, Peter. "Brief aus Wien." *Das Theater* 1, no. 1 (1909): 20.
———. "Der Freund." *Wiener Rundschau* 3, no. 1 (1898–99): 15.

———. "Eine neue 'Bar' in Wien." *Wiener Allgemeine Zeitung*, February 22, 1909.
———. "Hysterie." *März*, second October issue, 1909, 111.
———. "Kabaret 'Fledermaus.'" *Wiener Allgemeine Zeitung*, October 22, 1907.
———. *Wie ich es sehe*. 8–9 ed. Berlin: Samuel Fischer, 1914.
———. "Zwei anglo-saxonische Künstler." *Wiener Allgemeine Zeitung*, January 1, 1899.
Arnold, Franz [Rosa Mayreder]. "Der Wiener Styl." *Neue Freie Presse*, November 9, 1898.
———. "Die Ausstellung der Secession." *Neue Freie Presse*, January 17, 1899.
Bahr, Hermann. *Das Hermann Bahr Buch*. Berlin: S. Fischer Verlag, 1913.
———. "Das neue Ghetto (Schauspiel in vier Acten von Theodor Herzl)." *Die Zeit*, January 8, 1898.
———, ed. *Der Antisemitismus*. Edited by Hermann Grieve. Königstein: Jüdischer Verlag, 1979.
———. "Die Secession." *Die Zeit*, April 23, 1898.
———. "Die Vierte Ausstellung, Klimt, Engelhart, Andrei, Fräulein Ries." In Hermann Bahr, *Secession*, 122–27. 2nd ed. Vienna: Wiener Verlag, 1900.
———. *Gegen Klimt*. Vienna: Eisenstein, 1903.
———. Introduction to *Der Antisemitismus: Ein internationales Interview*, edited by Hermann Bahr, 1–4. Berlin: S. Fischer Verlag, 1894.
———. *Secession*. 2nd ed. Vienna: Wiener Verlag, 1900.
———. "Vereinigung bildender Künstler Österreichs: Secession." *Ver Sacrum*, January 1898, 8–13.
Bauernfeld, Eduard. *Erinnerungen aus Alt-Wien*. Vienna: Wiener Drucke, 1923.
Beer, Theodor. "Gibsons Zeichnungen." *Die Zeit*, May 16, 1896, 106–7.
Beer-Hofmann, Richard. "Camelias." In Richard Beer-Hofmann, *Novellen*, 85–112. Berlin: Freund and Jeckel, 1893.
———. *Der Tod Georgs*. Stuttgart: Reclam, 1999.
———. "Pierrot Hypnotiseur." In *Schlaflied für Mirijam, Lyrik, Prosa, Pantomime und andere verstreute Texte*, edited by Michael Matthias Schradt, 61–115. Oldenburg: Igel-Verlag Literatur, 1998.
Bing, Siegfried. *Artistic America, Tiffany Glass, and Art Nouveau*. With an introduction by Robert Koch. Cambridge, MA: MIT Press, 1970.
Bloch, Joseph Samuel. *Hellenistische Bestandtheile im biblischen Schriftthum: Eine kritische Untersuchung über Abfassung, Charakter und Tendenzen, sowie die Ursachen der Kanonisierung des Buches Esther*. 2nd ed. Vienna: D. Löwy, 1882.
Chipiez, Charles, and Georges Perrot. *Le Temple de Jérusalem*. Paris, 1889.
"Der Neubau auf dem Michaelerplatz: Sistierung des Fassadenbaues." *Wiener Allgemeine Zeitung*, September 29, 1910.
"Der Stadtrath gegen Klingers 'Beethoven.'" *Neue Freie Presse*, April 30, 1902.
"Die beanständete Fassade des Baues am Michaelerplatz." *Illustrirtes Wiener Extrablatt*, September 30, 1910, 7.
"Die Secession im eigenen Hause." *Neue Freie Presse*, November 12, 1898.
Editorial. *Neue Freie Presse*, May 31, 1895.
"Ein neues Kaffeehaus." *Neue Freie Presse*, April 20, 1899.
"Eduard Todesco." *Die Presse* (Vienna), January 17, 1887.
"Feuilleton: Kleine Wiener Chronik." *Die Presse* (Vienna), June 20, 1858.

"Feuilleton: Ueber die Neugestaltung Wien." *Die Presse* (Vienna), June 25, 1858.

Flögl, Mathilde. *Die Wiener Werkstätte, 1903–1928: Modernes Kunstgewerbe und sein Weg.* Vienna: Krystall-Verlag, 1929.

Folnesics, Dr. "Das moderne Wiener Kunstgewerbe." *Deutsche Kunst und Dekoration* 5, no. 6 (October 1899–March 1900): 253–81.

Förster, Ludwig. "Das Haus Nr. 154 in der Renngasse nächst der Freiung der freiherrlichen Familie Pereira-Arnstein gehörig." *Allgemeine Bauzeitung*, 1847, 241–43.

———. "Plan der Bauzeitung und Aufforderung an Männer von Fache, diesselbe durch Mittheilung zu Bereichern." *Allgemeine Bauzeitung* 1, no. 1 (1836): 237–40.

———. "Das Wohnhaus des Herrn Franz Klein in Brünn." *Allgemeine Bauzeitung* 13 (1848): 46–47.

———. "Die Baron Pereira'sche Villa auf der Herrschaft Königstetten im Tullnerboden nächst Wien." *Allgemeine Bauzeitung* 14 (1849): 107, 248–51.

———. "Wohnhäuser in Wien, Ecke der Ringstrasse, am Ausgange der Kärntnerstrasse links." *Allgemeine Bauzeitung* 27 (1862): 27–28.

Frauberger, Heinrich, ed. *Biographisches Lexikon der Wiener Weltausstellung 1873.* Vol. 4. Vienna: Engel and. Rotter, 1873.

———. "Gustav Ritter von Epstein: Banquier und General-Consul in Wien." In *Biographisches Lexikon der Wiener Weltausstellung 1873*, edited by Heinrich Frauberger, 4:9–13. Vienna: Engel and Rotter, 1873.

Fred, W. [Alfred Wechsler]. *Die Wohnung und ihre Ausstattung.* Bielefeld: Velhagen and Klasing, 1903.

———. *Giovanni Segantini.* (Vienna: Wiener Verlag, 1901).

———. *Lebensformen: Anmerkungen über die Technik des Gesellschaftlichen Lebens.* Munich: Georg Müller, 1911.

"Fremde Gäste in der Secession." *Neue Freie Presse*, January 13, 1899.

Freud, Sigmund. *The Interpretation of Dreams.* Translated and edited by James Strachey. New York: Avon, 1965.

Friedell, Egon, ed. *Das Altenbergbuch.* Leipzig: Das Wiener Graphischen Werkstätte, 1922.

——— and Alfred Polgar. "Die zehn Gerechten: Eine Kabarettrevue." In *Goethe und die Journalisten: Satiren im Duett*, edited by Herbert Illig, 67–72. Vienna: Löcker Verlag, 1986.

———. *Goethe, Eine Szene.* Vienna: Carl Wilhelm Stern, 1908.

Frimmel, Theodor. "Aus der Sammlung Todesco." *Blätter für Gemäldekunde* 1, no. 8 (1905): 148–51.

Fuchs, Eduard. *Die Juden in der Karikatur.* Munich: Langen, 1921.

"George Minne." *Ver Sacrum* 4, no. 2 (1901): 31–38.

Gomperz, Julius von. *Jugend-Erinnerungen.* Brno, Czech Republic: Verlag des Verfasser, 1902.

Gomperz, Theodor. "Eduard Wessel." *Neue Freie Presse*, January 29, 1879.

———. *Essays und Erinnerungen.* Stuttgart: Deutsche Verlags-Anstalt, 1905.

———. *Traumdeutung und Zauberei: Ein Blick auf das Wesen des Aberglaubens.* Vienna: Carl Herold's Sohn, 1866.

Grün, Karl. *Glückliches Wien! Die Stadt und ihre Kunstschätze.* Vienna: Beck, 1869.
Grüner, Oscar. *Moderne Villen in Meisteraquarellen.* Vienna: Verlag Friedrich Wolfrum, 1905.
Günther, Georg. "Karl Wittgenstein und seine Bedeutung für den Aufbau und Entwicklung der österreichischen Volkswirtschaft." In *Neue Österreichische Biographie, 1815–1918,* edited by Anton Bettelheim, 4:156–63. Vienna; Amalthea-Verlag, 1927.
Gurlitt, Cornelius. *Im Bürgerhause: Plaudereien über Kunst, Kunstgewerbe und Wohnungs-Ausstattung.* Dresden: Gilbers'sche Königl, 1888.
Hanel, Rudolf, ed. *Jahrbuch der österreichischen Textil-Industrie.* Vienna: Hölder, 1906.
Hatvany, Ludwig. "Ludwig Hevesi." *Pester Lloyd,* March 27, 1910. Accessed April 4, 2010. http://www.pesterlloyd.net/html/1910hatvanyhevesinachruf.html.
Herzl, Theodor. *Das neue Ghetto: Schauspiel in 4 Acten.* Vienna: published by the author, 1903.
Hevesi, Ludwig. *Acht Jahre Sezession (März 1897–Juni 1905): Kritik—Polemik—Chronik.* 1906. Klagenfurt: Ritter Verlag, 1984.
———. *Altkunst—Neukunst, Wien, 1894 bis 1908.* 1909. Klagenfurt: Ritter Verlag, 1986.
———. *Das Bunte Buch, Humoresken, aus Zeit und Leben, Litteratur und Kunst.* Stuttgart: Verlag von Adolf Bonz, 1898.
———. "Eine American Bar." *Kunst und Kunsthandwerk* 12, no. 4 (1909): 214–15.
———. "Feuilleton: Der Aristopath: Ein Daseinbild aus dem modernen Nerven Leben." *Fremden-Blatt,* December 25, 1906.
———. *Flagranti und andere Heiterkeiten.* Stuttgart: Adolf Bonz, 1909.
———. Introduction to *Ideen von Olbrich, Text von Ludwig Hevesi.* 2nd ed., 1904. Reprint, Stuttgart: Arnold'sche, 1992.
———. "Jef Lambeaux im Künstlerhause." *Die Wage,* December 17, 1899, 864–66.
———. "Kunst auf der Straße." *Fremden-Blatt,* May 30, 1899.
———. "Moderne Kaffeehäuser." *Kunst und Kunsthandwerk* 2 (1899): 196–97.
———. *Österreichische Kunst im 19. Jahrhundert.* Leipzig: Seemann, 1903.
———. "Sind die Engländer Juden?" In Ludwig Hevesi, *Die fünfte Dimension:. Humore der Zeit, des Lebens, der Kunst,* 247–60. Vienna: Carl Konegen, 1906.
———. "Wie soll man den Leopoldsätdter Tempel bauen? Ein Vorschlag zur Güte." *Pester Lloyd,* April 8, 1899.
Hirt, Aloys, ed. *Bilderbuch für Mythologie, Archäologie und Kunst.* Vol. 1. Berlin, 1905.
Hock, Stefan. "Lebensbild." In Franz Grillparzer, *Grillparzers Werke,* 1:vii–cxxiii. Berlin: Deutsches Verlagshaus Bong, n.d.
Hoffmann, Josef. "Das individuelle Kleid." *Die Wage* 1, no. 15 (1898): 251–52.
Hofmannsthal, Hugo von. "Der Schüler." In *Neue deutsche Rundschau,* edited by Oskar Bie, 12, part 2, 1204–11. Berlin: S. Fischer, 1901.
Israelitischer-Frauen-Wohlthätigkeit-Verein, 100, Vereinsjahr Jubiläums-, und Jahres-Bericht für das Jahr 1915. Vienna, 1916.
Kanner, Heinrich, and Isidor Singer. "Unser Blatt." *Die Zeit,* September 27, 1902.
"Karl Wittgenstein als Kunstfreund." *Neue Freie Presse,* January 21, 1913.
Kerr, Robert. *The Gentleman's House; or, How to Plan English Residences.* London: John Murray, 1864.

Kohut, Adolf. *Berühmte israelitische Männer und Frauen in der Kulturgeschichte der Menschheit.* Vol. 2. Leipzig: A. H. Payne, [1900–1901].
Kokoschka, Oskar. *Die träumenden Knaben.* Vienna: Jugend und Volk, 1968.
Köstlin, August. "Das Neue Wien." *Allgemeine Bauzeitung* 48 (1883): 1–2.
Kraus, Karl. "Darmstadt." *Die Fackel* 3, no. 81 (1901): 11–14.
———. "Das Haus auf dem Michaelerplatz." *Die Fackel* 12, nos. 313–14 (1910): 4–6.
———. "Der Löwenkopf oder Die Gefahren der Technik." *Die Fackel*, October 13, 1913, 178–84.
———. "Die Europäisierung der 'Zeit' oder 'Der kleine Kohn ist weg!'" *Die Fackel* 5, no. 137 (1903): 17.
———. "Ein ältere Firma." *Die Fackel* 12, nos. 315–16 (1911): 9.
———. *Eine Krone für Zion.* 3rd ed. Vienna: Verlag Moritz Frisch, 1899.
———. "Eine Kulturtat." *Die Fackel* 9, no. 236 (1907): 1–9.
———. "Ganz wider den Willen der Natur." *Die Fackel*, early April, 1901, 1–13.
———. "Salome." *Die Fackel* 5, no. 150 (1903): 1–14.
———. "Seit Wochen stehen in Norden." *Die Fackel*, early February, 1900, 1–5.
———. Untitled item. *Die Fackel*, May 1900, 22.
———. "Die diesmalige Ausstellung." *Die Fackel*, mid-November 1900, 19–20.
———. "Was einem der feingefühligsten Kunstgelehrten...." *Die Fackel* 2, no. 41 (mid-May 1900): 18–22.
———. "'Zeit'—Genosse." *Die Fackel*, 5, no. 136 (1903): 22–23.
Kupelwieser, Paul. "Karl Wittgenstein: Ein Charakterbild." *Neue Freie Presse*, January 22, 1913.
Lang, Marie. "Das Secessionsgebäude." *Wiener Rundschau*, no. 24 (1898): 939–40.
Lehmann, Adolph. *Allgemeiner Wohnungs-Anzeiger: Nebst Handels- u. Gewerbe-Adressbuch für d. k.k. Reichshaupt- u. Residenzstadt Wien u. Umgebung.* Wien, 1859–1922.
Leiter, Friedrich. "Die Männerkleider-Erzeugung in Wien." In *Untersuchungen über die Lage des Handwerks in Österreich*, 491–598. Leipzig: Duncker and Humboldt, 1896.
Levetus, A. S. "The 'Wiener Werkstätte,' Vienna." *Studio* 52 (1911): 187–196.
Loos, Adolf. "Briefkasten." *Das Andere*, no. 2 (1903): 8.
———. "Damenmode." *Dokumente der Frauen* 6, no. 23 (1902): 660–64.
———. "Das Heim." *Das Andere*, no. 1 (1903): 8–9.
———. "Das Princip der Bekleidung." *Neue Freie Presse*, September 4, 1898.
———. "Das Sitzmöbel." *Neue Freie Presse*, June 19, 1898.
———. "Die Herrenmode." *Neue Freie Presse*, May 22, 1898.
———. "Die Intérieurs in der Rotunde." *Neue Freie Presse*, June 12, 1898.
———. "Die Kleidung." *Das Andere*, no. 1 (1903): 8.
———. "Die Potemkin'sche Stadt." *Ver Sacrum* 1, no. 7 (1898): 15–17.
———. "Keramika." *Die Zukunft* 34 (1904): 366–70.
———. "Lob der Gegenwart," *März* 3 (August 18, 1908): 310–12.
———. "Mein erstes Haus!." *Der Morgen*, October 3, 1910.
———. "Mein Haus am Michaelerplatz." *Parnass*, special issue 2 (1985): ii–xv.
———. "Myrbach Ausstellung." *Die Wage* 1, no. 14 (1898): 229.
———. *Trotzdem 1900–1930.* 1931. Reprint, Vienna: Herold, 1988.
———. "Vom armen reichen Mann." *Neues Wiener Tagblatt*, April 26, 1900

———. "Weihnachtsausstellung im Öst: Museum, Bürgerlicher Hausrat—Das Leflerzimmer." In Adolf Loos, *Adolf Loos: Sämtliche Schriften*, edited by Franz Glück, 144–52. Munich: Herold, 1962.
Lothar, Rudolph, "Von der Secession." *Die Wage* 1, no. 49 (1898): 813–14.
Lux, Josef August. "Biedermeier als Erzieher." *Hohe Warte* 1 (1904–5): 145–55.
———. "Der Depeschen-Saal der 'Zeit' in Wien." *Deutsche Kunst und Dekoration* 11 (1903): 117–18.
———. *Die moderne Wohnung und ihre Ausstattung*. Vienna: Wiener Verlag, 1905.
———. "Korrekte Kleidung." *Offizielle Mitteilungen der Vereinigung der Herrenkundenschneidermeister Wiens und der Reichsverbande angehörigen Vereinigungen Österreichs*, September 1, 1907, 25–29.
———. "Sanatorium." *Hohe Warte* 1 (1904–5): 406–7.
———. "Stilarchitketur und Baukunst," *Der Architekt*, no. 8 (1902): 45–47.
———. "Villenkolonie Hohe Warte, erbaut von Prof. Joseph [sic] Hoffmann." *Das Interieur* 4 (1903): 121–83.
Mayer, Sigmund. *Die Wiener Juden, 1700–1900*. Viennan: K. Löwit Verlag, 1918.
Meier-Graefe, Julius. "Ein Modernes Milieu." *Dekorative Kunst* 4, no. 7 (April 1901): 249–65.
"Michael Goldman." *Offizielle Mitteilungen der Vereinigung der Herrenkundenschneidermeister Wiens und der Reichsverbande angehörigen Vereinigungen Österreichs* 3, no. 8, August 1, 1907, 72.
Muthesius, Hermann. "Unsere Wohnungen." *Hohe Warte* 1 (1904–5): 156–57.
Niemann, George, and Ferdinand V. Feldegg. *Theophilos Hansen und seine Werke*. Vienna: Anton Schroll, 1893.
Obituary of Jakob Rappaport. *London Times*, August 11, 1886.
Olbrich, Joseph Maria. "Das Haus der Secession." *Der Architekt* 5, no. 1 (1899), 5.
———. "Grabmal für die Familie v. Klarwill auf dem Dornbacher Friedhofe." *Der Architect* 5, no. 1 (1899), 6.
Oesterreichische Schachzeitung, 2, nos. 35–36 (September 1873): 268.
Panizza, Oskar. "Der operierte Jud." In Oskar Panizza, *Visionen der Dämmerung*, 213–42. Munich: Bei Georg Müller in München, 1923.
Polgar, Alfred. "Heinrich Eisenbach." In *Ja und Nein*, Vol. 3: *Noch allerlei Theater*. Berlin: Rowohlt, 1926.
Pötzl, Eduard. *Moderner Gschnas und andere Wiener Skizzen*. 4th ed. Vienna: Robert Mohr Verlag, 1901.
Ranzoni, Emerich. *Wiener Bauten*. Vienna: Lehmann-Wenzel, 1873.
Rappaport, Moritz. *An Ludwig August Frankl, zum 70. Geburtstag: Ein Sonettenkranz*, Verlag Steyremühl, 1880
"Recent Deaths." *Boston Evening Transcript*, August 13, 1886. Accessed September 1, 2012. http://news.google.com/newspapers?nid=2249&dat=18860813&id= wAk0AAAAIBAJ&sjid=fiMIAAAAIBAJ&pg=5020,2727977.
Saar, Ferdinand von. *Seligmann Hirsch*. Edited by Detlef Haberland. Tübingen: Max Niemeyer, 1987.
Sacher-Masoch, Leopold von. *Jüdisches Leben in Wort und Bild*. Mannheim: Verlag J. Bensheimer, 1891.

———. *Venus im Pelz*. 1869. Frankfurt: Insel Verlag, 1997.
Salzberg, J. Wolfgang, ed. *Häuser-Kataster der Bundeshauptstadt*. Vienna: Moritz: Perles, 1929.
Scapin [pseud.]. "Vally Wieselthier und Paul Poiret in New York." *Die Bühne*, January 17, 1929, 16–17.
Schaukal, Richard. "Ein Haus und seine Zeit." *Der Merker*, December 10, 1910, 181–84.
Scheu, Robert. "Adolf Loos." *Die Fackel* 11, no.283-84 (June 26, 1909): 25–37.
Schnitzler, Arthur. *The Road into the Open*. Translated by Roger Byers. Berkeley: University of California Press, 1992.
Seligmann, Adalbert Franz. *Kritische Studien: Von Plein-air. Japanische Kunst—Die Impressionisten—Die modernen Stilisten—Gustav Klimt—Unmoralische Kunstwerke—Anonyme Kritik. Ein Gespräch*. Vienna: Schroll, 1904.
———. "Secessionistisches." *Die Wage*, April 2, 1898, 233–34.
Simmel, Georg. "Die Rolle des Geldes in den Beziehungen der Geschlechter, Fragment aus einer 'Philosophie des Geldes.'" Part 1. *Die Zeit*, January 15, 1898.
———. *Georg Simmel in Wien: Texte und Kontexte aus dem Wien der Jahrhundertwende*. Edited by David Frisby. Vienna: WUV University Verlag, 2000.
———. "Koketterie" *Jugend* 2, no. 41 (1901): 672.
———. *Simmel on Culture: Selected Writings*. Edited by David Frisby and Mike Featherstone. London: Sage, 1997.
———. *The Sociology of Georg Simmel*. Translated, edited, and with an introduction by Kurt H. Wolff. Glencoe, IL: Free Press, 1950.
Sp., L. [Ludwig Speidel]. "Feuilleton: 'Bildende Kunst.'" *Neue Freie Presse*, April 6, 1866.
Speidel, Ludwig. "Feuilleton: Wohlthätigkeits-Vorstellung (Im Palais Todesco)." *Die Presse* (Vienna), April 3, 1868.
Spitzer, Daniel. "Wiener Spaziergänge," *Neue Freie Presse*, November 25, 1883.
St., G. "Wiener Frauen-Club." *Wiener Mode* 14, no. 7 (1901): 295.
Staberl jun. "Wiener Secession." *Neue Freie Presse*, November 11, 1900.
Sterne, Felix. "Automobilistische Wiener Firmen." *Allgemeine Automobil-Zeitung*, September 10, 1905.
Stoessl, Otto. "Das Haus auf dem Michaelerplatz." *Die Fackel* 12, nos. 317–18 (1911): 13–17.
Streiter, Richard. "Das deutsche Kunstgewerbe und die englisch-amerikanische Bewegung." Part 1. *Illustrierte Kunstgewerbliche Zeitschrift für Innen-Dekoration*, no. 7, July 1896, 106–8.
Strzygowski, Josef. *Die bildende Kunst der Gegenwart*. Leipzig: Quelle, 1907.
T., L. [Ludwig Tischler?]. "Die Neubauten der Ringstrasse in Wien." In *Zeitschrift des Österreichischen Ingenieur-Vereins*, edited by Joseph Herr, 16:170–74. Vienna, 1864.
Uhl, Friedrich. *Das Haus Fragstein*. Vienna: Manz'sche K. K. Hof-Verlags- und Univ.-Buchhandlung, 1878.
———. "Die Gesellschaft." In *Wien, 1848–1888*, edited by Friedrich Uhl, 2:521–32. Vienna: Carl Konegen, 1888.
"Unser Depeschensaal." *Die Zeit*, September 27, 1902.
"Vandalismus in Wien." *Der Zwiebelfisch* 3, no. 4 (1911): 138–40.
Vasili, Paul. *Die Wiener Gesellschaft*. Leipzig: Verlag von H. Le Soudier, 1885.
"Vereinigung der Herrenkundenschneidermeister Wiens." *Offizielle Mitteilungen*

der Vereinigung der Herrenkundenschneidermeister Wiens und der Reichsverbande angehörigen Vereinigungen Österreichs, September 1, 1907, 12.

Villari, Luigi. *Giovanni Segantini*, New York: T. F. Unwin, 1901.

Vincenti, Carl Ferdinand von. *Wiener Kunst-Renaissance: Studien und Charakteristiken*. Vienna: Verlag von Carl Gerold's Sohn, 1876.

Waerndorfer, Lili. "Eleonora Duse und Josef Hoffmann. Eine Erinnerung von Lili Waerndorfer." *Die Bühne*, January 1931, 44–45.

Wagner, Otto. *Moderne Architektur: Seinen Schülern ein Führer auf diesem Kunstgebiete*. Vienna: Schroll Verlag, 1896.

———. *Modern Architecture*. Translated with an introduction by Harry Francis Mallgrave. Santa Monica, CA: Getty Center for the History of Art and the Humanities, 1988.

Wagner, Richard. *Das Judenthum in der Musik*. Leipzig: Verlagsbuchhandlung von J. J. Weber, 1869.

Weininger, Otto. *Geschlecht und Charakter: Eine prinzipielle Untersuchung*. Vienna: Wilhelm Braumüller, 1903.

Wiener Werkstätte, "Das ästhetische Programm: Eine Schrift der Wiener Werkstätte zur Eröffnung der 'Fledermaus." In *Fledermaus Kabarett, 1907–1913: Ein Gesamtkunstwerk der Wiener Werkstätte*, edited by Michael Buhrs, Barbara Lesák, and Thomas Trabitsch, 154–72. Vienna: Christian Brandstätter Verlag, 2008.

Wilhelm, Paul [Wilhelm Dworaczek]. "Künstlerhaus." *Wiener Rundschau*, April 1, 1897, 394.

Winz, Leo. "Assimilation." *Ost und West*, October 1904, 641–54.

Wittels, Friz. *Der Taufjude*. Wien: M. Breitensteins Verlagsbuchhandlung, 1904.

"Wittgensteins Abschied." *Die Wage*, May 21, 1898, 358.

Wrede, Alphons Freiherrn von. *Geschichte K. u. K. Wehrmacht*. Vol. 1. Vienna, 1898.

Zuckerkandl, Berta. "Die Linie (Wie die Frau sich kleiden soll)." *Die Zeit*, January 28, 1899.

———. "Kunst und Kultur: Das Kabarett 'Fledermaus.'" *Wiener Allgemeine Zeitung*, October 19, 1907.

———. "Kunstindustrie." *Die Zeit*, January 9, 1897, 26–27.

———. "Künstlermoden." *Die Zeit*, March 16, 1901, 168–69.

———. *Zeitkunst Wien 1901–1907*. Vienna: Hugo Heller, 1908.

Secondary Sources

Achleitner, Friedrich. *Wiener Architektur: Zwischen typologischen Fatalismus und semantischen Schlamassel*. Vienna: Böhlau, 1996.

Aichelburg, Wladimir. *Das Wiener Künstlerhaus, 1861–2001*. Vol. 1. Vienna: Österreichischer Kunst- und Kulturverlag, 2003.

———. "Freunde und Mitarbeiter des Künstlerhauses." Accessed July 1, 2012. http://www.wladimir-aichelburg.at/kuenstlerhaus/mitglieder/verzeichnisse/freunde-und-mitarbeiter/.

Alofsin, Anthony. *When Buildings Speak: Architecture as Language in the Habsburg Empire and Its Aftermath, 1867–1933*. Chicago: Chicago University Press, 2006.

Altmann-Loos, Elsie. *Adolf Loos der Mensch*. Vienna: Herold, 1968.

———. *Mein Leben mit Adolf Loos*. Vienna: Amalthea-Verlag, 1984.
Anderson, Benedict. *Imagined Communities*. New York: Verso, 2003.
Anderson, Mark M. *Kafka's Clothes: Ornament and Aestheticism in the Habsburg Fin de Siècle*, Oxford: Clarendon Press, 1992.
Anderson, Stanford. "*Sachlichkeit* and Modernity, or Realist Architecture." In *Otto Wagner: Reflections on the Raiment of Modernity*, edited by Harry Francis Mallgrave, 323–62. Santa Monica, CA: Getty Center, 1993.
Arendt, Hannah. *The Origins of Totalitarianism*. New York: Harcourt, Brace, 1968.
Arnbom, Marie-Theres. *Friedmann, Gutmann, Lieben, Mandl, Strakosch: Fünf Familienporträts aus Wien vor 1938*. Vienna: Böhlau, 2002.
Aschheim, Steven E. "'The Jew Within': The Myth of 'Judaization' in Germany." In *The Jewish Response to German Culture: From the Enlightenment to the Second World War*, edited by Jehuda Reinharz and Walter Schatzberg, 212–41. Hanover, NH: University Press of New England, 1985.
Assmann, Aleida. "Opting In und Opting Out: Konformität und Individualität in den poetologischen Debatten der englischen Aufklärung." In *Stil: Geschichten und Funktionen eines kulturwissenschaftlichen Diskurselements*, edited by Hans Ulrich Gumbrecht und K. Ludwig Pfeiffer, 127–43. Frankfurt: Suhrkamp, 1986.
Augustin, Andreas. *The Most Famous Hotels in the World: Ana Grand Hotel Wien*. London: Treasury, 1994.
Baatz, Wolfgang, et al., eds. *Das Palais Epstein: Geschichte—Restaurierung—Umbau*. Vienna: Löcker, 2005.
Baltzarek, Franz, Alfred Hoffmann, and Hannes Stekl. *Wirtschaft und Gesellschaft der Wiener Stadterweiterung*. Wiesbaden: Franz Steiner Verlag, 1975.
Bammer, Anton. *Architektur als Erinnerung: Archäologie und Gründerzeitarchitektur in Wien*. Vienna: Österrichische Gesellschaft für Archäologie, 1977.
Barker, Andrew. *Telegrams from the Soul: Peter Altenberg and the Culture of Fin-de-Siècle Vienna*. Columbia, SC: Camden House, 1996.
——— and Leo Lensing. *Peter Altenberg: Rezept die Welt zu Sehen*. Vienna: Braumüller, 1995.
Barner, Wilfried. "Jüdische Goethe Verehrung vor 1933." In *Juden in der deutschen Literatur*, edited by Stéphane Moses and Albrecht Schöne. 127–51. Frankfurt: Suhrkamp, 1986.
Barnouw, Dagmar. "Loos, Kraus, Wittgenstein, and the Problem of Authenticity." In *The Turn of the Century German Literature and Art, 1890–1915*, edited by Gerald Chapple and Hans H. Schulte, 249–73. Bonn: Bouvier Verlag Herbert Grundmann, 1981.
Baroni, Daniele, and Antonio D'Auria. *Josef Hoffmann und die Wiener Werkstätte*. Stuttgart: Deutsche Verlags-Anstalt, 1984.
Bastl, Beatrix. "Ringstrassengesellschaft, Hansen Auftraggeber." In *Theophil Hansen: Ein Resümee*, edited by Beatrix Bastl, Ulrike Hirhager, and Eva Schober, 23–49. Weitra: Verlag Bibliothek der Provinz, 2014.
Bauman, Zygmunt. *Moderne und Ambivalenz: Das Ende der Eindeutigkeit*. Hamburg: Junius, 1992.
Bedoire, Fredric. *The Jewish Contribution to Modern Architecture, 1830–1930*. Jersey City, NJ: Ktav Publishing House, 2004.

Beer-Hofmann, Richard. *Briefe, 1895–1945*. With a commentary by Alexander Košenina. Oldenburg: Igel Verlag, 1999
———. *Der Briefwechsel mit Paula, 1896–1938*. Oldenburg: Igel Verlag, 2002.
Beller, Steven. "'The Jew Belongs in the Coffeehouse': Jews, Central Europe and Modernity." In *The Viennese Café and Fin-de-Siècle Culture*, edited by Charlotte Ashby, Tag Gronberg, and Simon Shaw-Miller, 50–48. New York: Berghahn, 2013.
———. *Vienna and the Jews, 1867–1938: A Cultural History*. Cambridge: Cambridge University Press, 1989.
———. "Who Made Vienna 1900 a Capital of Modern Culture." In *Kreatives Milieu, Wien um 1900*, edited by Emil Brix and Allan Janik, 175–80. Munich: Verlag für Geschichte und Politik, 1993.
Benedikt, Heinrich. *Die wirtschaftliche Entwicklung in der Franz-Joseph-Zeit*. Vienna: Herold, 1958.
Bergman-Carton, Janis. "Negotiating the Categories: Sarah Bernhardt and the Possibilities of Jewishness." *Art Journal* 55, no. 2 (1996): 55–64.
Bertschik, Julia. *Mode und Moderne: Kleidung als Spiegel des Zeitgeistes in der deutschsprachigen Literatur (1770–1945)*. Cologne: Böhlau, 2005.
Bilzer, Franz F. *Das K.u.K. Yachtgeschwader: Segelsport an der österreichischen Adria*. Graz: Weishaupt, 1990.
Bisanz-Prakken, Marian. "The Beethoven Exhibition of the Secession and the Younger Viennese Tradition of the Gesamtkunstwerk." In *Focus on Vienna 1900: Change and Continuity*, edited by Erika Nielsen, 140–49. Munich: Wilhelm Fink Verlag, 1982.
———. *Heiliger Frühling: Gustav Klimt und die Anfänge der Wiener Secession, 1895–1905*. Vienna: Verlag Christian Brandstätter, 1999.
Blom, Philipp. "Rebelling in a World of Façades: Style and Identity in Vienna around 1900." In *Birth of the Modern: Style and Identity in Vienna 1900*, edited by Jill Lloyd, 21–30. Munich: Hirner Verlag, 2011.
Blümel, Barbara, ed. *Das Österreichische Parlament: Parlamentarismus, Gebäude, Geschichte: The Austrian Parliament*. Vienna: Parlamentsdirektion Vienna, 2006.
Borsi, Franco, and Ezio Godolo. *Wiener Bauten der Jahrhundertwende: Die Architektur der Habsburgischen Metropole. Historismus und Moderne*. Stuttgart: Deutsche Verlags-Anstalt, 1985.
Botstein, Leon, and Werner Hanak, eds. *Quasi una fantasia: Juden in die Musikstadt Wien*. Vienna: Wolke Verlag, 2003.
Bourdieu, Pierre. *The Field of Cultural Production*. Edited and introduced by Randal Johnson. Translated by Richard Nice. Cambridge: Polity, 1993.
Bramann, Jorn K., and John Moran. "Karl Wittgenstein, Business Tycoon and Art Patron." In *Austrian History Yearbook*, edited by William E. Wright, 15–16:106–24. New York: Cambridge University Press, 1979–80.
Brubaker, Rogers, and Frederick Cooper. "Beyond 'Identity.'" *Theory and Society* 29, no. 1 (2000): 1–47.
Buhrs, Michael, Barbara Lesák, and Thomas Trabitsch, eds. *Fledermaus Kabarett, 1907–1913: Ein Gesamtkunstwerk der Wiener Werkstätte*. Exh. Cat. Österreichisches Theatermuseum. Vienna: Christian Brandstätter Verlag, 2008.

Burri, Michael. "Theodor Herzl and Richard von Schaukal: Self-Styled Nobility and the Sources of Bourgeois Belligerence in Prewar Vienna." In *Rethinking Vienna 1900*, edited by Steven Beller, 105–31. New York: Berghahn, 2001.

Cernuschi, Claude. *Re/Casting Kokoschka: Ethics and Aesthetics, Epistemology and Politics in Fin-de-Siècle Vienna*. Madison, NJ: Associated University Presses, 2002.

Chenoune, Farid. *A History of Men's Fashion*. Paris: Flammarion, 1995.

Cixous, Hélène, and Catherine Clément. *The Newly Born Woman*. Translated by Betsy Wing. Minneapolis: University of Minnesota Press, 1986.

Clark, Robert Judson. "Olbrich and Vienna." In *Kunst in Hessen und am Mittelrhein*, edited by Gerhard Bott, 7:27–51. Darmstadt: Eduard Roether Verlag, 1967.

Cohen, Shaye J. D. *The Beginnings of Jewishness: Boundaries, Varieties, Uncertainties*, Berkeley, University of California Press, 2001.

Cohn, Willy. "Richard Beer-Hofmann: Schlaflied für Miriam." In *Über Richard Beer-Hofmann, Rezeptionsdokument aus 100 Jahren*, edited by Sören Eberhardt, Charis Goer, 22. 2nd ed. Hamburg: Igel Verlag, 2012.

Colomina, Beatriz. "On Adolf Loos and Josef Hoffmann." In *Raumplan versus Plan Libre: Adolf Loos and Le Corbusier, 1909–1930*, edited by Max Risselda, 65–77. Amsterdam: Delft University Press, 1991.

———. "Sex, Lies, and Decoration: Adolf Loos and Gustav Klimt." In *Gustav Klimt, Painting, Design and Modern Life*, edited by Tobias G. Natter, 43–53. New York: Abrams, 2008.

Costello, Mary. "Adolf Loos's Kärntner Bar: Reception, Reinvention, Reproduction." In *The Viennese Café and Fin-de-Siècle Culture*, edited by Charlotte Ashby, Tag Gronberg, and Simon Shaw-Miller, 138–57. New York: Berghahn, 2013.

Czech, Hermann, and Wolfgang Mistelbauer. *Das Looshaus*. Vienna: Verlag Löcker and Wögenstein, 1976.

Dahm, Friedrich. "Die Baugeschichte des Palais Epstein—zur Rolle des Bauherrn und Architekten." In *Das Palais Epstein: Geschichte—Restaurierung—Umbau*, edited by Wolfgang Baatz, et al., 48–67. Vienna: Löcker, 2005.

Dankl, Günther. *Die "Moderne" in Österreich: Zur Genese und Bestimmung eines Begriffs in der österreichischen Kunst um 1900*. Vienna: Böhlau, 1986.

Daviau, Donald G. "Hermann Bahr and the Secessionist Art Movement in Vienna." In *The Turn of the Century German Literature and Art, 1890–1915*, edited by Gerald Chapple, and Hans H. Schulte, 433–62. Bonn: Bouvier Verlag Herbert Grundmann, 1981.

Davison, Neil R. "'The Jew' as Homme/Femme-Fatale: Jewish (Art)ifice, Trilby, and Dreyfus." *Jewish Social Studies* 8, nos. 2–3 (2002): 72–111,

Dijkstra, Bram. *Idols of Perversity: Fantasies of Feminine Evil in Fin-de-Siècle Culture*. New York: Oxford University Press, 1986.

Diniejko, Andrzej. "Benjamin Disraeli and the Two Nation Divide." Victorian Web. 2010. Accessed August 1, 2014. http://www.victorianweb.org/authors/disraeli/diniejko3.html.

Donald, James. *Imagining the Modern City*. London: Athlone, 1999.

Eberhardt, Sören, and Charis Goer, eds. *Über Richard Beer-Hofmann: Rezeptionsdokumente aus 100 Jahren*. Paderborn: Igel Verlag, 2012.

Eder, Franz X. "'Diese Theorie ist sehr delikat. . . .'": Zur Sexualisierung der 'Wiener Moderne.'" In *Die Wiener Jahrhundertwende*, edited by Jürgen Nautz and Richard Vahrenkamp, 159–78. Vienna: Böhlau Verlag, 1996.
Engelmann, Paul, ed. *Adolf Loos*. Tel-Aviv: Mafil, 1940.
———. "Das Haus auf dem Michaelerplatz." *Die Fackel*. 12, nos. 317–18 (1911): 18.
Farkas, Reinhard. *Hermann Bahr, Prophet der Moderne: Tagebücher, 1888–1904*. Vienna: Böhlau 1987.
Fenzl, Harald. "Alexander Zemlinsky: Karriereschritte seiner ersten Wiener Phase." MA thesis, Vienna University, 2009.
Fliedl, Gottfried. *Gustav Klimt, 1862–1918: The World in Female Form*. Cologne: Benedikt Taschen, 1989.
Fliedl, Konstanze "Arthur Schnitzler und Italien." In *Ferne Heimat, nahe Fremde: Bei Dichtern und Nachdenkern*, edited by Eduard Beutner and Karlheinz Rossbacher, 132–47. Würzburg: Könighausen and Neumann, 2008.
———. "Gedächtniskunst: Erinnerung als Poetik bei Richard Beer-Hofmann." In *Richard Beer-Hofmann: Studien zu Seinem Werk*, edited by Norbert Otto Ecke and Günter Helmes, 116–27. Würzburg: Königshausen and Neumann, 1993.
Frampton, Kenneth. *Modern Architecture: A Critical History*. 3rd ed. London: Phaidon, 2000.
Franz, Rainald. "'A True Memorial to the Viennese Flamboyant Style': Hans Makart's Room for Nicolaus Dumba." In *Makart Painter of the Senses*, edited by Agnes Husslein-Arco and Alexander Klee, 159–69. Munich: Prestel, 2011.
Friedman, Mira. "The Metamorphosis of Judith." *Jewish Art* 12–13 (1986–87): 225–46.
Fürst, Anton. *Das Palais Todesco*. Vienna: Österreichische Volkspartei-Bundesparteileitung, 1987.
Garelick, Rhonda K. *Rising Star: Dandyism, Gender, and Performance in the Fin-de-Siècle*. Princeton, NJ: Princeton University Press, 1998.
Gaugusch, Georg. "Die Familien Wittgenstein und Salzer und ihr genealogisches Umfeld." *Adler, Zeitschrift für Genealogie und Heraldik* 21, no. 4 (2001): 120–45.
———. "Österreichs Industrie gewidmet—Die jüdischen Stifter des Hauses der Industrie." In *100 Jahre Haus der Industrie, 1911–2011*, edited by Veit Sorger, 150–71. Vienna: Industriellenvereinigung, 2011.
———. *Wer einmal war*. Vienna: Amalthea Verlag, 2012.
Gelber, Mark H. "Interfaces between Young Vienna and the Young Jewish Poetic Movement." In *Jüdische Aspekte Jung-Wiens im Kulturkontext des Fin de Siècle*, edited by Sarah Fraiman-Morris, 61–74. Tübingen: Max Niemeyer Verlag, 2005.
Gillman, Abigail E. "Hofmannsthal's Jewish Pantomime." *Deutsche Vierteljahresschrift für Literaturwissenschaft und Geistesgeschichte* 3 (1997): 437–60.
———. *Viennese Jewish Modernism: Freud, Hofmannsthal, Beer-Hofmann, and Schnitzler*. University Park: Pennsylvania State University Press, 2009.
Gilman, Sander L. *The Case of Sigmund Freud: Medicine and Identity at the Fin de Siècle*. Princeton, NJ: Princeton University Press, 1993.
———. *The Jew's Body*. New York: Routledge, 1991.
———. *Sexuality: An Illustrated History. Representing the Sexual in Medicine and Culture from the Middle Ages to the Age of AIDS*. New York: Wiley, 1989.

Goffman, Erving. *The Presentation of Self in Everyday Life*. London: Allen Lane, 1969.
Goldschmidt, Hans E. *Quer Sacrum: Wiener Parodien und Karikaturen der Jahrhundertwende*. Vienna: Jugend und Volk Verlagsgesellschaft, 1976.
Gombrich, Ernst. *The Visual Arts in Vienna circa 1900*. London: Austrian Cultural Institute, 1997.
Graf Antonia, Otto. *Das Werk des Architekten, 1860–1902*. Vol. 1. Vienna: Böhlau, 1994.
Gravagnuolo, Benedetto. *Adolf Loos: Theory and Works*. Milan: Art Data, 1995.
Gronberg, Tag. "The Inner Man: Interiors and Masculinity in Early Twentieth-Century Vienna." *Oxford Art Journal* 24, no. 1 (2001): 69–88.
———. *Vienna: City of Modernity, 1890–1914*. Oxford: Peter Lang, 2007.
———. "The Viennese Coffeehouse: A Legend in Performance." In *Performance, Fashion and the Modern Interior, from the Victorian to Today*, edited by Fiona Fischer, 59–71. London: Berg, 2011.
Gruber, Karlheinz, Sabine Höller-Alber, and Markus Kristan. *Ernst Epstein, 1881–1938: Der Bauleiter des Looshauses als Architekt*. Vienna: Holzhausen Verlag, 2002.
Günther, Georg. "Karl Wittgenstein und seine Bedeutung für den Aufbau und die Entwicklung der österreichischen Volkswirtschaft." In *Neue österreichische Biographie, 1815–1918*, edited by Anton Bettelheim, 4, part 1, 156–63. Vienna: Amaltha-Verlag, 1927.
Haiko, Peter. "The 'Obscene' in Viennese Architecture of the Early Twentieth Century." In *Egon Schiele: Art, Sexuality, and Viennese Modernism*, edited by Patrick Werner, 89–100. Stanford, CA: Society for the Promotion of Science and Scholarship, 1994.
——— and Hannes Stekl. "Architektur in der industriellen Gesellschaft." In *Architektur und Gesellschaft von der Antike zur Gegenwart*, edited by Hannes Stekl, 251–340. Salzburg: Lehr- und Studienbehelfe, 1980.
Hamann, Brigitte. "Der Bauherr Gustav Ritter von Epstein." In *Das Palais Epstein: Geschichte—Restaurierung—Umbau*, edited by Wolfgang Baatz, et al., 42–47. Vienna: Löcker, 2005.
———. "'Von der Magie des historischen Ortes': Das Palais Epstein und sein Bauherr." *Jüdische Echo* (Vienna) 48 (October 1999): 302–7.
Hanak-Lettner, Werner. "Quasi una fantasia: Zur Dramaturgie einer Ausstellung." In *Quasi una fantasia: Juden und die Musikstadt Wien*, edited by Leon Botstein, 23–41. Vienna: Jewish Museum Vienna, 2003.
Harrer, Paul. "Wien: Seine Häuser, Menschen und Kultur." Vol. 2, part 6. Unpublished manuscript, 1948.
Haslinger, Ingrid. *Kunde: Kaiser. Die Geschichte der ehemaligen K. u. K. Hoflieferanten*. Vienna: Schroll, 1996.
Häusler, Wolfgang. "'Orthodoxie' und 'Reform' im Wiener Judenthum in der Epoche des Hochliberalismus." In *Der Wiener Stadttempel, 1826–1976*, edited by Kurt Schubert, Studia Judaica Austriaca, 16:29–56. Eisenstadt: Edition Roetzer, 1978.
Hecht, Louise. "Appropriation of Jewish Space on the *Wiener Ringstrasse*: Palais Schey and Its Tenants." Paper presented at the European Social Science History Conference, Vienna, Austria, April 26, 2014.
———, ed. *Ludwig August Frankl (1810–1894): Eine jüdische Biographie zwischen Okzident und Orient*. Cologne: Böhlau Verlag, 2015.

Heidrich-Blaha, Ruth. "Josef Kornhäusels Synagoge in Wien." *Jüdische Echo* (Vienna), 1988, 131–36.

Heimann-Jelinek, Felicitas. "Die Welt des Richard Beer-Hofmann / The World of Richard Beer-Hofmann." In *Zu Gast bei Beer-Hofmann; Visiting Beer-Hofmann: An Exhibition on Jewish Vienna at the Turn of the Century*, edited by Felicitas Heimann-Jelinek, 23–37. Vienna: Jüdisches Museum der Stadt Wien, 1998.

Henderson, Susan R. "Bachelor Culture in the Work of Adolf Loos." *Journal of Architectural Education* 55, no. 3 (2002): 125–35.

Hess, Heather. "The Wiener Werkstätte and the Reform Impulse." In *Producing Fashion, Commerce, Culture, and Consumers*, edited by Regina Lee Blaszczyk, 111–29. Philadelphia: University of Pennsylvania Press, 2007.

Hiebler, Heinz. *Hugo von Hofmannsthal und die Medienkultur der Moderne*. Würzburg: Königshausen und Neumann, 2003.

Hilger, Wolfgang. "Geschichte der 'Vereinigung bildender Künstler Österreichs': Secession, 1897–1918." In *Die Wiener Secession: Die Vereinigung bildender Künstler*, 9–66. Vienna: Böhlau, 1986.

Hirsch, Sharon. "Codes of Consumption: Tuberculosis and Body Image at the Fin-de-Siècle." In *In Sickness and in Health: Disease as Metaphor in Art and Popular Wisdom*, edited by Laurinda S. Dixon, Gabriel P. Weisberg, 144–65. Newark: University of Delaware Press, 2004.

Hoberman, John M. "Otto Weininger and the Critique of Jewish Masculinity." In *Jews & Gender: Responses to Otto Weininger*, edited by Nancy A. Harrowitz and Barbara Hyams, 141–53. Philadelphia: Temple University Press, 1995.

Hodin, Josef Paul. *Bekenntnis zu Kokoschka: Erinnerungen und Deutungen*. Berlin: Bei Florian Kupferberg Verlag, 1963.

——. *OK: Sein Leben, seine Zeit*. Frankfurt: Kupferberg, 1968.

Hoffmann, Edith. *Kokoschka: Life and Work*. London: Faber and Faber, 1947.

Höhle, Eva-Maria. "Vom Glacis zur Ringstrasse—Theophil Hansen und seine Zeit." In *Das Palais Epstein: Geschichte—Restaurierung—Umbau*, edited by Wolfgang Baatz, et al., 30–41. Vienna: Löcker, 2005.

Hollander, Anne. *Sex and Suits: The Evolution of Modern Dress*. New York: Knopf, 1994.

Houze, Rebecca. "Fashion, Disguise, and Transformation: Origins of the Modern Art Movement in Vienna, 1897–1914." PhD diss., University of Chicago, 2000.

Huey, Michael. "Das ästhetisierte Individuum: Das Subjekt und seine Objekte im Wien der Jahrhundertwende." In *Wiener Silber Modernes Design, 1780–1918*, edited by Renée Price and Wilfried Seipel, 343–52. Ostfildern: Hatje Cantz Verlag, 2003.

Humphrey, Caroline, and Vera Skvirskaja. Introduction to *Post-Cosmopolitan Cities: Exploration of Urban Coexistence*, edited by Caroline Humphrey and Vera Skvirskaja, 1–16. New York: Berghahn, 2012.

Immler, Nicole Leandra. "Das Familiengedächtnis der Wittgensteins: Autobiographische Praxis und ihre Strategien. Die Familienerinnerungen von Hermine Wittgenstein und die autobiographischen Bemerkungen von Ludwig Wittgenstein." PhD diss., Institut für Geschichte, Karl-Franzens-Universität Graz, 2005.

Inderwisch, Karin C. *Augen-Blicke bei Richard Beer-Hofmann*. Oldenburg: Igel Verlag, 1998.

Iven, Mathias, ed. *"Ludwig Sagt . . .": Die Aufzeichnungen der Hermine Wittgenstein*. Berlin: ParErga, 2006.

Jankowitsch, Regina Maria. "Mode in Wien, 1870 bis 1890: Eine gesellschaftspolitische Studie." MA thesis, Vienna University, 1987.

"Jewish Cemetery of Chernivtsi." Accessed July 25, 2015. http://www.academia.edu/5444863/Jewish_cemetery_of_chernivtsi.

Johnson, Julie M. "Athena Goes to the Prater: Parodying Ancients and Moderns at the Vienna Secession." *Oxford Art Journal* 23 no. 2 (2003): 49–69.

———. *The Memory Factory: The Forgotten Women Artists of Vienna 1900*. West Lafayette, IN: Purdue University Press, 2012.

Kalina, Suzanna. "Hugo von Hofmannsthal und der Tanz." MA thesis, Vienna University, 1993.

Kann, Robert A., ed. *Briefe an, von und um Josephine von Wertheimstein, ausgewählt und erläutert von Heinrich Gomperz*. Vienna: Verlag der Österreichischen Akademie der Wissenschaften, 1981.

———. *Theodor Gomperz: Ein Gelehrtenleben im Bürgertum der Franz-Josef-Zeit*. Vienna: Verlag der Österreichischen Akademie der Wissenschaften, 1974.

Kapfinger, Otto, and Adolf Krischanitz. *Die Wiener Secession: Das Haus. Entstehung, Geschichte, Erneuerung*. Graz: Böhlau, 1986.

Kelley, Susanne. "Perception of Jewish Female Bodies through Gustav Klimt and Peter Altenberg." *Imaginations* 3, no. 1 (2012): 109–21.

Kernmayer, Hildegrad. *Judentum im Wiener Feuilleton (1848–1903): Exemplarische Untersuchungen zum literarästhetischen und politischen Diskurs der Moderne*. Tübingen: Max Niemeyer Verlag, 1998.

Kinney, Leila W. "Fashion and Fabrication in Modern Architecture." *Journal of the Society of Architectural Historians* 58, no. 3 (1999): 472–81.

Kirschenblatt-Gimblett, Barbara, and Jonathan Karp. Introduction to *The Art of Being Jewish in Modern Times*, edited by Barbara Kirschenblatt-Gimblett and Jonathan Karp, 1–20. Philadelphia: University of Pennsylvania Press, 2008.

Klein-Primavesi, Claudia. *The Primavesi Family and the Wiener Werkstätte: Josef Hoffmann and Gustav Klimt as Friends and Artists*. Vienna: Art Book, 2006.

Kodek, Günter K. *Unsere Bausteine sind die Menschen: Die Mitglieder der Wiener Freimauererlogen, 1869–1938*. Vienna: Löcker Verlag, 2009.

———. *Zwischen Verboten und Erlaubt: Die Chronik der Freimauerei, in der österreichisch-ungarischen Monarchie (1867–1918) und der I. Republik Österreich (1918–1938)*. Vienna: Löcker Verlag, 2009.

Kohlbauer, Gabriele, and Wiebke Krohn, eds. *Beste aller Frauen: Weiblich Dimensionen im Judentum*. Vienna: Holzhausen, 2007.

Kokoschka, Oskar. *Letters, 1905–1976*. London: Thames and Hudson, 1992.

———. *My Life*. London: Thames and Hudson, 1974.

———. *Die träumenden Knaben*. New ed. Vienna: Jugend und Volk, 1968.

Koppelkamm, Stefan. *Der imaginäre Orient: Exotische Bauten des achtzehnten und neunzehnten Jahrhunderts in Europa*. Berlin: Ernst & Sohn, 1987.

Kornberg, Jacques. *Theodor Herzl from Assimilation to Zionism*. Bloomington: Indiana University Press, 1993.

Koss, Juliet. *Modernism after Wagner*. Minneapolis: University of Minnesota Press, 2010.

Koziura, Karolina. "Jewish Cemetery of Chernivtsi," accessed October 1, 2015. http://www.academia.edu/5444863/Jewish_cemetery_of_chernivts.

Kraševac, Irena. "Ivan Mešrović und sein Wiener Mäzen Karl Wittgenstein." In *Übergänge und Verflechtungen: Kulturelle Transfers in Europa*, edited by Gregor Kokorz and Helga Mitterbauer, 128–45. Bern: Lang, 2004.

Kravtsov, Sergey R. "Reconstruction of the Temple by Charles Chipiez and Its Applications in Architecture." *Ars Judaica*. 4 (2008): 25–42.

Krechting, Tim. *Richard Beer-Hofmanns jüdisches Denken: Eine theologische Werkanalyse unter Berücksichtigung der Historie von König David*. Hamburg: Igel Verlag Literatur und Wissenschaft, 2009.

Kristan, Markus. *Carl König 1841–1915: Ein neubarocker Großstadtarchitekt in Wien*. Vienna: Hozhausen, 1999.

———. *Josef Hoffmann: Villenkolonie Hohe Warte*. Vienna: Album Verlag, 2004.

———. *Oskar Marmorek: Architekt und Zionist, 1863–1909*. Vienna: Böhlau, 1996.

Kulka, Heinrich. Adolf *Loos: Das Werk des Architekten*. Vienna: Schroll, 1931.

Labanyi, P. "'Die Gefahr des Körpers.' A Reading of Otto Weininger's 'Geschlecht und Charakter.'" In *Fin de Siècle Vienna, Proceedings of the Second Irish Symposium in Austrian Studies held at the Trinity College, Dublin, 1985*, edited by G. J. Carr and Eda Sagarra 161–86. Dublin: Trinity College, 1985.

Lasher-Schlitt, Dorothy. "Grillparzer's Attitude towards the Jews." PhD diss., New York University, 1936.

Lathers, Marie. "Posing the 'Belle Juive': Jewish Models in 19th-Century Paris." *Woman's Art Journal*, spring–summer (2000): 27–32.

Le Rider, Jacques. *Modernity and Crises of Identity: Culture and Society in Fin-de-Siècle Vienna*. Translated by Rosemary Morris. New York: Continuum, 1993.

Lensing, Leo A. "Scribbling Squids and the Giant Octopus: Oskar Kokoschka's Unpublished Portrait of Peter Altenberg." In *Turn-of-the-Century Vienna and Its Legacy: Essays in Honor of Donald G. Daviau*, edited by Jeffrey B. Berlin, Journ B. Johns, and Richard H. Lawson, 193–220. Edition Atelier, 1993.

———. "Tiertheater: Textspiele der jüdischen Identität bei Altenberg, Kraus und Kafka." *Jüdische Echo* (Vienna) 48 (October 1999): 79–86.

Leuenberger, Stefanie. *Schrift-Raum Jerusalem: Identitätsdiskurse im Werk deutsch-jüdischer Autoren*. Cologne: Böhlau Verlag, 2007.

Lichtblau, Albert, ed. *Als hätten wir dazugehört: Österreichisch-jüdische Lebensgeschichten aus der Habsbugermonarchie*, 464–480. Vienna: Böhlau Verlag, 1999.

Lillie, Sophie. *Was einmal War: Handbuch der enteigneten Kunstsammlungen Wiens*. Vienna: Czernin Verlag, 2003.

Long, Christopher. *The Looshaus*. New Haven (CT): Yale University Press, 2011.

———. "The Origins and Context of Adolf Loos's 'Ornament and Crime.'" *Journal of the Society of Architectural Historians* 68, no. 2 (2009): 200–223.

Loos, Adolf. *On Architecture*. Selected with an introduction by by Adolf Opel and Daniel Opel. Translated by Michael Mitchell. Riverside, CA: Ariadne, 2002.

———. *Ornament and Crime: Selected Essays*. Selected with an introduction by Adolf Opel. Translated by Michael Mitchell. Riverside, CA: Ariadne, 1998.

———. *Spoken into the Void: Collected Essays, 1897–1900*. Edited by Peter Eisenman and Kenneth Frampton. Translated by Jane O. Newman and John H. Smith. Cambridge, MA: MIT Press, 1982.

Loos, Claire. *Loos Privat*. 1936. Vienna: Böhlau Verlag, 1985.

Lubbock, Jules. "Adolf Loos and the English Dandy." *Architectural Review* 174, no. 1038 (1983): 43–49.

Lunzer, Heinz, and Victoria Lunzer-Talos. *Peter Altenberg: Extracte des Lebens. Einem Schriftsteller auf der Spur*. Vienna: Residenz Verlag, 2003.

——— and Marcus G. Patka. *"Was wir umbringen": 'Die Fackel' von Karl Kraus*. Vienna: Mandelbaum Verlag, 1999.

Máčel, Otakar. "American Bar, 1907–8." In *Cafés and Bars: The Architecture of Public Display*, edited by Christop Grafe and Franziska Bollerey, 140–44. New York: Routledge, 2007.

Mahler-Werfel, Alma. *Tagebuch-Suiten, 1898–1902*. Edited by Antony Beaumont and Susanne Rode-Breymann. Frankfurt: Fischer, 1997.

Malmberg, Helga. *Widerhall des Herzens: Ein Peter Altenberg-Buch*. Munich: Langen, Müller, 1961.

März, Eduard. *Österreichische Industrie- und Bankpolitik in der Zeit Franz Josef I: Am Beispiel der k.k. priv. Österreichischen Credit-Anstalt für Handel und Gewerbe*. Vienna: Europa Verlag, 1968.

Mathis, Franz. *Big Business in Österreich: Österreichische Großunternehmen in Kurzdarstellungen*. Munich: Oldenbourg, 1987.

Mattiolo, Aram. *Jacob Burckhardt und die Grenzen der Humanität*. Vienna: Bibliothek der Provinz, 2001.

McGuinness, Brian. *Wittgenstein, a Life: Young Ludwig, 1889–1921*. London: Duckworth, 1988.

———. "Wittgenstein und das Judentum." In *Paul Engelmann: Architektur, Judentum, Wiener Moderne*, edited by Ursula A. Schneider, 57–77. Vienna: Folio Verlag, 1999.

———, Maria Concetta Ascher, and Otto Pfersmann. *Wittgenstein Familienbriefe*. Vienna: Verlag Hölder-Pichler-Tempsky, 1996.

McLeod, Mary. "Undressing Architecture: Fashion, Gender, and Modernity." In *Architecture: In Fashion*, edited by Deborah Fausch, Paulette Singley, Rodolphe El-Khoury, and Zvi Efrat, 39–123. New York: Princeton Architectural Press, 1994.

Meiszl-Novopacky, Ursula. "Der Kunstkritiker Ludwig Hevesi, 1843–1910: Sein Einfluss auf das Kunstverständnis in Österreich-Ungarn um die Jahrhundertwende." PhD diss., University of Vienna, 1989.

Mendes-Flohr, Paul. *Divided Passions: Jewish Intellectuals and the Experience of Modernity*. Detroit, MI: Wayne State University Press, 1991.

Meysels, Lucian O. *In meinem Salon ist Österreich: Berta Zuckerkandl und ihre Zeit*. Vienna: Herold Verlag, 1984.

Miller, Manu von. *Sonja Knips und die Wiener Moderne: Gustav Klimt, Josef Hoffmann und die Wiener Werkstätte gestalten eine Lebenswelt*. Vienna: Verlag Christian Brandstätter, 2004.

Moravánszky, Ákos. "The Aesthetics of the Mask: The Critical Reception of Wagner's Moderne Architektur and Architectural Theory in Central Europa." In *Otto Wagner:*

Reflections on the Raiment of Modernity, edited by Harry Francis Mallgrave, 199–239. Santa Monica, CA: Getty Center, 1993.

———. "Byzantinismus in der Baukunst Otto Wagner als Motiv seiner Wirkung östlich von Wien." In Die Kunst des Otto Wagner, edited by Gustav Peichl, 40–45. Vienna: Akademie der bildenden Künste, 1984.

Moser, Lottelis, and Helene Zand. "Die Zeit, ein 'Wiener Posten' der guten Europäer." In Pluralität: Eine interdisziplinäre Annährung, Festschrift für Moritz Csáky, edited by Gotthart Wunberg and Dieter A. Binder, 247–57. Vienna: Böhlau, 1996.

Müller, Ines. Die Otto Wagner-Synagoge in Budapest. Vienna: Löcker Verlag, 1992.

———. "Synagogen in Österreich—Eine Kulturhistorische Eingrenzung." In Synagogen in Österreich, edited by Pierre Genée, 115–21. Vienna: Löcker Verlag, 1992.

Müller, Martin Anton. "Emil Auspitzer." Hermann Bahr: Österreichische Kritiker europäische Avantgarden, 2013. Accessed on August 1, 2014. http://www.univie.ac.at/bahr/node/49641.

———. "Heirat mit Rosa Jokl." Hermann Bahr: Österreichische Kritiker europäische Avantgarden, 2013. Accessed August 1, 2014. http://www.univie.ac.at/bahr/node/27875.

Münz, Ludwig. "Die Gefährdung des Loos-Hauses auf dem Michaelerplatz." Wiener Zeitung, January 19, 1936.

——— and Gustav Künstler. Der Architekt Adolf Loos. Vienna: Schroll Verlag, 1964.

Natter, Tobias G. Die Welt von Klimt, Schiele und Kokoschka: Sammler und Mäzene. Cologne: Dumont, 2003.

———. "Fürstinnen ohne Geschichte? Gustav Klimt und die 'Gemeinschaft aller Schaffenden und Genießenden.'" In Klimt und die Frauen, edited by Tobias G. Natter and Gerbet Frodl, 57–74. Cologne: Dumont, 2000.

———, ed. Isidor Kaufmann, 1853–1921. Vienna: Jüdisches Museum der Stadt Wien, 1995.

——— and Gerbet Frodl, eds. Klimt und die Frauen. Cologne: Dumont, 2000.

Nebehay, Christian M. Vienna 1900. Vienna: Brandstätter, 1994.

———. Ver Sacrum 1898–1903. Vienna: Edition Tusch, 1975.

Neutra, Richard. Survival through Design. New York: Oxford University Press, 1954.

Neuwirth, Watraud. Josef Hoffmann: Bestecke für die Wiener Werkstätte. Vienna: published by the author, 1982.

———. Wiener Werkstätte: Avantgarde, Art Deco, Industrial Design. Vienna: published by the author, 1984.

Nierhaus, Andreas. "Vor-Bild Frankreich: Die Paläste der Familie Rothschild im Wiener Belvedere-Viertel." Österreichische Zeitschrift für Kunst und Denkmalpflege 62, no. 1 (2008): 74–86.

Nierhaus, Irene. Arch6: Raum, Geschlecht, Architektur. Vienna: Sonderzahl, 1999.

Noever, Peter, ed. Der Preis der Schönheit: 100 Jahre Wiener Werkstätte. Vienna: Hatje Cantz Verlag, 2003.

———, ed. Yearning for Beauty: The Wiener Werkstätte and the Stoclet House. Vienna: Hatje Cantz Verlag, 2006.

Nyíri, J. C., and Brian F. McGuinness. Introduction to Karl Wittgenstein, Karl

Wittgenstein: Politico-Economic Writings, edited by J. C. Nyíri and Brian F. McGuinness. Amsterdam: John Benjamins, 1984.

Österreichischer Gewerbeverein Interessensvertretung für Industrie, Gewerbe, Handel und freie Berufe. Chronology of the Austrian Trade Union at http://gewerbeverein.at.dedi787.your-server.de/de/zeittafel_1815–1938/1815_-_1938, Accessed August 1, 2014.

Olin, Margaret. "Nationalism, the Jews, and Art History." Judaism 45, no. 4 (1996): 461–82.

Ottillinger, Eva B. Adolf Loos, Wohnkonzepte und Möbelentwürfe. Salzburg: Residenz Verlag, 1994.

Oxaal, Ivar, Michael Pollak, and Gerhard Botz. Jews, Antisemitism and Culture in Vienna. New York: Routledge and Kegan Paul, 1987.

"Palais Epstein." In Das Österreichische Parlament: Parlamentarismus, Gebäude, Geschichte: The Austrian Parlament, edited by Barbara Blümel, 48–51. Vienna: Parlamentsdirektion Vienna, 2006.

Panizza, Oskar. The Operated Jew. Translated by Jack Zipes. New German Critique 21, no. 3 (1980): 63–79.

Pannosch, Fridrich. "Die Wohnnbauten der Architekten Julius Romano und August Schwendenwein in Wien, 1860–1865." MA thesis, Institut an der Universität, Vienna, 2005.

Patai, Josef. "Ludwig Hevesi." In Jüdisches Lexikon: Ein enzyklopädisches Handbuch des jüdischen Wissens in Vier Bänden, edited by Georg Herlitz and Bruno Kirschner, 2:1586. Berlin: Jüdischer Verlag, 1928.

Pichler, Gerd. "Das Kabarett Fledermaus: Ein Gesamtkunstwerk der Wiener Werkstätte." In Fledermaus Kabarett, 1907–1913: Ein Gesamtkunstwerk der Wiener Werkstätte, edited by Michael Buhrs, Barbara Lesák, and Thomas Trabitsch, 51–88. Vienna: Christian Brandstätter Verlag, 2008.

Pincus-Witten, Robert. "The Iconography of Symbolist Painting." Artforum 8 (January 1970: 56–62.

Pogacnik, Marco. Adolf Loos und Wien. Salzburg: Müry Salzmann Verlag, 2011.

Pollak, Michael. "Cultural Innovation and Social Identity." In Jews: Antisemitism and Culture in Vienna, edited by Ivar Oxaal, Michael Pollak, and Gerhard Botz, 59–74. New York: Routledge and Kegan, 1987.

Powers, Martin J. "Art and History: Exploring the Counterchange Condition." Art Bulletin 77 (September 1995): 382–87.

Praz, Mario. An Illustrated History of Interior Decoration: From Pompeii to Art Nouveau. New York: Thames and Hudson, 1983.

Priddis, Nathan. "Ashantee and the Colonial Gaze: A Study in Colonialism." Perspectives 15 (2007): 1–11.

Prokop, Ursula. Margaret Stonborough-Wittgenstein: Bauherrin, Intellektuelle, Mäzenin. Vienna, Böhlau Verlag, 2003.

———. "Zum Umgang mit Kunst und Ästhetik in der Familie Wittgenstein." Lecture delivered at the symposium Wittgenstein nach der Arbeit, Budapest, February 24, 2012.

Purdy, Daniel. "The Cosmopolitan Geography of Adolf Loos." *New German Critique* 33, no. 3 (2006): 41–62.
Read, Herbert. *Art and Society*. London: Faber and Faber, 1945.
Rebhann, Fritz Maria. "Die Zeit: Ein historischer Abriss." PhD diss., Vienna University, 1948.
Redl, Renate. "Berta Zuckerkandl und die Wiener Gesellschaft: Ein Beitrag zur österreichischen Kunst- und Gesellschaftskritik." PhD diss., Vienna University, 1978.
Reissberger, Mara. "Zum Problem künstlerischer Selbstdarstellung in der zweiten Hälfte des 19. Jahrhunderts—Die lebenden Bilder." In *Die österreichische Literatur: Ihr Profil im 19. Jahrhundert (1830–1880)*, edited by Herbert Zeman, 741–69. Graz: Akademisches Druck- und Verlagsanstalt, 1982.
Reiter, Cornelia. *Schöne Welt, wo bist du? Zeichnungen, Aquarelle, Ölskizzen des deutschen und österreichischen Spätklassizismus*. Salzburg: Müry Salzmann, 2009.
Rennhofer, Maria. *Koloman Moser: Leben und Werk, 1868–1918*. Vienna: Christian Brandstätter Verlag, 2002.
Ricoeur, Paul. *From Text to Action: Essays in Hermeneutics II*. Translated by Kathleen Blamey and John B. Thompson. Vol. 2. Evanston, IL: Northwestern University Press, 1991.
Riou, Jeanne. "Aesthetic Imagination as Network? Approaches to Thought and Death in Rilke and Richard Beer-Hofmann." In *Networking across Borders and Frontiers*, edited by Jürgen Barkhoff and Helmut Eberhart, 235–48. Frankfurt: Peter Lang, 2009.
Robertson, Pamela. "Margaret Macdonald Mackintosh: 'The Seven Princesses.'" In *Ein moderner Nachmittag, A Thoroughly Modern Afternoon: Margaret Macdonald Mackintosh und der Salon Waerndorfer in Wien*, edited by Hanna Egger, Pamela Robertson, Peter Vergo, and Manfred Trummer, 41–78. Vienna: Bóhlau, 2000.
Rochowanski, Leopold Wolfgang. *Josef Hoffmann: Eine Studie geschrieben zu seinem 80. Geburtstag*. Vienna: Verlag der Österreichischen Staatsdruckerei, 1950.
Roeck, Bernd. "Kunstpatronage in Vergangenheit und Gegenwart." *Neue Politische Literatur* 47, no. 1 (2002): 5–9.
Rose, Alison. *Jewish Women in Fin de Siècle Vienna*. Austin: University of Texas Press, 2008.
Rossbacher, Karlheinz. *Literatur und Bürgertum: Fünf Wiener jüdische Familien von der liberalen Ära zum Fin de Siècle*. Vienna: Böhlau Verlag, 2003.
———. *Literatur und Liberalismus: Zur Kultur der Ringstrassenzeit in Wien*. Vienna: J and V, 1992.
Rozenblit, Marsha L. *The Jews of Vienna, 1867–1914: Assimilation and Identity*. Albany: State University of New York Press, 1983.
Rudolf, Richard L. *Banking and Industrialization in Austria-Hungary: The Role of the Banks in the Industrialization of the Czech Crownlands, 1873–1914*. Cambridge: Cambridge University Press, 1976.
Rukschcio, Burkhardt. "Wien, Adolf Loos und das Haus am Michaelerplatz." In *Traum und Wirklichkeit, 1870–1930*, 422–36. Vienna: Wien, Bundesministerium für Unterricht und Kunst, 1985.
———. "Die Bedeutung der Bauherren für Adolf Loos." *Parnass*, special issue 2 (1985): 6–15.

———. "Studien zu Entwürfen, Projekten, Ausgeführten Bauten von Adolf Loos." PhD diss., Vienna University, 1973.

——— and Roland Schachel. *Adolf Loos: Leben und Werk*, Vienna: Residenz Verlag, 1982.

———. "Adolf Loos und das Kaffeehaus." *Parnass* 2, no. 5 (September–October 1982): 24–30.

Safran, Yehuda E. "Adolf Loos: The Archimedean Point." In *The Architecture of Adolf Loos*, edited by Yehuda Safran and Wilfried Wang, 26–35. London: Art Council of Great Britain, 1985.

———, ed. *Adolf Loos: Our Contemporary, Unser Zeitgenosse, Nosso Contemporâneo*. New York: GSAPP Books, 2012.

———. "Adolf Loos: Our Contemporary." In *Adolf Loos: Our Contemporary, Unser Zeitgenosse, Nosso Contemporâneo* edited by Yehuda E. Safran. New York: GSAPP Books, 2012.

Sármány-Parsons, Ilona. "The Art Criticism of Ludwig Hevesi." In *From Ausgleich to Jahrhundertwende: Literature and Culture 1867–1890*, edited by Judith Beniston and Deborah Holmes, 87–104. Leeds, UK: Maney, 2008.

Scherer, Stefan. *Richard Beer-Hofmann und die Wiener Moderne*. Tübingen: Niemeyer, 1993.

Schmidt-Dengler, Wendelin. "Decadence and Antiquity: The Educational Preconditions of Jung Wien." In *Focus on Vienna 1900*, edited by Erika Nielsen, 32–45. Munich: Wilhelm Fink Verlag, 1982.

Schorske, Carl E. *Fin-de-Siècle Vienna: Politics and Culture*. New York: Vintage, 1981.

Schneider, Ursula A., ed. *Paul Engelmann: Architektur, Judentum, Wiener Moderne*. Vienna: Folio Verlag, 1999.

———. "Vom 'Wittgensteinhaus' zum 'Café Techelet': Die sichtbaren und die unsichtbaren Werke Paul Engelmanns." In *Paul Engelmann: Architektur, Judentum, Wiener Moderne*, edited by Ursula A. Schneider, 115–54. Vienna: Folio Verlag, 1999.

Schülz, Jürgen Michael. "Hermann Bahr als Publizist in Berlin." In *Hermann Bahr für eine andere Moderne*, edited by Jeanne Benay and Alfred Pfabigan, 125–44. Bern: Peter Lang, 2004.

Schweiger, Hannes. "Shaw's Contributions to *Fin-de-Siècle* Vienna." In *Shaw: The Annual of Bernard Shaw Studies*, edited by MaryAnn Krajnik Crawford and Gale K. Larson, 135–46. University Park: Penn State University Press, 2005.

Schweiger, Werner J. *Wiener Werkstaette: Design in Vienna 1903–1932*. London: Thames and Hudson, 1990.

Segal, Harold B. *The Vienna Coffeehouse Wits, 1890–1938*. West Lafayette, IN: Purdue University Press, 1993.

Sekler, Eduard F. *Josef Hoffmann: Das architektonische Werk: Monographie und Werkverzeichnis*. Salzburg: Residenz Verlag, 1982.

Shapira, Elana. "Adolf Loos and the Fashioning of 'the Other': Memory, Fashion and Interiors." In *Interiors: Design, Architecture and Culture*, edited by Anne Massey and John Turpin, 2:213–37. Boston: Berg, 2011.

———. "Assimilating with Style: Jewish Assimilation and Modern Architecture and Design: The Case of the 'Outfitters' Adolf Loos and Leopold Goldman and the

Making of the Goldman & Salatsch Building." PhD diss. University of Applied Arts Vienna, 2004.

———. "An Early Expressionist Masterpiece: Oskar Kokoschka's *Children Playing* of 1909." *Zeitschrift für Kunstgeschichte* 64, no. 4 (2001): 501–36.

———. "Gaze and Spectacle in the Calibration of Class and Gender: Visual Culture in Vienna." In *A History of Visual Culture: Western Civilization from the 18th to the 21st Century*, edited by Jane Kromm and Susan Benforado Bakewell, 157–68. Oxford: Berg, 2010.

———. "Imaging the Jew: A Clash of Civilisations." In *Facing the Modern: The Portrait in Vienna 1900*, edited by Gemma Blackshaw, 155–71. London: Yale University Press, 2013.

———. "Jewish Patronage and the Avant-Garde in Vienna." In *Jüdische Sammler und ihr Beitrag zur Kultur der Moderne*, edited by Annette Weber and Jihann Radjai-Ordoubadi, 219–35. Heidelberg: Universitätsverlag Winter, 2011.

———. "Kunst und Repräsentation: Darstellungen jüdischer Salondamen in Wien um 1800." *Juden in Mitteleuropa*, special issue, 2009, 10-18.

———. "Modernism and Jewish Identity in Early Twentieth Century Vienna: The Patron Fritz Waerndorfer and His House for an Art Lover." *Studies in the Decorative Arts* 13, no. 2 (2006): 52–92.

———. "The Pioneers: Loos, Kokoschka and Their Shared Clients." In *Oskar Kokoschka, Early Portraits from Vienna and Berlin, 1909–1914*, edited by Tobias G. Natter, 50–60. Cologne: Dumont, 2002.

———. "Tailored Authorship: Adolf Loos and the Ethos of Men's Fashion." In *Leben mit Loos*, edited by Inge Podbrecky and Rainald Franz, 53–72. Vienna: Böhlau Verlag, 2008.

———. "Todesco, Förster, Hansen, and the New Hellenistic Jews on Vienna's Ringstrasse." In *Theophil Hansen: Ein Resümee*, edited by Beatrix Bastl, Ulrike Hirhager, and Eva Schober 273–300. Weitra: Verlag Bibliothek der Provinz, 2014.

Shavit, Yaacov. *Athens in Jerusalem, Classical Antiquity and Hellenism in the Making of the Modern Secular Jew*. London: Vallentine Mitchell, 1997.

Shedel, James. *Art and Society: The New Art Movement in Vienna, 1897–1914*. Palo Alto, CA: Society for the Promotion of Science and Scholarship, 1981.

Sichrovsky, Harry. *Mein Urahn, der Bahnbrecher: Heinrich von Sichrovsky*. Vienna: Braumüller, 1988.

Siebel, Ernst. *Der großbürgerliche Salon, 1850–1918: Geselligkeit und Wohnkultur*. Berlin: Reimer, 1999.

Silverman, Lisa. *Becoming Austrians: Jews and Culture between the World Wars*. New York: Oxford University Press, 2012.

Sjörgen, Cecilia. "Die Familie." In *Wittgenstein: Biographie, Philosophie, Praxis*, 99—117. Vienna: Wiener Secession, 1989.

Sluga, Hans. "Family Resemblance." *Grazer Philosophische Studien* 71, no. 1 (2006): 1–21.

Solomon-Godeau, Abigail. *Male Trouble: A Crisis in Representation*. London: Thames and Hudson, 1997.

Sontag, Susan. "Notes on 'Camp.'" *Partisan Review*, fall 1964. Accessed July 25, 2014. http://www.book.tubefun4.com/downloads/Sontag.pdf.

Spiel, Hilde. *Fanny von Arnstein oder die Emanzipation: Ein Frauenleben an der Zeitwende, 1758–1818*. Frankfurt: Fischer, 1962.

Spindler, Gabriele. "Zur Affinität von Interieur und Mode: Eine analysierende Gegenüberstellung theoretischer und praktischer Konzepte von Adolf Loos und der Wiener Werkstätte." MA thesis, Salzburg University, 1996.

Starl, Tim. *Lexikon zur Fotografie in Österreich, 1839 bis 1945*. Vienna: Album Verlag für Photographie, 2005.

Stewart, Janet. "Egon Friedell and Alfred Polgar: Cabaret in Vienna at the Turn of the Last Century." In *From Perinet to Jelinek: Viennese Theatre in Its Political and Intellectual Context*, edited by W. E. Yates, Allyson Fiddler and John Warren, 155–65. Bern: Peter Lang, 2001.

———. *Fashioning Vienna: Adolf Loos's Cultural Criticism*. London: Routledge, 2000.

Stögner, Karin. "Antisemitisch-misogyne Repräsentationen und die Krise der Geschlechtsidentität in Fin de Siècle." In *Wien und die jüdische Erfahrung, 1900–1938: Akkulturation—Antisemitismus—Zionismus*, edited by Frank Stern und Barbara Eichinger, 229–56. Vienna: Böhlau Verlag, 2009.

Strobl, Alice. "Kokoschka, der Klimttöter." In *Oskar Kokoschka und der frühe Expressionismus*, edited by Gerbert Frodl and Tobias Natter, 13–23. Vienna: Österreichische Galerie Belvedere, 1997.

——— and Alfred Weidinger. "Oskar Kokoschka, 'Mörder, Hoffnung der Frauen,' oder 'Der Todhass der Geschlechter.'" In *Dialog mit der Moderne: Fritz Wotruba und die Sammlung Kamm*, edited by Matthias Haldemann, 102–11. Zug: Balmer Verlag, 1998.

Szeps-Zuckerkandl, Berta. *Ich erlebte fünfzig Jahre Weltgeschichte*. Stockholm: Bermann Fischer Verlag, 1939.

Tielsch, Ilse. "Die Wochenschrift 'Die Zeit,' als Spiegel literarischen und kulturellen Lebens in Wien um die Jahrhundertwende." PhD diss., University of Vienna, 1952.

Tietze, Hans. *Die Juden Wiens: Geschichte, Wirtschaft, Kultur*. Leipzig: E. P. Tal Verlag, 1935.

Topp, Leslie. *Architecture and Truth in Fin-de-Siècle Vienna*. Cambridge: Cambridge University Press, 2004.

Tropper, Ulrike. "Die Sammlung Carl von Reininghaus." In *Pluralität: Eine interdisziplinäre Annährung, Festschrift für Moritz Csáky*, edited by Gotthart Wunberg and Dieter A. Binder, 258–72. Vienna: Böhlau, 1996.

Varnedoe, Kirk. *Wien 1900: Kunst, Architektur und Design*. Cologne: Benedikt Taschen Verlag, 1987.

Veigl, Hans. *Lachen im Keller: Von den Budapestern zum Wiener Werkel. Kabarett und Kleinkunst in Wien*. Vienna: Löcker Verlag, 1986.

Vergo, Peter. *Art in Vienna: Klimt, Kokoschka, Schiele, and Their Contemporaries*. London: Phaidon, 1975.

———. "Fritz Waerndorfer and Josef Hoffmann." *Burlington Magazine*, July 1983, 402–10.

———. "Fritz Waerndorfer as Collector." *Alte und moderne Kunst* 26, no. 177 (1981): 33–38.

———. "The Vanished Frieze." In *Ein moderner Nachmittag, A Thoroughly Modern Afternoon: Margaret Macdonald Mackintosh und der Salon Waerndorfer in Wien*, edited by Hanna Egger, Pamela Robertson, Peter Vergo, and Manfred Trummer, 18–40, 73. Vienna: Bohlau, 2000.

Vielmetti, Nikolaus. "Die Bedeutung des Tempels in der Seitenstettengasse für die jüdische Gemeinde in Wien." In *Voll Leben und voll Tod ist diese Erde: Bilder aus der Geschichte der jüdischen Österreicher, 1190 bis 1945*, edited by Wolfgang Plat, 130–42. Vienna: Herold, 1988.

Voglhuber, Eva. "Die Kunst des Wiener Jugendstiles und seine ägyptischen Formulierungen bei Fassaden- und Innenraumgestaltungen." MA thesis, University of Vienna, 1994.

Vossloh, Ute. "Kostüme-Entwürfe von Olbrich." In *Kunst in Hessen und am Mittelrhein*, 53–57. Darmstadt: Eduard Roether Verlag, 1967.

Vyleta, Daniel M. *Crime, Jews and News: Vienna 1895–1914*. New York: Berghahn, 2007.

Wagner-Rieger, Renate. *Die Wiener Ringstrasse*. Vol. 1, *Das Kunstwerk im Bild*. Vienna: Böhlau, 1969.

———. *Wiens Architektur im 19. Jahrhundert*. Vienna: Österreichischer Bundesverlag für Unterricht, Wissenschaft und Kunst, 1970.

——— and Mara Reissberger. *Theophil von Hansen*. Wiesbaden: Franz Steiner Verlag GmbH, 1980.

Waldhuber, Heinz, and Katrin Kruse. *Aristokratischer Chic auf der Insel Brioni, 1893–1919*. Vienna: Böhlau Verlag, 2006.

Walter, Bruno. *Theme and Variations: An Autobiography*. New York: Alfred A. Knopf, 1946.

Walter, Edith. "Die Funktion journalistischer Opposition: Die Leitartikeln der Tageszeitung 'Die Zeit,' Wien, 1902–1917." PhD diss., Vienna University, 1988.

Waugh, Alexander. *The House of Wittgenstein: A Family at War*. London: Bloomsbury, 2008.

Weidinger, Alfred. *Oskar Kokoschka, Dreaming Boy, Enfant Terrible: Oskar Kokoschka at the Vienna School of Applied Arts*. Vienna: Agnes-Werk, Geyer + Reisser, 1996.

Weixlgärtner, Arpad. *Führer durch die Dr. Albert Figdor-Stiftung*. Vienna: Verlag der Kunsthistorischen Sammlungen, 1932.

Werkner, Patrick. "The Child-Woman and Hysteria: Images of the Female Body in the Art of Schiele, in Viennese Modernism and Today." In *Egon Schiele: Art, Sexuality, and Viennese Modernism*, edited by Patrick Werkner, 51–78, 137–42. Stanford, CA: Society for the Promotion of Science and Scholarship, 1994.

———. "Kokoschkas frühe Gebärdensprache und ihre Verwurzelung im Tanz." In *Oskar Kokoschka: Symposion, abgehalten von der Hochschule für angewandte Kunst in Wien*, edited by Erika Patka, 93–99. Salzburg: Residenz Verlag, 1986.

Wigley, Mark. "White Out: Fashioning the Modern." In *Architecture: In Fashion*, edited by Deborah Fausch, Paulette Singley, Rodolphe El-Khoury, and Zvi Efrat, 149–268. New York: Princeton Architectural Press, 1994.

———. *White Walls, Designer Dresses*. Cambridge, MA: MIT Press, 1995.

Wijdeveld, Paul. *Ludwig Wittgenstein, Architect*. London: Thames and Hudson, 1994.

Windisch-Graetz, Franz. "Das Jagdhaus Hochreith: Zur Stilanalyse der Räume von Josef Hoffmann." *Alte und moderne Kunst* 12, no. 92 (1967): 28–32.

Winkler, Susanne. *Blickfänge einer Reise nach Wien*. Vienna: Museen der Stadt Wien, 2000.

Wittgenstein, Hermine, *Familienerinnerungen*. Edited by Ilse Somavilla. Innsbruck, Austria: Haymon, 2015.

Wittgenstein, Karl. *Karl Wittgenstein: Politico-Economic Writings*. Edited by J. C. Nyíri and Brian F. McGuinness. Amsterdam: John Benjamins, 1984.

Wittgenstein, Ludwig. *Briefe an Ludwig von Ficker*. Salzburg: Otto Müller Verlag, 1969.

Wunberg, Gotthart, ed. *Die Wiener Moderne: Literatur, Kunst und Musik zwischen 1890 und 1910*. Stuttgart: Reclam, 1981.

Zaunschirm, Thomas. *Gustav Klimt, Margarethe Stonborough-Wittgenstein: Ein österreichisches Schicksal*. Frankfurt: Fischer Taschenbuch Verlag, 1987.

Zuckerkandl, Berta. *Österreich intim: Erinnerungen, 1892–1942*. Edited by Reinhard Federmann. Frankfurt: Verlag Ullstein, 1970.

Zweig, Stefan. *The World of Yesterday*. Lincoln: University of Nebraska Press, 1964.

INDEX

Abels, Ludwig, 102, 197–98
acculturation: Altenberg's challenge to, 173; versus assimilation, 219–20, 231n6; Beer-Hofmann's cultural network, 154; Cabaret Fledermaus productions, 147–48; designing to different ideas of, 29–30, 139–41; Gomperz's promotion of, 25; Loos's and L. Goldman's dressing and undressing strategy, 210–11, 213; Loos's modernist critique of, 169–71; secessionists' redefinition of, 58–59, 61, 64; Singer's and Kanner's advocacy of, 119, 225; social trap of, 39–40, 138, 149–50, 205; Todesco's challenge to, 40–43; Todescos' Hellenistic, 24–27, 38–43; Wittgenstein's challenge to, 87–89, 92–93, 96

Altenberg, Peter: admiration for young women/girls, 152, 175, 177–78, 215; and American Bar, 168, 172, 183–86, *184*, *185*, 189–94; artistic self-representation of, 176–78, *178*, 183–84, 190–91; avant-garde self-identification of, 173, 174, 190–91, 193; and Beer-Hofmann, 151–53; bohemian lifestyle of, 169, 175–76, 224, 267n44; Cabaret Fledermaus role, 143, 146–47; crossing frontiers with style, 224–25; depictions of, *185*, 190–91, 270n112; fashion ideal of, 175; and Loos, 168–69, 171, 181–82, 201, 210; and Malmberg, 124; social transgressions of, 174–75

American Bar, 168, 172, 183–94, *184*, 268–69n84, 268n77
Anderson, Mark, 205
antisemitism: Alma Schindler's (later Mahler), 107; Bahr on, 72–74; caricatures of Jewish patrons' lives on Ringstrasse, 35, *36*, *37*; in *Der Floh*, 78–79, 245n91; and effeminate Jewish man stereotype, 14–15, 128, 129, 214; and Hofmannsthal, 76–77, 109–10; and Jewish conspiracy stories, 232–33n29; and Jewish patrons' self-identification, 18, 55–56, 121–22, 138, 172–73, 191–92, 195–96, 205, 222–23, 233–34n49; and Jews' supposed lack of honor, 257n62; Kraus and debate over Wilde's *Salomé*, 134; late nineteenth-century rise in, 61; Lueger's, 4, 61; Panizza's, 191–92; Saar's approach in *Seligmann Hirsch*, 40; secessionists' mission to overcome, 61, 71–77, 78–80; and Todesco's provocations, 40–43; and Waerndorfer's provocations, 129–30, 136–37

architectural style: importance to acculturation project, 29–30; importance to Jewish self-fashioning, 217; Jewish influence on, 2–3, 5–6, 13, 66. *See also* client-architect relationship; dressing metaphor in design

Arendt, Hannah, 8
Arnstein, Fanny von, 30, 91, 235n12
Arranged Table (Hoffmann), 141–42, 146
art, societal role of, 6–7, 50–51, 59, 63, 72, 80–81, 192–94
art nouveau, 12, 69, 100, 102, 108, 200
assimilation: versus acculturation, 219–20, 231n6; Bahr's prejudice against, 74, 124; criticism of, 74–75, 147–49, 169–70; Kraus as critic of, 121; Waerndorfer's identification with, 126
Assmann, Aleida, 31, 89

Athena, 24, 31, 77, 79, 83, 84–86, *85*; Klimt's *Pallas Athene*, 113–14, 124, 134
Aufricht, Emanuel, 217, 226, 271n136, 277n242
Auspitzer, Emil, 72, 244–45n69, 245n70
avant-gardists: American Bar, 168, 172, 183–94, *184*, 268n77; Café Museum, 180–81, *181*, 182–83; emancipation and cultural dress, 169–73; Goldman & Salatsch House and men's fashion, 13, 166, 172, 194, 196–216, *201*, *208*, 225, *228*; L. Goldman as, 194, 196, 202–3, 214, 215, 216–17. *See also* Altenberg, Peter; Loos, Adolf

Bahr, Hermann: and antisemitism, 72–74, 124; and Berl's hiring of Olbrich, 100–101; and *Die Zeit* journal, 117; on Klimt, 138; role in Beer-Hofmann villa project, 158; on secessionists, 64, 71, 72–74, 75–76; and Waerndorfer, 122, 124, 125, 136
Bauernfeld, Eduard, 23, 91
beauty: Olbrich's dream of, 76; and secession movement, 73; shame and, 185–86, 192, 211; and Wiener Werkstätte, 126, 138–39
Beer-Hofmann, Richard: crossing frontiers with style, 224–25; dandyism, 152–53, 154, 155, 157–66; as modernist Jewish club leader, 116, 151–55; on Orientalist style, 114, 158–59; reconstruction of Judaism, 154, 262n185; Todescos' tableaux vivants, 156; transformation of modernist aesthetic, 164–65, 265n233; villa, 151, 156–66, *157*, *160–61*, *163*, 263n10; and Waerndorfer, 153; and white-dress motif, *155*, 165–66
Beethoven sculpture (Klinger), 96–98, *98*
Beller, Steven, 1, 2, 174
Berl, David, 71, 100–102, *101*
Bertschik, Julia, 155–56, 176, 262n192
Bing, Siegfried, 102, 108
Bloch, Joseph Samuel, 27

body reclamation: in Altenberg's interiors, 177–78; in Waerndorfer's art and design choices, 128–37, 150–51
Bourdieu, Pierre, 171–73, 210
bourgeoisie: Jewish, 1, 3, 13, 32, 38; resistance to, 125, 129, 149, 174–75; and socialist credentials of *Die Zeit*, 118; and threat of Jewish sexuality, 152
British culture, Jewish affinity for, 187, 197, 201
Brummel, George Bryan "Beau," 8, 179
Burckhardt, Jacob, 34, 77, 237n50

Cabaret Fledermaus, 59, 116, 142–51, *145*, 260n130
Café Griensteidel, 116, 156
Café Museum, 180–81, *181*, 182–83
caryatids, 5–6, *6*, 24, 27, 33, 34, 43–44, *44*, 45, 46, 47, 53–54, 83–84, 154, 196, 207
celebrity: American Bar setting for Altenberg as, 190, 192; Beer-Hofmann's cultivation of, 154, 156; Jewish patrons' fashioning of, 8–9, 22–23, 109, 190, 219, 225
Cernuschi, Claude, 171, 214
classical style. *See* Greek revival style
client-architect relationship: Beer-Hofmann and Hoffmann, 162; Epstein and Hansen, 46, 49; L. and M. Goldman and Loos, 197, 201, 212, 215; Todesco and Hansen, 41–43
collectivist perspective, 1, 15, 59, 71, 81, 89, 123
covering and uncovering dynamic: at Goldman & Salatsch, 194, 196–216; in Jewish dandy's move from secession, 113; Loos's use of, 165–66; for secessionists, 60–61; social games role, 9–10; in Spitzer's music salon flirtations, 107; at Waerndorfer House, 133–35
crossing frontiers, style as tool for, 219–29
cultural authority: versus economic authority, 171–72; Epstein's, 22–23, 46–47, 49–51, 53; fashion as, 180,

204–5, 207–9; Hevesi's, 81–82, 83, 224; Jewish patrons' negotiation of, 15, 219–20; in land ownership, 28; of Loos and Goldman, 197, 200, 202–3, 211; of secessionists, 78–79; Todescos', 22, 23–24, 32–35, 38–39; Waerndorfer's challenge to, 136–37, 144, 147, 223; Wittgenstein's gestures, 87, 95, 250n172

cultural production: Beer-Hofmann's, 151–66, 157, 160–61, 163; Cabaret Fledermaus as, 143, 145–51; economic versus symbolic capital, 171–72; Epstein's, 53–55; fashion's role in, 9, 195, 201–2; in historicist transformation of Ringstrasse, 11; L. and M. Goldmans', 194, 196, 201–3, 214–15, 216–17; secessionists' mixing of Orientalist and Hellenist, 72; Todescos', 30–32, 55–56; and Viennese collaborative culture, 3

cutlery design for Wiener Werkstätte, 141–42

dandyism: and Altenberg's style, 176, 190; Beer-Hofmann, 152–53, 154, 155–56, 157–66, 224; as challenge to gender division, 152; covering and uncovering dynamic, 113; definition, 8; Goldman & Salatsch House, 194, 205, 213; as integration strategy, 8, 10; in Jewish patrons' self-fashioning, 80–81, 219, 220, 224, 227; Loos's, 179, 187, 190, 194, 205–6; in secessionists' fashioning of style, 60–61; and social mobility, 205–6; Spitzer's flirtation dramas, 104–5, 107; as style template for patrons, 8–9; Waerndorfer's, 126, 128; and woman performer, 150

Das neue Ghetto (Herzl): Bahr's reaction to, 74–75, 124, 190; Freud's reaction to, 221; Loos's reaction to, 170–71

Der Floh, 40, 78, 79, 211, 239n 81, 245n91

Der Schüler (Hofmannsthal), 109–10

Deutsche Zeitung, 72–73

Die Fackel, 121–22

Die Masken (Altenberg), 146–47

Die Wage, 58, 71, 87, 142

Die Zehn Gerechten (Friedell and Polgar), 147–48

Die Zeit: journal, 117–18; newspaper, 72, 116, 118–19, 120, 121–22

Drasche, Heinrich, 13, 32

dressing metaphor in design: American Bar, 187–88; caftan versus frock coat, 170–71, 205–6, 209, 233n33; Loos's "dressing principle," 204–7; Loos's views on fashion, 178–80; Secession House, 84; Waerndorfer House interior, 133, 139–40; Wagner's "principle of clothing," 65, 66, 67, 119, 203, 204. *See also* covering and uncovering dynamic; Goldman & Salatsch House

Dumba, Nicolaus, 13, 94, 233n48, 243n22

emancipation, 15, 25, 28, 169–73, 219–20, 222–23

Engelhart, Josef, 10, 64, 94, 103, 104, 125

Engelmann, Paul, 111, 112–13, 189, 215, 253nn237–38

Engländer, Richard. *See* Altenberg, Peter

Ephrussi, Ignaz von, 26–27, 31, 32, 235n15

Epstein, Gustav von, 4, 22, 43–55, 45, 65, 91, 95, 127, 219, 224. *See also* Palais Epstein

Epstein, Lazar, 47

Esther (Grillparzer), 25–26, 27, 28

Esther as cultural symbol, 5, 24, 25–27, 26, 55

European aesthetic/culture: through Hellenistic Jewish heritage, 25; Jewish historicists as Europeans, 28–38, 53–55; and Jewish modern identity, 5; Kraus's criticism of Singer's and Kanner's, 121–22; and Ringstrasse development, 11–13; tableaux vivants as expression of, 55–56; Waerndorfer's Gesamtkunstwerk, 125–26; Wittgenstein's renewal of, 86, 92–93, 99. *See also* Hellenistic Jews

European liberalism, 11, 29, 61, 117–18, 119

fashion: Altenberg's ideal of, 175–76; as cultural authority, 180, 204–5, 207–9; cultural production role of, 195, 201–2; culture of dressing up, 203–4, 211; Loos on, 178–79, 180, 182, 268n73; Loos and L. Goldman's contribution to, 215–16; secessionist style and women's, 135, 215; Zuckerkandl's aesthetic, 14. *See also* Goldman & Salatsch House

Felix, Eugen, 63, 64

femininity: in Altenberg's self-presentation, 175; and "effeminate" Jew stereotype, 14–15, 128, 129, 214; and gender ambiguity of dandy, 156; juxtapositions with masculine in Secession House, 83; Spitzer's villa design elements, 108; Todescos' caryatids as symbols of, 32–33; Waerndorfer House interior design, 133

feminist consciousness, 14, 70, 77

femme fatale, 6, 7, 80, 96, 113, 133, 134, 150

Figdor, Albert, 91

Figdor, Fanny, 89, 91, 92, 195, 248n136

Fischhof, Adolf, 117

flirtation: Altenberg's role in stylistic, 178; and American Bar, 192–93; in Beer-Hofmann's cultural productions, 151–54, 162–63, 164; Epstein's, 53; in Goldman & Salatsch House, 215; and Judith, 80–81; in Loos's architecture, 168; Palais Karl Goldschmidt, 154; Secession House as, 82–84; Spitzer's salon, 62, 104–7; Waerndorfer's expression, 135, 136, 150–51

Förster, Ludwig: Dohány Synagogue, Budapest, 65; Leopoldstadt Temple, Vienna, 65, 67; Palais Todesco, 6, 6–7, 10, 11, 22, 30–31, 32, 33, 33–34, 236n32

Frankl, Ludwig August, 91–92, 239n84

Franz Joseph I, 3–4, 10, 29

freemasonry, 71, 100–101, 134

Freud, Sigmund, 155, 164, 187, 217, 220–22

Friedell, Egon, 143, 147–49

Garelick, Rhonda, 8, 150, 154, 187

Gaul, Gustav, 45

Gesamtkunstwerk: Beer-Hofmann's rejection of R. Wagner's, 159; Beethoven exhibition (1902), 96; definition, 16, 59; Hansen's, 38, 41, 48; Klimt as binding force, 138; Olbrich's contribution to, 102, 105; R. Wagner's, 17, 58–59, 62; and secessionists, 58–60, 75–76; Spitzer's, 100, 107; and Todesco, 35–38, 41; in Waerndorfer House, 126, 135, 138

Gibson Room, Café Museum, *181*, 181–83, 186, 187

Gillman, Abigail, 158, 165

Gilman, Sander, 191–92

Goethe (Friedell and Polgar), 149

Goethe, Wolfgang Johann, as role model, 156

Goldman, Leopold: background of, 202; crossing frontiers with style, 169, 226; cultural production role, 194, 196, 202–3, 214, 215, 216–17; dressing and undressing strategy, 210–11, 213; fabric's role in interior design, 209; financing of store, 271n132; and Loos, 168, 216; patents, 203, 273nn172–73; pride in history of profession, 196, 206, 208, 217; social visibility of brand, 169

Goldman, Michael, 194, 195, 196–97, 200–201, 204, 206, 226, 271n133

Goldman & Salatsch House, 13, 166, 169, 172, 196, 197–216, 201, 208, 227, 228

Gombrich, Ernst, 2

Gomperz, Heinrich, 71

Gomperz, Max von, 86–88, 90

Gomperz, Theodor, 25, 35, 71, 233n33, 235n14

Greek revival style, 30–31, 33–34, 35, 38, 46, 52–53, 77, 245n90

Griepenkerl, Christian, 26, 52, *52*

Grillparzer, Franz, 23, 25–26

Gronberg, Tag, 174, 176

Grünfeld, Alfred, 59–60

Güdemann, Moritz, 54
Gurlitt, Cornelius, 41–43, 239n77
Gutmann, David, 90, 91, 97, 247n128
Gutmann, Wilhelm, 90, 97–98, 247n128

Hansen, Theophil von: and Epstein, 44, 46, 49, 49–50, 52; Gesamtkunstwerk, 41, 48; versus Hoffmann at Waerndorfer House, 126; and Todesco, 22, 24, 38, 41–43, 44, 49
Hellenistic Jews: Beer-Hofmann's self-identification, 158, 164; Epstein's self-identification, 46, 48, 53; Hevesi's Athena, 79, 84–85; as historicists' source for cultural authority, 25–27, 28–36, 39; Loos's and Goldman's opting in, 206; secessionists' mixing of Orientalist and Hellenist styles, 72, 83; Todescos' acculturation, 24–26, 38–43
Hellmann, Lili (Mrs. F. Waerndorfer), 125–26, 128, 136
Hellmann, Margarethe, 140
Hercules, 33, 34, 54, 237n48
Herzl, Theodor, 74, 75, 155, 157–58, 220, 221
Hevesi, Ludwig: on Cabaret Fledermaus, 143; cultural authority of, 81–82, 83, 224; dandy role, 60, 80–81; and *Der Floh* caricatures, 77–79; on Hoffmann's cutlery design, 141; on Judith dynamic, 80–81; on Loos's design aesthetic, 166, 179, 205; on modernist answer to Austrian prejudice, 138, 172; and Moser, 85, 85–86, 246n95; on Olbrich, 85; and Secession House, 63, 70, 77, 83, 84–86; support for secession movement, 60, 61, 62, 63, 64, 66, 70, 81; on Waerndorfer House, 128–29, 132–33; on Wagner's designs, 66–67
historicism, defined, 11
historicists: Epstein, 43–55; expression of modernization, 55–56; and Goldman store in Graben, 196–97; and Hofmannsthal, 110; versus modernists, 116, 126–27; Oriental style as threat to,

68; period review, 10–11; secessionist challenge to, 10, 68, 70, 71–72, 95–96; secessionists' development from, 84; Todesco, 22, 23–27, 35–43, 56, 99, 223, 237n47; Wittgenstein's challenge to, 88–92, 99
Hoffmann, Josef: *Arranged Table*, 141–42, 146; and Beer-Hofmann, 162; Beer-Hofmann villa, 153, 156–57, 158, 263n210; Cabaret Fledermaus, 143, 145, 145–46, 149; on Goldman & Salatsch House, 206; as rebel against historicists, 116, 126, 127; Spitzer's villa, 107–8; and Vienna Secession founding, 64; Waerndorfer House, 123, 126–27, 128, 129, 137–38; and Wiener Werkstätte, 139–41; Wittgenstein's Hochreit Hunting Lodge, 99, 140–41
Hofmannsthal, Hugo von, 55–56, 76–77, 106–7, 109–10, 143, 147, 150, 151, 152–53, 155, 156, 158, 184, 191, 228
Hohe Warte, artists' colony villas, 12, 102, 107–8, 127, 159
Hollander, Anne, 206–7
Hope I (Klimt), 133–34, 150
Houze, Rebecca, 119, 135, 203–4

identity. *See* Jewish self-identification
integration strategies: B. Zuckerkandl's, 14, 58, 59–60; caftan versus frock coat, 170–71, 205–6, 209, 233n33; dandy role as, 8–10, 17–18, 60–61, 80–81 107, 126; Loos's alternative, 169, 170, 207; modernism as, 75–76, 169–71, 225; public performances as instrument, 17, 25–27, 147–49; rise of antisemitism and changes in, 61; style and seduction as, 8, 15, 150–51

Jagerspacher, Gustav, 184, 185, 190
Jellinek, Adolf, 29
"Jewishness," 5–9, 19, 56, 58, 79, 107, 109–11, 138, 152–53, 193
Jewish patrons: ambivalence of acculturation, 2, 40, 74–75, 219–29;

contributions of, 3, 13, 18–19; existential strategy, 18, 55–56, 138, 195–96, 205, 233–34n49; introduction, 1–19; negotiation of masculine identity, 14–15, 128–29, 134–35, 175, 262n192; scholarly neglect of, 1–2; summary of use of style, 219–29. *See also* historicists; modernists and modernism; secessionists

Jewish self-identification: Altenberg's avant-garde, 173, 174, 190–91, 193; antisemitism and, 18, 55–56, 121–22, 138, 172–173, 191–192, 195–196, 205, 222–223, 233–234n49; Beer-Hofmann's modernist, 116, 153–66; and Cabaret Fledermaus, 143; Epstein's historicist, 46, 48, 53, 54; Esther's role in, 27; and gentlemen's fashion, 204–6; Jerusalem as romantic expression of, 23, 66, 68, 92, 96, 159–60, 187, 221; Loos on fashion and, 178–80, 205–6; Loos's avant-garde, 169–71, 190, 193–94, 216; patrons' self-mastery and, 79–80, 111–13, 151–54; secessionist strategies, 60–61, 68, 71–72, 95–96, 109–14; Shabbat as bride as romantic metaphor for, 130–32, 165–66, 173, 257n76; Spitzer as music salon host, 107; and stereotyping by gentiles, 7–8; tableaux vivants as expression of, 23–24, 55–56; Todesco's historicist, 6, 24, 32–33, 239n74; Waerndorfer's modernist, 114, 116, 123, 124–25, 126, 128–37; and Wagner's synagogue design, 65–68; Wittgenstein's modernist, 86, 87–89, 95–96, 99. *See also* acculturation; assimilation; dandyism; Hellenistic Jews; Orientalist style

Judaization, 14, 58, 214

Judith (biblical), 6, 7, 80–81, 96, 109, 232n25, 246n98

Jugend, 153–54, 214

Jugendstil design, 61, 66, 67, 100, 108, 119, 158, 180, 226, 227

Jung-Wien, 16, 17, 76, 110, 116, 144, 151, 153

Kanner, Heinrich, 72, 116, 117–19, 121–22, 124, 125, 225–26

Kaufmann, Isidor, 63

Klimt, Gustav: Bloch-Bauer portrait, 86, 95, 194; *Judith I*, 6, 7, 80; *The Kiss* from *Beethoven Frieze*, 96, 97; Kraus on "Jewishness" of, 58; Loos's admiration for, 215; and Mahler, 96; Margaret Wittgenstein portrait, 110–11; *Pallas Athene*, 113–14, 124, 134; and Secession, 10, 64, 70, 97; and Spitzer, 103; and Waerndorfer, 133–34, 137–38; Zuckerkandl's promotion of, 59–60

Klinger, Max, 93, 96–97, 98

Kneeling Boy (Minne), 122–23, *123*, 127, 137, 142, 176, 214, 255n31, 257n58

Kokoschka, Oskar, 127–28, 150, 190–93, *192*

Kornhäusel, Josef, 30

Kraus, Karl: acculturation debate, 42, 58, 100, 149, 170; and Altenberg, 188, 201; on Beer-Hofmann, 155, 157; on Goldman & Salatsch House as modern design, 210, 211, 213; versus secessionists, 100, 143–45, 242n2; and Loos, 18, 179, 188–89, 210; and *Salomé* debate, 134; on Singer and Kanner as "Easterners," 121–22; versus Zuckerkandl on Cabaret Fledermaus, 143–45

Künstlerhaus, 39, 63, 64, 73, 91, 100, 122, 173

Lang, Marie, 14, 77

Lensing, Leo, 193

liberalism, European, 11, 29, 61, 117–18, 119

Loos, Adolf: and Altenberg, 175, 181–83, 193–94, 201, 210; American Bar design, 183–84, *184*, 186–88, 193–94, 268n77; American sojourn, 179, 269–70n84; Café Museum, 180–81, *181*, 182–83; dandyism of, 179, 187, 190, 194, 205–6; on design as Jewish identification, 168–69; on fashion and self-identification, 178–80, 205–6,

268n73; Goldman & Salatsch ad, *201*; Goldman & Salatsch House design, 196, *197*–216, *208*, *212*; on Jewish emancipation, 169–71; and Kraus, 170, 173, 188–89; and L. Goldman, 166, 168, 194–95, 202–3, 206–9, 216–17; on men's fashion, 170–71, 178–80; and M. Goldman's fashion aspiration, 195; modernist transgressions of, 174–75, 192, 204, 207; opposition to secessionist movement, 105–6, 170–71, 173, 183, 192; Stössler's interior, 186; and white-dress motif, 165–66; on women's fashion, 180, 268n73

Loos-Haus. *See* Goldman & Salatsch House

Lothar, Rudolf, 58, 71, 87, 142

Lubbock, Jules, 179

Lueger, Karl, 4, 61, 73, 138, 195

Lux, Joseph August, 108–9, 212–13

Macdonald, Margaret, 126, 130–32, *131*

Mackintosh, Charles Rennie, 12, 108, 124, 126, 130, 136–37, 141, 223

Mahler, Gustav, 96, 107

male gaze, 183–86, 215

Malmberg, Helga, 124–25, 133, 136, 147

Marmorek, Oskar, 82, 100, 101–2, 220, 251–52n193

masculinity: Jewish patrons' negotiation of, 14–15, 154; juxtapositions with feminine in Secession House, 83; Loos and the Goldmans' fashion authority, 206–7. *See also* dandyism

Mayreder, Rosa, 14, 70, 96

Michaelerplatz Building. *See* Goldman & Salatsch House

Minne, George, 122, *123*, 124, 127–28, 130, 134, 136, 142, 176, 177, 214, 255n31

modernists and modernism: Beer-Hofmann's expression, 116, 151–66, *164*, 265n233; Cabaret Fledermaus, 59, 116, 142–51, *145*, 260n130; as emancipation of collective, 5, 81; Epstein's expression of, 53; Felix's suppression of, 63; and historicists, 10–11, 55–56, 85–86, 116, 126–27; and integration strategies, 75–76, 169–71; Jewish patrons' influence on Viennese, 1, 4, 5, 9–10, 222–23; and Orientalist style, 64–67, 199; as rooted in West and East, 83; sexualizing of Viennese, 152; Singer's and Kanner's *Die Zeit*, 116–22, *120*; Waerndorfer's expression of, 114, 116, 123, 124–25, 126, 128–37; Wiener Werkstätte, 137–42; Yiddish theater's role in, 144, 149. *See also* avant-gardists; secessionists

Moll, Carl, 100, 103, 123, 176, 255n29n31

Moorish-Byzantine style, 16, 54, 65–68, 95, 227. *See also* Orientalist style

Moser, Koloman "Kolo": cabaret designs, 144; and Hevesi, 85, 85–86, 246n95; Hohe Warte villas, 107; secessionist contributions, 64, 72, 83; and Waerndorfers, 125, 133, 134, *135*, 138, 139, 140, 227; Wiener Werkstätte, 12, 116, 139

Müller, Ines, 65–67

music rooms: Berl's, *101*, 101–2; Spitzer's, 100–109, *101*, *106*; Waerndorfer's, 130–33; Wittgenstein's, *116*

neo-Renaissance style: Palais Epstein, 43–44, *44*, 48–49; Palais Todesco, 31, 38–39

Neue Freie Presse, 34, 48, 70, 72, 74, 88, 95, 118, 142, 179, 195, 197

Olbrich, Joseph Maria: and Bahr, 73; Berl's music room, *101*, 101–2; dream of beauty, 76; and Hevesi, 85; Loos's critique of, 171; and O. Wagner, 11–12, 68–69; and R. Wagner, 100–101; Secession House design, 11–12, 61–62, *62*, 64, 68–69, 73; and Spitzer, 102–3, *104*, 105, 107, 108

Oldenburg, Peter von, 47, 52

Oppenheimer, Yella von, 39, 55–56, 143

Orientalist style: association with Other, 27, 64–65, 111–12; Beer-Hofmann's critique of, 114, 158–59; as declaration of Jewish Other, 111–12; Moorish-Byzantine, 16, 54, 65–68, 95, 227; in Palais Epstein, 47–48, 50, 54; secessionists' use of, 61, 68, 69–70, 72, 77, 83, 86, 92–93, 95–96, 109; in Wagner's architectural work, 64–68

Other, Jewish: Altenberg, 183; maintaining identification in modern context, 13–14; M. Goldman and Loos's cultural campaign on behalf of, 201–2; Orientalist association with, 27, 64–65, 111–12; secessionist negotiation of, 109, 111–12; Waerndorfer's self-expression as, 137; Wittgenstein's championing of, 95

Palais Ephrussi, 26, *26*, 27
Palais Epstein, 22, 43–55, *44*, *49*, *52*, 239–40n96, 241n140
Palais Karl Goldschmidt, 154
Palais Todesco, 5, 6, 22, 24–25, 29, 30–33, 35–43, *37*, 53–54
Panizza, Oskar, 191, 270n117
patrons. *See* Jewish patrons
Pereira-Arnstein, Ludwig von, 30
Pilz, Vincenz, 43, 46
Polgar, Alfred, 143, 147–49
Pollak, Michael, 5
Postal Savings Bank, 12–13, 119, 121, 255n24
prejudice and style. *See* antisemitism
"The Primitive" (Altenberg), 184–86

Rahl, Carl, 24, 35, *37*, 51–52
Ranzoni, Emerich, 48–49, 50, 52
Rappaport, Jacob, 89, 90, 191, 248nn137–38, 248nn141–42
Reinhardt, Max, 143, 153, 158
Reissberger, Mara, 27, 41, 49, 51, 53
religious themes in art, 39, 63, 93, 164
Ringstrasse, 10, 11–13, 15, 16, 25, 26, 28–29, 31, 32, *36*, 40, 43, 47, 48, 51, 53, 62–64, 68, 69, 84, 86, 89–92. *See also* historicists
Robertson, Pamela, 132

Rochowanski, Leopold, 141
Rodin, Auguste, 59–60
Romano, Johann Julius, 31
Rukschcio, Burkhardt, 179, 181, 274n189
Rumbach Synagogue (Budapest), 65–68

Saar, Ferdinand von, 39–40
Salomé: Moser's booklet for Waerndorfer, 134–35; Wilde's, 134–35
Salten, Felix, 144, 151
Schimkowitz, Othmar, 82–83
Schindler, Alma (later Mahler), 103–5, 107, 193, 225, 251n188
Schnitzler, Arthur, 136, 151, 156, 158, 173–74, 178, 183, 220, 258n92, 272n172
Schorske, Carl, 2, 29, 138
Schwendenwein, August, 31
Secession House: construction of, 82; dedication to classicist heritage, 77, 245n90; establishment as artistic rebellion, 63–64, 227; and Hevesi, 63, 70, 77, 83, 84–86; K. Wittgenstein's role, 61, 64, 68, 70–71, 86, 92–96, 247n128; as modern alternative to historicists, 72; Olbrich's design, 11–12, 61–62, *62*, 68–69; and secessionists, 60–62; Wittgenstein House as rebellion against, 109–14
secessionists: and Altenberg's celebrity, 193; avant-gardists as supplanters of, 172; Beer-Hofmann's critique of, 164–65; caricaturing of, 76, 78–79; challenge to historicists, 10, 68, 70, 71–72, 95–96; covering and uncovering dynamic, 60–61; and difference as aesthetic virtue, 75; Gesamtkunstwerk of, 58–60, 75–76; K. Wittgenstein, 68, 70–71, 86–99, *87*; Loos and L. Goldman's transformation of style, 214, 215; Loos's critique of, 105–6, 171, 183, 192; mission to overcome prejudice, 61, 71–77; modernist path of, 11–13, 64, 72, 137–42; Olbrich, 68–69; Orientalist style, 61, 68, 69–70, 72, 77, 83, 92–93, 95–96, 109; redefinition of accultur-

ation, 58–59, 61, 64; Spitzer's music room, 100–109, *101*, *106*; Waerndorfer, 94, 122, 123, 124, 127, 137–42; Wagner, 64–68; and Wiener Werkstätte, 141–42
Segantini, Giovanni, 93–94
Sekler, Eduard, 108, 146, 158
self-fashioning: Altenberg's bohemian style, 169, 175–76, 267n44; architectural style's importance to, 217; dandyism, 80–81, 219, 220, 227; Epstein's use of home in, 45–52; in exorcising of "Jewishness," 80–81; L. Goldman as progressive tailor, 199; L. Wittgenstein's abstract mathematical, 112–13; Waerndorfer's uniqueness, 127–37. *See also* Jewish self-identification
Seligmann Hirsch (Saar), 39–40
The Seven Princesses (Macdonald), 130–32, *131*, 138, 165
sexuality, cultural threat of Jewish, for gentiles, 152. *See also* flirtation
shame and beauty, 185–86, 192, 211
Simmel, Georg, 5, 9, 10, 42, 50–51, 90, 107, 113, 128–29, 154, 162, 163, 204, 211, 214, 220, 232n21
Singer, Isidor, 72, 116, 117–19, 121–22, 219, 225–26
social visibility: Altenberg's bohemian brand, 169; Beer-Hofmann's beard, 155; dialectics of decoration and collectivity/individuality, 89; *Die Zeit* as bid for, 121; dressing and undressing for, 211; influence on Jewish patrons' competition, 31; L. Goldman's tailoring brand, 169; Olbrich as design guide to, 102, 106; Waerndorfer's bids for, 137–38, 143, 149, 150; Wittgenstein's talent for, 89–90, 92–93, 99, 110–11
Sontag, Susan, 168
The Source of Evil (Segantini), 93–94
Speidel, Ludwig, 24, 25, 80
Spitzer, Daniel, 34
Spitzer, Friedrich Victor, 16–17, 60, 61–62, 100, *101*, 102–9, 103, *106*, 117, 130, 132, 163–64, 171, 193, 225

Springer, Max, 28, 32
Steinitz, Wilhelm, 46–47
Stewart, Janet, 147–48
Stiassny, Wilhelm, 68, 95, 154
Stonborough-Wittgenstein, Margaret, 110–11, 140–41, 165
Strzygowski, Josef, 64–65
style: as dynamic fashioning process, 4–5; and emancipation, 219–20; and identity, 232n16; importance in acculturation for Jews, 39–40; patrons' Jewish self-identification through, 18, 90; and possession in sacrifices of Jewish patrons, 214; social group competition, 31. *See also* self-fashioning
synagogues, 16, 29–30, 54, 63, 65–67, 68, 89, 95, 160, 202, 227

Telegraph Office, *Die Zeit*'s, 12, 17, 116, 118–19, 120, 121–22
Todesco, Eduard von, 22, 23–27, 35–43, 56, 99, 223, 237n47. *See also* Palais Todesco
Todesco, Hermann, 30, 31
Todesco, Sophie von, 23, 24, 25, 26, 29, 30, 32–33, 38, 55, 102, 143, 156, 211
Topp, Leslie, 2–3

Uhl, Friedrich, 28, 38

Ver Sacrum (journal), 75, 76, 81, 82, 93, 94, 124, 169, 172
Vienna: coffee house and Jewish outside relationship, 174; controversy in Goldman & Salatsch design, 210; Epstein's artistic connection to pilgrimage sites, 50–51; as focus for artistic and cultural changes, 59–60; Jewish patrons' influence on modernist identity, 1, 5, 9–11, 222–23; opposition to Orientalism, 64–65; rise of antisemitism, 4, 61, 73. *See also* Jewish patrons; Ringstrasse
Vienna Secession, 10, 63, 64. *See also* secessionists
Viennese Fabian Society, 118

Waerndorfer, Bertha, 139–40
Waerndorfer, Fritz: and Bahr, 122, 124, 125, 136; and Beer-Hofmann, 153; Cabaret Fledermaus, 142–51, 260n130; crossing frontiers with style, 223–24; and *Die Zeit* journal, 124, 125; and Klimt's *Pallas Athene*, 113–14, 124, 134; Kraus's attack on, 144; modernist self-identification, 114, 116, 123, 124–25, 126, 128–37; support for secessionists, 94, 122, 123, 124, 127, 137–42; Waerndorfer House, 123, 125–37, *131*; on Wittgenstein's hunting lodge, 99
Waerndorfer, Lili, 125–26, 128, 136
Waerndorfer House, 122–38, *123*, *131*, 139–40
Wagner, Otto: antihistoricism, 10; *Die Zeit* Telegraph Office, 116, 118–19, *120*, 121–22; and Epstein, 11, 54, 65–66; influence on Secession House, 69; Oriental architectural influences, 64–68; Postal Savings Bank, 12–13, 119, 255n24; "principle of clothing," 65, 66, 67, 119, 203, 204; Rumbach Synagogue (Budapest), 65–68; Steinhof Church, 67
Wagner, Richard, 58–59, 72–74, 103–104, 159
Walter, Bruno, 98
Weininger, Otto, 14, 130, 214, 220
Wertheimstein, Josephine, 25, 39
Weyl, Joseph, 68, 96
Wiener, Eduard, 32, 91
Wiener Werkstätte, 10, 12, 14, 17, 59, 86, 99, 111, 116, 118, 133, 137–42, 144, *145*, 146–49, 165, 184, 194, 210, 223, 224
Wiesenthal, Grete, 177
Wiesenthal Sisters, 150, 177
Wigley, Mark, 180
Wilde, Oscar, 134, 213, 219
Winz, Leo, 169–70

Wittgenstein, Hermine, 87, 94, 112, 247–48n129
Wittgenstein, Karl: challenge to acculturation, 87–89, 92–93, 96; crossing frontiers with style, 226; cultural authority, 87, 95, 250n172; and daughter Margaret, 110–11; and Gutmann brothers, 90–91, 97–98, 247n128; Hochreit Hunting Lodge, 99, 140–41; and Klinger's Beethoven, 96–98, *98*; and M. Gomperz, 86–87, 88; modernist self-identification, 86, 87–89, 95–96, 99, 109–14; and Rappaport, 89, 90, 248–49n142; Secession House role, 61, 64, 68, 70–71, 86–99, 247n128
Wittgenstein, Ludwig, 109, 111–12, 253n235
Wittgenstein House, 111–14
women: Adele Bloch-Bauer, 194; Altenberg's relations with, 177, 184–86, 266n39; Athena, 77, 79, 83, 84–86, 113–14, 124; depiction in Epstein's caryatids, 44; and *Die Masken*, 147; eroticism of Goldman & Salatsch design, 214–15; and Esther as cultural symbol, 5, 24, 25–27, *26*; femme fatale, 6, 7, 80, 96, 113, 133, 134, 150; Judith (biblical), 6, 7, 80–81, 96, 109, 246n98; Margaret's rebellion in Wittgenstein House, 111; Todesco's caryatids as symbols of, 32–33

Yiddish theater, 144, 148–49

Zemlinsky, Alexander von, 100, 105, 107, 193, 225, 252nn212–13
Zionism, 25, 61, 74. *See also* Herzl, Theodor
Zuckerkandl, Berta, 12, 14, 16, 58, 59–60, 104, 107, 137, 138, 143–44, 158, 172, 173, 191
Zweig, Stefan, 3–4